Two week
loan

Please return on or before the last
date stamped below.
Charges are made for late return.

IS 239/0799

INFORMATION SERVICES PO BOX 430, CARDIFF CF10 3XT

The French Defence Debate

The French Defence Debate

Consensus and Continuity in the Mitterrand Era

R. E. Utley

DC
423
$\cdot U8$

First published in Great Britain 2000 by
MACMILLAN PRESS LTD
Houndmills, Basingstoke, Hampshire RG21 6XS and London
Companies and representatives throughout the world

A catalogue record for this book is available from the British Library.

ISBN 0–333–79269–6

First published in the United States of America 2000 by
ST. MARTIN'S PRESS, INC.,
Scholarly and Reference Division,
175 Fifth Avenue, New York, N.Y. 10010

ISBN 0–312–23154–7

Library of Congress Cataloging-in-Publication Data
Utley, R. E., 1972–
The French defence debate : consensus and continuity in the Mitterrand era / R. E.
Utley.
p. cm.
Includes bibliographical references and index.
ISBN 0–312–23154–7
1. France—Military policy. 2. France—Politics and government—1981–1995. 3.
Mitterrand, François, 1916–1996. I. Title.

UA700 .U87 2000
355'.033544—dc21

99–089962

This book is printed on paper suitable for recycling and made from fully managed and sustained
forest sources.

10   9   8   7   6   5   4   3   2   1
09   08   07   06   05   04   03   02   01   00

Printed and bound in Great Britain by
Antony Rowe Ltd, Chippenham, Wiltshire

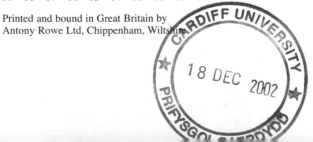

Contents

List of Abbreviations

ABM	Anti-Ballistic Missile
ASLP	*Air–sol longue portée* (air-to-surface long range missile)
ASMP	*Air–sol moyenne portée* (air-to-surface medium range missile)
AWACS	Airborne Warning and Control System
CCRAN	*Convention des cadres de réserve pour l'armée nouvelle*
CDS	*Centre des démocrates sociaux*
CEA	*Commissariat à l'énergie atomique*
CERES	*Centre d'études, de recherches et de l'éducation socialistes*
CFDT	*Confédération française démocratique de travail*
CFSP	Common Foreign and Security Policy
CGT	*Confédération générale du travail*
CIR	*Convention des institutions républicaines*
EU	European Union
EUREKA	European Research Co-ordination Agency
FAR	*Force d'action rapide*
FGDS	*Fédération de la gauche démocrate et socialiste*
GDP	Gross Domestic Product
IHEDN	*Institut des Hautes Etudes de Défense Nationale*
INF	Intermediate-range Nuclear Forces
MLF	Multilateral Force
MNF	Multinational Force
NATO	North Atlantic Treaty Organisation
NPT	Non-Proliferation Treaty
OAU	Organisation of African Unity
PCF	*Parti communiste français*
PLO	Palestine Liberation Organisation
PS	*Parti socialiste*
PTBT	Partial Test Ban Treaty
RPF	*Rassemblement du peuple français*
RPR	*Rassemblement pour la République*
SALT	Strategic Arms Limitation Talks
SDI	Strategic Defense Initiative
SFIO	*Section française de l'internationale ouvrière*
SNLE-NG	*Sous-marin nucleaire lance-engins*
UDC	*Union du centre*

UDF	*Union pour la démocratie française*
UDSR	*Union démocratique et socialiste de la Résistance*
UN	United Nations
UNIFIL	United Nations Interim Force in Lebanon
UNPROFOR	United Nations Protection Force
WEU	Western European Union

Acknowledgements

This book originates from doctoral research I undertook in the School of History, University of Leeds, from 1994 to 1998. I would like to take this opportunity to thank those people whose advice and encouragement were invaluable to me in the preparation of my thesis.

I would like to express my deep gratitude to Professor E. M. Spiers and Dr O. A. Hartley at the School of History, University of Leeds, for their time and patience, and their ever conscientious and constructive suggestions for the improvement of this work. I would also like to thank Professor J. F. V. Keiger, of Salford University, for allowing me to attend the University's seminars on the Mitterrand years, and to Professor Keiger and Professor J. Gooch, University of Leeds, for their helpful suggestions.

I am also grateful to those in France who took time from their schedules to help me to broaden my knowledge and understanding of the Mitterrand presidency in relation to issues of defence and security, especially M. Jacques Attali, M. Pascal Boniface, M. Jacques Boyon, Professor Maurice Vaïsse, and M. Hubert Védrine, and others who preferred to remain anonymous. Their insight, perspectives and, not least, practical assistance were, and remain, greatly appreciated.

My research was facilitated by the award of a studentship from the University of Leeds, and a study visit to Paris in January–June 1996 benefited from the award of grants by the Royal Historical Society, the Society for the Study of French History, the Gilchrist Educational Trust, and the Kathleen and Margery Elliott Scholarship Trust. I wish to thank all of these bodies for their financial support.

Earlier versions of some of the work contained in this book have previously been published elsewhere. The material on French military intervention in Bosnia and Rwanda formed the basis of an article for the journal *Civil Wars* (Summer 1998) and the material on military intervention in Lebanon and Chad constituted the basis of an article in the journal *Small Wars and Insurgencies* (Autumn 1999). I am very grateful to Frank Cass Ltd for permission to reprint this material here.

Finally, I wish to thank all my family and friends who have shown amazing understanding in recent years while I have neglected them completely, and especially Jonathan, without whose love and support I would never have finished. I am truly grateful.

Introduction

In the history of France since the Second World War two personalities are of particular importance. The first is General Charles de Gaulle, the head of the external French Resistance movement during the war, France's first postwar leader, and the founder of the Fifth Republic. The second is François Mitterrand, the seemingly implacable critic of de Gaulle's presidential regime, the first Socialist to attain the presidency of the Fifth Republic notwithstanding his previous criticisms, and France's longest-serving head of state since Napoléon III. This study considers the role of François Mitterrand in a domain more often associated with Charles de Gaulle: French defence. It will address the question of Mitterrand's role in, and responsibility for, the delineation of France's defence priorities during his presidency. It will also assess the impact of his governments' actions, and of the changing international context, on the accord which has been alleged to surround France's defence provision and priorities, and it will examine whether, under the Socialist president, continuity or change was more likely in a defence position which had existed largely unaltered since the early 1960s.

This study considers primarily the issues of consensus and continuity in French defence during the two presidential terms (*septennats*) of François Mitterrand. The reasons for this focus are both internal and external to French politics. Internally, the new Socialist predominance in France's political structures, in terms of the presidency from 1981 to 1995, and two separate periods, from 1981 to 1986, and from 1988 to 1993, as regards legislative power, had been hitherto unprecedented in the 23 years of the Fifth Republic. It could, therefore, reasonably be asked whether the new Socialist national leadership would provide an occasion for serious change, particularly perhaps in defence as France's

'Left turn' contrasted so sharply with the political tide in other Western countries. Externally, Mitterrand's period of office coincided with rapid changes in the international security context, coexisting with the reunification of Germany, the end of the Cold War and the collapse of the Soviet Union. Such events altered the very foundations of defence planning for the West in general, and for France in particular.

However, this study will not focus exclusively on the years 1981–95. As the subtitle suggests, the longer perspective of Mitterrand's political career during the Fifth Republic will also be taken into account, in view of the historical milestones of his accession to the presidency as a Socialist and the length of his tenure of office, as mentioned above. In addition, the length of his wider political career (from the Resistance during the Second World War, through ministerial positions under the Fourth Republic, to his role during the Fifth) sets François Mitterrand apart. His was a career spanning more than fifty active years in politics. Further, his prominence and stature grew over the course of his career, to which his unexpectedly strong challenge for the presidency in 1965, and a second close-run contest in 1974, bear witness. At the same time his influence as one of the most significant opponents of successive Right-wing governments also increased during the 1970s, through his unification of the Socialist Party under his own leadership in 1970, the Common Programme of Government with the Communists in 1972, and subsequent improvements in the Left's electoral performances. Finally, although it is not generally thought that Mitterrand was highly concerned with matters of defence and security, a closer examination reveals that he took a much greater role in, and responsibility for, the defence considerations of the political Left than is widely acknowledged, both prior to and during his period of office.

While it is not intended to undertake a comparative analysis of the actions of Presidents de Gaulle and Mitterrand in defence and military affairs,[1] certain consequences of de Gaulle's decisions on defence have continued to affect subsequent French governments, and so have conditioned a degree of continuity, constancy and consistency in France's defence since the General's leadership. Of these, the promotion of independent French action in defence matters (as in France's withdrawal from the integrated military command structure of the North Atlantic Alliance in 1966), the importance of concerns for French grandeur and status in international affairs (de Gaulle's 'certain idea of France'[2]), the refusal to subordinate France's interests and armed forces to external (particularly American) control, and the reorientation of France's defence around a nuclear capability are well-known. Their doctrinal and not least financial consequences for a medium power like France have exercised lasting influence over defence and security planning and priorities. Moreover, it has regularly been argued – not least by those involved in French politics – that these factors have given rise to a widespread public and political consensus surrounding France's defence. These associated issues of continuity, and the less clear-cut consensus in French defence will constitute the main features of this analysis.

The assertion of a growing consensus around France's defence gained credence at the end of the 1970s, and notably came to prominence after the accession to the presidency of François Mitterrand. It is well documented in both English- and French-language sources. External commentators have perceived an 'entrenched Gaullist consensus on defence matters',[3] and a 'broad consensus ... around the security policy established by de Gaulle'.[4] Similar analyses within the French material are to be found. Further, over the corresponding period, French public opinion also seemed to rally at least around the nuclear component of France's defence: in 1983, 66 per cent of those surveyed regarded the nuclear deterrent as 'positive' for France, as against 53 per cent in 1976, whereas the proportion of those who regarded the deterrent as 'negative' had fallen.[5]

Writing in the latter part of Mitterrand's presidency, respected analysts summarised the climate of opinion surrounding France's defence as one of 'national accord'.[6] This was reiterated by one of President Mitterrand's closest advisers, Jacques Attali, who suggested that a 'comprehensive consensus'[7] had existed on defence under Mitterrand. Moreover, the existence of the defence consensus was repeatedly argued in political spheres during Mitterrand's presidency. Such arguments were perhaps most explicit during debates in the Assemblée Nationale over the *loi de programmation militaire*[8] for 1987–91, formulated by Jacques Chirac's Right-wing government under the first period of *cohabitation*.[9] Of the minority Left, the prominent Socialists Jean-Pierre Chevènement (a future Minister of Defence), and Michel Rocard (a future Prime Minister), spoke respectively of 'the consensus on defence'[10] and the '*rassemblement* of the French people'[11] around their national defence. Among the majority Right it was suggested that 'a very wide consensus on the subject of defence policy,... and a deep consensus'[12] existed; indeed it was nothing less than 'a consensus on defence policy which rall[ied] the vast majority of the French people'.[13] Despite the concentration of timing, these remarks are nonetheless indicative of opinions expressed time and again during the Mitterrand presidency.[14]

Such assertions beg the questions, however, of why the idea of a consensus was so important, and why politicians were so keen to advance it. The significance of a defence consensus was indeed perceived to be considerable, notwithstanding partisan divisions. Firstly, there were international repercussions of such accord, as representatives of both the Left and the Right of the political spectrum agreed. The Socialist President of the Assemblée Nationale's National Defence and Armed Forces Committee, Jean-Michel Boucheron, suggested that consensus portrayed 'the external image of the cohesion of France'.[15] For the Right, Chirac had already expressed the view that consensus 'must, imperatively, be preserved ... because it constitut[ed] an exceptional asset for France, [whereby] the international standing of [the] country [was] all the greater'.[16]

There were equally argued to be military benefits of the apparent defence consensus. Consensus was regarded as 'the second pillar of France's deterrent'[17] after the actual nuclear component, a 'situation which exist[ed] in no other country of the Alliance'.[18] Moreover, the agreement surrounding France's defence 'count[ed] greatly for the credibility of [her] military force and of [her] diplomacy'[19] according to Defence Minister Chevènement in 1989, and 'the more people who agre[ed on it],... the more resolute and efficient [would] be [France's] defence'.[20] In Chirac's view the defence consensus was indeed 'the cement of national unity'.[21]

Nevertheless, despite the eagerness of some politicians to suggest an overwhelming defence consensus, its existence was not universally accepted. More cautious commentators believed that the alleged defence consensus had few, if any, foundations in reality. While the notion of consensus was widely promoted in 1987, the former Socialist Defence Minister (1985–86) Paul Quilès argued that at best, areas of partial accord existed between the political groupings,[22] but he articulated no less than six instances of inter-party divergence on defence questions.[23] This perspective reinforced that which Jacques Isnard, *Le Monde's* military analyst, had written as early as 1983: 'the national consensus on defence problems in France [was] only superficial ... a general accord on the missions and the organisation of the military system [was], in reality, largely unfounded'.[24] Such feelings were no less discernible more recently: the immediate reaction of one senior official within the French Defence Ministry, when asked about the defence consensus, was 'what consensus?'[25] It was his view that any accord which might seem to exist between the political parties on defence issues did so for the sole reason that so little debate of the principles and priorities of France's defence took place, or was even provided for.

Consequently, this work will consider a number of questions subsequently raised around the issues of consensus and continuity in French defence. Firstly, was there a consensus – and did it exist both prior to, and during, the presidency of François Mitterrand? How wideranging was any such consensus in reality, and how firm was it in practice? Furthermore, why were politicians in particular so keen to assert the existence of a broad and deep accord? Was the consensus itself continuous, or did it change over time? In which areas did continuity prevail, and where could significant change be seen under the Socialist presidency?

The study will consider the hypothesis that the French defence consensus was actually less solid than many suggested, and that at times it was little more than a tool of political expediency. It will be argued that this was apparent across the political spectrum. With regard to the scope and depth of the alleged consensus, it will further be argued that any agreement which existed was mainly a 'single issue' concern, focused on the principle of a nuclear component in France's defence panoply. Moreover, it will be suggested that the apparent consensus on (some) nuclear questions, and the particular desire of politicians to perpetuate it, masked divisions on other aspects of French defence – such as the role, equipment and responsibilities of the conventional forces. It will be argued that the widening cleft between declarations of consensus, and the instances on which consensus could be said to be based, was visible throughout Mitterrand's presidential terms. Furthermore, this work will hypothesise that, despite the political, practical and organisational continuities imposed on France's defence by previous decisions, certain substantial redirections and adjustments were made under Mitterrand, perhaps most notably in the spheres of autonomy and independence. Finally, the work will examine whether François Mitterrand's increasing tendency to treat France's defence posture less as an end in itself, and more as a political means to other political ends, undermined both that defence posture, and the associated arguments of consensus and continuity.

By concentrating on the debate which has been apparent in relation to France's defence during the Fifth Republic, not only within the parliamentary framework, but also in wider terms, this study will attempt to address the questions thus raised. It will be divided into two parts. Part I will consider these issues in relation to François Mitterrand's positions on defence after 1958. To this end, Chapters 1 and 2 will consider the period prior to his success in the presidential elections of 1981. Chapter 1 will seek to establish Mitterrand's position in relation to any defence consensus, and to examine the extent of defence debate, and subsequent consensus, during the first decade or so of the Fifth Republic. Chapter 2 will consider changes in these situations prior to May 1981, focusing on the evolution of the defence debate within the political groupings, and notably within the political Left; and Mitterrand's role therein, culminating in the conversion of both the Communists and the Socialists to the principles of nuclear deterrence in the late 1970s. Chapter 3 will provide a basic chronology of the defence decisions of Mitterrand's *septennats*, and will consider relations between Mitterrand and his Defence Ministers, particularly the increasingly strong role of the former in directing the decisions of the latter. Moreover, it will seek to identify any areas of significant continuity or adaptation in terms of defence planning, provision or action under the Socialist leader.

Part II will focus on major defence decisions and provisions during the Mitterrand presidency, considering where possible Mitterrand's role in such decisions, and the debate to which they gave rise. It will therefore take a more thematic approach, with Chapter 4 reviewing the defence budgets and military planning laws of the first *septennat*, the extent of debate and consensus which surrounded them, and their consistency with previous planning. The effects of *cohabitation* on the defence debate will be analysed, as will be Mitterrand's role in promoting, or otherwise, any defence consensus. Chapter 5 will consider France's overseas military involvement in Africa and the Middle East, particularly debate over the role of French forces in Lebanon and Chad. Given the precursors for such intervention under Mitterrand's predecessors, especially with regard to Chad, any adaptations in the commitment of French troops overseas will be assessed. Chapter 6 will examine the challenges facing France's defence and security arrangements in the light of developments in the international security situation, taking particular account of President Reagan's Strategic Defense Initiative and progress towards superpower arms control. It will consider the added impulses towards European defence cooperation provided by these factors. It will be argued that, by this time of fundamental challenge to the principles of international security, debate over defence in France was intensifying, as was the role of

François Mitterrand in defence concerns, and change was apparent in the provisions and priorities of France's defence.

Chapters 7, 8 and 9 will focus on Mitterrand's second presidential term, with Chapter 7 examining the end of the Cold War and France's defence planning for the 1990s, as manifested in the *lois de programmation militaire* of 1990–93, and 1995–2000, and the *Livre blanc* (White Paper) of 1994. It will consider Mitterrand's role in adapting to the changed security environment, and will suggest that even issues pertaining to the nuclear forces were no longer sources of agreement between the leadership and others in political or analytical circles. Chapter 8 will consider the theme of a Europeanisation of France's defence during Mitterrand's second term, and the particular influence Mitterrand himself had in the delineation of this course, especially in terms of relations with Germany. This constituted potentially significant change: however, within the change was continuity, as defence cooperation was to have specific limits. The debate which these priorities occasioned, in terms of France's actual military capabilities as well as in her relations with the Atlantic Alliance, will be examined. The politics of French troop deployment in the former Yugoslavia, in the context of a greater harmonisation of European policy, will likewise be covered. Finally, Chapter 9 will consider France's external military involvements in the Gulf War of 1990–91, the practicalities of intervention in the former Yugoslavia, and in Rwanda – each operation undertaken with close reference to the framework of the United Nations. These instances constituted an extension of the cooperative side of France's defence mechanisms. It will be argued that the debate which they engendered represented a changing climate of opinion in favour of an altered world role for France.

As mentioned above, this work will not constitute a comparative analysis of the defence policies of Charles de Gaulle and François Mitterrand, although elements of the earlier decisions inevitably had a bearing on the substance and context of the latter. Neither is it a study of defence policy formulation. Nor, finally, is it an examination of the position of the French Socialist party with regard to defence since its unification under Mitterrand in 1970, although all of the above would be fascinating topics for investigation. Rather, this will be an analysis of the proffered defence consensus and continuity within France, and the debate, or asserted lack of it, which surrounds them. In this context it takes as its parameters the political career of François Mitterrand during the Fifth Republic, to establish the relative health of the defence consensus over time and over issues. It will bear firmly in mind the considerable influence of such a prominent politician over the course of France's defence provision, particularly at the time of his presidency, which witnessed so many fundamental changes in international security.

It is hoped that this study will constitute a valid contribution to the work which currently exists on the subject of French defence, and indeed that it will help to fill certain gaps which are presently apparent. At the time of writing, the conduct of France's defence during the whole of Mitterrand's term of office has been little covered, and where it is considered it is often overshadowed by assessments of other aspects, particularly the economic or political aspects of the Mitterrand presidency. Moreover, the issue of consensus in French defence, while widely accepted, is little analysed, or is treated on a basis of individual issues.[26] In the light of the recent substantial changes in the French defence establishment, implemented by Mitterrand's successor, Jacques Chirac, it is hoped that this study might shed light on an imprecise and at times ambiguous factor – the defence consensus – which has been so widely asserted for much of the Fifth Republic, especially during the Mitterrand presidency.

Part I
Mitterrand and Defence

1
Years of Discord

> To watch over the defence of the country [was] the first
> mission of the Government ... security must be assured ...
> whatever its price.[1]

These words were spoken during the debate over the second *loi-programme relative à certains équipements militaires* for 1965–70 not, as might have been expected, by a member of the government or of the Gaullist majority, but by François Mitterrand, one of de Gaulle's harshest critics. However, though he may well have been in agreement with the government as to the latter's ultimate role in, and responsibility for, national defence and security, Mitterrand was an increasingly vocal opponent during the course of the 1960s of the means by which that defence and security were to be assured.

While Mitterrand became one of the most visible, and persistent, critics of the Gaullist model for France's defence, he was far from being its only opponent. The General's actions gave rise to prolonged and widespread debate, despite the leader's popular appeal[2] and the size of his party's Parliamentary majority.[3] Early Opposition within the Assemblée Nationale to the construction of a defence posture for France on the basis of nuclear deterrence and national independence raised cross-party concerns, and featured as strongly in Right-wing as in Left-wing critiques. Moreover, such opposition was especially significant with regard to any defence consensus because certain of the arguments then raised were to recur throughout the time period of this study. Despite the extent of discontent with de Gaulle's actions and imperatives in France's defence, however, by the time of the General's resignation from the presidency in 1969 many of his decisions had become more widely accepted. Nevertheless, it will be argued that the situation was far from constituting a broad agreement on the foundations of France's defence.

The principles of Gaullism in defence

The influence of Charles de Gaulle over France's defence, after his return to power in 1958, is widely accepted to have been considerable. Indeed, in matters of defence, the 'long shadow of de Gaulle'[4] and the 'Gaullist legacy'[5] are often affirmed. The Gaullist defence model so criticised in the 1960s by Mitterrand and others was predicated on certain tenets which the General held to be irrefutable.

Although defence had its own importance for General de Gaulle, it was perhaps of greater significance as a function of broader considerations. The military aspect of defence was at times no more important than its political aspect, and consequently, his assertion that 'for all [his] life, [he had] had a certain idea of France'[6] can be argued to set a guiding principle for his perceptions and policies. The 'certain idea' was inherently linked to his convictions regarding France's rightful place in the world, and particularly her status in relation to other world powers. It was fair to say that for de Gaulle, 'his country was endowed with very specific gifts of which the world could not fail to take account'.[7] Grandeur, rank and status were therefore key elements of the Gaullist world-view.

As de Gaulle maintained through his speeches and writings, the idea of rank was firmly intertwined with the requirement for France to be independent in her decisions and actions. This concern for independence, perhaps arising from disagreements with his allies during the Second World War,[8] and from doubts as to the reliability of others' commitment, led him to believe that 'it [was] intolerable for a great state to have its destiny subject to decisions and acts of another state, no matter how friendly it may be'.[9] The linkage of independence and defence was underlined during a notable speech in 1959; de Gaulle stating that 'at all times, the Government [had] as its *raison d'être* the defence of the independence and integrity of the territory'.[10] In pursuit of such independence and integrity, France must possess military means commensurate with the task in hand, not least because of the peculiar geographic difficulties involved in defending France from conventional attack, particularly from the east.[11] A modern, powerful armament – an atomic armament – and preferably French in its origins, was deemed a prerequisite for the politics which de Gaulle wished to pursue. It would convey prestige and status on France, and enable her to rank alongside the major postwar powers, which he identified as the United States, the Soviet Union and Great Britain on the grounds of their nuclear capacities.[12] Such a capability would also, he believed, allow France to act independently of her Western allies, should the need arise, thereby imparting political and diplomatic benefits. Finally, a modernised armament was to enhance France's military position, as above all, 'the defence of France must be French.... If a country like France sometimes wage[d] war, it must be *her* war. Her effort must be *her* effort ... it [was] essential ... that France defend[ed] herself by herself, for herself, and in her way.'[13]

The practicalities of Gaullism

If Gaullism in French defence was therefore characterised by concerns for the primacy of the state, for prestige and status, independence of decision-making and action, and a modern and capable military instrument based on the possession of an atomic armoury, how was this manifested in defence during the first decade or so of the Fifth Republic? In practical terms, de Gaulle's actions focused on a reordering of the French defence establishment to serve new ends by new means. In political terms, French defence was to assume a far greater role in advancing the independence of the state within the international framework.

De Gaulle's first priority was to resolve the Algerian situation, in order that he could extract the army from a debilitating and demoralising colonial conflict. This was to be a starting- as much as a finishing-point: colonial wars and theories of *la guerre révolutionnaire*[14] belonged to the past in de Gaulle's view, whereas atomic weaponry was the way of the future. Basically, 'for de Gaulle there was something absurd in investing (sinking?) the whole of France's military force in tracking down a few thousand guerrillas overseas'.[15] Indeed, as early as 'the first half of 1960, de Gaulle came to the conclusion that the running sore of Algeria had now continued for too long and was delaying the whole process of modernising France and her Army'.[16] Such a modernisation, based on the principles of nuclear deterrence and national independence, was provided for soon after de Gaulle's return to power, in the Ordinance of 7 January 1959.

The primary aim of the Ordinance was to ensure the security and integrity of the French territory, and the lives of its citizens. Respect for international alliances, agreements and treaties was an additional objective, but it was secondary to the defence of France itself. France's domestic and overseas responsibilities nevertheless dictated four kinds of mission for her armed forces, which in order of priority were: the task of deterrence, through the ability to launch a nuclear counter-strike against any aggressor; the defence of the nation, her institutions and military capacity; the conduct of military operations outside French borders to facilitate both national and European defence; and finally, French military intervention overseas in protection of French or allied territories. The emphasis was therefore placed firmly on national over cooperative actions, and likewise on nuclear over conventional means of deterring an attack on France, although conventional forces were not to be excluded entirely.[17]

The importance of the nuclear weapons capability to de Gaulle was reiterated by further legal measures he implemented to consolidate the control of the Head of State over the armed forces in general, and the nuclear forces in particular. As early as July 1958, he had legislated to emphasise political control over the military instrument.[18] The Constitution of the Fifth Republic, approved by referendum in September 1958,[19] reinforced political direction, making the President of the Republic 'the protector of the independence of the nation, of the integrity of its territory, of respect for treaties'[20] and 'Head of the armed forces ... [who] presid[ed] over the Higher Councils and Committees of National Defence'.[21] However, 'the Government ... [had] at its disposal the armed forces',[22] and in such a capacity was accountable to Parliament, where 'the Prime Minister [who was] in general charge of the work of the Government ... [was] responsible for National Defence'.[23] The role of the Prime Minister was repeated in the 1959 Ordinance, and in the Decree of 20 January 1962, which provided for the creation of the French Strategic Air Command.[24] However, a further Decree of 14 January 1964 returned ultimate responsibility for the deployment and utilisation of the strategic air force, and hence the nuclear weapons capability, to the President of the Republic[25] – Charles de Gaulle.

The prospects for an atomic-based reorganisation were greatly enhanced by the explosion of the first French atomic device at Reggane in the Sahara on 13 February 1960.[26] Added to this was the formulation of a *loi-programme relative à certains équipements militaires*, for 1960–64, which was presented to the Assemblée Nationale in October 1960. The *loi-programme*, relating to military procurement and laying down the expected financial commitments which would be necessary for its implementation, was not a comprehensive indicator of expenditure plans but nevertheless confirmed the strong bias in favour of the first-generation strategic nuclear force.[27] Its concerns were focused on nuclear weapons research, missiles for nuclear delivery systems, naval vessels and aircraft, and Mirage IIIs and IVs, the latter to be used as a means of missile delivery. A second *loi-programme* for 1965–70 envisaged orders for more Mirage IV bombers, but accepted that land- and sea-based components would assume far greater significance, due to continuing improvements in (particularly Soviet) air defences.

The focus on nuclear weapons development, and the role to which the nuclear capabilities were to be assigned, was indicative of the political as well as military implications of defence in de Gaulle's mind. The creation of a nuclear capability would both assist him in his relations with the French army, considering the difficulties over Algeria, and enhance France's political relations with regard to the major world powers and Germany.

It has been widely commented that de Gaulle intended to use military modernisation, and especially the nascent *force de frappe*, as a 'technical sop to the discontented army of Algeria'.[28] Indeed, this force constituted the 'clearest opportunity for de Gaulle to wrench the French officer corps clean away from its contaminated, corrupt past of self-absorbed political interference'.[29] De Gaulle himself was careful not to be explicit about any potential linkage between the two facts, although he strongly implied that this was the case at the end of 1961.[30] On the other hand, he was far more explicit concerning the benefits France could hope to derive from the possession of an atomic arsenal with regard to the major postwar powers.

De Gaulle's concerns with principles of equality and balance between the world's major powers was often expressed. It was of paramount importance that France should be one of the "Big Four", and should assume an appropriate role for that position: something of an arbiter between East and West.[31] Such a role was unquestionably to be reinforced by possession of an atomic armoury, for 'France, in equipping herself with a nuclear armament, help[ed] the equilibrium of the world.'[32] More accurately, perhaps, for de Gaulle, it could be understood that a nuclear capability would assist France in attaining a degree of diplomatic comparability with the three others of the 'Big Four', and to that end, 'if they wanted to invite [France] to renounce atomic weapons for herself, although others possess[ed] them and develop[ed] them in enormous quantities, there [was] no chance of her deferring …'. .[33] Hence,

French nuclear weapons were thought of not so much as a *force de dissuasion* as a *force de persuasion*. French nuclear armament had little to do with a military posture against a potential enemy.... However it had a great deal to do with the French position vis-à-vis the principal allies.[34]

Consistently with de Gaulle's perceptions of the roles of a defence capability, the emerging *force de frappe* was therefore to have significant implications both for France's internal and external politics. In respect of the latter, it was also to underline the French capacity for independence of decision-making and action. It would indicate particularly de Gaulle's resistance to any form of integration of French armed forces with those of other nations, and his abhorrence of external influence over France's military, and subsequent diplomatic posture. This was demonstrated by his progressive withdrawal of French troops from the NATO integrated military command structure, and his position on the issues of the Multilateral Force, the Partial Test Ban Treaty and the Non-Proliferation Treaty of the 1960s.

De Gaulle was damning in his assessments of the impact of integration on national defence. It was a situation whereby 'the people and the Governments [found] themselves more or less stripped of their role and their responsibilities in the domain of their own defence'.[35] To add insult to the perceived injuries of military integration, it amounted to a scenario 'where everything [was] controlled by the Americans who [had] at their disposal the use of the main weapons, meaning atomic weapons'.[36] Moreover, the Atlantic Alliance, and its military provisions, were deleterious to the individual European defence efforts which would otherwise be made, and thus decreased, rather than increased, the effectiveness of the defence of the West.[37] In each of these concerns, therefore, integration contradicted all the tenets of a Gaullist conception of defence.

Therefore, from a mixture of military and political justifications derived from his basic convictions regarding France's defence (and derived also perhaps from the US' and UK's rejection of de Gaulle's power-sharing suggestion for the Alliance, in the Memorandum of 1958[38]), Charles de Gaulle instigated the withdrawal of French troops from the Atlantic Alliance's integrated military command structure early in 1959, with the withdrawal of France's Mediterranean fleet. Increasingly de Gaulle criticised American initiatives and strategies in the opening years of the next decade, and then decided in 1963 similarly to remove the French Atlantic fleet from the NATO armoury.

From then on, through the recall of naval officers from the command organisation, a refusal to engage French aerial defence equipment without national authorisation, a distinct disinclination to reintegrate forces repatriated from Algeria under Allied command, and the refusal to participate in the Fallex NATO manoeuvres of 1965, steady progress was made towards de Gaulle's message to US President Johnson of 7 March 1966, announcing the termination of France's participation in the integrated military command structures of the Atlantic Alliance.

The withdrawal of French forces from NATO by the middle of the 1960s was not the only instance of de Gaulle's seeming intransigence, and irascibility, where French defence met foreign policy concerns, and especially where he believed France's nuclear capabilities were threatened. His determination to maintain an 'independent' criterion for the defence of France was apparent also in his rejection of proposals for a Multilateral Force (MLF), which implied sole American possession of nuclear weapons under hypothetical, joint US–European control. It has been argued that in this respect, 'de Gaulle's first priority was defeat of the MLF',[39] for it was 'a device aimed at undermining the strategic and diplomatic utility of the French national *force de frappe*'.[40] Indeed, one of the most prominent of France's nuclear strategists in the 1960s, General P. M. Gallois, went so far as to call it the 'multilateral farce'.[41] Therefore, as de Gaulle asserted, France was 'keeping to the decision that [she had] made: to construct and, if necessary, to use [her] own atomic force'.[42]

De Gaulle's reaction in this respect thereby conditioned, to an extent, his subsequent reactions to the major arms-control measures of the 1960s, the Partial Test Ban Treaty (July 1963) and the Non-Proliferation Treaty (July 1968). With regard to the former, however, there were reasons of practicality as well as of principle why de Gaulle could not commit France to such an agreement. Although de Gaulle had expressed his support for measures to counter nuclear testing in a letter to Khrushchev in July 1958,[43] he rejected the PTBT on the grounds that it was 'of only limited practical importance'[44] while no means were agreed to limit future weapons production, or to destroy existing stocks.[45] As superpower atomic capabilities were still, to all intents and purposes, unconstrained, it was de Gaulle's view that the PTBT could not be permitted to 'prevent France from equipping herself with the same kind of means, failing which … France's own security and her own independence would never again belong to her'.[46] For the French nuclear weapons programme in 1963, a test ban – even limited – was unacceptable, as France lacked data which the other nuclear powers had gained through extensive atmospheric testing, and had not yet mastered the techniques of miniaturisation which would permit underground explosions.[47] If the PTBT was seen as defective due to its incomplete approach to nuclear disarmament, the NPT was viewed likewise: as the French permanent representative to the United Nations General Assembly argued, the basic problem of achieving a real reduction in armaments, through the prevention of future production and the destruction of stockpiles, was not addressed.[48]

Consequently, by the later 1960s French defence had been apparently confirmed in its Gaullist orientations by the actions of the charismatic and tenacious French leader. Successive legislation, reinforcing his particular vision of France's duties and responsibilities, and accentuated by an ostensibly increasing independence of defence provision, had combined to suggest a convergence of opinion around de Gaulle's principles and priorities. Any consensus which existed, however, was hard-won, and insufficient attention has been given to the opposition encountered.

Defence: an expression of megalomania?

In expressing the opposition to de Gaulle's plans for re-ordering the French defence establishment, the debate over the *loi-programme* for 1960–64 is particularly important. It demonstrated widespread discord among the Parliamentary representatives as to the future course of France's defence – discord that was deeply felt and which engendered cross-party concern. The extent of disquiet was such that the *loi-programme* was ultimately enacted on a technicality, without the direct approval of either the National Assembly or the Senate.[49] Moreover, the debate merits particular regard due to the positions it set out, especially over cost, relations with the Atlantic Alliance, and the future prospects for France's conventional forces, which would recur in defence debates and increase in volume at least until the end of the Mitterrand presidency.

Resistance to the principles of de Gaulle's modernisation of French defence was perhaps a partisan affair. The concept of a nuclear deterrent for France was primarily criticised by the Left as a reflection of de Gaulle and his priorities. For the Socialists, it was nothing less than 'the expression of a megalomania to which it [was] high time to apply the brakes'.[50] Furthermore, Communists and Socialists concurred in believing that 'it [was] to the detriment of the true national grandeur that [the Government's] ambition to possess an instrument of military prestige ... would be realised',[51] for this would 'sacrific[e] the reality of [France's] needs and [her] commitments to the dreams of an unacceptable and illusory grandeur'.[52] In short, 'a national deterrent force respond[ed] neither to strategic nor to political facts'.[53]

The government's proposals for a nuclear force were also criticised according to the premise that they added nothing to, yet detracted much from, France's defence. The Socialist Schmitt argued that nuclear weapons did not enhance the country's ability to defend itself. He asserted that the resultant 'false security [was] the worst of illusions',[54] reinforcing the Communist position that any nuclear capacity constituted 'a mortal danger for the security and existence of [their] country'.[55] This was alleged to be so, even among Independent deputies, as any use of nuclear arms by the French 'would lead purely and simply to the removal of [their] country from the face of the earth'.[56] Such views were shared by some outside the political sphere – in an open letter to General de Gaulle, 90 academics from the Faculty of Sciences at the University of Paris urged that he should not 'sacrifice the nation's future by constructing an "outdated" and "unusable" military striking force'.[57]

If the principle of nuclear deterrence for France was opposed for partisan reasons, doubts over the credibility of the proposed force gave rise to universal criticism. The theme that the potential nuclear force would be outdated and unusable was recurrent. Expressing deep concern over the time which would be necessary to achieve a French nuclear capability, the Finance Committee, dominated by the Right, alleged that the programme risked being 'very profoundly outdated'.[58] At the opposite end of the political spectrum, the Communists were less concerned than scathing: 'the weapon that the Government propos[ed] ... [was] outdated from the beginning, outclassed in all its aspects'.[59]

Questions over France's industrial and technical capacity to produce the desired force similarly arose on all sides of the Parliament. The assertion of de Gaulle's Minister for the Armed Forces, P. Messmer, that the first elements of France's nuclear force would be operational from 1964[60] was perceived to be, at best, optimistic. Reports from the Finance Committee[61] and the National Defence Committee[62] reiterated that France would have achieved relatively little in her quest for a nuclear capability by the end of the proposed *loi-programme* (1964). Although a limited amount of atomic bombs could be produced by that date, further progress would have been hampered by the continued delay in commissioning the isotope-separation plant at Pierrelatte for the production of enriched Uranium-235, the requisite time for the development of a fusion bomb thereafter, and subsequent development and production of the delivery vehicles for the French weapons. These considerations led parliamentary observers to conclude that a more realistic target date for the emergence of de Gaulle's *force de frappe* would be 1967–68 at the earliest.[63] However, difficulties did not end even there: the Finance Committee believed that 'if the perfecting of bombs seem[ed] within the realm of normal possibilities between [1960] and 1964, it [was] not the same thing regarding missiles'.[64]

French difficulties in assuring a credibility for her nuclear capability were to be compounded by the government's choice of Mirage IV aircraft, of which it intended to order 50, as an interim delivery vehicle for France's atomic armoury. The inadequacy of the Mirage IV for a strategic bombing role was regularly asserted during parliamentary debates, as its 'range [was] only 2,500 kilometres ... and [its] speed ... [was] outclassed by that of the American B-70, itself outclassed in relation to Soviet rockets and to the US' Atlas and Titan rockets.'[65] Moreover, the government's apparent failure to capitalise on the benefits of submarines in the delivery of nuclear warheads was taken as an indication of the ultimate lack of credibility of the nuclear force: 'the French nuclear force, without rockets, without atomic submarines,... with bombs of a fifteen-year-old model carried by planes, [would] make no impression on the Soviet Union',[66] and would amount to 'nothing more substantial than a sinister comedy of irrationality'.[67]

De Gaulle's plans were thirdly criticised on the grounds of cost. For some parliamentary observers, the planned expenditure on nuclear forces constituted a 'financial adventure',[68] for 'atomic arms [were] very costly weapons,... [and] not only [were] the bombs expensive, but the missiles [were] more expensive still'.[69] The incalculable cost of the course of nuclear development risked being beyond the means of France, and thus an unrealistic objective: '[Would] there be a miracle? How [did] the Government expect to manage to equip France with ... a modern atomic armament in such a short time and with so little funding? It [was] clear that there [would be] no miracle.'[70]

Furthermore, concerns were voiced over the likely effect on France's conventional forces of such expenditure. By the beginning of the 1960s, there was extreme disquiet among members of the Assemblée Nationale regarding the state of French armed forces after the cumulative trials of the Second World War and 15 subsequent years of colonial conflict. De Gaulle's modernisation plans for the armed forces, in the form of the *loi-programme*, were henceforth criticised across the breadth of political opinion for what they did not do for France's conventional capabilities. According to the National Defence Committee, 'by a very great majority, [it] consider[ed] that the modernisation of the conventional forces had been sacrificed'.[71] It seemed that de Gaulle was compromising the very security that he aimed to enhance, by his focus on a nuclear orientation to national defence.[72] Consequently, both the Finance and the National Defence Committees asserted the inadequacy of the resources proposed for the military. The concerns of these prominent parliamentary committees were such that the government later accepted an amendment to the *loi-programme*, to provide an additional 400 million francs for the Army.[73]

Finally, de Gaulle's intentions were countered on the grounds of their adverse implications for France's participation in NATO, with the Government's assertions that a French nuclear capability would enhance the deterrence potential of the Western alliance being strongly contested. Socialists argued that the Government's proposals would result only in 'giv[ing] NATO, in a few years, rockets that it [had] in abundance, instead of the conventional forces it ask[ed France] for'.[74] Even the Right-wing parties were concerned by the prospect of a reduced participation in what de Gaulle's close associate, M. Schumann, referred to as 'the irreplaceable alliance'.[75] Given the difficulties over the realisation of a nuclear force, in cost and credibility, Gaullists and conservatives were concerned that the cooperative nature of France's defence should prevail. The *loi-programme* should not be a 'turning point towards the policy of national isolation'.[76] Indeed, if France nevertheless insisted on pursuing the nuclear option, it should be 'within the framework of NATO, and with the fundamental support of [France's] Atlantic allies'.[77]

It can therefore be seen that de Gaulle's defence imperatives, characterised by the development of a nuclear basis to the French armoury, and the associated reorganisation and modernisation of the armed forces to reflect this priority, were initially criticised across the political spectrum. However, after the first *loi-programme* had eventually been passed, and implemented, the Gaullist majority rallied to the General's principles as reflected by their support for successive defence and military budgets, and for the second *loi-programme* of 1965–70. Although concerns were still voiced over costs, credibility and the conventional forces, the broad lines of de Gaulle's defence stance were accepted. This was not the case at the other end of the political spectrum where François Mitterrand and his colleagues maintained their attack, especially during the 1965 presidential election campaign.

The role of François Mitterrand

It was not apparent from Mitterrand's earliest political activity that he would rise to prominence on the Left of the polity. His early political sympathies were more apparent on the Far Right, with biographers suggesting his loyalties lay somewhere near the *Croix de feu* (the most important of the extra-parliamentary leagues of the extreme Right) or *Action Française* (a Right-wing counter-revolutionary movement).[78] The significance, and the scope, of his involvement with Marshal Pétain and the Vichy regime during the Second World War have also consistently raised more questions than their explanations have provided answers.[79] Nevertheless, it is possible that even during the war Mitterrand's political convictions were imprecisely formed. Perhaps one of the most important of the events which shaped his political career was his meeting with the leader of Free France, and of external resistance to German occupation, Charles de Gaulle, in Algiers in November 1943.

Having left his post in Vichy France in January 1943, Mitterrand is said to have assisted in the formation of an effective Resistance network made up of former prisoners of war.[80] In this capacity, he met de Gaulle in the hope of securing the General's backing for himself as leader of the various ex-prisoners' Resistance movements. De Gaulle, however, preferred that the Resistance movements within France should be more closely controlled by the hierarchy of the Free French in London. Mitterrand was hostile, and the meeting was concluded in some anger by de Gaulle after half an hour. The legacy of the encounter was the 'personal antagonism and mutual political mistrust'[81] which it engendered between the two men.

Although Mitterrand's subsequent political development cannot be solely attributed to one meeting with de Gaulle, that meeting certainly coloured his positions thereafter. He aligned himself initially with the *Union Démocratique et Socialiste de la Résistance* (UDSR), an eclectic, if ostensibly Centre-Right, political grouping. However, unlike many of his colleagues in the UDSR, he refused to transfer his allegiance to the Gaullist *Rassemblement du Peuple Français* (RPF) created in 1947. The departure of UDSR members to the RPF in 1949 weakened the UDSR, but it meant that Mitterrand's position within the remaining grouping was greatly enhanced. He became its President at the UDSR's congress in November 1953, and under his leadership, and according to the principles of anti-Communism and anti-Fascism he professed, it gravitated a little more clearly towards the Centre Left.

Such factors undoubtedly contributed to Mitterrand's response to de Gaulle's return in 1958.[82] He became an unshakeable critic of Charles de Gaulle, of his challenges to French Republican traditions by his decrees, and by the Constitution of the Fifth Republic, and of his apparently anti-democratic style of leadership, by the elevation of presidential responsibility and the subjugation of the parliamentary role. Mitterrand's criticisms were wide-ranging, and certainly included questions of a defence or a military nature. His later assessment of events as 'the conspiracy hatched between the army and General de Gaulle'[83] is perhaps instructive in explaining the close interest he took throughout the 1960s in de Gaulle's legal and practical alterations to France's defence. As Mitterrand increasingly spoke for the majority of the Leftist opposition, he constituted a particular difficulty for de Gaulle and his governments.

François Mitterrand was certainly quick to challenge de Gaulle's Decree of January 1964, which gave the President ultimate authority over the strategic forces. Mitterrand had long been concerned by the enhancement of the presidential responsibility for the direction of France's affairs, at Parliament's expense. He was therefore highly concerned about the implications of such a concentration of powers as was provided for by the January Decree.[84]

Aspects concerning the control of the nuclear capability were but one factor in François Mitterrand's wide-ranging criticisms of de Gaulle's defence priorities. Primarily, Mitterrand was fundamentally at odds with de Gaulle's guiding principles, asking 'who [didn't] have an idea of France? [He had] several ...'.[85] He did not agree that de Gaulle's intransigence on the international stage constituted a furtherance of national security, stressing that 'grandeur [lay] firstly in fidelity to a certain conception of the world and of men ... the grandeur of France consist[ed] of refusing to confuse the love of the homeland with the insolence of national pride'.[86] Neither did he agree that French security was assured on the basis of nuclear deterrence. For Mitterrand, the world 'must hear again the voice of France, [for] that [was] the true strategy of deterrence'.[87] De Gaulle's conception of nuclear deterrence was unjustifiable, since on the basis of military, financial, civic and diplomatic considerations, 'the conditions for absolute deterrence, which alone would justify ... the existence of a national strategic nuclear force, [were] not fulfilled'.[88] Moreover, he doubted France's ability even to attain a nuclear force:

[He knew] the Gaullist argument: the balance of terror prevent[ed] war. It [was] enough for the weak, ten thousand times more weak than the strong, to reach the threshold of terror for him to be saved. France reach[ed] this threshold by her *force de frappe*.

As for [him]self, [he saw] the threshold which [was] always moving away, and France running after it, exhausted.[89]

An examination of François Mitterrand's pronouncements on defence and security issues in the 1960s indicates four recurrent themes. These were his opposition to a French defence constructed around a nuclear armoury; his concern that the dangers of nuclear proliferation should be reduced; his support for international disarmament and the dissolution of military blocs; and his preference for French participation in the Atlantic Alliance in fulfilment of her obligations (presumably until such time as the Western military bloc was dissolved). Each of these themes was regularly asserted during the presidential election campaign of 1965. Mitterrand's unexpectedly strong performance in the contest can be taken as evidence that his opinions, especially in his anti-nuclear stance, which was a central feature of his campaign, were far from a crippling electoral liability, and did not prevent his emergence as the leading opposition figure.

During the election campaign, Mitterrand benefited from the early endorsement of the Socialist party[90] and later the Communist Party,[91] regardless of his personal antipathy to their political position. Additionally, he was supported by the former Socialist Premier of the Fourth Republic, P. Mendès-France,[92] still a highly respected and influential member of the political hierarchy. The importance of such support for Mitterrand was twofold: firstly, it showed that the Left was prepared to rally to a cause and submerge its differences in pursuit of a greater goal, and secondly it showed that Mitterrand could be the figure to secure such accord. Mitterrand capitalised on this situation by a certain fluidity in his political affiliations during the latter half of the 1960s – in moves which could be argued to demonstrate blatant self-promotion, he shifted his allegiance from the *Rassemblement Démocratique*, under whose auspices he had returned to the Assemblée Nationale in 1962, to the *Fédération de la Gauche Démocrate et Socialiste* (FGDS), an alliance of Left-wing groups formed in 1965 to support his own presidential candidacy. His ill-timed and ill-conceived intervention in the crisis of May 1968 led to a loss of confidence in his leadership by the Left,[93] and the dissolution of the FGDS. Thereafter, Mitterrand fell back on the support for him which had existed in the *Convention des Institutions Républicaines* (CIR), a loose gathering of political 'clubs' which had supported Mitterrand since 1964. This base was to facilitate his accession to the *Groupe Socialiste* and its leadership in 1971.

Mitterrand's position on defence issues was contrary to that of the government on the majority of points. Like the broader Left, Mitterrand believed that there was fundamentally no place in French defence for a nuclear capability. In his words, it was 'ineffective, extravagant and dangerous'.[94] He proposed instead a 'categorical reconversion'[95] of all atomic energy installations from military to civilian purposes, and advocated the cancellation of the nuclear force.[96] As he was later to reiterate, 'the French nuclear force, far from ensuring the security of [the] country, and its autonomy in diplomatic, technological and military fields, creat[ed] an additional danger'.[97] Moreover, for Mitterrand, the costs were prohibitive: de Gaulle's 'sixty supersonic Mirage IV bombers [would] be old-fashioned in 1970, while each of them cost the price of two large secondary schools, or of six hundred council houses, or of the most modern hospital in the Parisian region'.[98] As stated at the beginning of this chapter, Mitterrand believed that the preservation of security was paramount, but his and de Gaulle's conceptions of such security diverged. As Mitterrand argued shortly before the 1965 election campaign, de Gaulle and his Governments 'defend[ed] not [France's] independence, but the theses of the most banal nationalism ... the remarks of the Head of State, repeated a hundred times, [were] more of a resort to propaganda than a serious political conception'.[99] For Mitterrand, 'the bomb was the worst solution for assuring France's security'.[100]

François Mitterrand's second concern was the danger of nuclear proliferation. In 1965, he argued that 'if France continued with her nuclear policies,... it would lead to wide nuclear dissemination and inevitable nuclear war',[101] for 'when France [had] her national *force de frappe*,... to whom, to which country [would] she forbid the possibility of possessing in their turn their own national nuclear force?'[102] For Mitterrand, 'the greatest danger for peace ... rest[ed] in the proliferation of nuclear weapons';[103] leading to his advocacy of adherence to the Test Ban Treaty of 1963, and his calls for French participation in United Nations talks on the non-proliferation of nuclear weaponry.[104] It was a theme to which he returned later in the 1960s, accusing de Gaulle and his party of a 'paradoxical theory of the benefits of atomic proliferation'[105] arguing that 'while General de Gaulle [was] plunging headlong into the nuclear arms race,... the Opposition regarded the spread of atomic weapons as the chief danger facing the world'.[106]

Thirdly, Mitterrand advocated international disarmament as a natural corollary to non-proliferation, and the only way to assure France's security. He argued that 'major French initiatives towards world disarmament'[107] would enhance France's status far more than possession of minimal nuclear capabilities of her own. Disarmament, for Mitterrand and his colleagues of the Left, was not merely a question of unilateralism, for it was inextricably linked with 'the progressive and simultaneous dissolution of military blocs, and the creation of a demilitarised zone in the centre of Europe'.[108] In the meantime, however, he urged France's return to the Geneva Disarmament talks, from which she had been absent since 1962, and reiterated his conviction that in 'Gaullist policies ... on disarmament, on the banning of nuclear tests and on the spread of atomic weapons ... a false notion of the grandeur of France [led] de Gaulle into political adventures which the Leftist opposition [found] impossible to endorse.'[109]

Mitterrand's position on military blocs perhaps explains a certain ambivalence which was apparent in the 1960s with regard to his perceptions of French relations with NATO and the Atlantic Alliance. In the earlier part of the decade, he was highly concerned by the deterioration of France's relations with her NATO partners, and by the diminution of French participation within the NATO structures. In 1963 he had asked whether it was 'not possible for France to be more co-operative in the framework of the alliances to which she [had] subscribed?',[110] as France 'needed her allies'[111] to whom de Gaulle was being 'unfaithful'.[112]

However, Mitterrand was no more keen than the government to invest France's future defence in the Multilateral Force. Contrary to the government, though, he did not accept that the French national nuclear force was the only alternative to the MLF.[113] In part this was attributable to his basic antagonism to the principles of nuclear deterrence; it was also attributable to his considered opinion that neither course was appropriate for France or the Western Alliance. He was unequivocal:

Parliament [was] not constrained to choosing between two bad military solutions which follow ... from bad political hypotheses. Parliament [did] not have to choose between a policy which would be submission to a foreign hegemony and sinking into nationalistic adventure.

The Multilateral Force [was] a bad solution. It divid[ed] the

Western Alliance while disturbing the Eastern bloc; it dilut[ed] responsibility without increasing effectiveness ... it creat[ed] the illusion of a greater unity of action whereas it add[ed] weaknesses; it offend[ed] national sovereignties without offering the compensation of real, joint political decision.... [114]

Over NATO, qualifications began to appear in Mitterrand's stance from the mid-1960s. As he emphasised the necessity for a dissolution of military blocs, he de-emphasised the value of NATO as a security organisation in its then current form. After de Gaulle's message to President Johnson of March 1966, Mitterrand agreed that 'the revision of the military accords ... correspond[ed] to the evolution of the international situation':[115] 'NATO ... belong[ed] to the past',[116] he insisted, because 'the situation [was] no longer that of the Cold War.'[117] Nevertheless, his harsh criticisms of the government's policies on military alliances persisted, for if there were justifications for de Gaulle's actions in principle, the style and consequences of the General's decision could not be condoned. He 'reproach[ed] de Gaulle for pursuing his policy of independence from the United States ... in such a hostile and insolent fashion and without offering France a reasonable alternative'.[118] Indeed, it was 'scandalous that the decision ... was taken in the absence of any alternative policy'.[119] For Mitterrand, de Gaulle's actions had been 'wrong in essence and rude in manner'.[120]

The confluence of Mitterrand's opinions in these matters with those of French public opinion was demonstrated by the presidential election result of December 1965. In a campaign where issues of defence and foreign affairs had featured prominently, Mitterrand received over 45 per cent of the votes cast in the decisive second round of the contest.[121] For a politician with no solid party base it was a significant and substantial achievement. Furthermore, that Mitterrand's position on defence issues was synonymous with that of the broader Left he represented was manifested very publicly in 1966 and in 1968. In a quest for greater electoral successes in 1967, the main Leftist groupings, Mitterrand's *Fédération de la Gauche Démocrate et Socialiste*, and the *Parti Communiste Français* (PCF), concluded an agreement whereby after the first round of voting, the lower-placed candidate of the FGDS and the PCF would withdraw from the contest in order to afford the higher-placed candidate an increased chance of success against their Right-wing opponents.[122] In a joint Communiqué issued to formalise the agreement, the parties concurred on the need for general disarmament, including the return of France to the Geneva Disarmament talks, and for France's signature of the PTBT as part of wider efforts to combat the danger of nuclear weapons proliferation. With regard to France's nuclear force, even by this late stage in the decade and in its development, the parties declared their 'fundamental hostility to the *force de frappe*'.[123]

After the Left's successes in the legislative elections of 1967, cooperation between Mitterrand's FGDS and the Communists was extended by the publication of a Common Declaration. The section of the Declaration which dealt with defence and nuclear issues was specifically amended to go further than the 1966 Communiqué, calling again for the renunciation of France's nuclear strike force, the conversion of the nuclear industry from military to peaceful ends, and the creation of denuclearised zones in the European continent. Further, the parties called for commitments by the major nuclear powers not to use their weapons in such denuclearised zones, for the destruction of existing nuclear weapons stockpiles and the dissolution of all military blocs.[124] Each of these points had been a major campaign theme for Mitterrand in 1965, and their re-iteration in 1968 demonstrated that the French Left had in no way yet rallied to the principles of nuclear deterrence for France.

Therefore, by the time of de Gaulle's resignation from the French presidency in 1969, although his plans for a nuclear-armed French defence establishment were well on the way to fulfilment there was far from a broad base of support about the best way forward. The main areas of contention in terms of the defence debates of the 1960s had undoubtedly been the reorganisation and modernisation of France's defence according to de Gaulle's precepts, and the subsequent implications of this course for France's international standing and relations. While concerns had been expressed about the adverse effects of extensive nuclear weapons development for the conventional forces, these had not in fact been specific, or prominent – as if the end of the protracted colonial conflicts in which France had been involved had provided the opportunity for consideration of other issues. However, this was not to remain the case into the 1970s; ironically, as debate and discord on nuclear questions diminished, protests over conventional force issues proved to be a persistent problem for the governments of Georges Pompidou and Valéry Giscard d'Estaing. Although the conversion of the Communists and Socialists to the principles of nuclear deterrence by the later 1970s was to mask the extent of difficulties and disagreements over defence thereafter, ambiguities and qualifications which had first appeared in the 1960s were to remain.

2
Towards a Defence Consensus?

Despite the implementation of de Gaulle's changed priorities for France's defence for over a decade, the debate over his provisions and principles was far from closed by the beginning of the 1970s. Indeed, debate encompassed issues of both the conventional and nuclear forces, and occurred at all points on the political spectrum, though rarely involving all political groupings on any one source of contention. Some of the most protracted debates were to be found within the *Parti Socialiste* (PS) after its creation in 1971, leading to profound changes between the defence stance it adopted at its inception, and that with which it entered the next decade. François Mitterrand's role within the Socialists' defence debates was particularly noteworthy, in that his public and private positions on such questions were often quite different, and typified some of the difficulties the Socialist Party faced in reorienting its defence priorities over the course of the decade. Considering that Mitterrand was elected to the French presidency at the beginning of the 1980s – at the beginning of what was to prove a difficult decade-and-a-half for defence and security questions – the positions he established during the 1970s are all the more significant. It will be argued in this chapter that the defence debate in France during the 1970s was buoyant, not only between but also within the political parties, and particularly among the Socialists, where Mitterrand took a greater part in the evolution of the Socialist stance than has generally been portrayed. It will be further argued that despite the conversions of the *Parti Communiste Français* and the *Parti Socialiste* to the principles of nuclear deterrence in May 1977 and January 1978 respectively, France was in fact little nearer to the broad consensus alleged to underpin the defence and security policies established by de Gaulle. Any consensus to which the decisions of the parties of the Left had given rise was in reality only limited and partial, and was indeed subject to many of the same qualifications as had been apparent in the 1960s.

The incorporation of many elements of the non-Communist Left into the *Parti Socialiste* at Epinay-sur-Seine in 1971, and the election of François Mitterrand to the leadership of the party he had only just joined, marked a new beginning for the Socialist Left in France. Under Mitterrand's leadership, the new PS was to gravitate more firmly to the Left than the previous main Socialist grouping in France, the SFIO,[1] and was to adopt a greater militancy of tone.[2] It was to commit itself to a programme of extensive nationalisation, social reform, and self-management by workers (*autogestion*). Thereafter, the party came to represent a far more dynamic element in French politics, and party membership, according to one source, had almost trebled by 1977.[3] In the intervening period François Mitterrand had only narrowly failed to attain the presidency,[4] and the party's tally of electoral successes between 1974 and 1977 was certainly impressive.[5] The reorientation of the *Parti Socialiste* was no less apparent in questions of defence and military affairs, although their eventual conclusions were perhaps more in line with existing conventions than might have been expected.

The Socialists' position on defence and military issues was laid down in 1972 after the Congress of Suresnes, in their Programme of Government, *Changer la Vie*,[6] and was reinforced by the conclusion of a Common Programme of Government with the PCF in June of that year.[7] Most importantly, the former declared the PS to be 'radically opposed'[8] to the military policy pursued by successive governments of the Fifth Republic, founded on France's possession of an atomic armoury. It advocated the construction of a defence institution based solely on conventional means. The Common Programme of Government, which increasingly came to be the primary reference point (in public) regarding Socialist policy intentions, reiterated these conclusions, asserting that 'general, universal and controlled disarmament'[9] would be the principal goal of a government of the Left, and demanding the 'renunciation of the strategic nuclear strike force in whatever form; an immediate halt to the manufacture of the French nuclear strike force,... [and] an immediate halt to nuclear testing'.[10] However, less than a full decade later, at the very time of Mitterrand's election to the presidency, such ideas were difficult to find. His presidential election programme, the *110 Propositions for France*,[11] while calling for 'progressive and simultaneous disarmament',[12] also required 'the development of an autonomous strategy of deterrence'[13] for France. The degree of reorientation of the Socialists' position on defence was therefore considerable.

The Socialists and the wider defence debates

It should not perhaps be unexpected that attention came to be focused on those aspects of Socialist reflection relating to nuclear deterrence; this was to be a major redirection in Socialist thinking. Moreover, throughout the 1960s, the nuclear element to the French defence posture had been progressively emphasised, in terms of strategy and resources, at the expense of the conventional forces.[14] Nevertheless, at the beginning of the 1970s, conventional-force concerns were prominent among defence-related issues. Debate occurred over the conditions of military service and conscription, and the role of the armed forces, both of which were particularly relevant in terms of the Socialists' defence deliberations, and the extant provisions of the Common Programme of Government. The prominence of debate over defence was also underlined at this time by the controversy between elements of the Army hierarchy and the Church, as well as by public disquiet over matters of the Army's land privileges, though the Socialists in particular had little involvement in such disputes. However, it was issues such as discord over resource provision, and its subsequent allocation between the nuclear and conventional forces, which engendered more widespread discourse, and which assumed greater significance given the proportion of the French national budget which was devoted solely to defence.[15] Anxiety over that resource provision was exacerbated by the deteriorating international economic situation, occasioned by the oil price rises of the early 1970s, giving cause for concern throughout the French Parliament. Consequently, conventional force issues were much to the fore in the defence debates of the early 1970s.

The widespread questioning of defence priorities which flared in 1973 over conscription and military service stemmed from reports of discontent and growing antimilitarism among conscripts from February of that year.[16] Concerns were initially focused on three areas: the poor state of repair of barracks, the insufficiency of both military tasks and recreational facilities to occupy conscripts' time, and the lack of access to a broad range of outside media. Delayed student reactions to an amendment to conscription legislation, in the form of demonstrations across France in April 1973, broadened support for the conscripts' cause.[17] M. Debré's amendment, debated in 1970, had suggested that young people should no longer have the right to defer their military service if they were called during the course of their higher education. Concerns were reinforced by discord over the length of military service (12 months), inadequacies of training, and low remuneration. Moreover, the discontent was prolonged: as the new president, Valéry Giscard d'Estaing, was engaged in a wide-ranging consultation on defence issues in summer 1974, conscripts in Nice and Draguignon were demonstrating against their living conditions and working environment.[18]

There was, however, something of a paradox in Socialist reactions to these developments, although the Common Programme of Government had, in effect, anticipated many of these very complaints. While reasserting the importance to the Left of the principles of military service, and a national defence based on popular mobilisation, the Programme proposed far-reaching reforms in that military service. According to the Common Programme of Government,

> military service, equal for everyone, [would] be of a length of six months. Within the limits fixed by the law, young people [would] be able to choose the date of their enlistment, according to the demands of their jobs or their studies. A democratic statute for soldiers and officers [would] be adopted. Military personnel [would] be able to receive freely newspapers and periodicals of their choice.[19]

Though they predated the conscript and student protests, it can be seen that there was a remarkable similarity between the causes of discontent and the particular concerns of the Socialists and Communists. Nevertheless, the responses of the Left – especially the Socialists – to the events of 1973 were minimal.

The inadequacies of the Socialists' position on the military service protests were publicly recognised in 1975, during the course of the first annual Congress of the *Convention des Cadres de Réserve pour l'Armée Nouvelle* (CCRAN). The CCRAN had been established in April 1974 on the initiative of C. Hernu and J.-P. Chevènement,[20] and was a forum in which (mostly retired) service personnel could gather to debate military matters in a manner sympathetic to the Socialist Party (while not directly constituting an organ of the *Parti Socialiste*). Under Hernu's leadership, the CCRAN took an increasingly progressive stance regarding the prospects for change in the Socialists' thinking on defence. Thus at its Congress in March 1975, at which François Mitterrand was present, the PS leadership was berated by a conscript for the lack of impact by the Young Socialists, within and outside the barracks, in furthering the cause of the Socialist Party and in capitalising on the conscripts' discontent.[21] Moreover, a Socialist student alleged that this lack of impact was wholly attributable to 'the absence of a definite defence policy within the PS'.[22]

Ironically, the reticence of the Socialists' position from the time of public protest contrasted sharply with the position of François Mitterrand prior to the unification of the *Parti Socialiste* at Epinay: in 1970, when Debré's proposals were initially debated, Mitterrand condemned the measures as 'discriminatory',[23] with regard both to the question of deferments and to the imposition of age limits by which military service was to begin. In 1971 he considered it 'intolerable'[24] that the government should not be initiating far-reaching reforms of military service. Such reactions exemplified the interest he had demonstrated in the conditions of military service throughout the Fifth Republic[25] – rendering the subsequent lack of substantive response by the PS to the protests of the early 1970s all the more uncharacteristic. That the Socialists became somewhat more vocal in their demands regarding military service from around the middle of the decade, with calls for reform in the living and working conditions of military personnel, and in their remuneration;[26] the creation of the *Convention des Appelés Socialistes*, within the framework of the CCRAN;[27] and proposals for ameliorating democratisation in military life to assist the pursuit of improved standards of living and service,[28] did little to compensate for the lack of response in 1973.

If reactions to the conscript crisis by the PS, and indeed the wider French Left, were somewhat muted, this was less so regarding debates from 1973 concerning the role of the Army. According to some elements of the military hierarchy, the best way in which to alleviate discontent among the armed forces was to increase their responsibilities in the realm of public affairs. Such was the analysis of three generals writing in *Défense Nationale*.[29] They advocated the collation of data from a wide range of ministries in order that the Army could deal effectively with 'an interior crisis' in national defence; a wider definition of the means of defence, to include 'military, civilian, economic and psychological' possibilities for response to a wider variety of threats to national security; and greater autonomy for military commanders in assessing situations arising.[30] Such views reinforced public and political perceptions that the armed forces' role in politics and society was increasing – the stimulus for this perception having come from the Minister for the Armed Forces, R. Galley. In a speech to reserve officers on 13 May, he had asserted that 'the Army remain[ed] the last resort of [France's] liberal society'.[31] Supported by pronouncements from prominent figures in the military leadership,[32] Galley's words gave extended cause for concern in 1973.

The prospect of the Army being viewed as a 'last resort' by the government of the Right, by implication internally, and more important justifiably, against the French themselves, was a particular worry to the Left of France's political spectrum. Fears were exacerbated by events in Chile, and notably President Pompidou's reactions to them, and by further developments in the interpretation of the role of the Army in the autumn. The removal from office of the democratically elected President Allende by a military coup, and Allende's subsequent death, affected certain members of the Left very deeply. François Mitterrand was personally very moved by the situation, as he recorded in *La Paille et le Grain*,[33] for Allende had been a friend as well as a political contemporary and a democratically elected Left-wing president. Pompidou's unsympathetic response[34] sparked widespread Leftist condemnation of the French authorities, over the Army's role in the service of government and society.

The Socialist journal *Frontière* was markedly virulent in its criticisms of the French authorities. Numbering Chevènement and G. Martinet, both prominent members of the PS, among its editorial staff, the journal had warned of how the government was preparing the Army 'for the defence of the bourgeois state'.[35] This reinforced Communist denunciations after Galley's speech in May, which alleged that 'for the principal task of the Army, the Minister [set] not the defence of the national territory, but the protection of big investors'.[36] Despite the assurances of General Maurin, the Chief of the Defence Staff, that 'the French Army [was] not at the service of capitalism'[37] the attack by senior figures of the Left was maintained, although not by François Mitterrand.[38] The comments of M. Rocard were typical of many, arguing that 'it [was] neither a nation nor a civilisation that [the Government asked] the military to defend, it [was] a political and economic regime, a social structure'.[39] Such perceptions were compounded by the apparent extension of the armed forces' remit in October.

The new mission for the Army seemed to place its activities firmly on a political level. According to documents made public by the media, the Army was now involved in investigating subversive, anti-government elements – 'enemies of the State'[40] – including the main political parties of the Left. In this capacity, Rocard argued, the Army was being asked to 'play the role of informants'[41] on the Left. Given that the government had also proposed to the armed forces as a theme for their manoeuvres, 'the Army intervenes to restore the government to power'[42] it is not difficult to understand the concerns of the Left, in particular, regarding the future role of the Army. Nevertheless, the debate was perhaps of greater significance to the Socialists at least in the context that it permitted an increased awareness, and an advancement, of their internal debate on defence – and indeed, it was exploited as such.[43]

The broader debates on defence

While the Socialists' concern over the role of the Army was made apparent, and their involvement in the debate over conscription and military service issues gathered momentum as the decade progressed, they took little part in debates over resource provision for the armed forces, and over the *loi de programmation militaire* proposed by Giscard's government in 1976. They had previously taken virtually no part at all in the controversy which arose between the elements of the Church and the Army, over the relationship between Christianity and the military profession, nor in the public protests over extensions to the Army's military training facilities. While this may have had several advantages, in demonstrating the extent of divergences in other parties and interest groups over defence in the 1970s, for example, it doubtless had the associated benefit of minimising the degree to which the Socialists' increasingly ambiguous defence position was made public, thus reducing the chances of provoking serious rifts within the Party. This was particularly evident at a time when the opinions of the Party hierarchy were evolving more rapidly than those of the rank-and-file membership.

The contention surrounding resource provision for France's defence set the parliamentary Right against the government for a large part of the decade, notwithstanding the Gaullist character of Pompidou's government, or the presence of the Gaullists as majority partners in Giscard's Right-Centre coalition. Allegations that insufficient financial means were being committed to defence surfaced as early as 1972, when the prominent Gaullist, Alexandre Sanguinetti (President of the National Defence Committee) argued that France risked being relegated to the lowest ranks of the powers in the Atlantic Alliance if spending on her armed forces was not immediately increased.[44] As the government was already engaged in a financial re-evaluation of the *loi-programme* for 1971–75, however, the prospects for adequate support of the services did not seem good. The worsening economic situation, linked to the oil price rises in the Middle East in 1973 and 1974, caused the monetary milieu of the armed forces to deteriorate further.

Indeed, by the time of the submission of its military budget in late 1975, the consequences of the international crisis were such that France was experiencing inflation in double figures, and rapidly rising unemployment,[45] both of which had been unprecedented during *les trente glorieuses*.[46] As the favourable French economic position had been one of the key factors in permitting the development of an autonomous nuclear deterrent capability, as well as maintaining conventional forces, the effects of the economic downturn on France's defence capacity were potentially serious. Such a realisation contributed to the discontent of the Right with the government line, so much so that the budget presented in 1975 was condemned as 'mediocre.... The increase in the volume of investments [did] not even correspond to the increased cost of living.'[47] No new weapons programmes were to be launched in 1976, and the timescale of those in progress would be extended to reduce their immediate financial impact. The adverse consequences for the armed forces aroused such concern that it prompted M. Debré, during the budget debate, to threaten that 'if the defence budget for 1977 [was] not better,... a certain number of [the Gaullist deputies would] draw conclusions from it, and [would] not refuse military credits, but [would] reject the entire national budget'.[48] Such concern was shared by some on the Left: as Chevènement argued, 'the essential choices [had] not [been] made to give credibility to France's defence ... the Government [had] an ulterior motive,... it practis[ed] a policy of deterioration'.[49]

The financial fears of the Right were reinforced by the government's *loi de programmation militaire*, submitted in 1976, since it sought to allocate a sum to the whole of the planning law, without separating this sum into projected credits for operational and equipment expenditure, as had previously been the case, and did not break down capital expenditure between the principal programmes.[50] This new innovation led to the project's condemnation as 'imprecise', 'ambiguous' and 'vague'[51] by the Gaullist J. Le Theule, *rapporteur* of the Finance Committee of the Assemblée Nationale. 'Imprecise' was also the term used by the *rapporteur* of the National Defence Committee, M. d'Aillières, who was a member of Giscard's own party.[52] The Left was also critical of the accounting device proposed by the Government, even declaring it unconstitutional. As an unnamed Socialist asserted, the whole plan amounted to 'a Bill which, if it was passed, would violate the rules of yearly budgeting.... It would be an open door to all abuses.'[53]

However, despite their evident concern, the Socialists' criticisms of the defence effort in the 1970s were quite muted. They were still less apparent in debates over other contentious military issues. Regarding an article by General Beauvallet, attempting to reconcile the positions of Christians in the Army with their profession, certain religious authorities took exception to the fact that the General had sought to determine how the Church should express itself on such a sensitive issue. A close interest in defence issues had been maintained by the Church since 1972, through concerns expressed over the arms trade.[54] The situation worsened considerably in the summer of 1973. By that time, to world-wide criticism, President Pompidou had instigated another series of atmospheric nuclear tests in the South Pacific. To compound international attacks, two French bishops reopened the controversy between the Church and the armed forces by condemning the action.[55]

The reactions of leading French military officials to these assaults were immediately evident: 'the military chiefs [were] apparently disappointed, astonished or exasperated by the attitude of certain ecclesiastical authorities ...'.[56] Admiral de Joybert, the Navy's Chief of Staff, was uncompromising, calling on the clergy to mind their own business.[57] For de Joybert, everyone should attend to their own area of competence: after all, 'he [did] not meddle with train driving or fish farming'.[58] While Hernu supported the right of the churchmen to express their thoughts, this was the nearest the PS came to an association with the dispute.

Concerns also arose in the 1970s regarding the military camps used by the Army for training and exercises. The 1970s saw an enlargement of the area of these camps, particularly through the construction of a new camp at Canjuers and the extension of existing military facilities at Larzac.[59] Reactions to the Canjuers proposals were not at all positive in 1972,[60] and the plans for the Larzac camp gave rise to a massive demonstration on the streets of Paris in 1973,[61] which was supported by 40 organisations including trades unions, the Socialist Party and the Communist Party. Such was the strength of feeling throughout France regarding the proposed changes at Larzac, that at a second public protest meeting at the Larzac site in summer 1974 the cause still attracted more than 100 000 people.[62] However, participation in the protest march was practically as far as Socialist involvement went in the 1970s: when François Mitterrand tried to address the summer meeting of 1974, he was actually booed down.[63]

Increasing debate on the Left

By the middle of the 1970s, however, the debate among the Socialists was increasing, and furthermore, it was becoming more overt. While the *Parti Socialiste* reiterated positions that had been set out by the Common Programme of Government, and repeated by François Mitterrand during his presidential election campaign of 1974,[64] serious reflection was well underway already, having been instigated by the Socialist leader himself at the Party Congress in Grenoble in 1973. The basic inconsistency between the public and private positions of the Socialist Party to which this gave rise were to persist even beyond the decision taken by the PS in January 1978.

The role of François Mitterrand in establishing defence as a topic for debate within the Socialist Party was considerable. It appeared that he recognised the fundamental inadequacies of both *Changer la Vie* and the Common Programme of Government, in relation to defence, at a very early stage. He argued at Grenoble in June 1973 that 'the duty, for a Socialist as for any other, [was] also to assume responsibility for the defence of his country'.[65] In a speech of which a significant part was dedicated to concerns over defence and military issues, Mitterrand further insisted:

A large party like [theirs did] not have the right to consider that the problem of the Nation's security [could] be the result of a sum of negations; [it could] not be, at the same time, against the professional army, against a military service which [was] long enough – when not against too short a military service – against the French atomic armament, against an atomic armament in alliance with those who possess it at the European level, against a possible nuclear armament, against a possible atomic and nuclear alliance with Soviet Russia, against Atlanticism, against neutralism....[66]

Such comments, reinforced by his personal perception that the stance of his 1965 Presidential election campaign had become untenable in respect of its anti-nuclear emphasis[67] and by his alleged encouragement to Hernu to reorientate the Socialist Party around a stance less averse to the nuclear force,[68] are indicative of the extent to which Mitterrand viewed significant changes in the provisions of the Common Programme of Government to be necessary.

Consequently, by the mid-1970s debate on defence was widespread at the higher levels of the PS, where Hernu had responsibility for defence questions, and he, along with Chevènement and R. Pontillon, most prominently, undertook extensive consideration of defence questions. It was clear from an early stage that Hernu, in particular, advocated a degree of nuclear capability for France,[69] and that later Chevènement, and the Left-wing faction of the PS that he led, CERES (the *Centre d'Etudes, de Recherches, et d'Education Socialistes*) also came to hold this view. However, the concurrence of these prominent party figures cannot be taken to indicate a predisposition for change among the majority of the PS in the defence principles of the Common Programme of Government. Factionalism within the Socialist Party was reinforced by widespread hostility towards nuclear deterrence. CERES itself, though vocal, was a minority group on the Left of the Party. In questions of defence and security, CERES was distinctly less Atlanticist than the other factions of the PS,[70] such as the much larger group of supporters of the old SFIO, which had favoured the Atlantic Alliance since its inception. Further, CERES's position on the Left, advocating class struggle and closer links to the Communist Party, meant it was regarded with suspicion by many.[71] Moreover, the long-standing opposition of many senior figures of the Socialist Party to a nuclear capability remained. There was disagreement even among those who were close to François Mitterrand: while Hernu was ardently in favour of the nuclear deterrent, P. Bérégovoy condemned it as 'ineffective on the military level, illusory on the diplomatic level and costly on the economic level'.[72] D. Taddei likewise considered it 'neither effective nor democratic'.[73] Mitterrand himself carefully avoided any commitment, reiterating that the policy of the *Parti Socialiste* remained that of the Common Programme of Government.[74]

Enhanced ambiguity among the Socialists

However, despite dissenting voices the PS was moving ever closer to acceptance of nuclear deterrence by 1976. As consideration of defence questions by its *Comité directeur* increased, the Party was seen to gravitate more firmly towards a formal breach with the terms of the Common Programme. The prospect of the enhanced proximity of a solid stance on defence by the Socialist Party did not, though, seem to permit a more authoritative intervention in the wider political debate which occurred at that time; namely, the debate over nuclear doctrine and the perceived Atlanticism of the government of Giscard d'Estaing.

The first major indicator of a significant reorientation in the Socialists' defence thinking in 1976 was the elaboration of an 80-page document on defence by the Party's National Defence Commission. As the appearance of the document almost coincided with the debate in the Assemblée Nationale over the *loi de programmation militaire* for 1977–82, the PS was placed in something of a quandary, for despite the provisions of the Common Programme of Government, the report envisaged a defence system under a Socialist government in which the nuclear deterrent force would constitute the cornerstone.[75] The extent of the contradiction between the public and private positions of the Socialists was thus becoming more visible.

The meeting of the *Comité directeur* of 12 June 1976 heard reports on defence, in its broader aspects, by Hernu, Chevènement and Pontillon – apparently at the request of François Mitterrand.[76] While the debate which ensued seemingly did little to advance a unity of position, the meeting was nevertheless significant as a sign of the increasing weight defence matters were felt to have within the Party, and for Mitterrand's admission, in conclusion, that the terms of the Common Programme on defence were increasingly at odds with the discussions taking place at the heart of the Party.[77] While recognising that only a National Convention could formally change the Socialists' stance, Mitterrand was keen that private reflections on defence questions should continue. Subsequently the debate focused more clearly on issues surrounding the nuclear force. At a meeting of the *Comité directeur* in November 1976, Hernu, Chevènement and Pontillon agreed that France should retain the means of assuring her security, and in particular that the nuclear force had become a reality of which it was necessary to take account.[78] While reiterating the importance of further consideration, François Mitterrand maintained that the PS's deliberations should safeguard France's 'autonomy of decision'.[79]

While the reports of these two meetings undoubtedly reaffirm the advanced stage of the Socialists' considerations on defence, they also raise further questions regarding Mitterrand's role in directing those considerations. Firstly, he requested reports from Hernu, Chevènement and Pontillon in June and November, when all three were known to be sympathetic to the ideas of nuclear deterrence that the Party officially repudiated. Moreover, he did not seek any expression of opinion by those who were still wedded to the official position, such as Rocard, who remained cautious in this matter, or Bérégovoy, who remained hostile to the nuclear force even in January 1978.[80] Secondly, when Mitterrand himself raised the issue of France's autonomy of decision, he chose to use a phrase more often associated with General de Gaulle as an argument for the nuclear force. From a writer who weighed the meaning of words carefully, this would seem an unusual oversight, adding credence to the argument that Mitterrand's role in amending the Socialists' position on defence was more significant than is usually suggested. Consequently, at a time when the leadership of the *Parti Socialiste*, at the highest levels, was involved in modifying its defence stance internally, but could not reveal the outcome of its deliberations, it is therefore less surprising that it should have remained so conspicuously reticent in debates over changes to France's nuclear doctrines, or over the Atlanticism, or otherwise, of the defence policy pursued by Giscard d'Estaing.

Giscard's modifications to the defence position aroused the hostility of both the Gaullists and the Communists – albeit for different reasons. The decision to halt the atmospheric testing of France's nuclear weapons in October 1974,[81] and a televised interview with Giscard d'Estaing in 1975,[82] gave rise to the perception that France's nuclear doctrines were changing and that the country would pursue more overt, conventional military cooperation with NATO in the future. The proposed *loi de programmation militaire*, debated in May 1976, was also seen to contribute to a reorientation of France's defence position. Further, when Giscard announced his intentions that France's armed forces should be improved until their standards matched those of the West German Bundeswehr,[83] and spoke of French defence being able to counterbalance the power of the Warsaw Pact countries only as part of the wider Atlantic Alliance,[84] Gaullist and Communist concerns intensified. The gravity of the situation was reinforced, for them, by an article from Giscard's Chief of Defence Staff, General Méry, envisaging France's participation in the NATO strategy of the forward defence of Western Europe, and the possibility of France's nuclear weapons constituting an area of enlarged sanctuary, rather than protecting solely the national sanctuary.[85] A speech by the president to the IHEDN, suggesting that France would be involved in any battle in Europe from the outset,[86] appeared to confirm a seemingly radical alteration to the foundations of defence planning.

After the proposal of the *loi de programmation militaire*, such were the perceptions of a European dimension to France's future defence, and of a shift towards American and West German security preferences, that the Bill was disparagingly referred to as *la loi Helmut Schmidt*.[87] Sanguinetti, for the Gaullists, alleged that it was 'designed to destroy the military apparatus and reconvert it to a European defence'.[88] In addition, it was declared that Méry's and Giscard's strategy modifications 'diverg[ed] absolutely from the political and military conception of Gaullism',[89] leaving France's conventional forces to be nothing more than 'NATO's rank and file'.[90] Other Gaullists were also perturbed by Giscard's options, as Debré affirmed: 'There [was] more a hesitation than a true retreat in French military thinking. But the ambiguity remain[ed] and there [was] a risk of a shift.'[91]

For the PCF, the proposed law 'prepar[ed] for a return to NATO and sanction[ed] "the abandonment of *tous azimuts* defence"'.[92] They were concerned that '"the enemy" was designated in advance:... it [was] the Soviet Union', despite the fact that Giscard had recently signed a declaration of friendship and cooperation with the USSR.[93] Indeed for the Communists, 'Giscard's policy [was] a *dangerous* policy, which [took France] back to the worst moments of the Cold War',[94] when the prevailing trend was one of détente. France's strategy was therefore 'the most belligerent of all Europe'.[95]

Given the state of Socialist defence considerations, the *loi de programmation militaire* made an extremely untimely appearance. At a time when the leadership was becoming more favourable to the idea of maintaining the French nuclear force, Giscard was proposing a conscious emphasis on conventional capabilities – and yet the Socialists could not argue for a reversal of priorities, for fear of being identified with the Gaullists, of offending the Communists, and not least of moving more quickly than the extent of their debates would permit, thereby risking the emergence of deep divisions within the wider Party membership.[96] J. Huntzinger, a member of the National Defence Commission who advocated the acceptance of the fact of the French nuclear deterrent, therefore confined himself to describing Giscard's plan as a 'great turning point'[97] in France's defence policy, and not necessarily a change for the better. Hernu focused his criticisms on the moves towards NATO – although many in the Socialist Party, including François Mitterrand, were long-time supporters of the Atlantic Alliance, the PS had come to rally around the principle of national independence. Consequently, Hernu, while perceiving limits to Giscard's legal alterations to France's alliance and associated defence stance, still noted that 'without a return to the integrated structures, there [was] at least a convergence and connivance with NATO',[98] whereby France was 'preparing for forward defence ... it

[was] thus no longer about maintaining the defence of the French sanctuary, but participating in the defence of the continent on West German soil'.[99] Members of the CERES faction believed that the condemnation of Giscard's Atlanticism should go much further,[100] thus illustrating the difficulties of the *Parti Socialiste* at this time in expressing a consensual position on questions of defence.

Towards acceptance of nuclear deterrence

Given the Socialists' prolonged, and increasingly public defence debate from the middle of the 1970s, and the hostility of the Communists to all developments in defence thinking on the part of the Socialists, it is perhaps surprising that the conversion of the PCF to acceptance of the principles of nuclear deterrence should have predated that of the PS. The Communists' decision, in line with their professed concern over the Atlanticist drift of government policy and its implications for the independence and security of France, but seemingly in direct contradiction to the previous hostility the PCF had demonstrated toward the nuclear deterrent,[101] did not, however, ameliorate relations between themselves and the Socialists. Divergences over defence questions persisted during the summer of 1977 and tensions between them worsened over the updating of the Common Programme of Government. Considering such factors, as well as the residual hostility of much of the PS membership to the nuclear force, the Socialists' formal acceptance of the French nuclear force was not necessarily a foregone conclusion.

The primary target for Communist attack throughout the 1970s had been Hernu.[102] The Communist daily, *L'Humanité*, took repeated exception to his preference for the nuclear force on the grounds that it followed the existing government line, and contradicted the bases of the Common Programme of Government.[103] The newspaper was particularly concerned by the positions of Hernu, Chevènement and Pontillon at the CCRAN Congress of March 1975: while they tended more openly towards the nuclear force, their stance was never disavowed by the Party leadership.[104] Harsh criticism of the evolving Socialist position was barely concealed; as *L'Humanité* argued, 'fidelity to the Common Programme of the Left [could] not put up with either duplicity or with the violation of the commitments signed before the people of France'.[105] The suspicions were, however, mutual,[106] and the poor climate of relations between the parties was not improved by the Communists' decision of May 1977.

The Socialists' internal defence debates continued after that date, although Hernu agitated for the early convocation of a National Convention to amend their defence stance following the Communists' shift.[107] Mitterrand however refused: he

> was more in favour of not initiating the debate, which [had] every chance of provoking rifts in the Party and in its electorate, before the next elections.[108] In the event of a victory of the Left, the recognition of the fact of the *force de frappe* would be passed 'painlessly' in the euphoria of victory.[109]

For the Socialist Party, however, the transition to acceptance of the nuclear force throughout the latter part of 1977 was far from 'painless', and the prospects of moving closer were slim. Even as the *Comité directeur* set a date for the National Convention, the journal *Faire* demonstrated the depths of persistent divergences by publishing a debate between Huntzinger and Taddei.[110] If elements of the Party hierarchy were still not reconciled to deterrence principles, it was little wonder that the wider membership remained sceptical.[111]

The advancement of the Socialists' debate was also hindered by the arguments in which they became embroiled with the Communists over the updating of the Common Programme of Government. Divergences between the two main signatories were apparent on almost every aspect; social policy, nationalisation and defence were only the most significant.[112] The breaking-point of the Union of the Left came in fact over nationalisation: the difficulties over defence were no less momentous.

During the course of negotiations, negotiators tried to reach agreement on four main criteria: general disarmament was to be sought by any government of the Left; a world conference, or at least a conference of nuclear powers was to be convened to that end; the French nuclear armament, in the meantime, would be maintained in working order; and finally, the ultimate decision would rest with the French people.[113] While the first two criteria may well have been generally acceptable, the latter were not. H. Védrine, Mitterrand's adviser, and later Strategic Counsellor at the Palais de l'Elysée during his presidency, insisted at interview that differences between the main signatories over the third point were manifold. Moreover, Mitterrand was determined that the parties should agree to the maintenance of the nuclear force *en état* – meaning in working order, and implying its development and upgrading so that it remained in working order. The

Communist Party, on the other hand, preferred the phrase to read *en l'état*.[114] To Védrine, this meant in the order in which the force existed in 1977, which, without modification, would soon become obsolete. The attention paid by the Socialist Party to the wording of any updated Common Programme was underlined at the time by Bérégovoy: 'words [could] mean many things,... and [the Socialists were] attentive to the use of certain words'.[115] In conjunction with the fourth point, namely Mitterrand's proposal for a referendum on the nuclear force, which the Communists interpreted as the Socialists' wish to avoid making any firm decisions,[116] the proposed criteria for agreement on defence questions were patently unacceptable to the Communists.

The difficulties over updating the defence provisions of the Common Programme demonstrate two aspects in particular. Firstly, they show that the Socialist Party had still not secured an acceptable common position regarding new defence commitments, and especially regarding the nuclear force. Secondly, they reiterate the interest François Mitterrand personally took in developing the Party's stance on defence. Notwithstanding his continued reluctance to express his own preferences regarding the nuclear capability – even at the height of the fruitless discussions with the Communists, he insisted that the Socialist defence policy was that set out in the Common Programme[117] – he took a leading role in directing that development.

However, irrespective of the years of deliberation by the PS, the National Convention which took place in January 1978 did not indicate that a consensus had been reached in the Party. The motion for discussion, presented unanimously by the *Bureau exécutif* of the PS (after three meetings which had been necessary, even with Mitterrand's arbitration, so a common text could be agreed),[118] achieved a 'subtle synthesis'[119] between advocates and opponents of a nuclear deterrent capability. The motion recognised the fact of the nuclear capability, with the maintenance, in working order, of the submarine component, while initiating nuclear disarmament by destroying the Mirage nuclear bombers and the land-based missiles of the Plateau d'Albion. The first condition was essential for advocates of the deterrent force; the second equally so for its opponents. In this way, by emphasising the importance the PS would attribute to disarmament, as had been pledged since the 1960s, the Party leadership evidently hoped to maximise support for its proposed changes. Indeed, within the wider programme the PS now adopted, the ultimate renunciation of the nuclear force which the Party was being asked to accept remained an objective, if it was so desired by the French people.[120] Nevertheless, the machinations of the

Party hierarchy failed to paper over all the divergences within the Party membership, and notably failed to prevent the presentation of an opposing motion at the National Convention, which forwarded a more complete disarmament plan, and a schedule for its accomplishment, by a group of Socialists whose loyalties were divided among all the main currents of the Party.[121] Despite the acceptance of the leadership's motion at the Convention, the contradictions in the Socialist stance remained, not least of which was precisely how a deterrence strategy would be maintained if the renunciation objective was also pursued.

As mentioned above, the extent to which the PS had undergone change in its provisions regarding defence policy during the 1970s was demonstrated during the presidential election campaign of 1981. Those provisions were indeed fundamentally altered; and although disarmament remained an option, it had less prominence than it had even had in 1978. In this respect, Mitterrand could not have disregarded the deterioration in the international situation: détente was dead, after the invasion of Afghanistan, the demise of the SALT process, the Soviet military build-up in Central and Eastern Europe, the NATO twin-track decision ... and not least the election of Ronald Reagan to the White House in 1980. At a time which was most definitely not right for disarmament, Mitterrand, once described as a 'consummate sniffer of the wind',[122] could not be other than acutely aware of it. His unequivocal support for the twin-track decision underlined this point. However, while the stance of the Socialists, as well as that of the Communists, had been reversed during the decade with regard to defence and the nuclear force, it must be said that this did not lead to any widespread consensus on defence in France at the end of the 1970s.

Into the 1980s

The argument of this chapter has been twofold: firstly, that defence debate in France in the 1970s was extensive, which necessarily affected suggestions of any subsequent consensus, and secondly, that the role of François Mitterrand in advancing the particular defence debates of the Socialist Party at that time was greater than has previously been portrayed. The degree to which consensus was not actually apparent by the end of the 1970s was reflected by the continuing discontent among the Right, in consideration of the financial means devoted to defence, and, for them, the unsatisfactory defence priorities that this entailed – while the necessity of defining priorities was not contested, that undertaken by the governments of Giscard d'Estaing met with almost universal disapproval. Notwithstanding the formal conversions of the Communist and Socialist Parties to the principles of nuclear deterrence, they were far from being in agreement among themselves and with each other on the way by which France's defence establishment was to move forwards into the 1980s, let alone in agreement with the Right of the political spectrum as to the underlying issues of strategy, such as the proportionate emphasis on deterrence and disarmament, to be pursued. Neither were the Socialists' dissatisfactions addressed in terms of the conventional forces in the 1970s. Discord over military service was never really settled, thus leaving that institution to enter the 1980s in much the same condition, and bearing many of the same contradictions, as it had entered the 1970s. Even the concerns of the Right over conventional forces were not resolved by the latter years of Giscard's presidency: insufficiencies of equipment and training, and questions of their role in relation to the nuclear forces, remained.

While debate and discontent persisted throughout the decade, the role of François Mitterrand in the Socialists' deliberations of defence issues is particularly interesting. It can be seen that he was not only directly but also indirectly involved in the progression of the Socialists' thinking: directly through the stimulus he provided for reflection from the time of the Congress of Grenoble, and more often, indirectly, by such actions as his presence at the Congress of the CCRAN, which was well-known to be progressive in its attitudes to defence, his apparently close involvement in the debates over the updating of the Common Programme of Government, and not least his encouragement of Charles Hernu to push forward the debate within the Socialist Party to move nearer to a more modern and pragmatic defence stance than it had previously adopted.[123] However, it seems that even after 1974 Mitterrand had not lost sight of the presidency, and he took care to remain above the day-to-day debates which were taking place in his Party, wherever possible. This was especially the case with the defence debates, which had the potential to be seriously divisive. Nonetheless, it appears that Mitterrand's influence over the Socialists' defence debates, though concealed to an extent, was formative over the course of their transformation in the 1970s.

3
Mitterrand and Defence: an Overview

The interests which François Mitterrand had demonstrated in questions of France's defence, prior to his accession to the presidency, were to be augmented and amplified thereafter. Mitterrand indeed was to embrace the concept of the presidential *domaine réservé* in defence and foreign policy issues that had been established by General de Gaulle. However, it was a characteristic of the Mitterrand presidency that his interests in, and influence over, France's defence were to become more apparent as the 1980s progressed than they were initially in May 1981. This was a consequence of both internal and external factors. As the role of the President increased, so that of his Defence Ministers arguably decreased. Nevertheless, if Mitterrand accepted his *domaine réservé* with ease, it would appear that over the course of his presidential terms, he was less concerned to preserve the notion of the consensus which was alleged to surround France's defence.

The Socialists in office, 1981–86

In the first years of Mitterrand's presidency, French defence was the responsibility of Charles Hernu. Through his role in the Socialists' defence deliberations of the previous decade, Hernu already enjoyed the support of much of the PS, and to a large extent the support of the military, due to his prolonged public stance in favour of the retention and development of the nuclear capability. Hernu's tenancy of 14 rue St Dominique in the years 1981–85 indicated three main themes which would come to characterise Mitterrand's early presidency in relation to defence: that Mitterrand's role in the running of France's defence was initially limited, at least ostensibly, although this did not extend to questions of the deployment of French troops overseas; that while continuity could be said to be a defining principle of the Socialist President and government in relation to defence priorities, certain changes could be discerned through the military budgeting and planning undertaken; and that the interaction between French defence concerns, and broader international defence and security issues, would come to dominate the calculations of the Defence Minister, and increasingly the President, towards the middle of the decade. After Hernu's resignation over the *Rainbow Warrior* affair in 1985, his replacement by the lesser-known P. Quilès furnished Mitterrand with an ideal opportunity to shift his attention more firmly towards defence and security questions.

In office, Hernu acted quickly to assert his authority over France's defence. His task was facilitated by the growing preoccupation of the rest of the Socialist government, including the President, with economic issues. Within weeks of the Left's electoral victories, the Defence Minister had made all newspapers and journals available in French barracks,[1] announced the end of the Larzac extension,[2] and declared himself in favour of continued research on the neutron bomb.[3] In terms of military planning, he announced the postponement of a new *loi de programmation militaire* due to the delays and shortcomings in the existing law,[4] but reiterated the Socialists' intentions to develop the nuclear force through the construction of two more nuclear submarines.[5] As the government and the President were faced with a deteriorating (and partly self-inflicted) economic situation,[6] underlined by a complete reversal in economic policy in 1982,[7] Hernu's role in the delineation and direction of France's defence was high-profile from the beginning.

From 1982 Hernu's role was still more accentuated, as the economic crisis facing France deepened, and the support of the political spectrum for the defence policy intended by the Left was called into question.[8] The effects of the recession on France's military budget in that year aroused the hostility of the Centre and Right.[9] Although the defence budget passed for 1982 had projected a rise in funding of 17.6 per cent (about 4 per cent in real terms),[10] the government first froze, and subsequently cancelled 16.6 billion francs of credits in the autumn of 1982.[11] The figure was argued by the Opposition to constitute 18 per cent of the year's planned military investment.[12] The national economic difficulties encountered by the Socialists were in a large part contributory to the difficulties Hernu faced in securing the passage of the defence budget for 1983.[13] The stagnation of the budget at 3.89 per cent of Gross Domestic Product (GDP), despite promises that it would increase to 3.94 per cent,[14] and the lack of security for such credits voted, meant that Hernu came under increasing pressure.[15] The rejection of the defence budget for 1983 by the Senate (the first refusal of a defence budget by the Senate during the Fifth Republic) was seen as a personal defeat for the Minister.[16]

As well as financial considerations, Hernu's attention was also focused on plans for a major reorganisation of the armed forces. A certain disquiet had been apparent within the services, most notably the Army, since the Prime Minister Pierre Mauroy's speech to the *Institut des Hautes Etudes de Défense Nationale* (IHEDN) in September 1982, where he had advocated a 'new model of army' for France.[17] The Army's fears over its future role were exacerbated by the 1983 defence budget: while resource allocations were increased for the nuclear forces, the figures for the Army were reduced. In addition, certain of the duties of the land army were transferred to the *Gendarmerie*. In this context, Hernu's speech to a meeting of the Western European Union (WEU) in Paris at the end of November 1982 was intended to reassure the Army about its future: according to Hernu, France intended to enhance the abilities of her ground forces to intervene rapidly, and with greater flexibility, in a European conflict.[18]

The extent of the armed forces' reorganisation to which Hernu aspired became apparent with the submission of the Socialists' *loi de programmation militaire* for 1984–88, in 1983. While its main theme remained the priority attached to the nuclear element of France's defence, the major provision for the conventional forces was the creation of a *Force d'Action Rapide* (FAR), and a reduction of manpower across the Services, with the Army shouldering most of the burden. That Hernu had not succeeded in carrying the whole of the military hierarchy with him in this respect was confirmed by the resignation of General Delaunay, the Chief of Staff of the Army, during the elaboration of the new planning law. Nevertheless, the adaptation was broadly accepted, with one newspaper referring to it as the greatest innovation in French deterrence strategy since the time of Charles de Gaulle.[19] When the planning law was debated in the Assemblée Nationale, the debate was, perhaps, surprisingly bereft of discord. Despite the dissatisfaction of the Opposition parties with the Bill – among the Right on the grounds of a perceived maladjustment of the military structure to the needs of modern defence,[20] and the inadequacies of financial provision, and among the Communists due to the Bill's designation of the Soviet Union as France's major potential enemy – it was passed largely without serious controversy.[21]

If the evocation of the Socialists' defence strategy was therefore Hernu's responsibility in the early years of the Mitterrand presidency, the same could not be said of decisions regarding the deployment of French forces overseas at that time. Straddling questions of both foreign and military policy, such deployments, occurring most notably in Lebanon and Chad, fell squarely within the traditional presidential *domaine réservé*, and were subsequently taken up by the new Socialist occupant of the Elysée Palace with the same facility his predecessors had shown.

From the outset of Israeli hostilities against Palestinian positions in Lebanon in June 1982 Mitterrand took a close interest in developments, demonstrating at least initially a certain sympathy for Israeli aims.[22] In the second major press conference of his presidential term on 9 June 1982, Mitterrand was markedly less firm in his condemnation of Israel than had been either the Quai d'Orsay or the Socialist Party.[23] However, as hostilities continued, and Israel, along with her main supporter the United States, showed what the French President and Foreign Ministry perceived to be a lack of concern for the fate of the Palestinians,[24] Mitterrand began to distance himself from his earlier position, to take a harder line against Israeli actions.[25]

Such increased consideration on the part of the French President for Palestinian affairs was translated into several high-profile diplomatic attempts to achieve a peaceful resolution of the crisis, through initiatives within the European Community, and jointly on the wider international stage with Egypt.[26] It was also manifested in the multinational peacekeeping force, comprising French, American and Italian forces, which was sent to Lebanon in August to evacuate Palestinian combatants. Indeed, French forces were numerically the strongest contingent. The rapidity of the French return to Lebanon after the precipitate international withdrawal of September 1982, together with the maintenance of troops in the conflict area in subsequent months, despite heavy losses in October 1983, were also largely attributable to the will of the French President. The primacy of the Elysée role in managing France's reactions to the crisis was clearly apparent.[27]

Such primacy was also apparent over French involvement in Chad. This involvement was not new; both de Gaulle and Giscard d'Estaing had sent French forces to Chad in previous years, and this single issue was argued to have been the 'nightmare and failure'[28] of each of Mitterrand's predecessors. In this light, Mitterrand diverted the Chadian President's initial call for French assistance, in October 1981, to the Organisation of African Unity (OAU). Subsequent French assistance to support the Chadian regime specifically excluded the prospect of military intervention. This was so even when the government of Goukouni Oueddeï was replaced by one under the former rebel Hissène Habré, who enjoyed American support – on the direction of the Elysée, France recognised the new authority and continued much as before in furthering Chadian reconstruction.[29]

The Chadian question became much more difficult after June 1983 when Libyan forces, in conjunction with the troops of the ousted leader Goukouni, relaunched hostilities. As Habré's regime was increasingly threatened, the French President came under sustained American pressure to intervene militarily – pressure which he resisted, while maintaining his attempts to encourage an inter-African solution. However, as Libyan forces advanced towards Chad's capital, N'djamena, thus threatening renewed destabilisation of the whole country, the situation for France became untenable. Military intervention to prevent further Libyan advances thereafter became inevitable, and on Mitterrand's decision, French troops were sent to Chad[30] in August 1983. The termination of the operation, in autumn 1984, was as much a decision of the President as had been its beginning: after secret talks with the Libyans, firstly through the Foreign Minister, Cheysson, and latterly through a top-secret meeting between Mitterrand and Gaddhafi themselves, withdrawal was instigated. Though the Libyan side of the agreement was never fully kept, the problem could be shelved by France until a resumption of hostilities in early 1986.

The significant features of the Chadian and Lebanese experiences were manifold. They included the extent of the role of the President and Foreign Ministry, to the exclusion of the Defence Ministry except in the implementation of presidential decisions; the precedent set in Lebanon for United Nations approval of multinational operations, which was to recur in the last third of Mitterrand's presidency; and the evidence in Chad that France under a Socialist president would still intervene abroad to protect its own, broadly defined, national interests. Continuity prevailed in ideas of France's rank and status, and her residual responsibilities with regard to her former African colonies. Demonstrations of French resistance to American pressures were also interesting, especially as a backdrop to the increasingly high-profile role Mitterrand took in questions of French defence *per se*, from 1985, with the extension of consideration of both the Strategic Defense Initiative and the superpower arms control process.

Arms control had had a particular relevance for François Mitterrand since he came to office, irrespective of his apparent reluctance to pronounce on other major aspects of the defence and security environment. Even before his election, he had supported the NATO twin-track decision;[31] and in a subsequent speech to the West German Bundestag in January 1983 he had pressed the wavering West Germans to maintain their commitment to the NATO deployment of US Cruise and Pershing II missiles.[32] He was, however, adamant that as France had taken no part in the NATO decision, having withdrawn from the integrated military command in 1966, she would not countenance such deployment on her soil. He likewise maintained that French nuclear arsenals could not be counted amongst any collective total of the West, as had been demanded by Soviet officials since 1982, and said so in as many words during his first presidential visit to the USSR in 1984.[33] However, the catalysts for the extended consideration which arms control and associated issues received in 1985 were several. First, the Americans had succeeded in making significant progress with SDI,[34] thus making SDI, and its potential consequences for the credibility of the limited French nuclear deterrent, more serious. Second, the US had reached the stage where it was inviting allied cooperation in the technological research and development of elements of the SDI programme. Third, consideration of questions regarding nuclear deterrence was more prominent at that time anyway in France because of the advent of the twenty-fifth anniversary of the first French nuclear explosion in the Sahara. Finally, the superpower arms control talks were due to resume in Geneva in March, meaning that the strategic situation from the French perspective, given the previous demands of the USSR regarding the French forces, remained decidedly uncertain.

Thereafter, it would seem that François Mitterrand took a firm decision to 'lead from the front' in 1985. Though the official viewpoint on the Strategic Defense Initiative, as forwarded by senior members of the President's staff in 1985, stated that a full realisation of any effective strategic defence was highly improbable,[35] it was particularly significant that according to Hernu, Mitterrand had previously ordered the modernisation of France's nuclear warheads to assist them in any penetration of potential enemy ballistic missile defences.[36] While implementing such measures, however, the French President was also determined that France should take some part in the exploitation of space: so much so that the Communist daily *L'Humanité* accused Mitterrand of betraying French independence to the Americans.[37] On the contrary, however, it was Mitterrand's preference that any French research into space issues should occur as part of a European initiative:

thus he proposed a European alternative to SDI, EUREKA (the European Research Co-ordination Agency), focusing on the peaceful civilian uses of space, in April 1985.[38] Nevertheless, the French were still actively considering the military implications of space exploitation, notably through the creation of a Space Studies Group within the Ministry of Defence.[39] After Hernu's resignation in autumn 1985 Mitterrand retained his fixation with space, to the extent that *Le Monde's* military correspondent J. Isnard perceived that the question of space defence had become an 'obsession' for the President,[40] and one which was reflected in the defence budget for 1986. The budget devoted credits to the development of a network of Syracuse communications satellites, and a system of Hélios reconnaissance satellites.[41] Moreover, Mitterrand was to have talks with West Germany's Chancellor Kohl in December 1985, to consider broader European space cooperation.[42]

Consequently, during the first five years of his Presidency, Mitterrand's visible role in the delineation of France's defence had increased, and his interests in questions of that defence had been extended. Behind the scenes, his influence over the direction of defence had been considerable, particularly over the elaboration of long-term defence planning, and in France's responses to the ever more rapid changes in the international security environment. In addition, his preference for a cooperative dimension to European defence, particularly between France and her neighbour West Germany, had also begun to surface. Nevertheless, his attachment to the principles of France's national independence, particularly in her own national defence through her possession of nuclear capabilities, and to the role of the President of the Republic in preserving that independence, was guarded with an increasing tenacity, which became fully apparent during the *cohabitation* with the Right, in 1986–88.

Cohabitation, 1986–88

Mitterrand's role in relation to France's defence from early 1986 was considerable, and encompassed five specific areas. Firstly, Mitterrand was concerned to reinforce the notion of the ultimate responsibility of the President of the Republic for matters of defence and security, in the face of a potentially serious challenge to his position from the forceful leader of the RPR, Jacques Chirac, after the successes of the Right in the legislative elections of March 1986. Secondly, Mitterrand was determined that France should retain her distance from the American SDI programme, on which his and Chirac's views were divergent. Thirdly, differences between the two men would also arise over Chirac's plan for a review, and redefinition, of the military policy pursued by the Socialists over the previous five years. Fourthly, the reappearance of the superpower arms control issue in 1987 presented Mitterrand with an opportunity to reiterate the primacy of his leadership, and finally the question of European cooperation in defence also figured prominently in French defence considerations – although on this matter, Mitterrand and his government were perhaps more in agreement than over any other defence issue. All of these factors combined to inflict grave damage on the image of a defence consensus in France: damage which was compounded by Mitterrand's *Letter to the French People*[43] of his presidential re-election campaign in 1988.

Mitterrand had begun to assert his constitutional role as head of the armed forces, particularly in respect of the nuclear forces, even before the election of March 1986. The publication of a collection of his speeches on defence and foreign policy at the beginning of 1986 reinforced the notion of the President's primary role in such questions. Reiterating that 'the Constitution ... made the Head of State the guarantor of national independence and territorial integrity', Mitterrand reminded his readers that 'to this end, the Government [had] the armed forces at its disposal, of which the President [was] the Chief. As the ultimate authority, he alone [could] command the use of the strategic force, that [was] to say, [France's] nuclear weapons.'[44] As the election approached, and speculation as to the likelihood of Socialist defeat increased, Mitterrand spoke in veiled terms of such a possibility, and the effects this would have on the direction of the defence effort:

> The only one to give the order for a nuclear engagement [was] the President of the Republic. It [was] a matter of seconds. It [would be] very difficult to deliberate, to consult. Taking counsel together in these conditions? The war [would] already [be] over....[45]

It was therefore already apparent that he had no intention of diluting his responsibilities for the ultimate defence of France. In addition, Mitterrand had let it be known to Chirac that in the event of the latter's victory, the President would insist on vetting appointments to certain key ministries. As well as his right to appoint the Prime Minister, Mitterrand also wanted to sanction the appointments of the

Minister of Foreign Affairs, the Minister of Defence and the Minister of the Interior.[46]

The President's desire to assert his authority over defence was further evident at the end of May. Following Chirac's declared intentions to modernise the land-based component of the nuclear force, and affirmations of support for the Strategic Defense Initiative, Mitterrand reasserted his attachment to France's independence in nuclear deterrence, and thus indicated indirectly his opposition to Chirac's position on SDI[47] during a visit to the military college at Saint-Cyr:

> [France would] not let herself be led into a conflict that she would not have clearly accepted. She [was] faithful to her alliances, she [was] loyal in her obligations. But [conflict was] a matter for her sole decision only....[48]

Mitterrand was widely perceived to be reinforcing his own position as head of the armed forces, while underlining the limitations on the role of the Prime Minister.[49] He also emphasised his own preferences over those of his Defence Minister, A. Giraud, who wished to redirect resources from the Army to the other services.[50] These were certainly timely indications to Chirac that the President would continue to take a close interest in defence, and that he would not shirk from expressing any differences of opinion with his government.

The Strategic Defense Initiative, which had prompted in part Mitterrand's words at Saint-Cyr, was to be a difficult issue between the President and the Prime Minister. It had been so as early as the second *Conseil des ministres* of Chirac's premiership, on 26 March, where it had given rise to an altercation between the two men. Over SDI, Chirac is said to have told the President that he wanted France to participate in the project, for 'it [was] one of [his] election promises'. Mitterrand in return was uncompromising: France would never participate as long as he was in office, and if Chirac insisted, Mitterrand would call a referendum on it. Moreover, Mitterrand argued, he would win.[51] Thereafter, the position of Chirac and his government on SDI seemed to vacillate.[52] A compromise was not apparently found until June, when Giraud announced in Washington that although French firms might participate in SDI research, as the Socialists had permitted the previous year, France would not make the political gesture of formal association with SDI.[53] While thus resolved, the difficulties over SDI between the President and Prime Minister showed the determination of the former to capitalise on his constitutional responsibilities for defence, and perhaps more importantly on the constitutional ambiguity surrounding the role of the prime minister and government, and the subsequent willingness of the Prime Minister in this case to amend his position for the sake of workable defence relations with the President.

The third area of difficulty between the Elysée and the Matignon in 1986 concerned the proposals of the latter to redefine France's military policy, and reorganise her armed forces. Difficulties had been foreshadowed from the beginning of Chirac's premiership. This was highlighted in April, when commentators observed that although the principle of Chirac's plans to introduce a new land component to the nuclear armoury was probably acceptable, the detail was probably not. Such a move would have the benefit of avoiding, in Hernu's phrase, 'putting all [France's] warheads in the same basket';[54] but there was scope for much disagreement over the form of such a second component – mobile or modernised fixed missiles, cruise or fixed trajectory ballistic missiles, or even the neutron bomb.[55] Moreover, the preferences of the President were known to lie with the submarine element of the nuclear deterrent capability. Therefore, although Mitterrand and Chirac had allegedly been keen to promote a consensus on 'the conceptual directions of the defence policy',[56] meaning the nuclear deterrence strategy, preference for a superpower balance of forces in Europe, and membership of the Atlantic Alliance, there was in fact little basis for agreement.

Chirac took two opportunities around the middle of 1986 to assert his own position with regard to France's defence capability, particularly with regard to his proposed force reorganisations. In July, he insisted that he would take a full part in the redefinition of military policy he had instigated, with the aim of forwarding a new *loi de programmation militaire* around the end of the year. Further, the redefinition would specifically deal with the problems of the Socialists' inadequate financial commitments to defence.[57] He reiterated his views in his speech to the IHEDN in September. Modernisation of the French military edifice would encompass the nuclear deterrent and satellite capabilities, and in addition France's conventional forces could see their role altered through a coupling of tactical nuclear weapons to the conventional forces.[58]

Nevertheless Mitterrand again disagreed, as he indicated on a visit to the training base of the 11th Parachute division at Caylus in October. His visit took place approximately a month before the decisive *Conseil de défense* which would pronounce on the detail of the forthcoming *loi de programmation militaire*. Reasserting his own prime authority over France's military and nuclear capabilities, Mitterrand indicated that

> the duty of the Government and of the Staffs [was] to try to find, on every occasion, a joint and harmonious definition of what they consider[ed] to be the interest of France. If the whole of these contingencies [could] not be brought to a joint decision, the moment [came] when one must act from authority. In that area, the authority belong[ed] to the President of the Republic.[59]

Moreover, Mitterrand declared that Chirac's conceptions of France's nuclear strategy were flawed; tactical nuclear weapons could not be separated from the whole of the deterrent capability, and their use by conventional forces would only undermine deterrence. The President's speech, represented as *'le nucléaire, c'est moi'*, reasserted the primacy of Elysée over Matignon in matters of defence. This was confirmed by the subsequent submission of the Right's *loi de programmation militaire* for 1987–91: although the Bill contained an element of being 'all things to all men', it clearly reflected the preferences and priorities of François Mitterrand, and was indeed supported in Parliament by Socialist deputies on that basis.

The question of superpower arms control which arose in 1987 by contrast demonstrated some similarity in the approaches of Mitterrand and Chirac to defence and security. After the acceptance of the zero option by Mikhail Gorbachev, the prevailing Right-wing attitudes were reserved at best, and outright hostile at worst, towards the zero option, whereas Mitterrand retained the attitude he had displayed earlier in the decade. He was supportive of the zero option on Intermediate-range missiles in Europe, while still refusing the inclusion of France's nuclear capabilities within this disarmament framework.[60] This was to remain his position even on the final INF Treaty conclusion,[61] and as such the strength of the President's conviction, supported in this instance by the Prime Minister Chirac, was sufficient to over-ride the objections from the wider Right.

Even more than over superpower disarmament, concord between Mitterrand and Chirac was apparent over the question of Franco-German cooperation in the realm of defence and security; a subject which promoted agreement within Chirac's broader government. After Chirac's electoral victory, this cooperative approach was sealed when the Prime Minister expressed his view that 'there [was] no security for [France] without security for her neighbours'.[62] He went further during his speech to the IHEDN of September, when he spoke of France's readiness to enhance defence cooperation with West Germany wherever possible, and to consult over any possible use of tactical nuclear weapons if the circumstances allowed.[63] When, in 1987, the West German government proposed a deepening of military cooperation between France and themselves, perhaps at the brigade level, the French authorities were almost unanimous in their support. Although Mitterrand showed some caution, citing the problem of historical differences,[64] he continued to promote the Franco-German defence collaboration he had sought since 1981.

Consequently, by the end of his first presidential term, François Mitterrand had established a significant interest in, and influence over, France's defence and security establishment, which had become more pronounced as his *septennat* had progressed. The demands of domestic politics had played a part in this development, as had the increasingly international aspect to such considerations, thus requiring the evident attention of the Head of State. However, the necessity for the open involvement in defence and security that Mitterrand perceived did not extend to submerging all differences between himself and his governments for the sake of the alleged consensus. He readily contradicted Chirac's government, and reasserted his personal authority over defence matters. Indeed he openly criticised Chirac on defence issues in his *Letter to the French People*, as for example with his disparaging assertions that Chirac had always ceded his own principles on defence to the will of the presidency.[65] The preferences of the President, it seemed, were paramount over those of any government, and Mitterrand could thus watch as politicians keen to preserve the illusion of agreement struggled to refocus the alleged consensus around the will of the President. With the election of a Socialist majority in the legislative elections called after Mitterrand's re-election, the combative style of Mitterrand's involvement was less obvious, but there was no concealing the firm hand of the President at the head of France's defence.

Return to power: the Socialists in office, 1988–93

In terms of defence, and of Mitterrand's relations with his Defence Ministers, the continuing strong role of the former, to the detriment of the potential for autonomous action of the latter, was one of the prominent features of Mitterrand's second term of office. Mitterrand's preferences in questions of financial provision and military planning for the armed forces, particularly in the post-Cold War context which developed during his presidency, in the use of those forces overseas, and in questions of France's nuclear deterrent, were predominant in many decisions taken and implemented by his governments. Perhaps the major consequence of this period for the French defence consensus was the increased debate which took place on the means and missions of France's defence, and the appearance of distinct limitations in the defence accord. These limitations were not necessarily new, but in the changed strategic circumstances of the post-Cold War world, and given the exposure to which they had been subjected by Mitterrand himself during his re-election campaign, their impact was enhanced.

In the first government of Mitterrand's second *septennat*, the post of Minister of Defence was taken by Jean-Pierre Chevènement. Chevènement was to experience significant difficulties in this position, mainly on account of the adverse economic situation, and its repercussions for military planning, but also because of increased disagreement with the President. Divergences became apparent over proposed budgetary cuts for the French military establishment, the future of French forces in West Germany and the deployment of France's troops in the Middle East during the Gulf War of 1990–91: the latter was sufficient to occasion the Minister's resignation.

Although the economic situation during the early years of Mitterrand's second term was less severe than that of the early 1980s, it still had serious repercussions for the entirety of the French national budget, and defence did not escape the search for cuts. Chevènement's concern for the maintenance of the defence budget at a level in accordance with the *loi de programmation militaire* passed for 1987–91 was expressed in an interview he gave to *Le Monde* in July 1988.[66] However, the very scale of the financial requirements of the Chirac government's planning law meant that it was a prime target for reduction, and in the context of its updating its provisions were revised in the first weeks of the new Socialist government. Furthermore, it was widely expected that credits would be further reduced, to finance the Socialists' social programmes.[67] The passage in November 1988 of the military budget for 1989 marked only a temporary agreement on the level of resource commitment to defence.[68]

The situation became still less certain in 1989. Chevènement was keen to maintain a spending level of around 4 per cent of GDP for defence.[69] However, the threat to the defence budget was maintained, with the likelihood of significant cuts being widely reported in May 1989.[70] This issue became a source of particular divergence between

Chevènement and Mitterrand and was further exposed by the elaboration of a new *loi de programmation militaire*, under Rocard's government, to cover the years 1990–93. The President's role in its delineation was widely perceived to be a primary factor; the defining principle of the forthcoming law was arguably Mitterrand's preference to 'keep everything, but … pay less'.[71] The budgetary cut imposed was confirmed by Mitterrand himself in a press conference in the latter part of May, where he insisted that the major defence programmes would be maintained despite a cut in resources of around 10 per cent.[72] While the Ministry of Defence disagreed with the Ministry of Finance and the Prime Minister's office over the means available for defence, the influence of the President was perceived to favour the latter.[73] The responsibility for the extent of the final budgetary cuts was firmly attributed to Mitterrand, as was the accountability for the lack of far-sighted strategic choices to see the French defence establishment into the twenty-first century and beyond.[74]

The timing of the presentation to the Assemblée Nationale of the *loi de programmation militaire* for 1990–93, which had caused so many disagreements even within the government and majority, in late 1989, was hardly propitious. Consideration of the planning law coincided with the beginning of extensive changes in the Eastern European strategic landscape, and the uncertainties this entailed,[75] but still the government pressed ahead. The lack of major choices regarding the defence programmes was confirmed. The programme included the modernisation of the strategic nuclear forces and the continuation of tactical nuclear weapons development; Leclerc tanks, multiple rocket launchers, satellite technology and improvements to the FAR for the Army; the maintenance of the new aircraft carrier, as well as the construction of more frigates for the Navy; and the development of new and improved capabilities for the Air Force, through the Rafale fighter and transport planes. Despite Chevènement's best efforts to defend the programme, and to argue a continuing vigilance over the French defence establishment in the changing international security situation,[76] it was not well-received.[77] Moreover, the substantial financial reductions contained in the planning law did not constitute the end of Chevènement's difficulties in maintaining defence spending. Despite his strong protests, the budgetary allocation for 1991 was further reduced in the summer of 1990.[78] Given the discord on the issue between Chevènement and his colleagues at the Finance Ministry and the Matignon, it had been the final arbitration of Mitterrand which ratified the cuts.

Thereafter, Chevènement's plans to reorganise the French armed forces developed in an inauspicious financial context, and in the atmosphere of heightened interest that this had provided for questions of defence. His plan, *Armées 2000*, envisaged the reinforcement of the operational capacity of the armed forces, and the coherence of the military establishment overall.[79] Among its other aims, it was undoubtedly an attempt to make savings in the defence budget by a process of rationalisation: rationalisation, however, had harsh consequences. The plan would instigate the removal of a certain number of military staffs, and the closure of some garrisons. As Chevènement argued, there were far too many local defence establishments in France, the Army alone having more than 1000.[80] Nevertheless, the plan was criticised because of its local repercussions, and it was roundly condemned for its effects on future military efficiency.[81] Moreover, it was argued, particularly by the political Centre, that the strategic changes of 1989–90 rendered the plan obsolete before it had even begun.[82]

It can thus be seen that in questions of finance provision and the major aspects of military planning Chevènement had little scope for autonomous action, and indeed little opportunity to influence the policy lines preferred by the Head of State. He could undertake a reorganisation of the armed forces, but could neither elaborate the main themes, nor instigate the necessary choices, of France's future defence. He further diverged from the President of the Republic over the aspects of Franco-German military relations in the post-Cold War period.

The priority afforded to improved relations with West Germany in the matter of defence and security provision by François Mitterrand was ostensibly well established by the time of his second *septennat*, having been cemented in the run-up to the 1988 election by acceptance of Germany's proposal for the creation of a joint Franco-German brigade.[83] Thereafter, however, it seemed that Mitterrand began to back-peddle. He used the occasion of a speech to the IHEDN – the first of his presidential terms – in October 1988 to define certain limits to the French commitment to European defence.[84] The sudden and seemingly uncontrollable changes which followed the fall of the Berlin Wall in 1989 reinforced a desire for caution in the matter of European defence and security on Mitterrand's part.[85] His subsequent assertion that French troops in Germany would be withdrawn after the conclusion of the '2+4' talks[86] caused consternation in France. No doubt surprised by Mitterrand's unheralded announcement, in response Chevènement effectively contradicted the Head of State, insisting that

Mitterrand had been merely anticipating events, and that any troop-withdrawal would take at least four or five years.[87] This difference indicated the extent to which Mitterrand had become prepared to act alone in defence questions, without agreement on a concerted policy line with his government. Similar tendencies were likewise apparent over the Gulf War of 1990–91.

According to observers, differences of opinion between Mitterrand and Chevènement over the Gulf War were apparent immediately after the Iraqi invasion of Kuwait. Within a week of the aggression, and the forceful American response, Chevènement was convinced that the conflict was being engineered by the United States for its own interests, and that French interests would only be served by strictly limited, national actions.[88] He was, therefore, firmly opposed to cooperation with the Americans in an economic embargo, although he considered that a French presence in the Gulf area would not be untoward, considering the evident violation of international law by Saddam Hussein, and the justification of the United Nations' Resolutions 661 and 662.[89] François Mitterrand, who favoured taking a firm line against Iraqi aggression, was already irritated by Chevènement's position – a situation which worsened almost immediately thereafter, when the Defence Minister maintained his refusal of French cooperation with the Americans and tried to delay the despatch of the aircraft-carrier *Clemenceau* to the Gulf, which Mitterrand had ordered.[90]

Considering that Mitterrand was keen for France to take a strong, supportive role in the management of the crisis, the continued reluctance of his Defence Minister, coupled with the apparent unwillingness of the military chiefs to condone fully the probability of a prolonged French troop commitment in the Gulf,[91] contributed to his exasperation. Chevènement's prominent role in the Franco-Iraqi Friendship Society,[92] and the Minister's propensity for giving anonymous comments to the press which directly contradicted the official presidential and government line,[93] did little to ameliorate his relations with Mitterrand, and the possibility of Chevènement's resignation was mentioned as early as August 1990. The irritation of the Head of State with his Defence Minister was still further inflamed after the sacking of the French embassy in Kuwait by Iraqi soldiers. While this development was said to have been a turning-point in Mitterrand's mind, sweeping away any doubts regarding French participation in a conflict, the Minister and military chiefs were still reluctant to contemplate French participation in a war effort. As it increasingly transpired that

Mitterrand wanted France to fulfil a traditional, Gaullist concept of international rank and status through her presence in the allied coalition against Saddam Hussein, and took every opportunity to prepare the French public for such an eventuality,[94] Chevènement's enthusiasm for such a course was most noticeable by its absence.

The catalyst for his resignation came after the war had actually begun, at the end of January 1991. Initially, it seemed that Chevènement had rallied to the idea of limited French participation in the allied effort. He reasserted his determination, for example, that French actions would be limited to Kuwaiti territory in a press conference of 18 January 1991,[95] thus interpreting very narrowly the coalition's UN mandate.[96] Nevertheless, at Mitterrand's instigation, French air forces went beyond the remit afforded them by their Minister on 24 January, and undertook missions over Iraq itself.[97] This development coincided with the President's authorisation of his military adviser, Admiral Lanxade, to appear on the political programme *7 sur 7*. Chevènement, who had not been informed, learnt of the forthcoming broadcast from the press, and in a situation which had become distinctly untenable, he resigned on 29 January.

Chevènement's replacement, Pierre Joxe, was altogether a safer pair of hands for Mitterrand, and the remainder of the land war passed without serious incident between the Elysée and the Ministry of Defence. The conclusion of the conflict did not, however, lead to any greater stability for the French armed forces: on the contrary, the Gulf War of 1990–91 gave rise to increased debate about France's defence capabilities, and the suitability of those capabilities for the threats they were likely to face in the future. Having exposed the extent of France's military shortcomings, the war became the departure-point for criticisms on all sides in Parliament. Financial difficulties remained a potent issue, and the need for alterations in military planning to take account of the changed international security situation was likewise prominent. The primary role of the President of the Republic in the delineation of defence decisions also remained a point of continuity, and indeed one which was exacerbated by Mitterrand's imposition of his own priorities regarding the future of the nuclear deterrent force, particularly in this matter the suspension of nuclear testing in the South Pacific from April 1992.

The prospect of further reduced financial provision for defence had been raised in May 1991, in a policy declaration by the new Prime Minister Edith Cresson.[98] In comparisons with spending cuts by France's allies, and in giving to understand that one element of the

French deterrent force was likely to be abandoned, Cresson returned questions of defence finance to the forefront of considerations regarding France's military planning. When the Parliamentary debate on the lessons of the Gulf War opened in June,[99] financial questions underpinned the discussion.[100]

The problem for Joxe persisted throughout the year. It was known by the middle of 1991 that the Finance Ministry hoped to make additional savings of approximately 8 billion francs from the defence budget for 1992,[101] through a 1 per cent funding cut in absolute terms (a 4 per cent cut in real terms).[102] The consequences of the cuts already imposed by the Finance Ministry were such that France was incapable of benefiting from any post-Cold War 'peace dividend'. The number of programmes already under way and behind schedule was a cause for concern. For the conventional forces, the month of August 1991 alone saw the European transport helicopter programme, the NH-90, cancelled, and orders for AMX-30 tanks, armoured vehicles, guns, military lorries, and the unarmed reconnaissance plane postponed.[103] Neither were the nuclear forces entirely free from cuts.[104] Dissatisfaction with the Socialists' resource provision for defence led Parliament to reject the 1992 defence budget.[105]

As financial difficulties persisted, so too did the need to reorganise the armed forces. Indeed, Joxe's reorganisation was more far-reaching than Chevènement's. Up to 24 000 military, and 4750 civilian personnel would be directly affected. However, in partial compensation for the loss of personnel, a *Direction du Renseignement Militaire* was to be created to exploit the possibilities of satellite intelligence, and a Staff was to be established to take care of the increasingly professionalised external intervention forces.[106] Despite protests from parliamentarians whose constituencies were directly affected, Joxe's measures were widely accepted in the light of the changed international situation, being very much a quiet revolution. Moreover, as it became apparent that French troops, at the will of the President, were to be committed in an increasing number of external forums, the need for the changes Joxe had instigated was underlined.[107]

However, Joxe was less influential in the matter of the nuclear forces. In the realm of nuclear deterrence the President remained the driving force, and proved himself reluctant to sacrifice his personal preferences for the prolongation of an assumed consensus. This was the case when Mitterrand excluded all matters relating to the nuclear forces from the defence debate of June 1991. The following month he instigated the renunciation of the S-45 mobile missile programme, so favoured by the *cohabitationniste* government of 1986–88, which was intended to replace the virtually obsolete fixed-silo missiles of the Plateau d'Albion.[108] The decision gave rise to significant discord. Then, in 1992, the Hadès tactical missile programme was frozen, after years of investment,[109] and Mitterrand decided to suspend France's nuclear test programme in the South Pacific. When coupled with the decision that France should adhere to the Non-Proliferation Treaty when it fell due for renewal in 1995, it was widely perceived that Mitterrand was destroying the credibility of the nuclear deterrent. As the legislative elections of 1993 approached, and the prospect of a second period of *cohabitation* seemed more certain, Mitterrand indicated that his suspension of nuclear tests was to last more than the initial year, and that this was an area on which he would maintain his prerogatives, despite the preferences of any incoming government.[110]

The first five years of Mitterrand's second term therefore demonstrated that the President was intent on maintaining the prominent role in defence and security questions that he had developed in the latter years of his first term, and that he would preserve the image of personal responsibility for many of the decisions which were taken. This was particularly the case in matters pertaining to the nuclear deterrence capability, constituting one of the pillars of the presidential *domaine réservé*. However, it was also evident from these years that Mitterrand was to be little more cooperative in the matter of maintaining the defence consensus in France, even when working with a government of the Left. Although politicians still sought to preserve the idea that accord supported defence provision,[111] the limitations of the notion were increasingly apparent. It was unlikely that this situation would change for the better during the period of Right-wing government which coincided with the end of Mitterrand's presidency.

Cohabitation II: 1993–95

Even before the onset of the second *cohabitation*, it could be seen that the alleged defence consensus was perhaps little more than a periodic political expedient. Areas of divergence between the President and the new government of Edouard Balladur were numerous, including the future of France's nuclear test programme; conscription; reorganisation of the armed forces to increase professionalisation; budgetary provision; and a prospective improvement in relations between France and NATO. The most significant of these in indicating the role of the President and the restrictions he reinforced on the defence consensus was that of the nuclear test programme. Against this backdrop, the Right-Centre government contributed to the profusion of defence planning the 1990s had already witnessed with a further reorganisation plan for the armed forces, a White Paper on defence (the first since 1972), and a new *loi de programmation militaire* to cover the years 1995–2000.

The position of the Right in France had evolved quite considerably on defence since the collapse of the Berlin Wall. Significant alterations in the organisation of the armed forces had been proposed by several prominent figures in the interim,[112] and had culminated in plans for a professional army elaborated by François Fillon of the RPR before the legislative elections of 1993.[113] Balladur and the wider RPR leadership had all agreed to such a course, which despite Mitterrand's reduction of the length of military service to ten months in July 1990[114] was anathema to the President. When restructuring plans were announced by the Defence Minister François Léotard in May 1993, such radical options as the transformation to a professional army were not apparent, but nevertheless, the proposed cuts and reorganisations went much further than those instigated by his Socialist predecessor. Each of the principal services would be affected.[115] However, the lack of a true broad consensus surrounding such moves meant that even the new majority was not agreed on the merit of such measures. Some members of the Gaullist side of the government coalition threatened to resign their seats in protest at the cuts, while the Mayor of Paris, Jacques Chirac, and his adviser on international affairs, Pierre Lellouche, added their voices to the storm of criticism.[116] The necessity for the *Livre blanc*, to place the restructuring of the armed forces into the context of a coherent long-term plan, was all the more evident.

The White Paper was thus presented in February 1994,[117] and though based on the deliberations of an expert Commission it no less reflected the internal political situation in France. The result was very much marked by *cohabitation*,[118] neglecting to take firm decisions on the future of the nuclear deterrent, which remained the preserve of the Palais de l'Elysée, but underlining the preference of the Balladur government for closer, formal cooperation with France's European and NATO allies, and for a leading French role in European security affairs.[119] A broad assessment of the potential threats facing France was undertaken, involving six crisis scenarios, but the primacy of the nuclear element of the French defensive arsenal and the need for its continued modernisation were maintained. Consequently, the lack of provision in the White Paper for a resumption of nuclear tests formed the basis of strong criticism of the government's efforts. However, it was in precisely this area that the influence of François Mitterrand was most apparent.

Mitterrand's involvement in the elaboration of the *Livre blanc* had only occurred at a late stage: a *Conseil de défense* in December 1993, only the third of Mitterrand's second *septennat*, constituted the first instance of the President's formal intervention in the Paper.[120] This was reinforced by an additional meeting on 16 February 1994 to confirm the provisions of the White Paper. In the meantime, though, it was suggested that the President had retained a closer influence on proceedings than might have been apparent through permanent contacts between his adviser, Védrine, and Balladur's Cabinet Secretary, Nicolas Bazire.[121] As a consequence, 'the agreement [was] ... the fruit of a compromise, turning to the advantage of the Elysée, particularly on the central question of nuclear deterrence'.[122] The nuclear test issue, which was pivotal to that central question, exemplified the extent to which the President's will prevailed over the *Livre blanc* and its terms for this major element of defence.

The repeated desire of many of the majority to see a rapid resumption of tests had been expressed frequently since Mitterrand's decision of April 1992.[123] Indeed, it had been one of the Right's electoral campaign themes in 1993,[124] and even as late as the publication of the White Paper, the Defence Minister Léotard reaffirmed his conviction that tests should recommence as soon as possible.[125] Given the extent of the government's divergence from the President's view, and the subsequent non-provision for the resumption of the test programme in the White Paper, it can be seen that it was not François Mitterrand who had to compromise in order to achieve an agreed text. The perception that Balladur's government had buckled under Mitterrand's pressures constituted a major criticism of the White Paper by certain figures of the Right, including Chirac[126] (despite Chirac's record in defence relations with Mitterrand in the 1980s). The best that could be said for the *Livre blanc* was that it preserved a semblance of defence consensus: Léotard went so far as to assert an 'active and renewed consensus'[127] on the bases of French defence among the whole of the executive. Other commentators were less afraid to question the alleged accord, observing that its survival was only due to the Paper's imprecision.[128] The reaction of Parliamentary deputies was therefore one of 'neither enthusiasm nor aversion':[129] hardly a suggestion of the solid consensus Léotard seemed to perceive. At least, according to the President of the

Assemblée Nationale's National Defence Committee, Jacques Boyon, the *Livre blanc* closed no doors, and would therefore be no constraint for an incoming government after the forthcoming presidential elections.[130]

Given Mitterrand's failing health, and perhaps his impression that he had already fulfilled his historical duty in terms of French defence, the remainder of his second *septennat* was less combative in the defence relations between the President and the government. Mitterrand played little part in the elaboration of a new military planning law for 1995–2000, which was placed firmly in the context of the *Livre blanc*, nor did he have any significant role in the budgetary deliberations of late 1994 over resources for defence. Furthermore, the President made few objections to the enhanced cooperation with NATO pursued by Balladur's government, although when Joxe had favoured similar measures, he had been regularly contradicted by Mitterrand, or his Foreign Minister Dumas.[131] Balladur's government instigated closer participation, at every level, between French and allied armed forces, including a French role in the WEU military exercise Purple Nova 94 under British command, and NATO's military exercise in Germany, Operation Counterguard, in December 1994:[132] both of which, while conforming in one sense to the President's desire for increased European defence cooperation, went beyond the boundaries of the cooperation that he had envisaged.

Taking Mitterrand's presidency as a whole, it can therefore be seen that his role in determining the means, missions, provisions and priorities of the French defence effort between 1981 and 1995 was far more expansive than is usually suggested. Even under Hernu's tenancy of the Defence Ministry the President's influence was striking. After Hernu, Mitterrand demonstrated an increased tendency to override his defence ministers, partly at times from consideration of personal political gain, and partly also due to an appreciation of his prerogatives, and preconceptions, regarding the primacy of his role. In this respect, Mitterrand demonstrated himself very much a President in the style of the Fifth Republic, if that presidential style, particularly in matters of defence and security, is taken as manifested by the Republic's founder Charles de Gaulle. There was continuity in presidential initiatives, in the willingness to intervene abroad, in the determination to discharge responsibilities to former African colonies, and in the resolve to uphold ideas of France's rank and status internationally.

However, as the enhanced role Mitterrand undertook in defining defence in France was partly a consequence of internal political factors, as during times of *cohabitation*, it was also a consequence of changing international circumstances, requiring a head of state to exercise firm leadership over the defence and security of his country in times of great strategic uncertainty. The defence consensus was in reality as thin under Mitterrand as it had been under any of his predecessors. It will be the intention of subsequent chapters to demonstrate in more detail the extent of the role of the President of the French Republic in questions of defence and security in these years, and to show that the defence consensus was indeed an instrument of political expediency used at times to good effect in eliminating critical debate. Nevertheless, debate over French defence was wide-ranging, and demonstrated continuities and consistencies of discussion and discord over time, and over issues.

Part II
Defence Debate during the Mitterrand Presidency

4
Defence Planning in the First Term

> I am certainly the Prime Minister of change, but there is at
> least one point on which continuity is essential: the impera-
> tives of defence.... The defence and security of the country
> constitute imperatives which transcend political choices.[1]

Pierre Mauroy's words, spoken so soon after the Socialists' election
victories of May 1981, thus defined the two characteristics which
would dominate discussions of defence planning and provision in
Mitterrand's first presidential term: continuity and consensus.
Continuity would be maintained largely by retaining the existing
balance of expenditure and emphasis between the nuclear and
conventional forces, retaining the primacy of the nuclear deterrent
capability. This was demonstrated in the defence budgets for 1982
and 1983, and in the Socialists' *loi de programmation militaire* for
1984–88. A professed consensus on these matters was reiterated
during parliamentary debates over such budgets and planning.
However, as Mitterrand's *septennat* progressed, the inherent limitations of these suggestions became apparent. While broad continuity
in the main defence orientations was largely dictated by decisions
taken over the previous two-and-a-half decades, innovations and
alterations were introduced which would have far-reaching consequences. Regarding consensus, as this became more forcefully argued,
its shortcomings only became all the more evident. This was particularly the case in discussions of the second *loi de programmation
militaire* of Mitterrand's presidency, for 1987–91. The increasingly
visible role of François Mitterrand in directing defence planning did
little to alleviate contradictions in France's alleged continuity and
consensus in defence.

That Mitterrand and his Socialist government intended to take a firm line in defence was apparent from the earliest days of Mitterrand's term. Almost immediately Mitterrand conveyed the impression of prevalent continuity in defence under an administration of the Left. His approach was observed to demonstrate nothing less than 'the faith of the converted';[2] within three weeks of his investiture he had visited the main nuclear command installations, Jupiter and Taverny, and within two months he had visited a nuclear submarine at the Île Longue base, where he announced that a seventh, new-generation nuclear submarine would be built to ensure a permanent presence of three submarines at sea instead of the current two.[3] His apparent determination to maintain a strong, independent French defence, based on nuclear deterrence, in the face of a deteriorating international situation (superpower arms build-up, and the uncertainties of the arms control process for a medium nuclear power such as France) was reiterated at the first meeting of the *Conseil de défense* of his term on 30 October 1981. Confirming the July announcement France was to have a seventh nuclear submarine to enter service around 1995. She would also have mobile ground-based missiles (SX) with a range of 3000km, from around 1993; and there would be an enhanced range of 350km for the Hadès tactical (prestrategic) weapons system, being developed as a replacement for the Pluton system from 1992.[4]

François Mitterrand was no less keen to assume the presidential mantle over the command and control of the French nuclear force, despite his early opposition to de Gaulle's legislation in this respect. At Île Longue he implied he would readily accept such responsibilities, suggesting that the significance of the submarine element of the French deterrent stemmed at least in part from its direct contact with himself, as President of the Republic.[5] He subsequently reiterated his own role in France's deterrence posture, asserting that 'the key element of the deterrent strategy in France [was] the Head of State, it [was himself]; everything depend[ed] on his determination',[6] for 'the responsibility of decision [for the use of the nuclear forces] rest[ed] on the President of the Republic, and on him alone'.[7] Hence, major changes in this area were to be unlikely under François Mitterrand.

However, continuity would not necessarily prevail for the non-nuclear forces. As the Chief of Staff of the Armed Forces put it, if 'France's defence policy [was] characterised by the concern for continuity,... continuity [did] not exclude, in the short term, certain shifts in the organisation and use of forces.'[8] He thus reinforced Mauroy's speech to the IHEDN in autumn 1982, which had called for the reorganisation of the Army.[9] Associated reports of manpower and funding cuts had caused much consternation among the armed forces.[10] As the financial environment in France worsened after the Socialists came to office, concerns regarding the maintenance of the nuclear priority, and its subsequent effects on the conventional forces, were enhanced.

A question of continuity?

The first indicators of the tenor of the Socialists' defence planning, the defence budgets for 1982 and 1983, suggested that for the time being no radical departures from existing priorities were likely. While this facilitated a certain 'honeymoon period' for the declaratory defence consensus, it did not prevent expressions of discord and dissatisfaction with the government's actions. The process of parliamentary debate was especially significant, indicating the extent to which assertions of consensus were, for the most part, very limited.

The parliamentary role in the definition of France's defence is something of a grey area – and was perhaps deliberately maintained as such by successive national leaders. Technically, parliamentary influence over the course of budgetary provision and medium-term defence planning is constitutionally assured: through its debate and passage of relevant bills and laws, Parliament is responsible for the determination of the basic organisational principles of national defence, and particularly the relation of those principles to French citizens regarding their national service. In addition, by approving, or otherwise, the annual budgetary provisions, it arbitrates on the means afforded to defence, thus gaining another lever with which to bring pressure to bear on the government's delineation of defence strategy. Finally, in the military sphere, Parliament is responsible for authorising declarations of war, and French conscript troops could not be fully committed outside France's borders without the express approval of Parliament.[11] In practice, however, the role and influence of Parliament over the course of French defence priorities and provisions has been limited. Debates on military policy occur infrequently, and with the exception of the yearly budgetary debates take place primarily on the presentation of military planning laws. This in itself is a constraint; although the *lois de programmation militaire* have entailed increasingly comprehensive military procurement decisions, they have revealed much less about the strategy and doctrine on which those procurement decisions have been based. Moreover, Parliament was not called upon to sanction any declaration of war in the 50 years to the end of the Mitterrand presidency, but French troops had been active almost all over the globe.[12]

Nevertheless, parliamentary defence debates were useful vehicles for determining the level of support for planning decisions openly expressed by deputies. Detailed discussions of such military planning are generally undertaken within the framework of the parliamentary committees (the National Defence and Armed Forces Committee, and the Foreign Affairs Committee, together with the Finance Committee, in the Assemblée Nationale), and each committee presents its findings in the context of the parliamentary debate, through the reports of its *rapporteurs* – reports dealing not only with the overall plans, but also with their specific impact on the various components of the armed forces. While the composition of the committees largely reflects the political structure of Parliament, they cannot be relied upon simply to rubber-stamp the provisions intended by the government, and do have a certain influence over the course of government planning. In addition to the committee reports, committee members and other interested deputies also contribute to parliamentary debates. It was the case under the Mitterrand presidency that the committee *rapporteurs* and members made good use of the Parliamentary forum to express their opinions – certainly not all complimentary – on the courses undertaken by his governments. In this context the debates over the defence budgets for 1982 and 1983, covering the last years of the previous Giscardian planning law[13] and as a prelude to the Socialists' own *loi de programmation militaire*, promised for 1984, took on added significance.

The budget presented in November 1981, for 1982, allocated 122 billion francs for military funding,[14] representing a 17.63 per cent increase in real terms over the budget for the previous year, and an increase of 0.045 per cent, to 3.895 per cent, in the proportion of GDP dedicated to defence.[15] It thus satisfied the broad criteria set out by Giscard's planning law for 1982, and maintained the priority afforded to France's nuclear capability,[16] providing for the completion of the sixth nuclear submarine, *L'Inflexible*, according to its anticipated timetable, and the continuation of the M4 missile programme. Giscard's planning law had also been intended to address concerns of under-investment in the conventional forces due to emphasis on the nuclear capability. The defence budget for 1982 was perceived to convey a will to correct delays that had developed, despite Giscardian efforts, in equipment provision for the conventional forces. The will and the reality, though, did not necessarily correspond.

For the Army, the discrepancy between the investment it should have received under the military planning law, and that which it actually had, was so great that it could not be corrected in 1982 alone. Rectification – the procurement of tanks, Roland ground-to-air missile launchers, artillery and armoured vehicles – was only to occur in 1983.[17] For the Air Force, previous funding inadequacies meant that none of the Mirage 2000s provided for in the *loi de programmation militaire* had been delivered by 1982, and despite the Socialists' attempts to increase financial provision for the Air Force it was still to be unable to maintain its previous fleet strength.[18] Difficulties were also envisaged over ammunition provision, the insufficiencies of the air-transportation capability and the deficiencies of low-altitude defence.[19] The Navy was to receive increased funding allowing expenditure on personnel and equipment to rise, although emphasis would remain with the nuclear submarine force[20] and overall tonnage would drop.[21] To compound potential difficulties, shortfalls in fuel provision were expected – calculated less, it was suggested, according to the needs of the armed forces, and more in line with the financial abilities of the State.[22] Significant improvements were only asserted in provisions for the *Gendarmerie*, where particular efforts were made in terms of manpower, in job creation and in quality of life.[23]

Through its adherence to the overall directions of the 1976–82 *loi de programmation militaire*, the Socialists' first defence budget was viewed by deputies as evidence of continuity in France's defence provision. As the Socialist *rapporteur* of the Finance Committee argued, it 'maintain[ed] the level of [France's] military capabilities, and safeguard[ed] the future'.[24] The Opposition, too, was apparently reassured by such continuity of the defence effort.[25] However, despite the continuity preserved by the budget overall, the details of the plan incurred criticism.

The provisions of the budget for the conventional forces were recognised as much for what they failed to do as for what they actually provided. There was concern that the government was potentially compounding the planning law's shortfalls. The government was 'procrastinating',[26] and it was argued that the subsequent aggravation of equipment inadequacies in the armed forces would compare to the situation of 1939 – if France failed to seize the opportunity to improve her services while it was still possible to do so then she would find herself ill-equipped and unprepared in the face of a deteriorating and dangerous international situation.[27] It was argued by the Opposition that, quite simply, defence was not an expenditure priority for the

Socialists.[28] The budget plan was 'disappointing',[29] and 'convey[ed] a slackening of the defence effort'.[30] Of the Opposition parties, the RPR abstained in the vote on the defence budget, in protest at its perceived shortcomings, and while the UDF[31] voted in favour, it registered deep concerns 'at a time when … international tensions [were] increasing'.[32]

The defence budget for 1982 was therefore only adopted amid a climate of a anxiety about the means available for defence. This was exacerbated during the course of 1982 as the government's financial position worsened. It was still more aggravated by the cancellation of a large amount of approved defence expenditure just before the presentation of the defence budget for 1983. The resources, amounting to 13.5 billion francs of *autorisations de programme* and 3.5 billion francs of *crédits de paiement*,[33] had been frozen since January 1982, before their suppression in October. The government's action – undertaken without consulting the Assemblée Nationale – alarmed many deputies, and did not augur well for the debate over the defence budget for 1983.

The budgetary proposals presented for 1983 were indeed characterised by the national climate of austerity. The defence budget was held at approximately 3.9 per cent of GDP, thus failing to fulfil the Socialists' promise[34] to increase that percentage to 3.94 per cent, and it showed an increase of only 8.5 per cent overall.[35] Nevertheless, the nuclear forces were allocated a disproportionate increase in funding, with *crédits de paiement* rising by 14.29 per cent. Funding requirements for the new nuclear submarine, the M4 missile programme, the development of the intermediate-range air-launched nuclear missile, the ASMP (*air-sol moyenne portée*), and the Hadès tactical nuclear weapons system were thus to be preserved.[36]

Provision for the conventional forces was less impressive, however. Annual expenditure for the Army was to increase by only 7.7 per cent,[37] casting doubt on likely operational effectiveness, as exercises would be curtailed. The position regarding equipment also gave cause for concern, as the prospects for acquiring the means promised for 1983, back in 1981, seemed slim.[38] The Air Force also suffered, as its funding allocation was argued not even to keep pace with inflation.[39] As no aircraft had been ordered in 1982 the government could not address the increasing shortfall in the Air Force's capability. The inadequacies of low-altitude air defence, and of long-range transport, also remained.[40] The Navy incurred a slightly lower rate of increase in its funding compared with the previous year, and the impact on its budget of the costly nuclear submarine element would have adverse consequences for the construction of conventionally armed vessels, which would diminish in 1983.[41] Again, the provision for the *Gendarmerie* caused most satisfaction, allowing for a substantial increase in manpower, and for the adaptation of the *Gendarmerie*'s role and responsibilities in counter-terrorism.[42]

The defence budget for 1983 was challenged from both Left and Right. The government was openly criticised by the Socialist *rapporteur* of the Finance Committee over the cancellation of credits, for 'it [was] not right that Parliament, which voted for a given budget, [saw] its prerogatives drastically reduced'.[43] The Opposition concurred, asserting that 'the Socialist government no longer grant[ed] priority to national defence'.[44] The budgetary plans for 1983 compounded what had been 'a black year for defence',[45] and the 1983 budget was perceived to be nothing better than a 'budget of stagnation'[46] which neither the RPR nor the UDF would support.

Nevertheless the government insisted that continuity was its defining principle in defence.[47] This position was reinforced by the Socialist president of the National Defence Committee, who argued that 'despite its moderate growth, the budget for 1983 [would] guarantee the continuity of French defence policy'.[48] However, members of the Opposition were unimpressed. Something of the flavour of their criticism was captured by J.-M. Daillet of the UDF: the government was

> swimming in a ocean of contradictions between [its] successive speeches and declared intentions on the one hand, and the means obtained on the other. Making a virtue out of a necessity, [it was] trying to camouflage [its] attitude in the uniform of continuity.[49]

As the extent of continuity in defence was debated, so too was the question of consensus. According to Mauroy in 1981 'a divided country [was] a weak country',[50] and thus the government seemed determined to pursue the theme of consensus, like that of continuity, not least as a means of deflecting discord which could have adverse effects on acceptance of its planning. The suggestion of consensus seemed perhaps to have limited validity: as the Socialists evidently intended no fundamental break in the defence budget for 1982 with the defence priorities of its predecessors, the Right professed the 'wide approval'[51] which existed in France over the Gaullist principle of defence based on nuclear deterrence. Even if there was in fact little solid consensus around defence provision and planning, other than adherence to the priority of the independent nuclear deterrent, the emphasis upon concord and consensus was to become something of a feature of French defence debates.

However, given the more difficult circumstances of the 1983 budget debate, as arguments of continuity had foundered, so did those concerning consensus. The Opposition's refusal to support the government's spending plans for defence, compounded by the subsequent refusal of the Senate to pass the defence budget,[52] and a motion of censure against the government's handling of defence planning and provision,[53] indicated the extent of dissatisfaction with the government's position on such a sensitive issue. Nonetheless in the view of the government's Communist partners, the 'alarmist declarations [of the Opposition] undermin[ed] the credibility of [France's] national defence',[54] and even the minority conceded that 'defence ought never to be the object of partisan attacks'.[55] The phenomenon of emphasising accord where there was little, instigated in the previous year's debate over the defence budget, was thus reiterated.

The defence budgets for 1982 and 1983 therefore indicated areas in which continuity could be expected under a government of the Left, and more importantly perhaps they suggested where adaptations might be found, as in the case of the conventional forces. They also demonstrated that while accord might well exist on the main themes underlying defence, there was substantial discord over the details. In practical terms these debates right at the beginning of Mitterrand's presidency outlined the extent of the challenge facing the French defence establishment in the 1980s, indicating something of the imbalance between investment in the nuclear and conventional forces, and the resultant weaknesses and shortcomings in the national military capability. Taken together, the debates over the defence budgets for 1982 and 1983 could be seen as a valuable foundation for the elaboration and discussion of the Socialists' subsequent military planning law.

The *loi de programmation militaire*, 1984–88

The military planning law submitted for debate in spring 1983 had been long awaited, given that the Socialists been in power for almost two years and that the previous law had officially expired in 1982. The law elaborated by the Socialists was a bold attempt to deal with changing international circumstances in the realm of security, and to manage the disparities which existed between the relative emphases on nuclear and conventional forces. It contained measures of both continuity and innovation, the latter particularly in regard to the conventional forces. Although it was adopted by a comfortable parliamentary majority, the debates to which it gave rise were in many ways consistent with those over the defence budgets for 1982 and 1983. Above all, they reiterated that consensus was limited.

According to Hernu's presentation of the *loi de programmation militaire* to the Assemblée Nationale, continuity certainly seemed to be the order of the day. He argued that France's defence rested on the principle of three circles, relating to the national territory, or sanctuary; the defence of Europe; and fulfilment of France's more distant defence commitments in her overseas departments and territories, and in many of her former colonies. To this end the government had three objectives, intending to maintain the highest levels of technology in the equipment of the armed forces; to maintain an effective deterrent capability through the modernisation of the nuclear forces; and to modernise the conventional forces to improve inter-service coherence and emphasise firepower, mobility and versatility.[56] To meet these aims the financial provision of the *loi de programmation militaire* amounted to 830 billion francs over the five years of its implementation,[57] indicating a significant increase in defence funding compared with the previous planning law.[58]

For the nuclear forces the key word was modernisation,[59] with the sixth nuclear submarine, armed with 16 multiple-warhead M4 missiles, to enter service in 1985 as planned. Four of the other five nuclear submarines were to be overhauled to take the M4 and other updated equipment. Furthermore, the seventh new-generation nuclear submarine was to be ordered in 1986–88. Eighteen Mirage IVs of the strategic air force were to be adapted to take the new air-to-ground medium-range missile, which they would carry until 1996, before they were replaced by mobile ground-based missiles. Seventy new Mirage 2000N aircraft were to be ordered to carry the ASMP on tactical nuclear missions, while 50 Super Etendards would also be adapted to carry it, and development of the Hadès system would continue.[60]

For the conventional forces the Air Force was to retain a fleet of fighter aircraft at the level of 450 planes. Most significantly, however, new means were to be ordered to improve high- and low-altitude detection of attack, and subsequent defence. The Navy was to receive a larger fleet tonnage at a level of 300000, though it would pass through a low point of around 270000 tonnes towards the end of the 1980s, due to decisions predating the Socialists' accession to power. The fleet would comprise two aircraft carriers, 12 submarines, of which at least eight were to be hunter-killer submarines, and 30 surface vessels including corvettes and frigates. A new nuclear-powered aircraft carrier was to be ordered after 1986. The *Gendarmerie* would benefit from increased manpower, partly due to an increase in its conscript numbers, and was to see its role extended to include organisation of the reserve forces and internal security missions, which had formerly been the preserve of the Army.[61]

The Army was to bear the brunt of the government's planned reorganisation. Its manpower level would be reduced by 22 000 over the timespan of the planning law to 290 000 (an additional manpower reduction of 13 000 would be distributed among the other services). The remainder of the Army would undergo a profound reorganisation to create a Rapid Action Force – *Force d'Action Rapide* – of 47 000 troops, to improve its capacity for external intervention both in Europe and further afield. It would be constituted around a significant helicopter strength of 250 for maximum mobility and versatility. In addition shortcomings in the Army's tank and artillery capabilities were to be addressed. It was anticipated that through the implementation of the law the Army would possess 1100 tanks, 400 combat helicopters, 450 modern artillery pieces and around 8000 armoured vehicles.[62]

The provisions of the *loi de programmation militaire* were largely well received by the relevant Committees, whose *rapporteurs* considered that they responded well to the immediate needs of French defence, and also safeguarded the future through the allocation of a quarter of the equipment budget to research and development.[63] Concerns for inter-force coherence, and the necessity for choices, were also met.[64] It was further considered that the creation of the FAR would benefit France's defence capabilities by improving the equilibrium between the demands of defending the national sanctuary, and the exigencies of alliance commitments.[65] Moreover, by taking the new step of naming the Soviet Union as France's ultimate potential enemy, it was perceived that the *loi de programmation militaire* marked an effective adaptation to the changing international realities, with regard to belligerent Soviet actions in Europe since the failure of détente, and the imperatives of European security.[66]

In the main themes of the military planning law, Hernu again undertook to place the Socialists' provisions firmly in the framework of continuity. He argued that the deputies '[should] notice a great continuity in the missions of [France's] forces, which transcend[ed] political changes'.[67] This continuity was asserted particularly in the clarification of France's continued commitment to the principles of deterrence by the weak of the strong. However, the Opposition insisted upon scrutinising the degree of continuity in the Socialists' military planning. Moreover, if continuity was questioned, consensus too was a matter for debate.

It seemed that the main directions of the Socialists' *loi de programmation militaire* did indeed give rise to some agreement among political opinion. Even on the Right, it was acknowledged that a 'very wide consensus [had been] established around the doctrine of national deterrence. It [was] an invaluable asset, not to be harmed under any pretext.'[68] However, in the broader aspects of the military planning law, no such consensus could be asserted:

> not only [did the government's] programme not correspond wholly to [France's] defence needs, it [was] more than likely that because of the financial means appropriated, [the government] would not even be in a position to give it concrete expression.
>
> That [was] what [the Opposition] fear[ed], that [was] what separated [the Parties], and that [was] what the French people must know.[69]

Consensus, therefore, was a limited phenomenon, as had been suggested by the previous debates over defence budgeting in 1981 and 1982.

The Opposition was particularly dismayed by the financial bases of the Socialists' military planning law. The sum of 830 billion francs which the government proposed to spend on defence was considered wholly unrealistic, as this was based on calculations of inflation of 8.5 per cent initially, falling to 5 per cent, before stabilising at 4 per cent.[70] Given that the authorities had only just released a monthly inflation figure of 1.4 per cent for April 1983 alone,[71] the government's calculations seemed 'abnormally low and optimistic'.[72] They were 'all the more illusory'[73] as inflation for military costs was always appreciably higher than the general level. Moreover, anxiety arose from the government's device of separating the military planning law into two distinct periods. The first, 1984–85, would see growth of around 1 per cent in military funding, whereas the second period from 1986–88 would see the growth rate enhanced.[74] The potential difficulty was compounded as the majority of the major projects contained within the planned law, such as the new aircraft carrier, were deferred until the second part of its execution, thus increasing the likely financial burden on those years.[75] It was observed that there was no guarantee of provision even remaining constant, let alone being revised upwards,[76] in 1985. Considering the Socialists' record in the economic sphere the prospects for defence funding seemed less than promising to the Opposition.

The *loi de programmation militaire* engendered further discord through its perceived effects on France's military capabilities. Léotard, for the UDF, insisted that 'there [was] continuously a gap, if not a gulf, between [the Minister's] assertions and realities'[77] which meant that the planning law was 'only an illusion; barely concealing a retreat in the nation's defence effort'.[78] More specifically, the gaps in the provision for the Army in particular, notwithstanding the reorganisation and the FAR, would lead to 'qualitative insufficiency'[79] of France's conventional forces, for 'the reorganisation of the Army [did] not give it the means for its missions'.[80] Moreover, the *Force d'Action Rapide* in itself was no 'great qualitative improvement ... [for it was] greatly disparate, if not to say heterogeneous'.[81] Its shortcomings would be exacerbated by the continuing non-provision of long-distance air transportation means, and the forthcoming shortfalls in naval projection – although one aircraft carrier was to be ordered in the mid- to late-1980s, two were due to go out of service in the 1990s.[82] This, added to anticipated reductions in tonnage, and the uncertainties regarding the potential of the *loi de programmation militaire* to fulfil its terms, augured ill for the French force-projection capabilities and for the subsequent ability to maintain any feasible world role.

Nevertheless, after the reasonably comfortable adoption of the *loi de programmation militaire*, the issues of a consensus and continuity in defence were little raised until the mid-1980s. Heightened concerns over the Strategic Defense Initiative in France, the course of superpower arms control, and Hernu's resignation over the damaging *Rainbow Warrior* affair, all coincided with increased speculation over the possibilities of a *cohabitation* between the Socialist President and a government of the Right. Such circumstances revived concerns over continuity and consensus, and emphasised the role of François Mitterrand in the determination of France's defence.

'The Constitution, the whole Constitution, and nothing but the Constitution'[83]

This was how François Mitterrand anticipated the division of responsibilities between himself and his new Gaullist Prime Minister after the victory of the Right in the legislative elections of March 1986: as was shown in Chapter 1, however, the interpretation of the Constitution in the matters of defence and security provided a number of useful ambiguities. Mitterrand thus added his own understanding of the document in these crucial aspects: he was to retain responsibility for the continuity of the State, national independence, territorial integrity and respect for treaties, while the remit of the new government would be to determine and conduct the nation's policies, and assure the implementation of commitments made before the French people.[84] There could be no doubt, therefore, over where the control of defence and security policy was to lie – or at least where François Mitterrand intended that it should lie. This was not altogether acceptable to Jacques Chirac. While relations between the President and Prime Minister in matters of defence and military planning demonstrated the imperatives of a certain continuity of action, they also demonstrated the inherent limitations of arguments suggesting consensus. The extent of the President's more overt influence on defence, as well as a certain desire of the Prime Minister to avoid fatal disagreement between the two offices over that issue,[85] demonstrated each of these points, which were further exemplified by the debates over the *loi de programmation militaire* proposed by the Right in 1987.

Despite Mitterrand's firm intentions regarding the direction of defence under *cohabitation* it became apparent that Chirac had his own ideas of his role and responsibilities in relation to defence. After a *Conseil ministériel de défense* held at the Suippes military camp in July, Chirac emphasised that 'as Prime Minister, and in that capacity responsible for national defence, [he] intend[ed] in this field as in others, to exercise fully the role which [was his]'.[86] He would therefore take a full part in the redefinition of military policy which was leading to the submission of a new planning law. Addressing the soldiers of the camp, Chirac demonstrated his acceptance, but only with limit-ations, of Mitterrand's constitutional responsibility for defence: the armed forces 'carr[ied] out an essential task, under the authority of the President of the Republic, Head of the armed forces, and *within the framework* of the policy defined by the government'.[87] The Prime Minister and President differed, therefore, over the relative responsi-bilities of their two offices with regard to the direction of defence.

It certainly seemed that Chirac would take a leading role in elabor-ating the new military planning law which the Right had promised even before its electoral success.[88] Reinforcing his criticisms of the Socialists' record on defence, Chirac underlined that 'there [was] no defence policy without a financial effort ... the goal [was] to see again, as soon as possible, a sufficient rhythm of growth in the military credits'.[89] Furthermore he envisaged certain changes in planning for France's nuclear forces. Although basing the new planning law on substantial modernisation of the nuclear capability, which was unlikely to create serious discord, his priorities over a mobile, land-based component, and over tactical nuclear doctrine,[90] were likely to bring him into direct opposition to the Elysée.

The assertion of authority over defence by the President of the Republic, which had begun as the new government was installed, and been prepared even during the election campaign, was reiterated soon after. In choosing to deliver his first major speech since the legislative elections at the most prestigious military academy in France, the officers' training college Saint-Cyr-Coëtquidan, François Mitterrand was reasserting his control over defence. Although his main speech focused primarily on the consequences of SDI for France, he took the opportunity to issue a veiled warning to the government about its known plans to alter the structures of the armed forces, presumed to be to the detriment of the Army.[91] He reiterated his concerns over the government's progress in defence planning later in the year. In a visit to Caylus, the training base for France's 11th Parachute Division, shortly before a decisive meeting between the President and government over the forthcoming planning law, he reminded Chirac and his colleagues that ultimate responsibility for the delineation of defence still remained with the President of the Republic. He was particularly concerned about Chirac's proposals for the development of mobile missiles, and their likely consequences for the successor missile to the M4 – the M5 – for the nuclear submarines, as well as the Prime Minister's suggested doctrinal modifications in relation to the tactical nuclear weapons capability.[92]

To an extent the disagreement had been anticipated – 'you could feel it coming'[93] according to observers, given Chirac's attempts to supersede the presidential *domaine réservé* in defence – but nevertheless it gave rise to quite widespread debate about the defence consensus. It was suggested that the Elysée and Matignon had previously compromised to preserve the image of a consensus which did not really exist;[94] and indeed that although 'the French believ[ed] not without some naivety, or pretend[ed] to believe, through the simple concern for intellectual comfort, that a consensus exist[ed] between the majority and the President of the Republic, nothing [was] less true'.[95] Accordingly, the defence budget for 1987 contained 'something for everybody': Mitterrand ensured continued priority for France's nuclear submarine force, and secured the survival of the Plateau d'Albion missiles, while Chirac maintained the mobile missile project which the President no longer favoured. This indicated a fundamental lack of agreement about the future of France's defence and deterrence. It failed to make the basic strategic choices for a medium power like France because the authorities were unwilling to make fundamental choices.[96] The same lack of firm choices, to avoid giving rise to damaging discord, was evident in the planning law submitted by Chirac's government in 1987.

The *loi de programmation militaire*, 1987–91

The military planning law presented to Parliament in April 1987 was the culmination of a 'bitter'[97] debate between the Palais de l'Elysée, the Hôtel Matignon and the Ministry of Defence, and reflected the preferences of the President inasmuch as it maintained the priority of the submarine element of the strategic capability, at the expense of significant investment levels sought by the government for further development of a mobile missile capability.[98] Mitterrand indeed applauded the final project as 'serious, reasonable and coherent'.[99] This is not to say, however, that the planning law abandoned any of the programmes favoured by the government, and the legislation considered by the Parliament in April 1987 was particularly wide-ranging. Twenty-seven equipment programmes were specified. For Chirac, the military planning law constituted an 'unprecedented increase'[100] in France's defence effort over that made by the Socialists. It expressed a preoccupation with modernisation and technology, providing for nuclear, conventional and space programmes,[101] and represented a conscious adaptation of France's defence mechanisms to perceived dangers.[102] The allocation of 474 billion francs at 1986 values to the implementation of the law was by no means over-generous, given the breadth of the aims and the continuing financial pressures, but it conveyed an 11 per cent funding increase in the first year (already in progress) followed by a steady growth of 6 per cent per annum thereafter.

Although none of the 27 programmes was allocated specific funding, provisions for the armed forces were to unfold as follows. For the nuclear forces, which constituted ten of the major programmes, the development of new-generation nuclear submarines was planned, as was that of the new M5 missile, and that of a new strategic element – unspecified, but meaning the mobile missile. Progress on the Hadès programme, and the refitting of the existing nuclear submarines with the M4 missile, would continue.[103] For the Army, the programme law planned the acquisition of the Leclerc battle tank, helicopters for support, combat, transportation and battlefield surveillance roles, armoured vehicles, anti-tank weapons, multiple rocket launchers, and improved communications. The Air Force would receive the Mirage 2000N for nuclear missions, American AWACS planes, the future fighter aircraft, under development, air defence systems and short-distance transport planes. For the Navy the nuclear-powered aircraft carrier was envisaged, as were hunter-killer submarines, anti-aircraft and anti-submarine corvettes and frigates, ocean-going minesweepers and an array of new missiles. The *Gendarmerie* could expect its role in times of crisis or conflict to be greatly expanded, requiring augmented means and mobility, and improved communications, as well as its peacetime anti-terrorism role enhanced. In addition, the military planning law made firm commitments in the field of space technology, with the Hélios observation satellite and the Syracuse II communications satellite.[104]

The extent of the provisions made in the *loi de programmation militaire*, coupled with its dual support by the President and the government, limited the discord which might otherwise have been outwardly expressed. Indeed, only the Communist Party voted against the adoption of the law, resulting in a vote of 536 in favour of the law with 37 against (with one abstention).[105] Yet the military planning law still attracted criticisms: its methods of financial calculation and provision were a source of some division, and the project was soundly criticised on the part of the PCF. Nonetheless, the main characteristics were again projected as continuity and consensus: continuity in the maintenance of the traditional French defence effort; and an alleged consensus between the political parties (excluding the Communists) on the major orientations of France's defence. Despite prolific assertions of continuity and consensus, though, the limitations of both were easily visible.

Criticism and scepticism regarding the financial aspects of the *loi de programmation militaire* focused on the consequences of the growth anticipated by the government, the scale of achievements envisaged, and the restrictions on parliamentary control that the planning law implied. The difficulty of reconciling the financial provisions of the law with the prevalent economic situation was recognised by the *rapporteurs* of both the National Defence and the Finance Committees, each a member of the governing majority. Expressing doubt, F. Fillon, for the former, argued that the implementation of the law presupposed the fulfilment of the economic and financial hypotheses that had governed the elaboration of the programme – otherwise all might be called into question.[106] Furthermore Y. Guéna, for the latter, was concerned by the prospects for the broader national budget of the greatly increased provision for defence. Given that the law anticipated an average growth of 7 per cent per annum over its five-year life there would have to be a considerable increase in the proportion of the national wealth awarded to the defence effort, since at least for the first two years of the planning law GDP was expected to grow only by 3 per cent annually.[107] Although there could well be benefits from the increased expenditure on equipment for France's trade balance, through arms exports, other consequences might not be so favourable.

A lack of financial realism in the bill was asserted among the Opposition, despite their intentions to approve it. M. Rocard argued that 'it must escape no-one that the multiplicity of programmes [made] it financially difficult, if not to say impossible, to see them all to fulfilment, and simultaneously'.[108] By inserting so many programmes, he insisted, the government was merely avoiding making necessary choices. Additionally, the Opposition argued, the failure to plan for operational expenditure and manpower costs marked an unacceptable omission. The government had created a 'total and deliberate impasse'[109] regarding these costs. This was exacerbated by the device of allocating a whole sum to the programme law, and providing no specific funding for individual projects.[110] As Chevènement argued for the Socialists, more precision was required in respect of national defence, in order to facilitate effective control of military direction and expenditure by Parliament.[111] And the Parliament was little impressed by the government's provision for a progress report at the end of 1988, with power to adjust future expenditure,[112] especially as the Right had so criticised a similar measure taken by Hernu four years previously. In addition to such criticisms, the Communist Party asserted that the planning law was simply 'profoundly bad',[113] plunging France headlong into the 'dangerous policy of over-armament'.[114]

However, arguments of continuity and consensus were prominent and in this respect, the Socialists in particular argued forcefully that the *loi de programmation militaire* elaborated by the Right was little different in many ways from that which it replaced. In its maintenance of the primacy afforded to the nuclear forces, and especially the submarine element, contrary to certain of the government's wishes, in its maintenance of the structure of the armed forces, including the

FAR, contrary to the government's many criticisms of this body, and as none of the 27 major programmes were actually new, representatives of the *Parti Socialiste* in the National Assembly insisted that 'on the positive side, the planning bill [lay] within the continuity of the preceding laws'.[115] The laws were argued to be so similar in principle that 'a simple updating would have sufficed. In fact, this [new planning law] only concern[ed] an extension of the preceding law. How, then, could [the Socialists] oppose it?'[116] Apart from the admittedly significant factor of the finance devoted to military equipment, in view of the 17 billion franc deficit alleged by the Right in just the first two years of the 1984–88 military planning law,[117] it was asserted that 'in short, [the Right's] bill add[ed] little, if anything, to that which preceded it'.[118]

It must be said, however, that the Socialists were in something of an awkward situation in the Parliamentary debate on the defence law. Although it was proposed that the law should allocate far more to defence than many of the Socialists would wish, and while it did little to clarify areas of divergence on defence between the parties, they were constrained to vote for the bill through a previous announcement apparently made after pressure on the PS from the Elysée.[119] There was a need to gain some political capital from the unprecedented step of replacing a planning law before its expiry – therefore, by effectively accusing the majority of a lack of imagination, the Socialists could claim something of the high ground in discussions of defence provision. In asserting continuity, the Socialists also avoided any acknowledgement of shortcomings in their own law. Nevertheless, notions of continuity promoted in the debate did in fact largely disregard the implications of the financial commitment contemplated by the majority for defence. As would become increasingly clear in Mitterrand's second term, discord over finance was more than surface-deep, and was indicative of fundamental differences of approach to France's defence.

If continuity was, therefore, more prominently featured in Socialist (Opposition) critiques of the planning law, the assertion of consensus was emphasised more by the majority. For the government, the Prime Minister argued that 'the unity of a people around its defence [was] an essential asset for a nation',[120] which was an 'irreplaceable strength'.[121] For the Defence Minister, such consensus 'by itself … add[ed] to the power of [France's] weapons. Inside France, it cement[ed] national unity. Outside France, it consolidat[ed] France's] credibility'.[122] For a deputy of the UDF, the consensus gave France an 'incalculable advantage'[123] over her European allies, conveying extra power and ensuring the respect of those European partners.

However, the Opposition was at this time apparently less convinced of the existence of consensus. The Socialists' position was cogently expressed by former Defence Minister Quilès, who saw a partial consensus in France around defence issues.[124] This partial consensus hinged on the principles of independence of decision, deterrence by the weak of the strong, and solidarity within alliances. Specifically, however, he identified six particular differences between the majority and minority in defence questions, which were not wholly treated by the proposed planning law: the possible extension of the French nuclear guarantee to her allies; the doctrine for use of prestrategic (tactical) nuclear weapons; the issue of chemical weapons; the means of defence, in money and manpower; approaches to disarmament; and appreciations of a European defence.[125] Furthermore, Chevènement's views highlighted the limitations of the Socialists' approval of the law: it was only acceptable because it conveyed the preferences of the President, rather than the Prime Minister, over the modernisation of the nuclear force.[126] Similarly, for Rocard the bill had validity because it 'reaffirm[ed] a certain number of vital principles that the President of the Republic [had] not ceased to defend'.[127] If the Socialists' acceptance of consensus was qualified, the PCF's view was negative: consensus was 'a lie ... there [was] not a "consensus" among all the French people, far from it.... And neither [was] there a "consensus" among all the political forces....'[128]

Consequently, while assertions of continuity and consensus dominated parliamentary discussions on defence planning in Mitterrand's first *septennat*, they had limited foundation in reality. The arguments of continuity were perhaps the more convincing, but even these were restricted in scope. As Hernu had argued in the early 1980s, 'defence policy [was] defined by the President of the Republic, and conducted by the government. It [was] marked firstly by continuity. Which continuity? That which consist[ed] of resting France's security on deterrence.'[129] Twenty-five years' investment in nuclear deterrence imposed this continuity, one which Hernu himself had worked hard to have accepted by his colleagues on the Left in the 1970s, but one which also provided room for manoeuvre in other areas.

This was perhaps the main benefit to be gained from emphasising continuity – the rallying of opinion behind assertions of a basically unchallenged defence strategy left the way open for potentially significant adaptations in the structures and organisation of other elements of the armed forces. This was particularly the case with the conventional forces, most notably the Army, where innovations in role and responsibility, largely through the creation of the FAR, were to involve a whole new European shift in France's defence over the course of the Socialist presidency. While such shifts may have been at least in part a reaction to the course of events, as well as the pursuit of a deliberate and cohesive long-standing policy, they were nevertheless facilitated by focusing attention on the prevalent consistency of the emphasis on nuclear deterrence. Hence, continuity was something of a fluid concept, concealing change as much as it reflected constancy.

Like aspects of continuity, one of the advantages of the purported consensus was also its imprecision, although a certain accord did seem to exist on the basis of nuclear deterrence. Although by the early 1980s it was argued that 'a consensus [had] finally been achieved in France on independence and nuclear deterrence',[130] it only served to highlight the extent to which similar arguments did not apply to the wider aspects of defence, such as the position of the conventional forces in France's defence panoply, and the level and distribution of investment in the military capabilities.

It can therefore be seen that continuity and consensus, while the dominant themes in discussions of French defence and military planning in Mitterrand's first term, were far from defining characteristics. Nevertheless, their shortcomings only seemed to enhance their utility as concepts around which to rally the French – politicians and legislators perhaps rather more than the public – in relation to their defence. Consensus and continuity, however, were not sacrosanct, as was to be seen in other defence and military matters as Mitterrand's presidency progressed.

5
Military Intervention in Lebanon and Chad

If François Mitterrand assumed a prominent role in defence planning from the outset of his presidency, this was also to be the case in the translation of that planning into practice, particularly in the deployment of France's forces outside her borders. Pertaining to questions of both foreign and defence policy, this fell squarely within the remit of the Presidential *domaine réservé*, which despite its Gaullist connotations was fully exploited by Mitterrand. This was primarily evident in the major military deployments of his first *septennat* in Lebanon and Chad. While demonstrating a certain continuity with the actions of preceding governments, both in terms of the scope of the presidential role and in the reasons for French intervention, the deployment of troops in Lebanon and Chad was also significant with regard to its exposure of areas of policy change, and the limitations of consensus. Ironically, Mitterrand's main support emanated from the Right of the political spectrum, while the Left, his traditional power base, proved the source of much criticism.

Even before Mitterrand came to office it seemed that he would take a firm line in certain questions of external policy. In his pre-election *110 Propositions for France*, for example, numbers four and five treated Lebanon and Chad specifically:

> 4. Peace in the Middle East by ensuring the security of Israel's established and recognised borders, the right of the Palestinians to a united Lebanon.
> 5. The independence of Chad....[1]

Linked with concerns he had shown over a long period – going back to when he was Minister for Overseas Territories during the Fourth

Republic[2] – and reinforced by his more recent criticisms of the external policy (read African policy) of the preceding government,[3] it was to be expected that French military action in these areas of contention would be a distinct possibility. Combined with his overwhelming sense of history, and his perception of France's particular role and responsibility in relation to her former areas of influence, together with the perceived bearing of France's actions in these areas on her wider international status, these factors proved impossible to resist: despite some hesitations displayed over Lebanon in 1982, and Chad from 1983, substantial French assistance was committed thereafter – leading France into lengthy, and costly, military interventions.

The French intervention in Lebanon

France's intervention in Lebanon from August 1982 was characterised by Mitterrand's prominence in the determination and elaboration of all its phases. The primacy of the Elysée contrasted with the minimal influence of the government, even allowing for the domestic difficulties with which it was preoccupied. While a certain continuity was apparent in the motivations for France's actions within the framework of the Multinational Force (MNF), there were also differences – not least among which was the emphasis placed by Mitterrand on explicit approval from the United Nations for the commitment of French troops abroad.

The French military commitment to Lebanon from the summer of 1982 can be divided into three phases. The first, and arguably most successful for France and Mitterrand, covered the period from Israel's attack on Palestinian positions in West Beirut in June 1982, to the end of the first MNF mission to evacuate Palestinian fighters from Beirut in September.[4] French troops arrived in Beirut in the middle of August to supervise the evacuation, alongside American and Italian units. The evacuation was implemented from 21 August to 1 September[5] and was followed by the rather hasty withdrawal of the MNF. The French were last to leave, withdrawing from Beirut on 14 September.[6]

The second phase, far more protracted and costly for the French, began almost immediately thereafter. The assassination of the Lebanese President-elect, Bashir Gemayel, and the massacres of Palestinians in the refugee camps of Sabra and Shatila by the Israeli-backed Lebanese Forces, between 14 and 17 September,[7] provoked international outrage, and a rapid commitment from Mitterrand that French forces would return to Beirut to deal with both the civil-war situation and the problem of the Israeli invasion. On this occasion, however, the mission of the international forces in Lebanon, supplemented now by a British presence, was less well-defined and became decreasingly acceptable to the warring factions. Attacks on French forces escalated: the worst of these occurred in October 1983 when a lorry packed with explosives destroyed the French barracks in West Beirut, killing 58 soldiers.[8] Mitterrand reacted firmly, making a lightning visit to Beirut[9] and authorising a retaliation raid on the positions of Shia Muslim extremists, and their alleged Iranian backers, in November.[10] The presence of French troops in Beirut continued until March 1984 when the MNF was withdrawn. The French contingent was again the last to leave.[11] It was replaced by a detachment of military observers, constituting the third phase of France's intervention in Beirut, which remained until 1986.[12]

Mitterrand's perception of the difficulties in Lebanon was deeply rooted in his knowledge of France's role in Lebanon's history, and of ties that had joined the two countries since the time of the French mandate over Syria and Lebanon after 1919. His longer appreciation of the situation had been gained from conversations with such leading Lebanese figures as Kamal Jumblatt, the leader of the Druzes, in the 1970s.[13] His commitment was affirmed by some of his closest advisers: according to Védrine,

> Regarding Lebanon, French passivity offended him greatly. France's particular responsibility with regard to that country was so obvious, to his mind ... [Védrine did] not remember having heard him justify it other than through general allusions to France's mission, and her history....[14]

As Mitterrand said, it was a commitment based on 'the historic role that [France played] in Lebanon, for the unity of [that] country. And as France [had] decided to be present in Lebanon, she [would] remain there ...'.[15]

Mitterrand decided, in principle, to commit French troops to the MNF as early as 25 June 1982.[16] However, his acceptance of the American proposal in this matter was conditional on a formal request for the intervention force being made by the Lebanese government, and the concurrence of all the warring factions in Beirut to the deployment. In July he added the requirement for explicit consent by the PLO, and the assent of the United Nations, as well as stipulating the necessity for a clearly defined mandate for the MNF.[17] Moreover,

Mitterrand increased his personal identification with diplomatic initiatives to resolve the crisis, as with the Franco-Egyptian initiative (the Mitterrand–Moubarak Plan)[18] placed before the UN Security Council in July–August.[19]

Mitterrand's leading role was even more apparent at the onset of the second phase of the engagement. On 16 September, between the assassination of Gemayel and a new Israeli offensive on the one hand, and knowledge of the massacres at Sabra and Shatila on the other, Mitterrand sent his Foreign Minister, Claude Cheysson to Beirut to demonstrate French support for the legitimate Lebanese government. After the discovery of the refugee-camp massacres, consultations between Paris and Washington began immediately over the return of the MNF to the Lebanese capital. The French return was announced by Mitterrand at 11 p.m. on 20 September.[20]

Mitterrand's reactions to the Lebanese crisis were at least consistent with the longer-term principles of France's foreign affairs under the Fifth Republic, even if there was little precedent for the use of the means of defence in a multinational action overseas. Indeed, whatever caveats Mitterrand advanced, it is uncertain whether such a cooperative venture with the United States would have been contemplated under his predecessors – even under the allegedly Atlanticist Giscard d'Estaing. Nevertheless, Mitterrand's actions were rooted in a desire to maintain France's international credibility, through the maintenance of her regional influence in the Middle East, as well as in his sense of history, and thus it was arguably more advantageous to participate in the MNF, with national distinctions, than to remain aloof. Mitterrand's machinations in his Middle Eastern policy balanced his own long-standing support of Israel with the more familiar French support for the Arab states,[21] and combined this with a nominal independence from the American line. In a country where perceptions of rank and status, and perceptions of diplomatic and military credibility, were so important, Mitterrand's qualifications were significant in establishing accord around the military options pursued by the Elysée.

Indeed, it was the *lack* of a solid French response to the initial Israeli invasion which gave rise to criticisms of Mitterrand. The daily newspaper *Le Quotidien de Paris* condemned 'the hesitations, the procrastination, the circumlocution of the President of the Republic'.[22] From within the Socialist Party itself, criticism of the slow public condemnation of the invasion was also strong:

France weigh[ed] her words, want[ed] to balance her assessment....

In that she [was] wrong ... in the very hour of [Lebanon's] misfortune, and of the loss of its freedom through clear-cut external aggression, France turn[ed] up her nose and limit[ed] her support.[23]

The perceived lack of commitment to the fate of Lebanon was seen to have wider implications for France's position in the Middle East – 'in this pussyfooting, these contradictory attitudes,... it [was] hazardous, to say the least, to try to discern a coherent policy. France [would] have succeeded in the rare feat of being seen badly from all sides.'[24] With the approach of a concerted French action, criticisms abated, with the result that after the troops' withdrawal in mid-September numerous concerns for their reinstatement were voiced. Hence, Mitterrand's announcement of the return of the French MNF contingent to Beirut after the refugee-camp massacres constituted

> one of the great moments of national unity.... Before such acts of horror, [France's] divisions between Left and Right no longer [made] sense.... All the parties [had] reacted favourably to the initiative of the President of the Republic to send the French contingent back to Beirut.[25]

Mitterrand had therefore achieved a broad consensus on the deployment of French troops, both for the limited action represented by the first phase of the commitment, and for the recommitment of forces after the outrage of the Sabra and Shatila incidents. This was all the more valuable to him as it deflected attention from France's domestic difficulties: in the summer of 1982 the Versailles summit had not succeeded; the second devaluation of the franc since the Socialists had come to office had failed to stabilise the French economy; and prices and salaries had been frozen. In addition, for Mitterrand personally, at such a time of difficulty for the Socialist government, the first phase of the Lebanese intervention had been broadly successful: the MNF's limited mandate – the evacuation of the PLO fighters from Beirut – had been successfully completed, the French contingent had suffered no loss of life, and the troops had been extricated with little difficulty. Mitterrand had had his own personal Falklands Crisis, a short and successful external military intervention – and one he had envied Margaret Thatcher.[26]

The second phase of the French military commitment to Lebanon was far less successful, however, and far less a focal point for consensus. A year after the return of the French contingent Mitterrand had little positive to show for its now prolonged presence. Moreover the escalating attacks to which French forces had been subject led directly to the warning issued by Paris, in September 1983, that in the future the French contingent would retaliate.[27] Consequently after four *légionnaires* had been wounded in the shelling of Beirut, and two more soldiers had been injured when their lorry was hit by a rocket-propelled grenade, on 22 September four Super-Etendard jets carried out the first MNF air strikes against artillery positions in the mountains overlooking Beirut.[28]

It was at this point that the divisions of Left and Right on the matter of policy in Lebanon in general, and on the air strikes in particular, were clarified. For the Right Chirac welcomed the strikes, although he reproached the government for the 'vagueness' of its wider Lebanese policy.[29] The retired General Bigeard, for the UDF, likewise supported the action.[30] To counter such approval from the Right, however, was a greater amount of criticism from the Left. Even *Le Monde* took issue with Hernu's assertion that the French air strikes had constituted an immediate and total response to continued attacks, arguing that one air strike by four jets was not an adequate riposte to 17 deaths and 35 injuries in one year.[31] Criticisms further Left in the political spectrum were more harsh. The leader of the PCF, G. Marchais, called for negotiations within the UN to resolve the civil war, or else an immediate repatriation of the French troops. Considering that four Communist ministers appointed by Mitterrand still participated in Mauroy's government, Marchais' comments were damning.[32] The extreme Left similarly called for the withdrawal of French forces from Lebanon, for the only goal of 'imperialist France ... [was] to exploit the peoples of the Middle East'.[33]

The bombing of the French Army headquarters in Beirut, the Drakkar barracks, the following month, served to regroup opinion around the line pursued by the Elysée. After the President's visit to Beirut in the aftermath of the bombing, which had been undertaken without informing the Prime Minister, or the Defence Minister, until Mitterrand had arrived in the Lebanese capital,[34] and his announcement that French troops would remain in Beirut, it was suggested that French opinion 'closed ranks,... despite underlying misgivings about the role and purpose of the Multinational Force'.[35] Mitterrand's lightning visit was widely approved. For *Le Monde*, the attacks had only 'reinforc[ed] the determination of the President of the Republic not to withdraw before terrorism and not to flee what he consider[ed] to be France's responsibility'.[36] J.-L. Delecourt, of the *Mouvement de la*

Gauche Populaire, applauded Mitterrand's 'courageous and symbolic visit to Beirut',[37] while the leader of the *Centre des Démocrates Sociaux* (CDS), P. Méhaignerie, agreed that 'the French forces must stay in Lebanon. The CDS approv[ed] unreservedly of the journey of the President of the Republic to Beirut ...'.[38] F. Léotard of the UDF similarly welcomed Mitterrand's move.[39] However, while the visit itself was saluted, its implications for France's military commitment to Lebanon were less a source of accord.

The Left's disunity, even in the mainstream, was striking. If French troops were to remain in Lebanon, as Mitterrand evidently wished that they should, the PS believed that changes were necessary in their role and responsibilities. It insisted that 'France must demand the definition and control of the mandate of the intervention forces from the UN, and anticipate [those troops'] reorganisation.'[40] Nor were such sentiments restricted to Socialists outside the government: Cheysson reportedly infuriated the President on the day of the Drakkar attack by declaring that '[France] must ask if [her] forces' military role [was] really necessary.'[41] However, *Le Monde* took the view that the handover of responsibility for the MNF to the UN was not actually an option, for 'the international community [was] not ready to assume its responsibilities'.[42] Indeed, while *Le Figaro* agreed that the mission of the MNF must be 'profoundly revised', this must actually occur 'in the sense of an enlargement' of its role.[43] In the final analysis, the French '[were] in Lebanon because France's interest [was] to preserve, or rather to rebuild, its unity and independence ... [and] in this drama, if [France] renounced being there, [the French themselves] would put the full stop to [their] influence in the region'.[44]

Even the fragile consensus which had existed so far was challenged by the retaliation raids undertaken at Baalbek in the Beka'a Valley in November. The attacks were initially supported, at least by the Right and Centre, as well as by the public,[45] as they had been intended to 'prevent new terrorist actions against the French forces in Lebanon'.[46] Coming within hours of a televised warning by Mitterrand, that the authors of the Drakkar attack would not go unpunished, 'the French [were] delighted that the outrage [had] been avenged and the Nation's honour saved'.[47] Both J.-M. Daillet for the UDF, and M. Debré for the RPR, expressed satisfaction with Mitterrand's order for air strikes.[48] However opinion soon shifted – regarding both Mitterrand's conduct, and the wisdom of the air strikes at all.

Many criticisms focused on the possibility of an escalation of the dangers facing the French forces in Lebanon as a result of the French attack. The 'reprehensible character of cold-blooded reprisals, the dangers of escalation and of terrorist responses, as well as the alteration of France's image abroad' meant that the raid 'risk[ed] rapidly appearing as an error, heavy with consequences'.[49] Harsh criticisms were also directed at Mitterrand himself: it was perceived that the maintenance of public support had weighed heavily in his decision. Although 'it would be indecent to write that the reprisals decided by M. François Mitterrand ... had the sole objective of making him regain the favour of the opinion polls',[50] *Le Figaro* made the point anyway. For a member of the Executive Bureau of the PS, 'it [was] a brilliant operation on the communication level. Political marketing [was] what determined François Mitterrand ... he hop[ed], through this operation, to reinforce his image in French opinion'.[51] The RPR and UDF groups issued separate, but almost identical statements, limiting suggestions that the Opposition concurred in the military policy conducted by Mitterrand.[52] The reactions of the former Prime Minister and Foreign Minister, Maurice Couve de Murville, were particularly sharp:

> Miracles [could] happen. It was a simple coincidence, but a fortunate coincidence: before 16 November, the day of the recent televised broadcast by the President of the Republic, it seem[ed] that atmospheric conditions did not allow the fulfilment of the Baalbek operation, although it had been planned, organised and executed for a long time. On the following day, 17 November, the conditions chang[ed]: the raid [could] be attempted.[53]

For Couve de Murville, therefore, with a large amount of sarcasm, meteorology confirmed that there had in fact been no domestic political calculation involved.

Criticisms of the raid were exacerbated by doubts over its effectiveness. While Lebanese police reports had originally suggested that 39 people were killed by the French attack,[54] later reports alleged that the damage inflicted had not been as great as first thought and that 'the Super-Etendard jets appear[ed] to have totally missed their stated targets, firing most of their rockets into a vineyard'.[55] According to one French newspaper, 'the only thing of which [the French] could be assured, three days after the Super-Etendard raid ... in Lebanon, [was] that it did take place'.[56] Although it was recognised that part of the problem lay with the government's imposition of a blackout on operational details, a certain degree of genuine confusion and deliberate misinformation seems to have been in evidence.

Thereafter, the French military commitment to Beirut was reduced.[57] Observers began to question openly the wisdom of remaining in Beirut where allied soldiers had become little but targets for snipers and suicide bombers. The French death toll had risen to 82,[58] a figure which was rapidly making a continued troop commitment untenable. Redeployments around Beirut continued, followed by the relocation of a quarter of the Beirut contingent to the UNIFIL forces in the South, at the end of January 1984.[59] The failure of Mitterrand's renewed efforts to have a UN force deployed in Beirut to relieve the MNF in the New Year[60] led to an almost inevitable withdrawal of French troops, along with those of their co-contributors. The French, departing after the other MNF contingents, had completed their withdrawal by the end of March.

The third phase of France's military presence in Beirut – the stationing of 80 military observers in the mountains around Beirut[61] – maintained Mitterrand's commitment to the Lebanese capital, thereby avoiding accusations of abandonment. This phase was not called into question until the beginning of 1985, when the observers were attacked twice in a week, and two soldiers died in an ambush.[62] As attacks increased, and as the Lebanese hostage crisis worsened, opinion turned against even the limited presence France retained in Beirut. The onset of *cohabitation* in 1986 marked the opportunity for change,[63] especially after the death of a seventh observer in March, although it was argued that a withdrawal had long been under consideration by Mitterrand and the former Socialist administration.[64] However, it had been delayed for political reasons, to highlight divisions among the Right: whereas Chirac had called for a reduction in the number of potential French hostages in Lebanon,[65] certain of his colleagues had urged Paris to increase support for the Christian community.[66] Although Mitterrand did not object to the withdrawal, responsibility for its announcement and implementation was left to the new government, thus enhancing the appearance of Mitterrand's firm stance over Lebanon.

It is not the focus of this chapter to comment on further divergences between Mitterrand and Chirac over the French contribution to the UNIFIL operation, and in particular over the effectiveness of the United Nations in addressing the situation in Southern Lebanon. The fact that those soldiers remained within UN forces in Southern Lebanon beyond his *septennats* is testament to Mitterrand's determination and commitment, both to Lebanon itself and to cooperative interventions under the auspices of international organisations.

Rather, it has been the intention of this section to demonstrate that Mitterrand had actively sought the primary role relating to France's military commitment in Lebanon after the Israeli invasion of 1982, and that he exploited the presidential *domaine réservé* fully in maintaining that commitment. Mitterrand's convictions relating to Lebanon found certain parallels in the interventions he authorised in Chad in 1983, and again in 1986, and where the second of these interventions, Opération Epervier, likewise outlasted his presidency.[67]

French interventions in Chad

While there had been little precedent for the French intervention in Lebanon in the Multinational Force, the same cannot be said regarding military actions in Chad. Having come to power against a backdrop of hostility to France's African policy, Mitterrand and the Socialists were to find that reality did not ultimately permit reorientation. Nevertheless certain policy modifications were attempted, in the promotion of regional, cooperative efforts to alleviate the Chadian situation; in endeavours to avoid making a French military commitment in Chad at all; and in the designation of that part of Chad for which France was subsequently willing to fight. However, the interventions to which France was led proved that continuity was the dominant factor, and moreover, that continuity in a military commitment to Chad facilitated consensus. Still, although accord was apparent over the fact of the French troop deployments in Opération Manta, those deployments gave rise to debate over wider French military roles, especially in conjunction with the commitment to Beirut.

As Mitterrand came to power, the civil war in Chad was once again at crisis-point. The precarious Government of National Unity, under the former Northern rebel Goukouni Oueddeï, was under threat from the rebel forces of the former Defence Minister Hissène Habré. Thousands of troops from Libya's Islamic Legion occupied Central and Northern Chad, after Goukouni's requests for assistance to the Libyan leader, Colonel Gaddhafi, had allowed the latter to declare a full-scale merger of the two countries in January 1981. French troops, which had been a major factor in Chadian affairs in the late 1970s before their withdrawal at Goukouni's instigation in May 1980, were again being reinforced in the Mediterranean and in various francophone states surrounding Chad.[68] It was into this context that the policy orientations attempted by Mitterrand and his ministers were inserted.

The dilemma which Chad constituted for François Mitterrand is apparent from his *Réflexions sur la Politique Extérieure de la France*. His sense of history, and his conception of France's international role and responsibility, were again in evidence, despite his view of the limitations of France's legal commitment to Chad.

... the reality was this: since 1976, no cooperation, assistance or security agreement [had] bound [France] to Chad any longer. However, [he] considered that [France had] two sorts of obligations there. The first [was] that despite the difficulties encountered by France in that country [under de Gaulle and Giscard d'Estaing] ... [France could] not make a complete break with more than three-quarters of a century of involvement with Chad. The second [was] that France, without taking advantage of any particular mission, represent[ed] economically, politically, culturally, for a large part of the African continent, an incomparable factor of equilibrium and progress, and that real treaties of military alliance unit[ed France] with several francophone states. All, or nearly all of them, [were] worried by the ambitions of M. Gaddhafi. And all, or nearly all of them, expect[ed] France to protect them.[69]

His sense of obligation was no doubt heightened by links he had maintained since his ministerial career in the 1950s.[70] He determined that the three principles of 'independence, unity [and] integrity of Chad'[71] would direct France's responses to the continuing civil war, irrespective of who led the government in N'Djamena. However, the dilemma was this: he despaired of 'the amazing ability that Chad [had] to live permanently in provisional situations',[72] and notwithstanding his protestations of concern for Chadian unity and territorial integrity he was unwilling to engage French troops in the hostile, rebel-held terrain of Northern Chad.[73]

Mitterrand's preference for dealing with the government in power led to the first changes in France's policy towards Chad. Previously Paris had favoured a victory of Hissène Habré but under Mitterrand, bearing firmly in mind the Libyan presence in Chad, France supported efforts to find a solution by the Organisation of African Unity. Diplomatic backing, together with small-scale military assistance, was thus directed at Goukouni Oueddeï. The aim was 'to bolster Oueddeï's self-confidence sufficiently so that he would feel able to ask the Libyans to leave'.[74] Manifestations of this policy included Goukouni's visit to Paris in September 1981,[75] and the provision of engineers,[76] military and technical assistance for retraining Goukouni's army (to take place in Cameroon),[77] and light weapons and ammunition for the government forces.[78] In urging the creation of an OAU force, primarily through his speech in Cancún in October 1981,[79] Mitterrand reiterated this line. In short, in view of his hostility to the African policy of his predecessors Mitterrand's 'policy of stabilisation [was] intended to avoid Giscardian-style military operations and to seek local solutions to disputes without superpower involvement'.[80] The Libyan departure after much African pressure (and for other reasons of Gaddhafi's own) in November 1981 seemed to prove the wisdom of Mitterrand's policy modifications.[81] However, Goukouni's overthrow by Habré in June 1982 created further difficulties for France, and gave rise to criticisms of the Mitterrand approach.

Habré's triumph, and moreover, his recognition by the OAU as the legitimate Chadian leader, demonstrated the limitations of the policy of offering support to Goukouni Oueddeï. In one sense, all that changed for France was the figurehead – as Mitterrand said, he did not like the man as among other failings he was in the hands of the Americans, 'but [France] must support him because he now represent[ed] the country in its entirety'.[82] In other respects, however, much changed. As Mitterrand was facing criticism for his hesitation to condemn Israel over the invasion of Lebanon, so too he was criticised for his inadequate response to the Chadian crisis. Mitterrand's reactions were compared unfavourably with those of Giscard d'Estaing in December 1980.[83] His policy was accused of lacking direction: 'in reality, France [was] forced to go forward blindly in this matter, no longer knowing what exact goal she [sought] to achieve'.[84] Goukouni's flight to Tripoli, where he received full backing once again from Gaddhafi, instigated a hardening of attitudes in Paris towards Libyan intervention in Chad, and indicated that, despite the attempts of 1981 to reorientate French policy, continuity would prevail. France would be committed to military intervention to support the government of Hissène Habré.

Active military intervention by France in Chad under François Mitterrand began in summer 1983. As it had become increasingly apparent that the resurgence of Goukouni's forces in the North was directly attributable to Libyan backing, it had become more difficult for Mitterrand to resist Habré's calls for assistance. Although as late as 24 June, after the capture of the Northern oasis town of Faya-Largeau by Libyan forces and Goukouni's soldiers, the President had reiterated that there was 'no question of intervening in Chad',[85] his position changed four days later after a visit to Chad by the Minister for

Cooperation and Development, C. Nucci. On that day France despatched weapons and military advisers to Chad,[86] and in an interview Mitterrand announced what was to be a fundamental break with his policy thus far: 'France [would] respect her commitments towards Chad without limits.'[87]

However, Mitterrand's intentions were based on a strict interpretation of the 1976 agreement between France and Chad. While it provided for French technical advisers to assist the Chadian government, it specifically precluded the use of French troops in internal political situations, and in the restoration of order. Consequently, a massive airlift operation was undertaken, delivering more than 200 tonnes of equipment in the first few days.[88] The authorities' continued insistence on the application of the agreement allowed Mitterrand to declare in mid-July that France would not send troops to Chad: '[France had] assisted the legitimate government of Chad by all the means at [France's] disposal, according to the terms of the 1976 agreement. But [France had] no reason to go beyond that.'[89] Moreover, Hernu stated as late as 7 August that the intervention of French soldiers was not an option.[90] Nevertheless he ordered the first troop-deployments on 9 August. By mid-August 500 well-armed paratroopers had been sent to N'Djamena[91] – a figure rising within a week to 3000[92] – and in launching Opération Manta, Mitterrand's France had made its largest military commitment abroad since the Algerian war.[93]

Support for Mitterrand and his policy in Chad varied across the political spectrum. His best support came, as in the case of Lebanon, from the Right, but even the support of the Right was somewhat qualified. Significant differences again arose between the presidency, the Foreign Ministry, and the wider Socialist Party; and criticisms hardened, through the point of view of the Communists, to that of the extreme Left. On the positive side of the balance sheet, Mitterrand was applauded for having 'chosen the path of difficulty at a moment when French affairs [were] in a pitiful state, and when the country would need all its strength to resolve its own problems'.[94] Chirac was supportive: the President and government were

> trying to do what they [thought] best. [France had] an agreement, and so, [France] provid[ed] weapons ... [he did] not condemn this action at all, [he] agre[ed] with it completely; it [was] in accordance with the application of [France's] agreements with Chad, and it [was] equally in accordance with the traditional idea that the French government recognis[ed] governments in place.[95]

Indeed, as General Bigeard commented after the rapid reinforcement of troops in Chad, 'the Opposition [was] in agreement with [the government] on the Chadian affair much more than the majority'.[96]

However, the Opposition's assessments were not all positive. The leadership was argued to have been tardy in recognising the Libyan invasion for what it was: 'the French government was slow to see it, and slower still to react. When at last its eyes opened,... it was too late to drive back the invader at little cost',[97] according to former Foreign Minister J. François-Poncet. The government's misguided perception of the Chadian conflict 'blinded it to the nature of attacks on the national unity and territorial integrity of that country'.[98] There was widespread conviction that if the Socialists had taken a firm line over Libyan incursions into Chad in the beginning, then the apparent uncertainties of a commitment determined by accident rather than by planning would have been avoided.[99] However, as P. Gallois admitted, the Opposition had not been particularly vocal in its criticisms for 'as soon as you [spoke] of war, it [was] the "sacred union"'[100] – only later were doubts given full expression.

This may have been the case for the Opposition, but as Bigeard had observed, the majority was more openly divided. Despite Mitterrand's reasons for increasing the French role in Chad, it was observed that 'even in [Mitterrand's] immediate entourage, serious reservations [were] felt on the part of those who, already, had dangerously under-estimated the extent of the Goukouni-Libyan offensive.... The Quai d'Orsay [was] clearly endeavouring to lighten the weight of the French commitment to Chad.'[101] Its preferred solution was confederal, to bring an end to the state of civil war which had existed since the 1960s, and its Minister, Cheysson, differed openly from Mitterrand in his assessment of the involvement of Libyan troops, and on the likelihood of an enlarged French commitment in Chad.[102] While the attitude of the Elysée hardened, that of the Quai d'Orsay gravitated around amicable relations with Libya, and its allies. The decision to commit troops to Chad was argued to have been 'difficult and embarrassing for the Socialists'[103] due to their divisions, as proved by its announcement late at night, after the main evening television news, and after the majority of the French newspapers had already gone to press.

Further Left the criticisms were more severe. For the Communists, not only had Mitterrand's commitment of troops actually gone beyond the requirements of treaties, it contravened France's basic interests. According to P. Juquin of the Party's leadership, on the contrary 'it [was] in France's interests to remain as far outside as possible ... from what [he did] not hesitate to consider already as a quagmire, or a Chadian hornet's nest'.[104] The extreme Left was still more vehement in its criticisms of the intervention. It constituted

an escalation as dangerous as it [was] contrary to the interests of the nation. Words [were] not strong enough to describe the situation which France [was] plunging into by intervening in Chad ... [the Socialists] reviv[ed] fully the traditions of the Fifth Republic, which want[ed] Africa to be the private hunting ground of one of the major imperialist powers on the planet.[105]

Rouge returned to the charge after the scale of the French commitment under Opération Manta had become known, alleging that it was 'dictated by one sole consideration: to preserve at all costs the framework of neo-colonialist accords which [bound] Chad to the Hexagon within the Franc Zone'.[106] Nothing less than the immediate withdrawal of the French troops would serve to rectify the situation.

However, as the course of events was to demonstrate thereafter, French forces in Chad would not be fighting to recover the North of Chad for Hissène Habré. In line with Mitterrand's conception of a *Tchad utile*[107] – an economically and politically viable entity comprising the south of the country below the 15th parallel – France would play a deterrent role, dissuading Libyan and rebel incursions into the south, and would not run the risks of a full-scale military engagement in the barren desert terrains of the north. After the bomb attack on the Drakkar building in October 1983 the Chadian approach held obvious attractions: it avoided combat with the rebels for the most part, thus avoiding loss of life and excessive domestic criticisms. In fact, by the beginning of 1984, *Le Point* was reporting that soldiers 'were beginning to wonder if the greatest danger which lay in wait for them was to die of boredom'.[108] However, as the situation in Lebanon was deteriorating to such an extent that the French contingent was to be withdrawn, the Chadian situation was also worsening. After a rebel attack on the government position of Ziguey, a French fighter and its pilot were lost over western Chad,[109] bringing home to the Manta forces, and to public opinion, 'that this forgotten and apparently frozen war was nevertheless a real war'.[110] More overt criticisms began to creep into domestic assessments of Chadian developments, with the RPR's spokesman on international affairs insisting that the loss of the Jaguar was a 'consequence of the shilly-shallying and inconsistencies of the

Socialist-Communist government'.[111] To counter accusations of stagnation which arose thereafter, the French advanced their demarcation line 100km to the north, maintaining their deterrent posture, but extending their surveillance and exclusion zone.[112]

The role of the forces in Chad was further called into question in April 1984, when nine soldiers were killed in a mine-clearing accident.[113] In commenting on the subdued reactions of parliamentary opinion to the loss of life, the daily *Le Matin* remarked that despite the questioning of the government's commitment to Chad which was now necessary, the French '[did] not get involved in controversy over corpses'.[114] This was all the more surprising as the fear of becoming enmeshed in Chad had apparently permeated the Opposition. The scope of, and reasons for, the French participation were considered more widely than had previously been the case. While one commentator on the Centre-Right concluded that France should stay in Chad, he insisted that the French people should know exactly why, and condemned as 'reprehensible'[115] the way in which the French intervention thus far had been undertaken without a firm and precise goal, other than a concern for the maintenance of an order which had never existed. Moreover, in a year of involvement France had succeeded in nothing more than acquiescence in the *de facto* partition of the country, between the Muslim north and Black African south, that Gaddhafi had always sought.[116]

The agreement subsequently concluded between France and Libya, providing for the withdrawal of French (and supposedly Libyan) troops, was hailed as an 'outstanding success for French policy in Africa'[117] by the Socialist leader L. Jospin. Likewise for the UDF, Mitterrand had secured a positive agreement which '[came] within the scope of the policy pursued for years by France'.[118] Vigilance was called for, however, by both the PCF and the Gaullists.[119] As time passed, the tenuous nature of the success was noted: if the 'thorny'[120] problems surrounding the French withdrawal – namely that the Libyans had failed to withdraw – were not resolved, the situation would constitute a serious diplomatic defeat for Mitterrand and his government.[121] Against this backdrop, Mitterrand's secret meeting with Gaddhafi in November 1984 was not welcomed, especially as the Americans announced on the same day that Gaddhafi had not implemented his side of the agreement. Mitterrand was most sharply criticised by the Right of the political spectrum: 'the failure of his mission was manifest; as was its imprudence'.[122] Mitterrand's subsequent acknowledgement of the continued Libyan presence in northern Chad, and his failure to return French troops to counter Gaddhafi's forces, confirmed the fears of the Right: France was abandoning her role and responsibilities as protector of her former colonies, leading to a lasting weakening of her credibility in Africa and the world.[123]

The second intervention undertaken in Chad during the Mitterrand presidency, Opération Epervier, was launched after renewed Libyan aggression and Chadian instability at the beginning of 1986. From the outset Mitterrand seemed keen to avoid allegations of vacillation. It was immediately decided to send arms to Habré's forces,[124] and in response to reports that fighting had occurred south of the French-imposed demarcation line French troops based in the Central African Republic were placed on alert.[125] Furthermore, after a direct appeal for assistance from the Chadian government, France instigated Opération Epervier, and jets attacked the Libyan air base of Ouaddi Doum, in northern Chad (which the Libyans had built after France's departure in 1984).[126] Contrasts were drawn with the previous troop commitment: Epervier was to be, numerically, much smaller than Manta, but it was to be more aggressively armed, and in particular would have greater air power.[127] Mitterrand, it was argued, was determined to avoid the impression of weakness.[128]

The legislative elections of March 1986 which brought Chirac to the Matignon were to have little effect on the French operation. In fact the President and Prime Minister agreed that further expansion of Libyan influence over Chad should be prevented, without engaging in direct combat with Tripoli itself. This was the justification for their refusal of involvement in the American air raid against Libya of April 1986, and their refusal of overflight rights to the USA.[129] Both Mitterrand and Chirac let it be known that they had no intention of engaging in full-scale hostilities with Libya.[130] As one observer noted, 'the exploitation of a success or a failure [in Chad] for partisan ends seem[ed] to have been removed. Consensus [was] necessary.'[131] Such apparent consensus was reiterated after Habré began an offensive to regain the Aouzou Strip, against his northern border with Libya, which had been under Libyan occupation since 1973. Replying to Habré's subsequent calls for French assistance, Mitterrand insisted that France '[had] always recommended the recourse to international arbitration' and that Habré's action 'only therefore commit[ted] himself and the forces of his country, a sovereign country, and [Mitterrand] repeat[ed], independent'.[132] The response had been elaborated after a full consultation between the President and Prime Minister, and was supported by both the PS and RPR.[133] The re-establishment of diplomatic relations between Chad and Libya late in 1988 permitted the reduction of the Epervier commitment, but the presence itself was maintained, to monitor the situation and demonstrate a continuation of French interests in Africa.

The implications of intervention

While the military operations authorised by Mitterrand in Lebanon and Chad were significant in demonstrating the President's will to commit French troops overseas, they were also important as indicators of sentiment regarding wider aspects of France's defence and military capabilities. The Lebanese commitment, begun as consideration of the Socialists' *loi de programmation militaire* was under way, was therefore valuable for the points it raised about the ability of the French troops to undertake sustained actions abroad. The deployment in Chad, which was begun after the planning law had been passed by the Parliament, underlined why some of the changes it contained were so necessary, and pointed to areas where adjustments might still be required.

The military interventions which characterised Mitterrand's first *septennat* underlined the limited ability of French forces to fulfil the missions assigned by the Presidency, due to reliance on a conscript base for so much of their manpower. The fact that the commitment of conscript troops overseas had to be sanctioned by Parliament meant that France's low number of professional soldiers was fully stretched in Lebanon and Chad – the three units of the 11th Parachute Division were so stretched in the MNF and UNIFIL that their commander relocated to Lebanon.[134] The lack of professional resources, at a time of increasing commitments, led the Ministry of Defence to undertake a survey of incoming conscript recruits to ascertain which would be prepared voluntarily to serve abroad – a device that would allow the government to bolster its numbers of soldiers serving outside France, while avoiding the referral of troop commitments to Parliament.[135] The operational consequences of France's conscript base were demonstrated at the beginning of Opération Manta, when the government could not immediately send a fuel detachment to support the operation, as all its soldiers were conscripts. This position arose despite plans for the *Force d'Action Rapide*, and the Defence Ministry responded by adjusting again its force reorganisation plans, ensuring that in the future such essential logistic units would be entirely professionalised.[136] With the continuation of French participation in military interventions into the 1990s, although increasingly in international rather than purely national frameworks, the problem of limited professionalisation remained. Fortunately for France, the numbers of conscripts volunteering to serve abroad was consistently higher than had been anticipated, and the phenomenon of conscript troops volunteering to serve overseas was to be fully exploited, particularly in Bosnia.

A further consideration which emanated from the interventions in Lebanon and Chad concerned operational costs and military shortcomings. Reservations were expressed over reliance on non-military methods of transport, thus vindicating the fears which had been expressed in the parliamentary debates over budgets and military planning. For the deployment of Opération Manta in particular, civilian cargo and passenger planes, along with their crews, were requisitioned.[137] The lack of sufficient transportation had still not been rectified by the time of Epervier, when DC-8s were chartered to assist in the deployment of troops. Highlighting the insufficiencies of the French armed forces, the transportation problems also contributed to concerns over costs. Given broad considerations that there was little spare money in the defence budget, the cost of the simultaneous commitments in Lebanon and Chad was cause for concern. It was even a private worry of the troops involved, some of whom believed that it would have a direct bearing on the French political will to see operations through to their full conclusions.[138] Fears were heightened as the French economic climate worsened, and concerns over the capacity of the defence budget to absorb the unquantifiable costs of interventions of undetermined length were reiterated.[139]

If cost and capability were under question, so too was strategy. The lack of a clear mandate for the second MNF commitment, and the operation in Chad from 1983, led J. François-Poncet to declare that in both cases the government's measures were 'sadly similar. They convey[ed] the same timidities, the same contradictions. If the government did not right the helm, it would lead to the same impasse, and finally to the same failure.'[140] The interventions were 'in accordance with the Socialist tradition. Hardly [were] they in power than it [was] war. Remember the pitiful Suez expedition of the Guy Mollet government ...'.[141] Indeed, 'with the Socialists it [was] always the same in any case. They [did] not want war. They said the same during the events in Algeria or Indochina. And then in the end, they always put [France] in it.'[142]

The French interventions in Lebanon and in Chad during the first *septennat*, in particular, of François Mitterrand, again indicated the primary role that Mitterrand intended to play in military matters, especially regarding the commitment of armed forces to overseas action, where he considered that such action was dictated by France's interests and responsibilities. His sense of a historical duty on France's part, coupled with his perceptions of France's international credibility, was paramount. However, external intervention under Mitterrand was also to show discontinuity with that undertaken by his predecessors. The Socialist President had a distinct preference for military action under the auspices of international bodies such as the UN, or the OAU. It seemed that for Mitterrand the French role and responsibility in such countries as Lebanon and Chad received its wider justification only in the context of international approval. Moreover, it seemed that particularly in the Chadian case, he was prepared to set a more realistic aim for the French forces than that which his predecessors had established. Limiting ideas that France was the *gendarme* of Africa, Mitterrand's forces would fight in Chad to preserve the south from Libyan incursion, thus denying the Libyan leader access to the remainder of Black Africa, but they would specifically not intervene to reconquer the north of Chad for its government in N'Djamena. These were important amendments to the French stance, allowing Mitterrand to avoid excessive commitment to unwinnable wars in the African continent.

The change which was apparent within the continuity of the Socialists' interventions overseas in the 1980s was not as widely challenged in France as perhaps might have been expected. The dominant continuity of the French commitment to her former areas of responsibility was perhaps a unifying factor. Nevertheless, the interventions in both Lebanon and Chad demonstrated that, despite the presidential *domaine réservé* in foreign and defence affairs, the consensus which surrounded Mitterrand's actions and principles was limited. The continuity and consensus in France's defence were no more solid in these matters than they were in the other major preoccupation of Mitterrand's first *septennat*: the vexed problem of superpower arms control.

6
The Security Challenge of the 1980s

At the beginning of the 1980s François Mitterrand was acutely aware of the challenges facing the international security environment, and France's position within it. The period of détente which had characterised superpower relations for the greater part of the 1970s had ended, replaced by a resurgence of Cold War tensions between the USA and the USSR. Soviet aggression and expansionism had been reinstated through military involvement in Angola and Ethiopia in the later 1970s, and had been reiterated by the invasion of Afghanistan in 1979. Moscow's threat to Europe was perceived to have increased with the deployment of intermediate-range nuclear force systems such as SS-20 missiles and Backfire bombers. In the West, the twin-track decision taken by NATO in December 1979[1] heightened the sense of confrontation. In addition, the electoral victories of Margaret Thatcher in 1979 and Ronald Reagan in 1980 indicated that a stronger line would be taken against Soviet belligerence in the future.

Mitterrand's accession to power, therefore, occurred against a backdrop of deteriorating East–West relations, and coincided with a time of unprecedented international challenge in the realm of security. The deployment of the Euromissiles[2] and the course of superpower arms control negotiations in Geneva, reinforced in the 1980s by President Reagan's Strategic Defense Initiative and further developments in the field of arms control, posed fundamental political and military problems for Mitterrand and his governments. Moreover, their potential consequences for the French military establishment gave rise to prolonged and widespread debate. Mitterrand's role in directing France's response to such multiple challenges assumed a particular prominence during his first *septennat*, as the new President demonstrated again 'the faith of the converted' in relation to the French nuclear capabilities. He came to embody both a certain continuity and a degree of national accord around the priority of maintaining the French nuclear force. However, his approach was manifold: while underlining the national emphasis and self-reliance implied by the nuclear capabilities, he multiplied initiatives in the more cooperative, European sense. Nonetheless, if there was some agreement around the broad principles of maintaining the nuclear capability, and the opening to Europe, the same could not be said regarding the deeper conclusions and inferences to be drawn from the security challenges of the 1980s.

'La crise des Euromissiles'[3]

Mitterrand's position on the superpowers' INF deployments was established even before his accession to the presidency. For Mitterrand, the deployments represented nothing less than 'the number one problem for peace in Europe'[4] as they increased the risks of decoupling American security from that of Washington's alliance partners, and thus enhanced the perceived possibility of a limited nuclear exchange between the superpowers in Europe. Developments in the Western security framework during the 1970s regarding the neutron bomb as a tactical (battlefield) nuclear weapon[5] enhanced this perspective. On the contrary, and consistently with positions he had established since the 1960s, Mitterrand's preferred way forward lay with negotiated superpower arms control based on the principle of 'neither Pershing nor SS-20s'.[6] This position, associated with the incoming President's overriding concern for 'a world balance of power ... and a sufficiently balanced situation in Europe',[7] was to remain the defining characteristic of his policy in relation to INF deployment, arms control and European security in the 1980s.

As Mitterrand insisted in December 1981, his 'first concern was to preserve the balance of power between East and West, this equilibrium being a requirement for peace'.[8] Disequilibrium, for Mitterrand, was a direct cause of vulnerability, which would endanger all European countries.[9] His tenacity was affirmed in an uncompromising speech to the UN General Assembly, in September 1983:

> peace between nations [could] only last on the basis of a real equilibrium. Such [was] the teaching of history ... the only approach possible to the problems which [lay] before [nations was] to establish these equilibria, or to re-establish them when they [had] been

broken, to guarantee their stability, to reduce forces progressively to ever lower levels....[10]

As he had argued in 1982, 'the choice which [was France's was] peace.... For peace to prevail, and it must prevail, the balance of forces between the two powers who dominat[ed] the world must be maintained.'[11]

If Mitterrand was therefore a regular proponent of equilibrium between the superpowers, and of an equivalence in their respective intermediate-range nuclear forces, it was his speech before the West German Bundestag in January 1983 which demonstrated the full extent to which he would support the Atlantic Alliance in this matter. Addressing the West German Parliament on the twentieth anniversary of the Franco-German *Traité de l'Elysée* of 1963, at a time when West Germany was divided over the prospect of INF deployments in the Federal Republic from the end of the year, and only two months from crucial legislative elections, the French President seized the opportunity to issue a rallying cry over the Euromissiles. Moreover, his call was not undertaken lightly: two of his closest advisers testify to the particular care which had gone into the speech's preparation.[12] The result was a fundamental pronouncement on Mitterrand's perception of the need for American INF deployments:

> nuclear weapons, the instrument of deterrence ... remain[ed] the guarantee of peace, as long as a balance of forces exist[ed].... But the maintenance of this equilibrium impl[ied] to [his] mind that whole regions of Europe [could] not be depriv[ed] of a response in the face of nuclear weapons directed against them. Anyone who would wager on a 'decoupling' of the European continent from the American continent would call into question the balance of forces, and thus the maintenance of peace....[13]

It was consequently apparent that Mitterrand would go to great lengths to promote the prospects of timely Western INF deployment, even if (or perhaps especially because) such deployments did not concern directly his own country.

While maintaining solid support for INF deployments by NATO members, Mitterrand undertook an equally staunch advocacy of superpower disarmament, coupled with a firm insistence that French nuclear capabilities had no place in such negotiations. Around the same time as the USSR began to seek compensation for British and

French nuclear systems in return for any agreement with the United States in the Geneva arms control talks,[14] he emphasised how 'it [was] inconceivable that France should renounce the force she [had], and therefore she [would] not participate in negotiations of [that] type. She [would] not agree to being included.'[15] His determination did not waver: a year later he 'reconfirm[ed] vigorously his refusal to see the French nuclear force taken into account'[16] in the superpower arms talks. As the Geneva discussions continued, the potential threat to the French deterrent capabilities increased. In December 1982 French forces were directly challenged. According to the Soviet leader Andropov, Moscow was prepared to reduce the number of its INF missiles targeted at Europe to 150, implying the dismantling of all the old SS-4s and SS-5s, and 90 of the new SS-20s, if NATO abandoned deployment of the planned 572 Cruise and Pershing II missiles. The Soviet figure of 150 SS-20s would then correspond to the numbers of strategic missiles possessed by France and Britain.[17] Such a proposition was totally unacceptable to the French Head of State:

> France [did] not participate in the Geneva Disarmament Conference. And in [that] matter, [the French would] not cut back a single one of [their] missiles.... [He could] only say to Mr Andropov: 'Discuss what you like with the United States of America; come to an agreement; as for thinking that France could reduce her present armament, even by the smallest amount, it [was] not even worth thinking about!'[18]

As he emphasised in the United Nations, 'one [could] only compare what [was] comparable';[19] and the French nuclear capability was incomparable to that of the superpowers in both size and nature. Mitterrand's reaction to the Andropov proposals indicated clearly the seriousness of their potential consequences for France.

While the substance of Mitterrand's position was little challenged in France, the contradictions and complications to which aspects of it gave rise were not lost on certain of his critics. On the plus side the French political parties, with the exception of the Communists, took a broadly similar view of the threat posed by the SS-20 deployments, and the necessity of NATO's INF counter-deployments. Giscard's UDF had long been in favour of a more balanced force-level in Europe between the Warsaw Pact and the Atlantic Alliance, to defuse tensions and increase stability. In traditionally Gaullist fashion, the RPR had maintained distance between France and NATO over the INF issue but the disequilibrium constituted by the unmatched installation of SS-20s and Backfire bombers had been noted with concern. As for the Socialists, the threat of the SS-20s, based on their mobility and precision, was universally recognised, and equilibrium followed by disarmament was a shared objective of both Mitterrand's wing of the Party, and the Left under Chevènement. By comparison the position of the PCF was largely isolated: it refuted suggestions of threat from the Soviet INF systems, which it argued were essentially defensive, and condemned American belligerence and imperialism in seeking to deploy counter-measures in Western Europe.[20]

Mitterrand's rejection of French participation in arms control engendered broad agreement through its reflection of French independence, and its concern for the credibility of the French nuclear capability. Despite his support for the Atlantic Alliance it was apparent that Mitterrand would not forsake autonomy and independence of decision in French deterrence. As Prime Minister Mauroy reasserted, '[France's] nuclear systems constitut[ed] a totally independent strategic system, at the service of a doctrine which [was France's] own.'[21] Even the Communist daily *L'Humanité* concurred that 'the defence of [their] country could not depend on negotiations in which [France] would not participate'.[22] The national independence that Mitterrand maintained thus found a broad measure of favour in France.

As the inclusion of French nuclear forces in the Geneva talks was unacceptable in principle, so it was too in practice, due to the challenges this would entail for their credibility and survival. The French deterrent capability was inherently limited: as Mitterrand himself had noted before the UN General Assembly, France possessed 98 nuclear warheads, while each of the superpower arsenals numbered eight to nine thousand,[23] indicating a basic difference of nature between the French force in comparison with those of the superpowers. Despite the range of the French missiles (from 3500 to 4000km) they could not, he argued, be compared in the same category as the INF systems of the USA and USSR, because they were of a fundamentally different strategic conception – a view which was commonplace.[24] Hence, Mitterrand's reaction to the Andropov proposals had been 'totally legitimate: the French nuclear forces [had] an exclusively deterrent character, [had] only been devised according to a strategy of deterrence, and, moreover, [were] only capable of an anti-cities strike'.[25] The force was therefore non-negotiable, and could not be linked to US and Soviet concessions. Not only would this set a precedent for consideration of the whole force in arms control talks, but it would place a foreign power, in this case the Soviet Union, in control of France's prospective nuclear modernisation, by linking superpower force levels to those of Britain and France.[26] Mitterrand's staunch refusal to contemplate such moves was widely supported, as was proven after the speech to the Bundestag. While Mitterrand may have been disappointed that the French public was more preoccupied with the economy, he was applauded across the political spectrum, from Marchais of the PCF to Chirac: 'France [had] on this point, a vigorous, realistic and individual policy which, contrary to what [was] happening with [her] neighbours, ralli[ed] more than it [tore] apart.'[27]

Nonetheless, Mitterrand was criticised for having become involved in a debate with which France was not concerned, and for having shown an unwise degree of support for the United States and NATO – thereby threatening the very independence he sought to maintain. Indeed the challenge to the French nuclear force issued by Moscow 'show[ed] the trap into which [the French leadership] therefore risk[ed] falling: for, in the end, it [could] seem contradictory to proclaim the absolute independence of the French defence system in relation to the East–West strategic balance ... and to take a position on what [was], or [was] not, this balance'.[28] Coupled with the President's Bundestag speech, which was partly interpreted as an endorsement of Reagan's zero option in arms control,[29] and the subsequent security declaration made at Williamsburg by the world's seven leading industrialised nations (G7), including France (a declaration which supported the main points of the USA in the Geneva negotiations), Mitterrand was accused of jeopardising France's independence and aligning France more closely with NATO than had been the case since 1966.[30] Consensus therefore was limited, and as Mitterrand's *septennat* continued, the advent of SDI in particular indicated the continued threat posed to the French capability in the 1980s.

The Strategic Defense Initiative

The announcement of President Reagan's Strategic Defense Initiative (SDI) on 23 March 1983 marked something of a watershed in France's strategic calculations, heralding the onset of what was to be a prolonged period of reflection concerning the bases of French defence and deterrence. According to Reagan, SDI was to be a 'comprehensive and intensive effort to define a long-term research and development programme', which would do nothing less than 'change the course of human history' by making nuclear weapons 'impotent and obsolete'.[31]

Reagan argued that if strategic ballistic missiles fired at the United States or its allies could be destroyed before they reached their targets, then international stability and security would be enhanced and nuclear arms control could be encouraged, as offensive weapons would have no logical place in an environment where defence prevailed. Consequently, nuclear deterrence would cease to be the defining characteristic of strategic relations, by implication calling into question the defensive arrangements of all the nuclear-capable states. Officials and observers alike in France perceived SDI to be an inherently destabilising project which would only heighten international tensions, and it was seen as a challenge on every level for France's defence provision and doctrines.

François Mitterrand was unequivocal on SDI. For him it was nonsensical and inopportune, coinciding with the very moment that the superpowers were beginning to debate disarmament seriously. It was nothing less than an 'offensive military strategy'[32] which gave little consideration to America's European allies. The French President thereafter embarked on a double mission of reaffirmation of the French nuclear deterrent capability, and promotion of the need for a common European approach to the security challenges of a rapidly changing international strategic environment.

Mitterrand's fears found echo in broader analyses of the American project. Firstly, it was perceived that SDI would result in an extension of the arms race. The Prime Minister Laurent Fabius claimed that both Soviet and American efforts in missile defences 'entail[ed] considerable risks [for arms control], each protagonist ... tempted to respond by the deployment of additional offensive systems'.[33] Similarly, Hernu argued that 'the strongest possibility remain[ed] that of a resurgence of the offensive arms race'.[34] This view was equally current outside official circles, with Reagan's logic as to the potential obsolescence of nuclear weapons being 'at the very least, questionable, and ... paradoxical'.[35] Even accounts purporting to find something positive in SDI could not avoid the conclusion that the relaunch of the arms race was just as likely as any benefit for international peace.[36]

Secondly, fears were raised by Hernu's successor Quilès over SDI's international repercussions. He was particularly concerned that 'zones of unequal security within the [Atlantic] Alliance'[37] could appear. Despite the semblance of detached independence that Prime Minister Fabius tried to maintain, it was clear that France was as much concerned for herself as for her partners in the Atlantic Alliance,[38] challenging the assertion of certain observers, for example under the auspices of the Oxford University Strategic Studies Group, that the French were in fact unconcerned by SDI and its implications.[39] Officials' fears were reiterated by security analysts in France, who considered that unequal security provision, and the residual threats to Europe from Soviet conventional forces, gave cause for anxiety.[40]

Thirdly, the political context which had allegedly generated SDI exacerbated French concerns. Immediately after Reagan's announcement in March 1983, *Le Monde* attributed the programme simply to his domestic considerations, such as the difficulty his administration was facing in pushing its defence budgets through Congress.[41] This assumption recurred in French strategic observations, with analysts attributing SDI to the American defence lobby, and to those with a desire to conquer perhaps the last 'new frontier' facing the USA.[42] For Fabius, SDI was simply one result of mutual superpower competition based 'above all on a will to power',[43] which made it all the more likely to engender change in the prevailing strategic circumstances of the Cold War.

Concerns over SDI were equally apparent in practical terms, and indeed contributed to Hernu's designation of 1983 as an *'année terrible'*[44] for French defence. The doctrine and credibility of the nuclear forces were called into question by SDI, which threatened to demolish the potential effectiveness of a strategy such as France's deterrence *du faible au fort*, as was acknowledged explicitly by Mauroy only months after Reagan's speech.[45] Compounding the difficulties facing France, as Quilès commented, was the fact that 'the SDI research programme weaken[ed] the consensus on the concept of nuclear deterrence'.[46] Extra-governmental analysts concurred.[47] Consequently, the French authorities began a concerted effort to maintain popular support for nuclear deterrence, in arguments which indicated the concern in official circles that such deterrence could become redundant as a strategic concept.

The leadership's main political offensive against SDI was launched from 1985. Not only had the Americans made significant technological progress by then,[48] and invited their Alliance partners to participate in the research and endorse the project; but 1985 saw further challenges to acceptance of the nuclear capability through the *Rainbow Warrior* affair. Mitterrand took the prominent role in reaffirming the primacy of nuclear deterrence from 1985 – economic problems at home were easing, although he faced political difficulties, and the prospect of *cohabitation* loomed. The response to SDI thus afforded the welcome opportunity to achieve a public success on defence. In addition, American diplomatic pressure regarding SDI required the firm response of the Head of State. Finally, the fiasco of the sinking of the *Rainbow Warrior* in Auckland harbour by French secret services, and the resignation of Hernu to which it gave rise, further required a bold effort by the President to reassert the commitment to a strong nuclear capability, and maintain public opinion accordingly.

At the launch of the sixth French nuclear submarine, *l'Inflexible*, in May 1985, Mitterrand reiterated his staunch support for deterrence.[49] This had been carefully calculated, according to sources close to him, to emphasise France's attachment to nuclear deterrence just as the Americans seemed to give the impression that it was dying, through developments in anti-missile defences. Mitterrand expanded on his opposition to SDI, and particularly to the Americans' invitations for European participation, in June. He resented not only the substance of Washington's requests, but also the manner in which they had been delivered: 'the American proposals to Europe were made in a hurry ... they [were] asking [the Europeans] to participate as subcontractors, without consulting [them] on the objectives'.[50] For both of these reasons Mitterrand retained his deep suspicions of the American plans, and rejected the possibility of official French endorsement.[51]

Unlike SDI, of course, the crisis which arose over the *Rainbow Warrior* affair was entirely of the French government's own making. The destruction of the Greenpeace vessel *en route* to protest against France's latest series of nuclear tests at Mururoa in the South Pacific, and the international condemnation to which this gave rise, served again to undermine the official position on defence and deterrence. Mitterrand, it seemed, considered nothing less than a major gesture on his part would serve to rectify the situation, and thus it was announced on 10 September 1985 that the President would visit Mururoa on 13 September, to demonstrate his commitment to the nuclear tests in particular, and to the nuclear capability more widely. As Isnard commented 'undoubtedly, Mr Mitterrand [had] a liking for surprise trips, above all when they [were] supposed to be symbolic, and when they [fell] into a context, national or international, where it [was] necessary to affect opinion'.[52] Moreover, following his lightning visit to Lebanon in October 1983, and a recent visit to New Caledonia to address a wave of discontent,

it [would] be the third time that François Mitterrand [had] indulged in a real dramatic turn, and thrown all his weight into an affair

where France's interests [were] at stake on the international stage....
[He used] the surprise effect to dramatise the event, to make his
personal intervention yet more formal.[53]

In the context of the manifold challenges to French deterrence by
1985, Mitterrand's trip took on added significance, and also served to
indicate how the President would use questions of defence and security to promote his own political goals.

Notwithstanding the government's attempts to rally the French
polity and people around the principles of nuclear deterrence, and the
means to meet the challenge, the matter of the finance and technical
abilities required to realise the government's nuclear modernisation
plans was more divisive. As even General Lacaze observed, SDI was 'the
major challenge with which [France was] going to be confronted'.[54]
Given the austerity measures affecting France since Mitterrand's accession, Lacaze was definitely pessimistic over the prospect of meeting the
financial costs. As the financial climate for defence had deteriorated so
much by the onset of *cohabitation* that the incoming government
considered necessary a new military planning law, France's financial
inability to respond to the challenge of SDI was lent credence.
Cohabitation also indicated that the government's position on aspects
of SDI was not universally held. After Chirac had pledged closer French
participation in the research programme in the election campaign,
and continued to emphasise his preference for participation in the
initial months of his premiership,[55] it was apparent that the scepticism
and distance of Mitterrand and the Socialists were contested elsewhere
on the political spectrum.

The European question

SDI exacerbated issues of the relationship between, if not the interdependence of, French and wider European security. It reiterated that
in some ways the French defence posture was already irretrievably
intertwined with the physical and doctrinal positions taken by NATO.
The limitations of independence were clearly apparent. Although
Fabius tried to maintain the distinction between French and European
security the difficulty was evident: as the Prime Minister recognised,
'the security of Europe, and hence [French] security, depend[ed] on the
cohesion of the Atlantic Alliance'.[56] Nonetheless if closer relations with
NATO in the search for European security were a significant factor, they
were not the only option. They were to be pursued simultaneously with

a drive for greater West European cooperation in defence and security, which would be separate from that which occurred under the influence of the United States. The construction of Europe constituted one of the cornerstones of France's external policies under Mitterrand's presidency,[57] and his attendance at the Hague conference of 1948 was repeatedly cited as proof of his commitment to the cause.[58] Moreover, he was equally convinced that European cooperation must be extended to include security. This was also a position of some long standing: he had initially supported the principle of the European Defence Community in the 1950s, although he abstained in the final vote,[59] and he had favoured a European defence capability during his presidential election campaign of 1974.[60] Even by the mid-point of his first presidential *septennat*, Mitterrand insisted that 'the idea of Europe [was] inseparable from the idea of defence'.[61] France under Mitterrand was therefore instrumental in the pursuit of a greater European defence capability, initially through the intensification of relations with West Germany, and secondly through the drive for broader European defence cooperation with resurrection of the Western European Union.

Reaction to the positions taken by the Socialist President and government in the early 1980s in this respect was largely favourable. The drive towards better relations with the United States and the Alliance, on the one hand, and the search for a European base to France's policies on the other, echoed the policies pursued by their predecessors, and Mitterrand thus gained the support of Giscard's UDF.[62] Further Right, reactions were also largely positive, contrary to what might have been expected at the turn of the decade. In this respect, Mitterrand was fortuitously placed to profit from a reversal of the RPR position on European affairs, away from the very negative attitude it had displayed before the European elections of 1979 which had proved so out of line with popular opinion. Chirac consequently approved of the Left's moves 'for the reinforcement of European solidarity within the framework of the Atlantic Alliance'.[63] The Socialists equally benefited from the unexpected, if nuanced, support of the PCF. Its leader Marchais merely regretted that the Leftist leaders' conceptions of security equilibrium seemed to exist at different levels.[64]

SDI was an additional factor in promoting moves towards European cooperation in the field of high technology, through the impulse it provided for the creation of EUREKA, the European Research Coordination Agency, in April 1985.[65] Mitterrand had pursued the possibilities of enhanced European cooperation in this field since promising 'new initiatives'[66] for research coordination in September

1983. In his speech at The Hague in February 1984 he similarly called for greater efforts within the European Community in joint technological projects, in the search for a European defence; and for an active policy of coordination for the exploitation of space, through the launch of a European space station.[67]

The breadth of favour which this stance found was considerable. Under the Socialist governments of 1981–86 the main Opposition parties diverged little from Mitterrand's cooperation with France's European partners in defence and security. The UDF's position was reiterated in 1985 in a party publication advocating full and formal participation in the Atlantic Alliance, discussions with West Germany over French tactical nuclear weaponry, and enhanced cooperation with both West Germany and Britain.[68] While the RPR's 1985 position was less prescriptive, it similarly referred to the 'need to consider and resolve the problems of [France's] defence in the spirit of close solidarity with [France's] partners and European allies',[69] and suggested consultation with West Germany over tactical nuclear weapons within the context of the 1963 Treaty. However, the path to such conviction had involved, at least for the RPR, a degree of financial realism. Even by the time that the government's financial crisis had begun to affect defence, at the end of 1982, it was recognised that one direct consequence was the drive for more cooperative European security arrangements – a view shared, it seems, by Mitterrand and his advisers.[70]

The Centre-Right's position was consolidated under *cohabitation*. In fact, during Chirac's premiership, government remarks closely echoed Mitterrand's propositions. For Chirac, 'France [was] a European power: in this capacity she could not be indifferent to the fate of her neighbours.'[71] And quite unequivocally, 'in the hypothesis where West Germany would be the victim of an attack, who [could] doubt that France's engagement would be immediate and unreserved?... France could not consider the territory of her neighbours as a "glacis".'[72] As with the President, the new government's positions were tied to conceptions of the WEU and Alliance: not only was it the case that 'European solidarity must be embodied in the WEU, whose vocation ... [was] to create a new European defence spirit',[73] but in addition, 'a European defence [was] not conceived of outside the Atlantic Alliance'.[74] France would 'commit herself to maintaining modern units whose size, and effectiveness, [could] represent a satisfactory share of the means of the Alliance',[75] while 'participat[ing] actively in the reflections which must be initiated at the heart of the Atlantic

Alliance, in the face of the political and military challenges of the years to come'.[76]

The debate which therefore occurred over SDI and its effects on French defence was illustrative not only of the political perspectives relating to France's nuclear capabilities, but also of the very practical considerations of how France's capabilities and strategy would be adversely affected. Moreover, it was indicative of the extent to which France's defence and security would in future be conceived in a more cooperative framework, potentially diluting the autonomy criterion which had previously been applied to French defence. While this was a matter of preference on the part of the President, and the major political parties, it was also a necessity. Concord was most evident in assessments of the international consequences of SDI, and in conclusions of its intrinsic danger for international security relations, but there had been far less agreement on the capacity of France's defence to withstand the pressures which bore upon it, and this element was highlighted as the arms control process gathered pace in 1986 and 1987.

Arms control and the Gorbachev phenomenon

Mikhail Gorbachev's accession to the Soviet leadership in April 1985 marked a new phase in the strategic challenges faced by France. The renewed vigour that Gorbachev imparted to the arms control process constituted a particular affront to the French nuclear force, both directly, in terms of his calls for French disarmament, and indirectly, given the eventual agreement between the superpowers in December 1987. While Mitterrand maintained the position he had on arms control before his victory of 1981, wider consensus was a far less certain factor, especially after the onset of *cohabitation*.

Gorbachev's primary challenge to the French deterrent force came during his official visit to France in October 1985. Gorbachev seized the opportunity to reiterate his commitment to the arms control process, and to call for direct negotiations between the USA and the USSR on the one hand, and between France and Britain and the Soviet Union on the other.[77] While welcoming the prospect of conversations with Moscow on many subjects, Mitterrand firmly declined the possibility of disarmament talks, taking pains to reaffirm the position he had previously set out for France.[78] The French reluctance to enter into disarmament negotiations with the Soviets was publicly confirmed during the press conference which concluded Gorbachev's visit.[79]

Such firmness was largely supported by observers. Although the weekly *Témoignage Chrétien* argued that the proposals could in fact favour détente, and thus benefit the whole world,[80] others were more sceptical. Gorbachev's proposals were recognised as 'skilful',[81] both for their manipulation of international public opinion by the Soviet Head of State on his first, and therefore closely watched, official visit abroad, and for their timing, as they were made only weeks before the planned summit meeting in Geneva between Reagan and Gorbachev. The ulterior motives to the proposals therefore contributed to their unacceptability. Moreover, they were based on a fundamental mis-conception of the French nuclear force, classifying it as a European factor (such a designation was enhanced by the call for a joint negoti-ation by the French and the British regarding their forces), and allowing the potential for Soviet influence over modernisation of the French deterrent.[82] Gorbachev's proposals therefore constituted 'a trap'.[83]

Discord began to appear after Gorbachev's next proposals in January 1986, issued only one day before the resumption of bilateral super-power talks in Geneva. On 15 January Gorbachev called for the elimination of all superpower nuclear weapons by the end of the century. The new proposals were conditional on the renunciation of SDI by the Americans, and called again for the inclusion of French and British forces, through a pledge by Paris and London not to increase their nuclear arsenals.[84] In the opinion of Jacques Attali, Gorbachev's proposals were 'dangerous: [they] would leave Europe, in the long term, at the mercy of Soviet conventional power'.[85] A highly placed adviser across the political spectrum was also hostile. For Pierre Lellouche, adviser to Chirac, Gorbachev's plans constituted a 'poisoned gift'[86] to France, and to the arms control process, because of their provision for freezing French and British forces.

Consensus dissipated with the clarification of Gorbachev's January proposals the following month. In February, Moscow made the first indications that SDI could be separated from the question of the INF systems under discussion in Geneva. Lellouche feared that 'the Reagan Administration [was] in the process of falling, head first, into the trap which Soviet diplomacy was setting for it'.[87] On the contrary, however, the Elysée was gravitating towards an entirely different posi-tion as it emerged from the prudent silence it had observed since Gorbachev's January proposals. During 1986 and 1987, the principle of cautious welcome was to be maintained, even when this diverged from the views of the *cohabitationniste* government.

The first major public disagreement between Mitterrand and Chirac over arms control occurred in the aftermath of the superpower summit at Reykjavik, in October 1986. The summit had come close to agreeing substantial nuclear disarmament, to reduce superpower strategic forces by 50 per cent and to implement the zero option in relation to their longer-range intermediate nuclear forces (those with a range of 1000 to 5500km) in Europe. It failed only because Reagan had eventually refused to comply with the renunciation of SDI for which Gorbachev called. In the face of such a fundamental challenge to the European security order, the French President and government differed greatly in their responses. While Mitterrand retained his conviction that the preferred solution to European security concerns would be found through the formula 'neither Pershing nor SS-20', leading figures of both the Centre and the Right proved to be far more attached to the presence of the American missiles on European soil, and the coupling of American and West European security to which this was perceived to give rise.[88]

The public position of the Elysée on Reykjavik was broadly favourable. It purported to view the summit as having borne much promise for successful arms control negotiations in the future, and Mitterrand emphasised this view during a visit to London to discuss the superpower summit with Margaret Thatcher on 16 October: 'People [had] spoken of failure at Reykjavik, but [he had] the feeling that on numerous points, there were advances, and that it only remain[ed] to give them concrete expression during the course of further discussions.'[89] Furthermore, speaking at the Franco-German summit in Frankfurt at the end of the month, he reiterated that 'regarding the zero option, everything which aimed for disarmament [had to] be approved'.[90]

On the contrary, Foreign Minister Raimond expressed his concerns over the 'fearsome prospect'[91] of the disappearance of America's nuclear armoury from Europe. Criticisms increased with the publication of an interview with Chirac in the weekly *Valeurs Actuelles*, where the Prime Minister declared himself to be 'quite cautious on the zero option',[92] and insisted that Europe should guard against anything which might lead to the decoupling of West European defence from that of the United States. Chirac's growing preoccupation with the prevention of decoupling was expressed unequivocally at the beginning of December, before the Assembly of the WEU in Paris. For Chirac, although '[Europe could] only rejoice at the Soviet Union's declared intention to dismantle most of its SS-20s, [the Europeans] must nevertheless prevent the possible repatriation of American missiles from weakening the ties between Europe and the United States'.[93] Such views could only underline the difference of approach to the problems of disarmament between the President and his government. These were exacerbated in 1987, as arms control progress continued, and the very real prospect of the withdrawal of American INF systems from Europe emerged.

In February 1987 Gorbachev formally removed the precondition for arms control which had been presented by demands for the renunciation of SDI. The reactions of the two French leaders were again discordant. The initiative in responding to the announcement was taken by the Quai d'Orsay: 'taking into account the conventional and chemical weapons disequilibrium in Europe, the objective must be to avoid the denuclearisation of Western Europe';[94] a statement which displayed perfectly the government's reticence over Gorbachev's latest initiative in arms control. However, in contrast with the reaction of the Defence Minister, Giraud, Raimond's position seemed quite favourable. In the meeting of the *Conseil des ministres* which followed Gorbachev's announcement, Giraud insisted that in dropping his calls for an end to SDI, 'for an exceedingly modest price Mr Gorbachev [had] obtain[ed] a complete change of the nuclear balance in Europe. The situation [was] of an extreme gravity. [They were] witnessing a sort of European Munich.'[95] Furthermore, he was not alone in his analysis – the same view was held by former Prime Minister Barre,[96] and by J.-M. Daillet, president of the UDF's Defence Commission.[97]

Mitterrand's position was much more favourable. According to Attali, the President was determined to examine the proposals with real interest, while maintaining his position that the necessary preconditions for any conceivable French participation in disarmament talks[98] had not been met. However, the danger for France stemmed not so much from Gorbachev's proposals as from the likely response by Reagan: 'the principal danger [was] the dream and madness of Mr Reagan, who [had] accepted at Reykjavik the complete withdrawal of nuclear forces. [Europe had] come within a hair's breadth of catastrophe ...'.[99] While Mrs Thatcher employed the direct approach in informing Reagan of the folly of the Reykjavik proposals,[100] for Mitterrand the only possible course was to seek a true unity of views with the other West European nations, so that Europe could begin to speak with one voice in defence of its own security. To advertise the President's position, the Elysée issued a declaration at the end of the *Conseil des ministres* which was altogether more favourable to the Soviet proposals than had been the response of the Quai d'Orsay: in the President's view, 'the prospect of the elimination or reduction of the American and Soviet intermediate-range nuclear forces [was] in accordance with the interests of France and of peace'.[101] While this view was supported in the *Conseil* by Chirac, he made known to Mitterrand that he had suppressed his personal opinions in order to maintain a semblance of consensus on deterrence and disarmament.[102]

If the French authorities were therefore unable to agree in February 1987, this was all the more true after Gorbachev's Prague speech of April, during which he not only accepted the zero option Reagan had proposed in 1981, but extended it to include the shorter-range intermediate nuclear forces with a range of 500 to 1000km. This time, however, Chirac could not hide his disquiet. The double zero option 'would create a dynamic in favour of the denuclearisation of Western Europe ... that it would be perhaps impossible for [France's] allies to control.'[103] Giraud considered it to be the last stage before the 'Finlandisation' of Europe. Lellouche concurred as to the dangers of the double zero, adding that it constituted a 'free gift for the conventional supremacy of the USSR'[104] and sounded the 'death knell of NATO's doctrine of flexible response'.[105]

Conversely, Mitterrand proffered reassurances that the latest situation constituted no threat to France. As he reiterated, France's forces remained unaffected by the Soviet proposals, as they were a principal system, strategic in nature, which by definition still had no place in discussions of supplementary, non-strategic systems. Moreover, according to the French President, the zero option did not call into question international stability and security, since the basic deterrence which existed between Moscow and Washington would continue, as their main intercontinental forces were not the subject of agreement.[106] Decoupling, he insisted, was not a possibility.[107] Mitterrand again prevailed over his government, but the point was made – if anything, consensus was less apparent at this late stage in the arms control process than it had been earlier in the decade when French capabilities were more directly threatened. The unmistakable implication was that French deterrence and security were far more closely linked to American capabilities, and to the security dimensions prevalent in Europe, than many cared to admit.

The political majority was not, however, alone in its assessments of the dangers of the disarmament process, and in the shortcomings of the Treaty which was concluded at the end of 1987 by Reagan and Gorbachev. The treaty was regarded as fundamentally flawed; and it was considered that concessions made by the West far exceeded any which had been made by the USSR. For one analyst, the INF Treaty would 'weigh heavy on the fate of peace and freedom in Europe and in the rest of the world'.[108] The agreement was a 'trap',[109] which constituted the invalidation of nuclear deterrence.[110] The American negotiators had been deluded by 'the rhetoric of false symmetry'[111] into concluding a dangerous and destabilising bargain, for

> the 'elimination' agreement eliminat[ed] nothing at all on the Soviet side, since the Kremlin [could] convert, overnight, the long-range intercontinental missiles into intermediate-range missiles intended for European targets, while the American Parliamentary system [made] the return of intermediate nuclear forces to Europe impossible.[112]

The consequences for European security, and by extension for French security, gave rise to the second source of disquiet for analysts in the INF Treaty, as the effects of the zero and double-zero options on Europe were argued to be highly significant. The result would be 'the denuclearisation of Europe, and division between the Europeans and the Americans'.[113] Few commentaries argued that the INF Treaty did not adversely alter the security situation.[114]

The only solution to the impending crisis therefore was to inject new momentum into the search for a European defence entity. The significance of Reykjavik was pivotal: through its demonstration that the superpowers were prepared to arbitrate on Europe's fate without even consulting the Europeans, it indicated that (Western) Europe would have to take a much firmer line in the delineation of its own security concerns in the future.[115] It was perceived that Chirac's initiative before the WEU fell squarely into this framework. Taking into account the challenges thus posed for Western European security in Iceland, it was asserted that 'European defence was definitely born at Reykjavik',[116] and further argued that 'whatever the result of the Soviet–American negotiation, Mr Gorbachev's spectacular proposal [of February 1987 would] have had the merit of moving forwards the union of the Europeans in respect of their defence'.[117] The subsequent obligation on the part of the Europeans to create a West European pillar within the Atlantic Alliance,[118] and for France to take the leading role in the establishment of a common European defence identity to combat the threats to her security provided by the arms control process, was similarly asserted.[119]

It can therefore be seen that the course of the superpower arms control process during Mitterrand's first *septennat* had, in fact, many more consequences for France than initial considerations might have suggested. While the official French response to the disarmament talks, most prominently asserted by President Mitterrand himself, confirmed the French commitment to the principles of nuclear deterrence, and as such benefited from a degree of national accord in the public and political spheres, this was not necessarily the case regarding the future of deterrence. However, on this point, the constraints and ambiguities of consensus were further demonstrated, for on occasion discord was consciously not expressed, so as to maintain suggestions of consensus which, particularly during *cohabitation*, were so highly prized by members of the French government.

The constraints of consensus also led to the situation whereby adverse comments as to future French defence and deterrence capabilities were expressed in consideration of another issue. Over arms control and disarmament, then, the issue of Europe served a dual purpose. On the one hand, it was clearly and positively perceived that the way forward for aspects of French defence lay within the European context; on the other, considerations of the injurious consequences of SDI, and more particularly of the INF Treaty, served to conceal that the implications applied equally to French capabilities, and that Europe, though undefined, in reality meant Western Europe, and included France. Thus the arms control process of the 1980s, spanning the Euromissile deployments; Mitterrand's overt support for the Atlantic Alliance; SDI; the accession of Gorbachev to the Soviet leadership; and the unprecedented disarmament of 1987 all highlighted the actual limitations of French independence in her defence mechanisms. It underlined the extent to which interdependence was the true factor, and emphasised that there was precious little consensus in truth.

An additional conclusion to be drawn from the arms control process was the extent to which the President was prepared to use defence considerations as a means to secure other personal and domestic political ends, especially from 1985. Not only did this enhance his own standing, but it had the supplementary benefit of working against his Gaullist prime minister from 1986 – a prime minister who was to be his principal rival during the presidential elections of 1988. Ironically, it was Chirac's concern to preserve the appearance of a certain consensus on defence policy, and to subjugate his opinions to those of the president on occasion, which helped Mitterrand to triumph. Hence, Mitterrand could begin his second term safe in the knowledge that his personal authority over defence and deterrence – the bastion of any Gaullist president – was underscored.

Thus, the constraints of consensus were particularly significant in the 1980s in hiding the real depth of divergence between the executive and the legislative, officials and observers, analysts and commentators on the credibility and capabilities of French deterrence and defence, but they were also significant in their inability to conceal such divisions totally. In this manner, it was confirmed that the first term of François Mitterrand witnessed an almost unprecedented debate over fundamental questions of the principles of French defence; a debate which was to be amplified in his second term, and which was to have repercussions on the cascade of military planning which was undertaken during that time.

7
The End of the Cold War: a Crisis for French Military Planning?

The symbolic fall of the Berlin Wall in November 1989, and its consequences for the European political and military landscape, caused fundamental upheaval in the security calculations of many of the world's leading states. Such radical change was a particularly acute challenge for France, where the end of the Cold War called into question almost all of the accepted military certainties. The changes were of profound significance for France's military planning, and for the partial, precarious consensus alleged to surround defence. They gave rise to extended and at times bitter debate over both the finance and structure of defence. The coincidence of these debates with the imminent end of the useful service-life of some of the existing nuclear capabilities augmented doubts as to the wisdom of continuity in defence and deterrence. The chaos thus created for French military planning was intensified by an alleged inability of the national leadership, even at the highest levels, to define a coherent, considered and adequate response to the new security environment – despite a succession of military planning laws and various armed forces reorganisations, and not least despite the elaboration in 1994 of the first defence White Paper in over 20 years.

The nature of the challenge

Throughout the lifetime of the Fifth Republic France's military planning had been determined, and facilitated, by the Cold War context. This had been apparent even under Charles de Gaulle: notwithstanding the General's best efforts to suggest otherwise, the concepts of rank and independence he promulgated, and his attempts to construct a third force position for France in international affairs, were in a large measure dependent upon the bipolarity of superpower relations. The continued rivalry of the superpowers, together with increased security cooperation between France and West Germany, and sustained French membership of the Atlantic Alliance after her withdrawal from the integrated military command, conditioned the future shape of French defence. Such a confluence of factors provided a propitious environment for the development of France's nuclear force, while also providing for the external conventional and nuclear military safeguards which could protect France from attack, if the case arose. As one of Chirac's foreign policy advisers asserted, 'In the Cold War, France found comfort and flourished.'[1]

The extent to which France's defence was determined within this framework was underlined by the subsequent reliance on nuclear deterrence capabilities, and the relative downgrading of conventional capabilities which was associated with it. Furthermore, the orientation of France's defence and deterrence was confirmed by the evident unfeasibility of the *tous azimuts* doctrine for a medium power such as France. Indeed, the very range of the French nuclear capabilities, reinforced by the placement of France's reduced conventional forces within the European theatre, meant that those capabilities could only conceivably be used in one direction. Thus, irrespective of the best Gaullist rhetoric, France's defence was placed firmly in the Western camp. All of these aspects were intensified under François Mitterrand: despite the socialist credentials of the French President he was no favourite of Moscow,[2] and in many instances the feelings were entirely mutual.[3] Mitterrand's support for NATO's INF deployments, and the explicit designation of the Soviet Union as France's principal potential enemy, for the first time, in the Socialists' *loi de programmation militaire* for 1984–88, reinforced France's position in the Cold War system.

The end of the Cold War therefore undermined almost all of France's doctrines and structures of defence. Its effects were amplified given its suddenness, and scale, and the lack of clarity in response to the developments on the part of the political hierarchy. Politically, despite Mitterrand's longstanding criticisms of the division of Europe through Yalta,[4] his equally aged dislike of military blocs,[5] and his claims, published posthumously, to have anticipated the fall of the Berlin Wall, the reunification of Germany and the collapse of Communism,[6] there is no evidence that he had formed any contingency plan to deal with these prospects. Neither is it certain that he had any conception of their consequences for France's security. Rather, his concerns over the changes unfolding in Europe were more apparent, as demonstrated during his consultations with Mikhail Gorbachev, over the reunification of Germany.[7] Notwithstanding Mitterrand's concerns, however, the military implications were equally serious: as a respected French analyst of international affairs observed,

> for the first time in several centuries, French national territory [was] no longer threatened with invasion; the defence of France, defined as defence of a territorial body on or beyond the north-eastern border, [was] now meaningless.... France [had] thus just watched the simultaneous disappearance of the *psychological and political geography* within which it operated, *the power scale* on which it positioned itself, and *the definition of its defence forces' missions*....[8]

Therefore, France was in urgent need of new defence planning. However, economic, military and political factors stultified France's reactions to the changes, and stifled attempts at planning adaptations.

Financing the defence effort

In line with debates over defence planning during Mitterrand's first term, discord over the financial means available was to dominate defence debate in his second. The difficulty of resource allocation was one with which the President became more perceptibly involved than at any time during his first *septennat*. However, rather than reinforcing accord and consensus, his interventions served instead to heighten appearances of division, not only between the Left and Right of the political spectrum, but also within political groupings, and not least, within governments.

Under France's Socialist governments of 1988–93[9] any remaining consensus over defence planning and resource allocation was sorely tested. The likelihood of resource restrictions was perceived among the Opposition from the earliest weeks of Mitterrand's second term, for at least two reasons. The first related to the national economic climate: France was faced with a significant, and worsening, budget deficit, which Prime Minister Rocard and Finance Minister Bérégovoy were keen to reduce. The second related to the inferred preferences of the President himself: even during his re-election campaign he had been suspected of wanting to reduce military expenditure.[10] Anticipation of funding cuts for defence was confirmed with the presentation to the Assemblée Nationale of a new *loi de programmation militaire* for 1990–93 in October 1989.

Allocating 182.36 billion francs to defence in the budget for 1989, the government increased expenditure by only 2.1 per cent, in line with France's low rate of economic growth, thereby reducing slightly the proportion of GDP allocated to defence from 3.73 per cent to 3.69 per cent.[11] While equipment expenditure was maintained, savings were found in operational expenditure, including manpower costs. The budget for 1988 had already shown a shortfall of 2 billion francs between the requirements of the planning law and the actual financial provision; the budget for 1989 added a further shortfall of 4 billion francs,[12] resulting in an expenditure deficit of 6 billion francs in only two years. It was alleged that if the budget was characterised by a certain continuity, then it was no more than a 'continuity in insufficiency'.[13] Unable to accept the budget plan, the main Opposition parties, the RPR and the UDF, abstained from the vote.

After divergence between members of the government and the presidency, the revision of the military planning law for 1987–91 confirmed fears of significant cuts. Contrary to the widely reported view of Chevènement, that a figure of no less than 450 billion francs, of the 476 billion francs provided for in the planning law, would be sufficient to maintain the commitments of that law,[14] Rocard and Bérégovoy had wanted to reduce the allocation to 400–420 billion francs for 1990–93.[15] The dispute was only resolved by Mitterrand's intervention, during a press conference on questions of defence and foreign affairs, when he set the sum available for defence at 430–435 billion francs.[16] The sum eventually provided to cover the period 1990–93 was 437.8 billion francs, conveying a saving of around 40 billion francs (approximately 10 per cent), in comparison with the means anticipated under the previous planning law.

Nevertheless, the modernisation of the nuclear forces was emphasised, including the refurbishment of existing submarines to carry the new M4 missile; continued development of a new-generation nuclear submarine (SNLE-NG); the replacement at the end of the century of the missiles of the Plateau d'Albion; and improved tactical nuclear capabilities through the introduction of the Hadès short-range weapons system in 1992, and the establishment of three squadrons of Mirage 2000N bombers armed with the ASMP missile.[17] There were to be delays, however, in the delivery of the SNLE-NG, and the number of Mirage 2000N squadrons planned had been reduced from five to three. For the conventional forces, the balance sheet was more ambiguous. The Army's flexibility and mobility were to be improved with the new Leclerc tank; new helicopters from 1997; and more firepower. Cuts were made though in 155mm artillery, terminal guidance ammunition and the AMX-30 B2 tank. The priority of the Rafale fighter, still under development, was maintained for the Air Force, which would also benefit from the purchase of four AWACS aircraft and enhanced weaponry, but the order rate for the Mirage 2000 was reduced (from 33 per year to 28) with adverse consequences for the preservation of a fighter fleet-strength of 450 planes. Naval capacities were to be substantially improved, with modernised hunter-killer submarines, new frigates and landing craft, an ocean-going minesweeper capability and new maritime patrol aircraft. Difficulties were expected, however, in the replacement of the Crusader aircraft operated by the Navy, which would become obsolete in 1993, and were due to be replaced by a naval version of the Rafale, although the latter would not be ready until at least 1996. The capabilities of the *Gendarmerie* would be reinforced, particularly through the delivery of enhanced communications equipment.[18]

As the government and its supporters argued, the proposed planning law contained a mixture of continuity and caution in its reactions to international developments. As Chevènement insisted,

if the détente which [was] governing the international climate ... allow[ed] France to nurture a justified hope for peace it must not, for all that, lead [France] to change the course of [her] defence policy. [French] policy [was] defensive; it [was] based on deterrence, within the framework of strict sufficiency.[19]

His view was reiterated by the Socialist *rapporteurs* of the Defence and Finance Committees: the Bill 'clearly preserv[ed] the fundamental missions of [France's] defence'[20] and 'coherence ... [was] guaranteed, since the principle of sufficiency [was] confirmed'.[21] However, the Bill also created discord across the political spectrum. It was declared unconstitutional – a vote on this was only narrowly defeated by the government[22] – and it was rejected by the influential cross-party Foreign Affairs Committee.[23] In fact such was the extent of opposition to the proposed law, and the probability of its defeat in a vote, that Rocard was compelled to mirror the actions of M. Debré almost thirty years earlier[24] and stake acceptance of the law on a series of confidence votes in his government.

For the main Opposition groupings the financial bases of the revised planning law were unacceptable. Indeed, the timing of the Socialists' extensive resource reductions, coinciding almost exactly with the culmination of events leading to the fall of the Berlin Wall – but decided well in advance – did not augur well for their easy passage through Parliament. The cuts were deemed an 'amputation',[25] which was 'justified by neither the economic and financial situation, nor by the evolution of the threat',[26] especially as economic performance had exceeded the forecasts of the 1987–91 planning law. Hence, according to the Centre and Right, France's defence requirements were being badly neglected by the Socialists. Capabilities were 'gravely compromised'[27] by the delays in weapons development and reductions of orders. A 'contradiction' would occur 'between the concern to equip [France's] forces with coherent equipment, and the heterogeneity which [would] emerge from the extension of programmes'.[28] Moreover, it appeared that the cuts were devoid of any revision of France's strategic requirements, as the proposed planning law '[did] not bear witness to a deep reflection on the military consequences of the new diplomatic developments, or on the evolution of the balance of forces in Europe. It [was] only an exercise in planing down the defence credits …'.[29] Quite clearly, for the main Opposition, 'the defence effort [was] no longer the priority of this government, [and] in that, the government called into question the national consensus'.[30]

Nevertheless, at this point there was little apparent consensus to preserve. If the government had been divided over the financial means of the planning law, despite its defence by Chevènement in the National Assembly, and the Right was generally disgusted by its inadequacies, the Communists were equally hostile, but for entirely different reasons. The PCF was in 'total opposition'[31] to the plan, whose dominant factor was not the cuts it contained but the *extra* resources it allocated for defence in the coming years.[32] It was argued that this contradicted the course of international developments, which 'should logically have led to the reduction of France's military equipment credits'.[33] For the Communists, the satisfaction of pressing social needs was far more important than an increase in the defence effort, leading to their proposal to redirect 40 billion francs from the defence budget to education and civil research.

The forcing of the planning law through Parliament did not, however, indicate any greater commitment on the part of the Socialist government to respect the funding obligations it had undertaken. This was apparent only months later, with reports of a dispute between the Finance and Defence Ministries recurring by July 1990. Such was the desire of the former, to make savings at the expense of the latter, that Bérégovoy was demanding a cut of six to seven billion francs from the budget for 1991 alone, compared with what had been provided for in the planning law.[34] The resolution of the defence budget disagreement within the government was once again provided by François Mitterrand, who ratified a cut of almost six billion francs in the 1991 allocation, against the wishes of his Defence Minister.[35] The subsequent announcement that the planning law was to be replaced eroded further any confidence in the Socialists' military planning, as was demonstrated from all sides with the submission of the defence budget for 1991, in November 1990.

The budget set the financial provision for defence at nearly 195 billion francs – an increase of 2.7 per cent over the previous year, confirming a stagnation in real terms, as the Socialists acknowledged.[36] While it incorporated timely efforts to improve military pay and conditions as French troops served in the Gulf, its predominant features were the reduction of equipment expenditure and proposed manpower cuts. For the main Opposition it was both short-sighted and precipitate, taking little account of the uncertainty of the future threat and moving too quickly towards defence reductions.[37] Even the Socialist *rapporteurs* recognised the inadequacy of the resource allocation, asserting that a continuation in this vein would endanger the modernisation of the armed forces.[38] The criticisms were still harsher from the Communists: the government was evidently 'blind'[39] to the new international context of disarmament, and was maintaining military expenditure at an artificially and unjustifiably high level. The budget was rejected by the Assemblée Nationale, and its eventual adoption was only possible after Rocard had staked the existence of the government in another confidence vote.[40]

The situation had little improved when the defence budget for 1992 was submitted to the National Assembly. The sum available was 195 billion francs – an increase of 0.5 per cent over 1991 – while the national budget had increased by 3.1 per cent. With inflation at 2.8 per cent, purchasing power for the armed forces was reduced by approximately 2.3 per cent in real terms, and the proportion of GDP granted to defence decreased from 3.37 per cent to 3.26 per cent. The shortfall between the *loi de programmation militaire* and the budget allocation was 7 billion francs.[41] Operational expenditure was cut, and 24 380 jobs were to be lost, principally in the Army. The stagnation of equipment expenditure marked a 2.8 per cent fall in purchasing power due to inflation, and of particular note, funding for the nuclear capabilities was cut through the abandonment of the S45 missile, the reduction of the Hadès tactical capability from 120 to 30 missiles, reduced funding for the *Commissariat à l'énergie atomique* and the extension of the SNLE-NG programme by a further six months. The only parts of the defence budget to demonstrate any significant increase were space and intelligence. After the shortcomings exposed by the Gulf War, credits rose by 17.5 per cent. For the conventional forces the prestige programmes were maintained, but delayed; no fighter planes were ordered; the ocean-going minesweeper and the eighth hunter-killer submarine were cancelled; two-year delays were introduced for the Tigre helicopter and the new-generation anti-tank helicopter; and production levels of the Leclerc tank were to run at 40 per year, instead of the 100 initially planned. Finally, there was no indication of how the budget related to the planning law anticipated for 1992.

In fact, no new planning law was debated in the Assemblée Nationale in 1992, although the government proceeded on the bases of the Bill it had elaborated. Relating to planning from 1992, to a reference point in 1997, although formal provision only went as far as 1994, it was considered to be a 'law of transition'[42] whose execution, and even its relevance, were highly uncertain. Despite the lack of formal debate it was known that the planning law had set equipment expenditure at 308 billion francs, and an overall finance level of 662.4 billion francs until 1997. Funding for the nuclear forces was reduced, although expenditure for space and intelligence was to increase, and resources for the conventional forces were also to increase, by more for the Navy than the Army and Air Force.[43]

The uncertainties and perceived inadequacies of the military planning situation had a direct bearing on the fate of the defence budget for 1993.[44] The allocation for defence was set at 198.9 billion francs, conveying an increase in absolute terms of 1.4 per cent over the previous year, but a decrease of 1.4 per cent in real terms. The proportion of GDP granted to defence was again reduced, to 3.14 per cent. The equipment budget remained constant, resulting in a decrease in real terms due to inflation, but the operational budget remained constant in real terms. Manpower reductions were also a feature of the budget, numbering 22 400 posts, and again targeting the Army in particular. Some provision was made to finance external military interventions; but the fact that the Finance Ministry had cancelled 4 billion francs of credits from the previous equipment budget, from September to November 1992, meant that the real cost of such operations would only be met by a reduction in the future equipment capability of the armed forces. Despite the arguments of the Socialist majority in the

Assemblée Nationale that the reductions were far less than those in the budgets of France's allies, the French budget was only passed after the failure of yet another vote of confidence.

Consequently, the period of Socialist government from 1988 to 1993 had been immensely divisive among French parliamentarians, over the direction and financing of the defence effort. The position of the Centre and Right, the main Opposition, was clear: the Socialists had abandoned defence as a national priority, as proven by the reduced proportion of GDP allocated to defence, from 3.895 per cent in Hernu's first defence budget for 1982 to 3.14 per cent in the budget for 1993. The position was equally clear at the other extreme of the political spectrum, where the Communists sought a substantial redistribution of the expenditure allocated to the defence effort. Even members of the government and the Socialist Party had begun to demonstrate disquiet over their governments' commitment to defence. These positions did not augur well for broader aspects of military planning at such a time of international challenge.

The problem of the peace dividend

> Meet ... Jean-Pierre Chevènement of France, a man to whom peace dividends are anathema.[45]

While the other major Western nations, following the American lead, sought to benefit openly from the peace dividend in the aftermath of the Cold War, this was not to be the case in France. Partly because France's leadership seemed to lean towards retrenchment, rather than revision, in its response to the changes in Eastern Europe and beyond,[46] and partly because of the pre-existing discord over the level of defence expenditure, this was not to be an argument to which France could easily subscribe. The need for a reorganisation of French defence to adapt to changing international circumstances was little questioned; the linkage of financial cuts to the end of the Cold War, in search of *les dividendes de la paix*, was far more contentious.[47]

Economically, there was every reason after the fall of the Berlin Wall and the collapse of Communism for France to seek to gain from a peace dividend. France's poor economic performance at this time had begun with a slowdown of economic growth in 1990, which was aggravated in 1991. The downturn in growth had exacerbated the fact that the government's economic calculations had simply been far too optimistic in the first place; after growth levels of 3.7 per cent in 1989, and

2.6 per cent in 1990, the Finance Ministry had planned on 2.7 per cent for 1991. However, by the middle of that year a maximum increase of 1.5 per cent was anticipated. To add to the difficulties, tax revenues were also far lower than expected, compounding the budget deficit, whose reduction had been a Socialist priority since 1988.[48]

However, successive budgetary reductions meant that little remained to be diverted from the defence budget without creating a political and military crisis. Divisions throughout the body politic made the realisation of any peace dividend almost impossible. Militarily, too, crises loomed as equipment of all types, conventional and nuclear, approached obsolescence, and the pay and conditions of military personnel lagged ever further behind their civilian counterparts. Unforeseen costs, such as the French contribution to the Gulf War, magnified the problem. In addition any realisation of a peace dividend implied a reassessment of the priorities and commitments of the defence apparatus. No such reassessment was forthcoming under the Socialists after the Cold War. This is not to suggest that certain reorganisations of the armed forces were not undertaken – the difficulty was that these were designed to correct deficiencies identified in the 1980s and, like the cuts in the defence budget, they had been decided well in advance of the strategic upheavals of the post-Cold War environment. Hence, it was not necessarily pressure from the military which made Chevènement resist a peace dividend, nor any belligerence on the part of the Minister. Rather, it implied recognition that despite the poor economic climate, ironically, if France could not afford her defence at the onset of the 1990s, then neither could she afford the luxury of a peace dividend. Into this somewhat contradictory, and certainly complex situation, was placed the future of France's conventional and nuclear forces.

The future of the conventional forces: organisation and equipment

Within the confines of a broadly continuous military policy favouring the nuclear forces, the reassertion of conventional capabilities which had begun under Giscard was maintained under Mitterrand. Nevertheless, Hernu's improvements in conscript conditions and his creation of the *Force d'Action Rapide* in the 1980s were overshadowed by the reorganisations of Mitterrand's second term. Each Defence Minister of the second *septennat* undertook extensive force restructuring and rationalisation – each, it seemed, more extensive than the last.

Given the condition of the conventional forces at the end of the 1980s such tasks were widely accepted as necessary, but they were complicated by both the end of the Cold War and the financial limitations facing each of the governments of the period. The increasing hostility of the Right to the successive reforms was much in evidence – especially to the reforms of the Centrist Léotard under the second *cohabitation* of 1993–95.

The first of the major armed forces reorganisations was Chevènement's plan, *Armées 2000*, formally announced on 20 June 1989.[49] It was designed to 'reinforce the operational capabilities of [France's] forces, and the coherence of [her] military system';[50] a coherence which had previously been obscured.[51] Consequently the Army in particular would be reorganised, with the six existing military regions being reduced to three.[52] To reinforce the operational capacity of this simplified organisation the responsibilities of the First Army, stationed at Metz, would be increased, and France's three army corps would be reduced to two, which would be stationed in Baden and Lille. Interservice cooperation would be developed, initially in support functions. Early indications suggested the dissolution of 15 units, including nine regiments, and the abolition of 23 military staffs.[53]

Reaction to the plan was generally divided, between adverse local and some military opinion, and the more balanced political reaction, on this occasion even from the Right. Local protests emerged from areas scheduled to lose their regiment or unit, where that regiment or unit constituted a major factor in the local economy and society. A typical case was that of Barcelonnette, which was to lose the Alpine brigade stationed there, and whose citizens launched a strong campaign to retain a military presence in the area.[54] On the military level, the coincidence of the proposed reforms with the recent difficulties over financial provision caused concern, notwithstanding the military's own efficiency drive with the Orion plan.[55] Fears centred on the conjunction of the financial cuts and the reduced numbers of military regions, districts, units and regiments, and over the possible operational consequences thereof.[56] Nevertheless, political reactions were characterised by calm – even the RPR spokesman Fillon acknowledged 'a courageous choice'.[57]

However, as the pace of international change quickened after 1989, questions arose over the applicability of Chevènement's restructuring in the new security circumstances. Even before the trial implementation of *Armées 2000* began on 1 September 1990 further change was contemplated, considering the government's continuing financial difficulties and Mitterrand's unexpected announcement in July 1990 that all French forces were to be withdrawn from Germany.[58] Added to these considerations, France's participation in the Gulf War of 1990–91 increased pressures for reassessment. The reforms subsequently announced by the new Defence Minister, Pierre Joxe, were more wide-ranging than Chevènement's original plan had ever been. Joxe's reorganisation was based on manpower cuts of up to 70 000 by 1997, from a starting point of 285 000 in 1991, and would take into account the 50 000 or so French troops to be withdrawn from Germany by 1995.[59] However, the main part of Joxe's reform plan was not announced until 1992.[60] Amounting to a 'true revolution',[61] Joxe's plan was also designed to address some of the more glaring French military shortcomings exposed by the Gulf War.

Primarily, the new reforms would develop an autonomous French intelligence capability. The Defence Minister was a determined advocate of such capabilities,[62] particularly after the dependence of French forces in the Gulf on American information. The restructuring would therefore build on his creation in 1991 of a *Direction du Renseignement Militaire*, which grouped the previously disparate intelligence services of the armed forces, and on the increased funding for space research in the budget for 1992. Secondly, Joxe's reforms further modified France's force structures to fulfil any type of mission, with minimal notice, based on the 'dual principle of projection and flexibility'.[63] Extending the rationalisation of *Armées 2000*, such a reorganisation would inevitably have consequences for the armed forces. For the Army, the 8th Infantry Division, three reserve regiments, six regiments of the Second Army Corps, and numerous engineering and support services would be dissolved. The Air Force would lose over fifty fighters, and the Navy would see its functions further concentrated on the ports of Brest and Toulon in search of financial savings. Medical services would likewise be rationalised. The target level for Army manpower was confirmed as 225 000, but final cuts in the other services were less clear.[64]

Reaction to Joxe's measures was again divided, largely between those who recognised their utility, and those who would be affected by the cuts. F. Fillon, for example, commented upon the 'cogency'[65] of the reforms, but as one analyst noted, 'courageous measures ... [were] often painful'.[66] Thus, it was argued that Joxe's announcement had come as a 'bombshell' for the 93 local communities it affected.[67] For the main Opposition, the measures constituted a 'neutron bomb' for the Haut-Rhin area, according to its representative, J.-J. Weber (UDC –

Union Démocratique du Centre),[68] and for G. de Robien, the UDF mayor of Amiens, the removal of the 8th Infantry Division from Picardie left his town 'systematically forgotten and neglected'.[69] Socialist figures were equally concerned by the Joxe plans. C. Trautmann, mayoress of Strasbourg and a member of the European Parliament, wrote to Joxe specifically to ask him to reconsider, and the mayor of Cherbourg, J.-P. Godefroy, insisted that 'it [was] out of the question to accept such decisions'.[70] The Communist-backed unions, the CFDT and the CGT, also condemned the plans, and strikes and protests were organised in the areas affected.[71] Nevertheless the reforms were implemented, albeit with some concessions to the economic concerns of local communities.[72] The political discord to which they had given rise was almost eclipsed, however, by reactions to the reforms announced one year later by François Léotard.

Part of the difficulty with the Léotard reforms was their similarity with those which had preceded them. If the Opposition had long lost faith in the Socialists' military planning, it can perhaps be assumed that the Centre-Right, once in power during the second *cohabitation*, might have expected a more concerted effort. Still, with reference to external constraints on defence, Léotard extended the reorganisations already undertaken. Thus, the Army's future manpower level was confirmed as 225 000; the dissolution and rationalisation of units continued; the Navy's functions were yet further concentrated on Brest and Toulon; more Air Force bases were to close; and three military hospitals would be shut.[73] Moreover, Léotard failed to address the issue of equipment. Given the apparently ever-decreasing Socialist defence budgets, and the difficulties of securing investment expenditure for military hardware, the reforms of Léotard's Socialist predecessors had aimed to improve equipment levels through the reduction of the number of units, allowing the distribution of the equipment of the disbanded divisions among those remaining. Léotard's plans followed in the same vein, exacerbating problems which had already arisen, and offering little practical assistance in the matter of obsolete *matériel*.

Adverse reaction from all sides was apparent in response to the local consequences of Léotard's cuts: at Lorient, the Socialist mayor J.-Y. Le Drian, and the CGT union, strongly protested the 'absurdity' of plans to close the submarine base, while the Socialist mayor of Verdun, J.-L. Dumont, declared himself 'appalled' by the proposed dissolution of the 3rd Marine Artillery regiment.[74] Across the political spectrum, mayors and deputies from the Limousin region in particular threatened resignation over such proposals as the removal of the Staff of the 15th Infantry division, and the closure of the air base at Romanet.[75] However, the strongest opposition concerned the principle, rather than the consequences of the measures, and on this aspect Léotard's reforms served as a catalyst for demonstrating the true limitations of the consensus on defence issues, even among the governing coalition.

The RPR's response to Léotard's plans was harsh. The president of the Parliamentary RPR condemned such 'decisions taken in haste'.[76] P. Lellouche likewise criticised the reorganisations because they 'weaken[ed] the armed forces considerably',[77] having been undertaken with no clear strategy for the future. Léotard was accused of organising 'the wholesale slaughter of [France's] armed forces'.[78] On the contrary, J. Mellick for the Socialists hailed the measures as 'courageous',[79] and J.-M. Boucheron called Léotard's plans 'sound, and necessary'.[80] As Isnard commented in *Le Monde*, 'a new element [had] appear[ed]: the Minister of Defence [was] largely supported by the representatives of the Opposition, and condemned by his own political allies'.[81] The lack of consensus was emphasised; all the more so since Léotard's proposals had in fact *avoided* the known areas of contention, such as the future of national service and France's relations with NATO, altogether. Therefore, although the necessity of some form and degree of reorganisation of the armed forces was acknowledged to adapt France's forces to the challenges of the post-Cold War world, there was in fact little agreement on the scope or shape of such reorganisations. Such lack of accord was similarly evident in the discussions of military service which gathered pace in the aftermath of the Cold War.

The future of the conventional forces: national service

In the context of the widening defence debate in France, conscription and national service constituted another significant area of discord. The heightened concern of the Socialists to address the problems of national service was apparent soon after Mitterrand's re-election. As the debate over conscription simmered, its topicality was increased by the combined factors of armed forces reorganisations, and Mitterrand's unexpected announcement of a shortened military service from 1992. Consequently, the feasibility and desirability of a professional army for France was more widely considered, but on this topic as on many others at the beginning of the 1990s, little accord was apparent.

Following Hernu's efforts to improve the conditions of conscription in the early 1980s, Chevènement's commitment to the cause was equally staunch. By that time concerns were mounting over the short-comings of national service in relation to republican ideals of equality and universality of service.[82] Equality was called into question by the development from the 1960s of non-military forms of service, and the regular incorporation of the cream of France's youth into such forms of service as participation in business and commerce or teaching information technology.[83] Universality was also doubtful, as by the late 1980s almost one in three Frenchmen eligible for service at any one time were exempted on medical or social grounds, and almost four out of five graduates avoided actual military service.[84] Consequently Chevènement reiterated the necessity of 'modernising military service, improving it, diversifying it',[85] and established enquiries to define the extent of the problems.[86]

Nevertheless, his options in the short term were limited – primarily by financial considerations. Conscription allowed the maintenance of a large army at relatively small cost. The financial savings to be made through conscription, in comparison with the costs of a professional army, had been confirmed by studies both within and outside France.[87] The extra cost of maintaining a professional army had also been considered by J. Fontanel, in a benchmark comparative study with Britain, which had concluded that the British salary expenditure on armed forces was 60 per cent greater than that of France, for a manpower level of less than 175 000, and excluding the costs of the civilian support staff.[88] Given France's unreliable economic health, and the general drive, particularly at that time, for financial savings in defence, the prospective costs of a professional army could be considered prohibitive.

However, with military reorganisations and associated manpower reductions, the necessity for a reconsideration of national service became more pressing. Debate was heightened by President Mitterrand's announcement in July 1990, with little warning and seemingly little consultation of his government,[89] that the length of military service was to be reduced from twelve to ten months, with effect from 1992.[90] Reaction to the measures was reserved, especially on the Right. At best, Chirac cautiously welcomed the initiative.[91] Elsewhere on the Right, reaction was more severe. General Bigeard of the UDF was 'frankly hostile' to any reduction in the length of military service, considering the uncertainties of the international security environment.[92] Neither was a possible electoral impulse for Mitterrand's announcement lost on other commentators who noted that the measures, which were bound to be well received by the public, would be introduced in time for the legislative elections of 1993.[93] The dilemma which ensued over conscription or a professional army highlighted the differences in the French polity over defence.

The major opportunity for the expression of political discontent was the parliamentary debate over the government's modification of the National Service Code. Joxe insisted that conscription was the object of a broad consensus among the French people, and that to preserve the republican traditions of the French armed forces its maintenance remained a necessity.[94] To this end, the Ministry of Defence was to instigate further studies into improving the equality and universality of service. The government was, mostly, supported by the Left of the political spectrum. Nevertheless, while the reduction of military service to ten months was both 'possible and necessary' – possible due to the military changes in Europe and necessary to take account of such – it was important that service should not be reduced further, and imperative that the conscripts' military and living conditions were improved.[95] On the Centre and Right of France's politics, however, the differences in approach to the problems of national service and conscription were broader, and the solutions propounded more diverse.

The UDF and the UDC each retained a degree of basic support for the principle of conscription. The UDF favoured increasing the number of units without conscripts, to provide enhanced capabilities for external action, while retaining conscription and an effective network of reserves which was adapted to modern circumstances.[96] The UDC position was slightly more nuanced, for although the grouping advocated the principles of national and military service, the exercise of that service over previous years had come to mean that it no longer fulfilled the republican aims which had been set for it.[97] Thus the government's measures to rectify the changed situation were 'inadequate and incomplete', and indeed the method of their delivery – an unheralded announcement by the President – had been 'demagogic', presenting the deputies with a *'fait accompli'*.[98] Of the main Opposition parties, however, the reactions of the RPR were the most radical. According to their spokesman, François Fillon, 'conscription [had] become scandalously inegalitarian', giving rise to 'an unacceptable, and unfortunately irreparable, social discrimination'.[99] Consequently, 'the only choice, as much in keeping with the strategic reality as the development of [France's] society, [was] the passage to a professional army'.[100] Although the announcement followed consultations among the RPR deputies, Fillon's view was not universally held. If there was disarray therefore among the RPR, there was certainly disarray among the wider Centre-Right Opposition, who had not been consulted before Fillon's declaration.[101]

The publication of the RPR's programme for a professional army[102] prior to the legislative elections further highlighted divisions, at least among the RPR itself, as Baumel asserted his opposition to a professional force[103] and Fillon continued his advocacy of it.[104] The intermediate position was taken by Boyon, who called for greater debate, in the public as well as the political sphere, over the future of conscription.[105] However, as the debate broadened into 1993, it became further apparent that Fillon's position was not a majority view. Even the military hierarchy was not convinced by his arguments. Prominent military figures such as the former Chief of Staff of the Armed Forces, General Schmitt, and the Commander of the 2nd Armoured Division, General Paris, preferred the concept of improved, mixed armed forces, to retain large reserves of trained personnel, at the least cost.[106] Only the renegade General F. Valentin advocated the rapid transition to a professional army, to allow France to fulfil the changing nature of her missions in the new international circumstances.[107]

The course of the second *cohabitation*, under the Centre-Right government of Edouard Balladur, did little to clarify the debate over conscription. Neither did the publication of the *Livre blanc* in 1994. In fact, as one analyst noted, 'the White Paper implicitly acknowledged the underlying lack of consensus inasmuch as it devoted thirteen pages to refuting the arguments of those opposed to national service ...'.[108] A decisive choice was not made until Chirac's presidency, under whose leadership, and true to positions the RPR had begun to establish in the early 1990s, France moved towards a professional army.[109]

The future of the nuclear forces

The *cohabitation* of 1986–88 had shown that Mitterrand perceived all issues relating to France's nuclear forces to fall squarely within his own *domaine réservé*: the course of his decisions regarding the nuclear capability in his second term amply demonstrated that continuity was the order of the day in this respect, at least, even if those decisions called into question the future of that capability. There were four main areas in the context of the nuclear forces where Mitterrand exercised his presidential authority – the cancellation of the S45 mobile missile project, the limitation of the Hadès tactical nuclear weapons system,

the imposition and subsequent extensions of the nuclear test moratorium, and the controversy over the new M5 missile. With the
imminent end of the useful service life of nuclear capabilities
conceived and produced from the 1950s and 1960s,[110] each of
Mitterrand's decisions took on potentially greater significance, and
were therefore contested by the parties of the Right in particular.

The successor missile to the S35 of the Plateau d'Albion, and a
replacement for the Mirage IVs which had entered service in the late
1960s, were particular sources of dispute, in debates which were both
confused and exacerbated by the apparent inconsistencies of the political hierarchy. In a televised speech in March 1991, Mitterrand had
insisted that modernisation would involve no alteration of France's
defence strategy: 'the deterrent force [was], and [would] remain, its
pivot'.[111] However, only weeks later in her speech to the National
Assembly outlining the government's main policy themes, Prime
Minister E. Cresson was less reassuring, intimating that one element of
France's strategic triad was to be abandoned.[112] Despite Mitterrand's
attempts to remove nuclear force questions from the arena of debate,
by his exclusion of such matters from the defence debate of June 1991,
their importance, and the potential contradictions of the leadership in
this matter, meant that such an attempt would inevitably fail.

This was underlined by the decision to cancel the S45 mobile missile
programme, taken at a meeting of the *Conseil de défense* under
Mitterrand's chairmanship on 10 July, and notified to the industrial
firms involved two days later.[113] The press reports of the decision, a
week later, constituted Parliament's notification. The choice was
firmly attributed to Mitterrand – indeed his hostility to the mobile
missile plans had been apparent from the mid-1980s[114] – and the
President was much criticised for not having announced it himself.
According to Chirac, his leadership had deteriorated into little more
than 'a monarchical exercise of power'.[115] As one deputy commented,
there would be little point in debating the forthcoming *loi de programmation militaire*, as its major decisions had already been taken.[116]

If the manner of the announcement was inflammatory, its meaning
was still more so. Effectively, it was argued, Mitterrand had eliminated
one component of the strategic triad, by renouncing the potential
replacement for the Albion missiles without reference to Parliament
and without providing the opportunity for debate. Moreover, he had
abandoned an element which was the Right's best hope of maintaining the credibility of the deterrent force into the next century. Chirac
called upon Mitterrand unequivocally to reconsider a decision which

was 'heavy with consequences'[117] for the future of French defence. Fillon argued that the President had decided, 'in reality, to base deterrence from 1998 on the nuclear submarines only'[118] – and furthermore, this had been undertaken without any serious consideration of a replacement to preserve the credibility and the future of the nuclear panoply.[119] Despite Socialist arguments that the S45 had only 'correspond[ed] to the strategic situation of the past',[120] and Léotard's view that the mobile missile was 'extremely costly, fragile through its vulnerability and relatively weak in its effectiveness',[121] the RPR insisted that Mitterrand had made a 'bad choice'[122] which would only detract from the credibility of the deterrent force.

The deceleration of the Hadès programme was perhaps less contentious. The end of the Cold War, and the changes in Central and Eastern Europe, as well as Mitterrand's concerted, and broadly supported, efforts to improve Franco-German relations, had cast doubt on the desirability of this battlefield system. Even with its increased range of 480km, if it was ever fired Hadès would still only fall in the 'new democracies' if launched from French positions in western Germany, or on eastern Germany itself if it was fired from France.

As with the mobile missile project, Mitterrand had never been an adherent of short-range, tactical nuclear weapons capabilities. For Mitterrand the nuclear capability was more a political than a military instrument; it was not a means of fighting wars. It was a tool of war prevention. Consequently his announcement in September 1991 that the Hadès programme was to be greatly restricted could not have been unexpected, especially given the added weight of his convictions against the mobility of land-based nuclear weapons. Although he had sanctioned the establishment of the first Hadès brigade, from 1 September, only weeks earlier,[123] the President declared unequivocally in a press conference later that month that he had 'considerably reduced ... the Hadès capability in relation to the initial forecasts.... Thirty missiles ... [would] be stored.... No Hadès [was] deployed.'[124] This was the first public confirmation of a trend that had been developing throughout Mitterrand's second *septennat*; discreetly, outdated tactical nuclear weaponry had not been replaced on a one-for-one basis since 1988, and Mitterrand's announcement served to acknowledge the reduced role of those capabilities in the French armoury.[125]

Reactions to Mitterrand's press conference did not tend to take into account the Hadès decision, as attention had been focused on the greater part of the President's subject matter, which had been Europe. In this respect, the freezing of the Hadès capability at the 15 launchers already manufactured (one launcher fired two missiles) was an intelligent ploy, for it avoided outright cancellation, and the stockpiling of the missiles meant that at least in theory a residual capability remained. Moreover, Mitterrand's move broadly corresponded to the evolution of opinion: P. Séguin, of the RPR, had called overtly for the cancellation of Hadès in view of European developments, since at least December 1989.[126] His position was shared by Fillon, and also by the Socialists G. Fuchs and F. Heisbourg.[127] Popular feeling, too, was moving away from support for Hadès, as was apparent from a pacifist demonstration in favour of its abandonment in March 1990. Nevertheless, in the broader context of defence and deterrence, the Hadès decision contributed to the growing questioning of France's nuclear capabilities. It was followed by measures to reduce the number of France's pre-existing nuclear-artillery Pluton regiments,[128] and by the withdrawal of that system altogether at the end of its service life. The moratorium on nuclear testing, announced in April 1992 at the will of the President, further extended debate over the prospects for the French nuclear forces, and exacerbated fears that Mitterrand was denigrating the defence effort with little idea of any long-term planning, and for domestic political ends.

The moratorium on nuclear testing was announced on 8 April 1992 by the new Prime Minister Bérégovoy.[129] It came only just before the start of the annual test series in the South Pacific – all but the most final preparations had been made. Linking his decision with a call to the other nuclear powers to do likewise,[130] Mitterrand apparently tied the French force more closely to disarmament processes than had ever previously been the case. This was reiterated by the decision of June 1992 to adhere to the Non-Proliferation Treaty.[131] Furthermore, in a press conference, the President revealed a view that considering international developments, France 'must diversify her priorities',[132] developing, in particular, better space-based intelligence and observation. After the reduction of the credits awarded to the nuclear forces, for the first time, in the defence budget for 1992, the way was therefore open for much speculation and debate over the President's intentions for the future priority of French deterrence.[133]

Unsurprisingly, Mitterrand's decision was welcomed by environmental movements, such as the Green Party and *Greenpeace-France*[134] and by the governments of South Pacific states.[135] It was also supported by the public: a survey showed nearly 60 per cent of the French people opposed nuclear testing.[136] However, it was less well received elsewhere. Léotard, for the UDF, was cautiously positive, qualifying France's new contribution to disarmament and the reduction of nuclear tests as a 'useful and intelligent objective'.[137] Chirac, for the RPR, was much more severe: Mitterrand had set out on the 'path of renunciation' of nuclear deterrence, by taking a decision of 'unilateral disarmament ... [which ran] the risk of weakening the defence of [France] and that of Europe'.[138] Even the government's financial difficulties could not be argued to have driven the decision, since at best, 500 million francs could be saved from the original outlay of 3.6 billion francs.[139] In view of recent electoral progress by the Greens in France, it was alleged that the decision had been 'inspired exclusively by domestic political considerations'.[140] Caustically, one observer noted, Mitterrand was not 'the first of the French, but the last of the ecologists'.[141]

The moratorium which Mitterrand had initially imposed for the rest of 1992 was subsequently extended to match that of the superpowers, until July 1993. As the prospective end of the moratorium approached, popular feeling in favour of continuing the moratorium, mobilised by the *Mouvement de la paix* (close to the PCF), was manifested through a demonstration of over 3000 people on the Plateau d'Albion.[142] However as France at that point did not have the technical expertise to proceed to simulated tests, the technical experts of the *Commissariat à l'énergie atomique*, charged with the conduct of the tests and the development of the nuclear capabilities, considered a resumption of testing to be a 'necessity'.[143] Even when the CEA's PALEN programme (*préparation à la limitation des expériences nucléaires*) was fully operational, the CEA management argued, a number of tests would still be necessary due to the limitations of simulated tests.[144]

The indefinite extension of the moratorium, by a joint decision of the Elysée and the Prime Minister's office in July 1993, fuelled the debate. While Balladur's *cohabitation* government planned to create a committee of experts to assess the impact of the test suspension on France's nuclear forces, the main part of Mitterrand's moratorium was unchanged.[145] As such it aroused the lively hostility of the Right, especially from the government's allies, the RPR. For J. Baumel, 'it [was] a very bad decision',[146] especially as military analysts considered necessary further tests on France's new warhead, the TN75, for the M45 missile and the ASLP missile,[147] as a matter of some urgency. The extension was condemned by the Front National.[148] The positive reaction of the Greens,[149] and the movement *Génération Ecologie*, was little apparent elsewhere.[150]

Debate and discord barely subsided thereafter, as the need for a number of extra tests became more keenly argued, and as the international moratorium was called into question. The occasion for this latter was the Chinese nuclear test of October 1993. In February, Mitterrand had said that France would not be the first to break the test suspension; his reaction was therefore of particular significance at this point. That reaction, in the form of another joint communiqué with the Matignon on 6 October, was the maintenance of the French moratorium.[151] It was not well received by the Right.

Indicating the extent of the Right's discord over decisions taken by the President (and the Left) and Balladur's Centre-Right, Chirac estimated that in order to maintain a credible deterrent, France was 'obliged'[152] to carry out 10 to 20 more tests before data for simulation could be considered reliable. J.-L. Debré, also of the RPR leadership, argued that 'by preventing the resumption of nuclear tests, the President of the Republic [dealt] another blow to France, and her capacity for independence, for political reasons'.[153] Nevertheless, as the Balladur government began to distance itself from Mitterrand by openly considering the probability of more tests in the future, the President announced a further extension of France's moratorium until the end of his presidency.[154]

The final area in which Mitterrand intervened over nuclear forces came at the beginning of 1994, and amounted at least in part to an exploitation by the President of the evident division over defence between the parties of the governing coalition, in the approach to the elections of 1995. His intervention was also interpreted as undermining yet further the future of France's nuclear deterrent. The subject of debate was the M5 missile. The M5, successor to the M45, was designed to equip France's new-generation nuclear submarines from around the year 2005. It was to have a range of 8000km and would carry between 10 and 12 nuclear warheads (the new TN100). It was also costly: around 200 million francs had been spent on it by mid-1992,[155] and the programme in total was expected to cost up to 40 billion francs.[156] While the military specialists of the RPR declared their view that the M5 constituted the future of the French strategic missile capability, the Balladur government was far less convinced.[157] To compound what was, in effect, yet another disagreement between the main parties of the majority, Mitterrand intervened to express his support for the M5. Moreover, as a possible solution to the problem of replacing the practically obsolete missiles of the Plateau d'Albion, he suggested the development of a land-based variant, the S5.

However, Mitterrand's intervention was quite clearly perceived to be a 'trap',[158] on financial, technological, strategic and political grounds.

Financially, if the M5 plan was to be fully and immediately funded, as the Head of State seemed to suggest, it would dominate the defence budget for years to come, to the detriment of all other equipment. Technologically, it was a challenge to say the least, for to be fully effective it was to carry the miniaturised and more accurate TN100 warhead, but Mitterrand's moratorium on testing meant that development of the TN100 was open to question. The President's suggestion that the M5 could instead carry a modified version of the TN75 was not feasible, for reasons of the additional financial and technological difficulties it would pose, and also for the strategic questions it would raise about the quality and credibility of French nuclear weapons into the next century. Mitterrand was thus accused of a surreptitious abandonment of the deterrence that had served him so well during his presidency.[159] The challenges to consensus were evident; they were compounded by the internal political damage being inflicted on the majority, through exposure of the extent of differences even between Chirac and Balladur – each of whom was a candidate in the presidential elections of 1995.

Nevertheless Chirac maintained the charge, with the explicit argument that the M5 was the only means of assuring the credibility of the French nuclear force.[160] The M5 argument was closely linked, for Chirac, to the continuing problems of the nuclear test moratorium – contrary to the President, he believed that it should be equipped with the TN100, as planned, which urgently required more nuclear tests.[161] Nevertheless, the Balladur government, mindful of the financial constraints that Chirac's demands would impose, retained its position on the M5. Léotard even criticised François Mitterrand in a public session of the Finance Committee of the Assemblée Nationale, on the grounds of the 'unreasonable'[162] costs which would be incurred through early development of the M5, and particularly through attempts to develop a land-based variant. The M5 programme was subsequently deferred in the military planning law elaborated for the years 1995–2000.[163]

Each of these areas demonstrated the lack of consensus not only between the position of the President and the Socialists, and that of the Right of the political spectrum, but also between the parties of the Right themselves. Furthermore, the issues which gave rise to Mitterrand's attentions were far from an exhaustive catalogue of nuclear-force debates in the post-Cold War period. Rather, they were symptomatic of deep divisions which existed over anything more specific than whether or not France should have a nuclear capability.

Thus, debates which were continued in the public domain over, for example, an adaptation of France's nuclear doctrine – from deterrence *du faible au fort* (by the weak of the strong) to deterrence *du faible au fou* (by the weak of the mad) – to take account of nuclear proliferation in the Third World,[164] and the nature of the second nuclear component if one element of the strategic triad was abandoned, indicated the extent to which perceptive and profound new planning was vitally necessary to adapt France's defence and deterrence structures to the challenges of the future. This was not necessarily provided, however, by the major defence planning document of the latter years of Mitterrand's presidency – the *Livre blanc*.

Planning for the twenty-first century: the *Livre blanc*

> France's defence [was] no longer applicable only at her immediate borders. It depend[ed] on the maintenance of international stability, and on the prevention of crises, in Europe or outside Europe, which would place [France's] interests and [her] security in danger if they degenerated.[165]

In attempting to adapt France's defence to such requirements, the *Livre blanc* established six crisis scenarios with which France could be faced in the subsequent twenty years, in order of probability. The resurgence of a major threat against western Europe was considered the least likely scenario in the short term, while the prominence of regional crises, involving France's vital interests or not, were perceived to be the greatest danger facing the French defence systems.[166] In decreasing order of probability thereafter, were the possibilities of attack on the territorial integrity of France's overseas possessions, the implementation of bilateral defence agreements, and operations in support of peace and international law. In addition, the *Livre blanc* professed openness to Europe, in matters of both arms production and procurement, and in its preference for multinational military cooperation within the framework of France's alliances, including the Atlantic Alliance, should the need arise. However, while recognising the prominence of the conventional force role, the *Livre blanc* still reasserted the primacy of nuclear deterrence.

Political reactions to the *Livre blanc* were perhaps best described as cautious. The RPR recognised it as 'courageous',[167] and 'necessary after ten years of [Socialist] incoherence and the weakening of the defence system'.[168] The UDF likewise supported the government's legislation.

For the Left, there was similarly a basic welcome for the *Livre blanc*,[169] but significantly this welcome was founded on one of the areas which was to become a source of contention among the majority, namely the maintenance of the nuclear test moratorium.

Indeed, although the White Paper was initially favoured, albeit with some reservation, by the majority, criticisms of its deference to the wishes of President Mitterrand soon made it yet another example of division between the parties of the Right and Centre-Right on defence. Mitterrand's influence over the *Livre blanc*, in that it was unlikely to challenge his own deterrence priorities, and over the test moratorium, had been signalled even before its publication.[170] This led to clashes between Balladur and Léotard on the one hand, and Chirac on the other, over the Paper's non-restoration of nuclear tests.[171] As opinion settled, the perception emerged that the *Livre blanc* had been altogether marked by *cohabitation*.[172] While Léotard argued that it had indeed been a product of an active French consensus on defence, this being one of its strengths,[173] others even among the majority claimed that the government had produced a document that '[ran] the risk of evading embarrassing questions because of *cohabitation*'.[174] On the contrary, it was argued by members of the RPR that the *Livre blanc*'s best quality was its proximity to the presidential elections: as J. Boyon, the President of the Defence Committee of the Assemblée Nationale maintained, it had closed no doors to the next government.[175] As had also been perceived outside France, the *Livre blanc* was no magic solution to the difficulties France's defence was facing; 'rich in ideas and recommendations for the long term, ... it [was] considerably less forthcoming about where France's defence [was] heading in the next few years'.[176] It raised more questions than it answered, avoiding choices over whether the Army was to be a professional or a conscript force, and over the development of the nuclear forces into the millennium. It therefore fell squarely within the tradition of military planning under Mitterrand's second term.

In short, the end of the Cold War not only provoked a particular challenge for immediate French military planning, but moreover engendered a profound examination of planning for the future. However, contrary to other states, who seized the opportunity for a fundamental reassessment of their defence and security provisions, France was more unable than unwilling to take the same course. The necessity of reform was widely acknowledged, but the potential for effective implementation was severely hampered.

Primarily, the economic constraints on the French defence mechanism were stifling. The financial effort required even to keep abreast of new strategic and security developments had always been only just within France's reach: the rapidity and the extent of the changes from the end of the 1980s risked taking them out of France's range altogether. In addition, the resources available for defence had been under particular threat even prior to the developments associated with the end of the Cold War and its aftermath. The weight of the domestic financial burden was such that the defence allocation was always a prime target. Consequently, each of the other areas of debate and dispute which existed before was highlighted and exacerbated by the end of the Cold War.

Secondly, there was a dearth of strategic vision in France in relation to a coherent medium- to long-term military development schedule. This was not solely attributable to the Socialists, as the Right maintained: French force structures and emphases had been established from the beginning of the Fifth Republic. Twenty-three years of Gaullism in defence planning had given rise to a certain rigidity, which had proved detrimental even before the end of the Cold War, without any sign of solution thereafter. The events of 1989–91 served to complicate and confuse matters still more. Combined with repeated financial pressures, the chances for necessary change were further restricted. Hence, the reorganisations of the conventional armed forces attempted by Mitterrand's defence ministers were almost doomed to failure even as they began. Moreover, they set a precedent for what needed to follow – if reform was not possible in an area which, relatively speaking, escaped the intervention of the president, then this augured ill for the prospects of fundamental reorganisation in areas which did not, and where the President favoured retrenchment, on the one hand, in a traditional French deterrence strategy, moving away from potential battle-fighting capabilities, and on the other, tended ever more towards the use of defence questions for domestic political ends.

Thirdly, the concept of consensus was now in crisis. Its weaknesses had already been evident at the end of François Mitterrand's first *septennat*, over matters of finance for the defence effort, and the management of the nuclear capability. These were exacerbated during his second term, and expanded to include, more overtly, issues relating to the non-nuclear forces. The end of the Cold War, and the crisis in military planning which followed, drove deeper the divisions both between and among the political parties over the future of defence, and demonstrated the limitations of that consensus.

8
Towards a European Defence?

The cooperative stance which increasingly came to characterise France's defence relations with her Alliance, and particularly European, partners during François Mitterrand's second *septennat* was one of the most striking features of defence development under his leadership. Assertions of independence which had surrounded the French position at the outset of Mitterrand's terms of office had given way to rhetoric about a common foreign and security policy, leading to a common defence, in the Maastricht Treaty on European Union, and had evolved to such an extent that within months of the end of Mitterrand's terms, France could undertake a near-complete return to the fold of the Atlantic Alliance. The genesis of this reorientation, which had begun under Mitterrand's first term of office, was given added impetus by the upheavals in the Cold War security order which took place from 1989. Challenging many of the foundations of France's defence posture, the impact of the changes on France was considerable.

Given the favourable reactions which greeted moves towards a more collaborative French stance in defence in the 1980s, especially regarding Europe, the objective of the increasingly outward-looking posture of French defence was not significantly contested within France – at least in the first years after the symbolic fall of the Berlin Wall. However, if the end was largely uncontested, the means to that end gave rise to more discord, as political proponents of the Atlantic and the European approaches to French defence took opposite positions in the debate. Moreover, although the political hierarchy maintained, and indeed expanded, a commitment to cooperative security on the Continent and beyond, the European ideal proved difficult to achieve, giving rise to a significant questioning of the very principle of a common European defence.

Europe and the German Question: '2+4'?

As previously noted, Mitterrand had demonstrated himself to be a forceful advocate of the European ideal in all fields, including defence, in the 1980s.[1] Such a goal would be sought through a tangible improvement in relations between France and West Germany, especially in military matters, and through the associated revitalisation of the Western European Union. Moreover, the President had shown himself willing to identify personally and extensively with the amelioration of Franco-German and Franco-European efforts in this field; an identification which would be maintained into the 1990s. However, even the convinced European in Mitterrand appeared at times unable to navigate consistently the complex issues surrounding the reunification of Germany and its implications for Europe, and particularly for France.

The strength of Mitterrand's European convictions was reiterated in his *Lettre à tous les Français*, of 1988. As Mitterrand insisted to the French people, 'France [was their] homeland, Europe [was their] future.'[2] He warmed to his theme before the IHEDN in October 1988, arguing that the Europe to whose pursuit he would 'devote'[3] himself, '[would] not exist without being capable of assuring her own defence'.[4] Thus, he would build on the successes of his first term, especially in security relations with Germany, to constitute the core of the European defence of the future.

However, as post-Cold War events unfolded, the scale of the change in the European security context became apparent. France was faced suddenly with the prospect of a reunited Germany, of huge political, economic, demographic and not least military potential, at the heart of Europe. Such reunification potentially undermined the cornerstone of France's security stance, which had been the continued division of the power responsible for the humiliations of 1871, 1914 and 1940. While the German potential was re-emerging, the second strand which had facilitated France's defence posture since the Second World War, namely the United States' physical military and political commitment to Europe, was also under threat. Thirdly, to compound the problem, the *raison d'être* of the ultimate French security guarantee, the Atlantic Alliance, was called into question by the progressive collapse of Communism in the Soviet bloc, the dissolution of the Warsaw Pact, and the disintegration of the Soviet Union itself. Mitterrand was no less concerned than his compatriots over the implications of such developments for France, notwithstanding the solidity of the Franco-German relations he had engineered since 1981.

Indeed, the German question was a principal concern by the turn of the 1990s, both among and beyond the leadership. Analysts of the changing international security situation were remarkably frank in their assessments: as a former ambassador pondered, 'how could the unquestionable right of the German people to self-determination be reconciled with their French neighbours' desire for security, still deeply marked by the memory of three successive invasions in less than seventy years?'[5] The concerns of the French political hierarchy were personified in the approach of the President to international developments. His abstract consideration of the possibility of German reunification within ten years, in a press conference in Bonn just before the breach of the Berlin Wall,[6] together with a speech he gave in Strasbourg outlining concern over the consequences of the changes in Central and Eastern Europe for continental stability, and stressing that the question of German reunification was in a large part dependent on the will of the Soviet Union,[7] gave the impression of a statesman whose primary emotion was apprehension, rather than enthusiasm, for the course favoured by his principal diplomatic ally. Mitterrand's visits to the USSR and Eastern Germany, in December 1989, entrenched the perception of his reluctance to consider a rapid and near-revolutionary change in the status of West and East Germany.[8] This was reinforced by his comment to George Bush, also in December 1989, that 'if [they did not] keep both horses pulling evenly, there [was] going to be an accident':[9] that accident being the rapid reunification of the Germanies.

As Mitterrand was concerned with questions of security and stability, so too was his electorate. It was argued that 'a large majority of the French people would accept the hypothesis of a long and carefully planned unification if their security could be guaranteed';[10] and this guarantee was to take the form of a double commitment on the part of Germany, unified or not, to the Atlantic Alliance and the WEU, the latter in association with a wider European defence capability. It was argued that for France,

> the maintenance of Atlantic integration and the acceleration of Western European construction in a federalist spirit [had] clearly represented,... since the fall of the Berlin Wall, the best framework for German reunification, and the best even for managing its effects.[11]

The strength of feeling for a greater European (and especially French) element in the control of Germany after the end of the Cold War was apparently broadly felt: it was suggested that for political as well as military reasons, 'for France, [the possibility] of having more of Germany, and less of Europe, was excluded'.[12]

The reservations towards German unification, and the impulse to respond to it with European security initiatives, were particularly evident in French reactions to the '2+4' Treaty of September 1990, and in analyses of the consequences of the Gulf War, in 1991. The 2+4 Treaty, signed by East and West Germany and the four powers previously enjoying occupation rights in Germany throughout the Cold War (the United States, the Soviet Union, Britain and France), provided for German unity to occur within the framework of the Atlantic Alliance, and for the confirmation of Germany's borders. Certain concessions were also made by the newly-united Germany's government over the size of her armed forces, the continued renunciation of weapons of mass destruction, and over financial support for the withdrawal of occupying Soviet troops from the former East Germany.

The French order of priorities in disposing of this final act of supremacy over the post-1945 Germany was encapsulated in Mitterrand's insistence on referring to the negotiations, and agreement, as the 4+2 talks, emphasising the residual role of the external powers in directing the affairs of Germany.[13] His spokesmen in the ratification debate reiterated the benefits for France, and for European security, of the Moscow Treaty. The Foreign Minister, R. Dumas, underlined the continuity of Franco-German relations sealed within the accord,[14] and M. Vauzelle, the president of the Foreign Affairs committee, asserted the ways in which the agreement provided for the resolution of French security concerns – as in the question of borders, the renunciation of chemical, biological and nuclear weapons, and Germany's membership of the Atlantic Alliance.[15]

However, the preoccupations of the Opposition were not entirely alleviated by the 2+4 Treaty. On the Right, while professing faith in the continued validity of privileged Franco-German relations, the RPR insisted that given the dynamism of the new German entity, if such relations were to remain privileged, 'France must regain a political, economic, military and cultural power allowing her to speak from an equal footing with [her] neighbour across the Rhine.'[16] This acknowledgement of a degree of French weakness was taken up by the UDF, which expressed concern that although many provisions were indeed made to address security fears, there was no mention of the 'vital question' of broad European defence.[17] The reactions at the opposite end of the political spectrum were, perhaps predictably, more extreme, but interestingly were based on similar concerns. For the Communists, French weakness relative to the new strength of Germany, along with the weakness of existing collaborative structures, was determining: the French thus must 'not shelter under the illusion of thinking that the power of the reunified Germany could be "contained" in some manner in integrated structures ... the truth [was] that no structure [could] contain, by itself, the influence of Germany'.[18] However, the conclusion reached varied from that of the government and Rightist opposition; instead of the European option, which the Socialists and the mainstream Right and Centre favoured, the PCF advocated the demilitarisation of Germany under the auspices of pan-European security structures.[19]

The debate which followed the end of the Gulf War, ostensibly to consider its military lessons for France, also considered in a large part the prospect of an effective European defence capability. Broadly speaking, the same objective of a European defence identity was a source of consensus among participants in the debate; only the Communists again differing.[20] However, by this stage divergence over the achievement of the objective was more apparent. For the Centre and Right the need for a European defence capability was one of the primary lessons of the Gulf War, and one which the Socialist administration seemed unable to acknowledge. For A. Paecht of the UDF, '[France was] condemned to European solidarity not only in the realm of conventional weapons, but also in that of nuclear weapons ... [France] should be the embryo of a nuclear defence of Europe, allied in this respect with Great Britain.'[21] Due to her own inadequacies and the course of international developments, J. Briane of the *Union du Centre* insisted that France in fact had no choice in the matter; she 'must play the European card'.[22] However, the RPR was critical that despite the longstanding, and formerly secure preferences of the President in this respect, the Socialists would not go far enough to achieve it. For F. Fillon, European security plans were 'all the more illusory, and condemned to failure, because [France] dare not – because [the government] dare not – follow [them] to [their] logical conclusion'[23] – a full pooling of France's military resources with her European and NATO partners. Only the Communists rejected the European path, arguing that it constituted a threat to peace; the party maintained that the only way to preserve the basis of France's defence position, namely its independence, was to reject the idea of European defence altogether.[24]

Consequently, the extent to which the foundations of French defence and security interests were challenged by the end of the Cold War, and the prominence of concerns to effect some control of Germany, coloured the debate about France's defence and security relations in the post-Cold War world. While there was support for a combination of the European and Atlantic methods, the French government distinctly favoured the solely European option at the beginning of the post-Cold War period.[25] Only as the shortcomings, and pitfalls, of this position became apparent was a more pragmatic approach adopted, integrating the continental and Atlantic aspects which had been favoured by the Centre and the Right since at least the outset of the changes in the international security environment.

Europe and NATO, vs Europe or NATO

In accordance with the desire of Mitterrand's governments, of all political hues, since his accession to the presidency, the preferred way forwards to achieve both control of Germany, and a wider European capability in the area of defence, had been the reinforcement of the WEU. Arguing that 'the Alliance [could] not remain unchanging in a changing world',[26] and indeed that NATO's military doctrine had effectively been bankrupted by the end of the Cold War,[27] J.-P. Chevènement asserted the priority of the European over the Atlantic commitment: 'Conscious of the necessity for the European countries themselves increasingly to take charge of their security interests, France [was] determined to contribute actively, and primarily at the heart of the WEU, in the efforts necessary for this continuous construction of a European pillar of the Alliance.'[28] The emphasis on an autonomous European approach to the provision of European security was reiterated by initiatives to deepen the integration of the European Community, in which France found a willing partner in Germany. Consequently, from the latter part of 1990 greater Franco-German efforts were made in the field of European defence and security.

The efforts undertaken built on the achievements of Mitterrand's first *septennat*. Mitterrand had pursued close Franco-West German security relations throughout his period of office, since he raised the question with Chancellor Schmidt specifically in February 1982.[29] Under Kohl's Chancellorship, the relationship improved further, providing for the revival of the security provisions of the 1963 *Traité de l'Elysée* in January 1983, and the creation of the Franco-German

Defence and Security Council to ease their implementation.[30] The powerful imagery of Kohl and Mitterrand joining hands at a commemoration of the battle of Verdun, in September 1984, confirmed the extent of the changes in France's security relations with her European neighbours, and with West Germany in particular. As Attali noted, it was a picture which '[would] epitomise, better than any other, the effort of the decade'.[31] The substantiation of the image continued in subsequent months. In June 1985, for example, an opinion survey revealed that for the first time since the Second World War, a majority of the French people favoured an automatic commitment to the security of West Germany if the latter came under attack.[32] Only days later, on the occasion of a Franco-German military exercise, Hernu unequivocally applauded the 'intense relations in the field of defence and security'[33] between the two countries. Subsequently, according to Mitterrand's adviser Védrine, West Germany's pressure on France to deepen and diversify their security relations intensified.[34] Its result was unprecedented. In February 1986, an agreement concluded between Mitterrand and Kohl provided for the installation of a Paris–Bonn hotline; studies on the practical use of the *Force d'Action Rapide* in Germany; and on a West German initiative, consultation between the French and German leaders over the possible use of France's short-range nuclear weapons in Germany. While Mitterrand would not accept any co-decision, the text of the agreement was nevertheless near-revolutionary:

> Within the limits imposed by the extreme rapidity of such decisions, the President of the Republic declar[ed] himself willing to consult the West German Chancellor on the possible use of French prestrategic weapons on German soil.[35]

Significantly for the objective of legitimising a European defence capability in Mitterrand's second term, he and Kohl gained American backing for the prospect of a European Security and Defence Identity at the NATO summit in London in July 1990.[36] At the October meeting of the European Council in Rome thereafter, the twelve members reached agreement on the objective of a Common Foreign and Security Policy (CFSP), which was developed further by Mitterrand and Kohl in December, when they addressed a joint letter to their European partners calling for the elaboration of the CFSP in close cooperation with the WEU.[37] In 1991, the two leaders emphasised their commitment to a European defence capability with the publication of a joint document on security, proposing the creation of a Franco-German Corps from the Franco-German Brigade. The Corps, later the Eurocorps, would be under French leadership; it would include forces from other European countries; and it would be responsible to the WEU. Its primary focus was therefore to be European, rather than Atlantic. To extend the European dynamic constituted by the Corps, the Franco-German document also advocated Qualified Majority Voting by the Corps' participants on certain foreign and security policy issues.[38] The joint initiative was also noteworthy for its reversal of Mitterrand's decision of July 1990 to withdraw French troops from Germany, and the acceptance by France of the principle of peacetime military integration. Confirmed by the provisions of the Maastricht Treaty, in relation to a common position on defence and external policy concerns,[39] it would seem that by early 1992 significant progress had been made towards the goal of a European defence capability.

Nevertheless, as the course of international developments demonstrated, the path to a European defence capability was a difficult one. External events, combined with increasing domestic pressures, and reluctance among France's allies, engendered a certain reorientation of the French government's position towards Europe *and* NATO, rather than the initially preferred Europe *or* NATO. The impediments to the latter option were political and practical, domestic and external. Politically, opposition within France to the government's policy ambiguities continued to find expression. This was exacerbated by the political and practical difficulties which were indicated by the positions of France's European partners, and the structure of existing European security arrangements. This was manifested by generally adverse external reactions to the establishment of a European security architecture and extension of the role of the WEU, and also practically by the reactions to the Eurocorps proposal in 1991–92. The deterioration of the situation in the former Yugoslavia, and the inability of the Europeans to resolve the crisis themselves, exposed further the practical difficulties of a solely European approach to security problems.

The ambiguities of the government's position in relation to the future of the Atlantic Alliance had been apparent almost from the beginning of Mitterrand's second term. Even Chevènement noted in 1990 that 'the Atlantic Alliance remain[ed] an element of stability';[40] for according to Prime Minister Rocard, it 'remain[ed] the uncontested framework to take responsibility for the interests that [its members had] in common; no-one look[ed] to call it into question ...'.[41]

Nevertheless, as the Defence Minister suggested, 'the prospects opened up by a certain American disengagement [from Europe could] only reinforce the necessary modernisation of the Alliance.... If it [was] normal that the Europeans [would] play a greater role in their defence, their responsibilities must be better noted at the heart of the Alliance'.[42] French aims, therefore, were especially geared towards achieving a reform of NATO which would reduce the role of the United States, thus allowing the pursuit of a clearer European defence capability, and which would provide a greater capacity within the resultant Alliance for leadership by France. In this manner, reform rather than renunciation was the aim, in order that the guarantee of European security marked by the American commitment to the continent should be preserved.

Consequently, France's relations with the Alliance in the early 1990s came to be characterised by an increase in the perceptible interaction, if not overt cooperation, between France and NATO. Not only did France take part in NATO's 1990-91 Strategy Review[43] but she also agreed to the Alliance's new Strategic Concept at the Rome Summit meeting in November 1991.[44] However, it was to be more difficult than French officials might have imagined to attain a reform of the Alliance along the lines they favoured, and instances of discord between the two continued to outweigh those of accord. The 1990 London Summit was a case in point: while NATO members agreed to rely more heavily on multinational corps in the future, France did not adhere to this declaration, and additionally rejected the possibility of a greater out-of-area capability for the Alliance.[45] While the Summit endorsed the prospect of the European Security and Defence Identity, its assumption that the USSR was no longer the principal enemy of the West overturned much of France's recent strategic doctrine.[46] Difficulties were similarly apparent over NATO's creation of a British-led Rapid Reaction Corps in May 1991: consistent with the rejection of this idea in 1990, Mitterrand refused any French involvement.[47] Therefore, by this point, the French authorities were becoming increasingly entangled in a complicated web of defence and security calculations, and the 'two steps forward, one step back' principle which began to characterise their relations with NATO precipitated debate across the political spectrum.

The emphasis on reform, rather than renunciation, was indeed widespread: at the poles of the political spectrum, prominent analysts concurred on the necessity of maintaining the Alliance framework into the post-Cold War world. As Heisbourg argued, 'the Atlantic

Alliance no less retain[ed] its utility, both political and military. The threat fad[ed], but the danger linked to the upheavals in what [was] still the Soviet Union remain[ed].'[48] Lellouche also favoured close relations with the Alliance: 'for the moment, dismantling the Alliance would be both premature and dangerous'.[49] Beyond this conservative approach to the maintenance of the Alliance, others among the Centre and Right argued for a far greater French commitment to the cause of Atlantic security. In this respect, Balladur's views in favour of a significant *rapprochement* had been known since the beginning of the upheavals in the European security order,[50] and came to be widely held among his colleagues on the Centre and Right. Thus, Mitterrand's rejection of French participation in NATO's Rapid Reaction Corps aroused particular disquiet. In a Parliamentary question, G. Mesmin of the UDF criticised the President's reiteration of the 'empty chair' policy with regard to the Atlantic Alliance, which ran counter to the course of international developments. Not only did it disregard the lessons of the Gulf War, which had shown the need for narrow coordination in future military operations between all the forces of the West, but it also sabotaged France's desire to play a leading role in the construction of any European defence.[51]

Domestic opposition to the positions of Mitterrand and his governments was reinforced by the continued hostility of many of France's European partners towards any significant redirection of the European security framework away from the Atlantic Alliance. The British position in particular was not helpful to the French cause. British reluctance to expand greatly the role of the WEU was expressed by the Foreign Secretary, G. Howe, as early as 1989, when he argued that 'it [did] not [help] the WEU if one over[sold] its achievements or underplay[ed] its problems ... it [was] in a phase of consolidation rather than of radical evolution'.[52] The consolidation to which the Foreign Secretary referred was to anchor the WEU firmly within NATO, rather than to take it in the direction envisaged by the French; a fact which was confirmed by London's proposal for the WEU to relocate to Brussels, the home of the Atlantic Alliance, and the decision to appoint the same Permanent Representative to both NATO and the WEU.[53] The significance of this decision, which was also taken by Portugal and the Netherlands, was not lost on the French.[54] Moreover, Britain was ambivalent about arguments in favour of a new European security architecture. As the Permanent Representative on the North Atlantic Council argued, he doubted the appropriateness of architectural metaphors.... It [was] not a question of separate buildings or separate rooms with separate existences ... the ultimate aim of all the organizations active in European security [should] be to create a Europe and North America whose individual member states work[ed] together to produce an effective and indivisible collective security.[55]

The preference for an indivisible Atlantic-based collective security was no less important for the Italians, as was reflected by the Anglo-Italian declaration on defence in preparation for the Maastricht Treaty,[56] and indeed by the position of the United States. According to Secretary of State Warren Christopher, 'the United States ... welcom[ed] the development of a European security and defence identity,... [but] NATO must develop closer ties with the Western European Union ... [they] must act on the premise that although the military capabilities of the two institutions [were] separable, they must not be seen as separate'.[57]

Political ill-will on the part of France's allies towards a European defence capability, at the expense of the American commitment to Europe, was also compounded by operational complications. As the French analyst Le Hégarat noted, the perceived chain of responsibility between the EU (after 1992), WEU and NATO was over-complicated, and in practice unworkable.[58] Moreover, there was a multitude of difficulties in relation to membership of the EU of neutral states such as Ireland, which would not therefore participate in WEU activities. Even if a WEU-led operation could be put into the field, it was militarily and politically compromised by a lack of its own means and the preference of the majority of its members for action in the NATO framework.[59] In sum, the shortcomings of the WEU, linked to adverse reception of the Eurocorps proposal, and the difficulties of European Union, especially in the foreign policy and security area as demonstrated by the Yugoslav crisis, undermined the best attempts of the French government to promote the European security ideal.

The Franco-German Corps, later the Eurocorps, was proposed in October 1991, at the initiative of the French and German leaders, in a letter to their European partners. The Corps was to build on the basis established by the Franco-German Brigade, created in October 1989, extending the manpower of the new unit from the 4200 of the Brigade, to 45 000–50 000, to be operational by the end of 1995, and in which other members of the European Union were invited to participate. The Corps was formally announced in May 1992.[60] Militarily, the Corps was to make qualitative as well as quantitative improvements over its predecessor, the Brigade, for the integration was to occur at the level of commands, and not the more problematic joint basing scheme of the Brigade.[61] However, its impact was more noteworthy on the political scale, as it was to constitute the 'embryo of a European army'.[62] Proposed before, but formalised after, the signature of the Maastricht Treaty, the Eurocorps '[gave] concrete expression to this will for the implementation of a joint European defence'.[63] Also it would allow Germany to consider security problems potentially occurring outside NATO's structures and geostrategic remit.[64] As such, it was almost guaranteed to give rise to difficulties between France and Germany, and their Alliance partners: as was noted even within France by the pro-Europeans of the UDF, the initiative raised more questions than it answered.[65]

Certain of France's partners, including Britain and Italy, immediately voiced reservations as to the prospects of an erosion of NATO as a European security institution.[66] The Bush Administration, in addition, was particularly concerned by the prospective Eurocorps, in case it would distract German troops from their NATO commitments.[67] Despite Mitterrand's arguments 'that it would be wrong to try to present the two as contradictory. That [was] what [he] tried to explain to George Bush ...',[68] the two structures were almost inevitably to be perceived as such. Moreover, in the context of the shifting French attitudes towards NATO since around 1990, and Mitterrand's known preferences for greater European military integration, even the subsequent clarification of the Eurocorps' missions, effectively double-hatting it for NATO as well as European service, could not alleviate the suspicions of France's allies.[69] Militarily, also, the Eurocorps was questionable in the perceptions of its opponents, not least because half of the 1st Armoured Division, designated for the Corps, was made up of conscripts – and its operational effectiveness outside Europe was thus circumscribed.[70] For France's Alliance partners, who preferred the NATO structure to untried, and unattractive, European alternatives, the Corps was nothing less than 'Mitterrand's Trojan horse, an instrument to hijack the Alliance'.[71]

Limitations of the European approach

Differences in reaction to the disintegration of Yugoslavia on the part of the European partners also conspired to raise questions about the prospect of an indigenous European defence capability, such as that advocated by Paris and Bonn. The onset of civil war in the former

Yugoslavia, and Germany's extension of diplomatic recognition to Slovenia and Croatia, without the definition of a common position with her European partners, cast serious doubt on the likelihood of a Common Foreign and Security Policy. It raised concerns among the other European partners, for if France and Germany could not agree on such a significant issue, what chance was there for the rest of Europe to agree?

The crisis in Yugoslavia was indeed instrumental in proving the inadequacy and even impotence of the WEU, and EU. Likening the conflict to that which had faced French forces in Indo-China, one analyst argued that the reason for the failure of the Europeans to resolve the crisis was the patent lack of a political concept to define and determine their response.[72] As the former Chief of Staff of the Armed Forces, General Maurin, argued, 'the reactions of the European nations faced with the Yugoslav conflict were particularly disparate, and demonstrated well the deep divergences existing between them as to the concept relating to intervention missions by their respective forces'.[73] The basic failing was therefore political, and the political failing was the most difficult for France to surmount. Indeed, although the European Union arguably had the capacity for influence, it '[could] be only a partial, limited actor',[74] for it remained nothing more than an association of states.

Consequently, given the difficulties apparently inherent in the search for Mitterrand's holy grail of a European defence capability, certain harsh realities had to be taken into account. Perhaps primary among these was the imperative of improving Paris' relations still further with NATO, for the suspicion and hostility to which the Franco-German efforts had given rise had clearly indicated that 'Europe and NATO' was to be a more workable security solution than 'Europe or NATO'. Indications of this change in France's position, suggesting further moves towards the NATO allies, came in Prime Minister Cresson's policy declaration to the National Assembly in May 1991, when she placed much greater emphasis on French military action alongside her allies.[75] This increased speculation that a degree of realignment with NATO could be expected.[76] It was reinforced in her speech to the *Institut des Hautes Etudes de Défense Nationale* later in the year, when she declared that '[France] remain[ed] faithful to [her] alliances.... The battle for democracy [had] been peacefully won. But if that impl[ied] that the Atlantic Alliance [was] modernising, *the tie of solidarity that it establish[ed] between its members for the preservation of the common values they [had] must remain.'*[77] However, only weeks after

Cresson's speech, the difficulties of France's new stance towards NATO were underlined at the Alliance's Rome summit. While Mitterrand adhered to the Alliance's new Strategic Concept, at least in public with good grace, it was suggested that in fact he had been outmanoeuvred into accepting a document which asserted the primacy of NATO over European security,[78] and had bad-temperedly accused NATO of 'preachifying'.[79] Nonetheless, his determination to pursue the Europe *and* NATO approach was reaffirmed in June 1992:

> An alliance without a precise, firm objective [lost] a little of its soul; however, [he] remain[ed] a supporter of the Atlantic Alliance, while considering, like [his] predecessors, that France [did] not have to enter the integrated military command of this Alliance, and that as a nuclear power, she must retain her national decision-making capacity, but also her solidarity for joint defence. Today, no other force than that of NATO [was] capable of ensuring the security of [European] countries; so let us be realistic....[80]

Mitterrand's new-found realism thus extended to significant additional cooperation with NATO in the realm of defence and security. It allowed the formal adoption by NATO of non-Article 5 missions,[81] such as peacekeeping, at the June 1992 meeting of Alliance foreign ministers, and the resolution of some of the tensions regarding NATO and the Eurocorps with the signature in January 1993 of a three-way agreement between France, Germany and NATO, providing for French forces within the Eurocorps to come under the operational command of NATO in the event of crisis. It was also manifested in Mitterrand's authorisation in December 1992 for French officers to participate in NATO military staff work, preparing for a potential United Nations mandate to implement a Bosnian peace settlement, or to protect safe areas. More progress was made in April 1993, when the head of France's mission to Military Committee, General Pélisson, began to participate with a 'deliberative' rather than just a 'consultative' voice (observer status) in meetings dealing with peacekeeping missions.[82] Notwithstanding such unprecedented moves, however, it was a case of too little, too late, for the main Opposition.

The European debate in France

For the Right, as for the Centre, if Mitterrand was moving nearer to NATO his progress was insufficient. Indeed such was the distance between their relative positions in the approach to the elections of 1993 that relations with NATO were expected to constitute a source of significant discord thereafter. The extent of the Gaullists' preference for much closer cooperation with NATO far exceeded that of Mitterrand. While the President had regularly limited the attempts of his Defence Minister, Joxe, to deepen France's ties with the Atlantic Alliance[83] beyond those he contemplated himself, leading figures in the RPR advocated yet more profound cooperation and coordination. As Jacques Chirac argued forcefully for the Right at the beginning of 1993,

> With respect to Europe, [the RPR was] forced to note that the substantial reduction in the American military presence [had] not stimulated any decisive European process, far from it. Several of [France's] partners had even begun considerably to reduce their armed forces and [were] placing themselves more than ever under American protection, incarnated through NATO. [He] conclud[ed] that if France want[ed] to play a determining role in the creation of a European defence entity, it must take into account this state of mind of its partners, and reconsider to a large degree the form of its relations with NATO. It [was] clear, in effect, that the necessary rebalancing of relations within the Atlantic Alliance, relying on existing European institutions such as the WEU, [could] only take place from the inside, not against the United States, but in agreement with it.[84]

What Chirac said, and what Mitterrand meant, may well have amounted to similar things, but the will of the Right to countenance specifically what the President evaded, and preferred to cloak in reassertions of France's traditional caveats of independence and autonomy, indicated the difficulties of consensus even on this issue. In fact, there was by no means a concerted position on the part of the French political classes on anything beyond the principle of cooperation. Questions relating to the scope or nature of cooperation in particular were still subject to debate and discord. This was to be reiterated under the Balladur government when the most that can be said is that, subject only to certain alterations, French policy in this respect marked time, coloured as much by forthcoming electoral calculations as by any major initiatives – and this despite the elaboration of the *Livre blanc*.

The *Livre blanc*, in fact, reiterated the preference of the government for an increasingly cooperative position in relation to defence and

France's European partners, while reinforcing also the new government's desire to deepen France's relations with the Atlantic Alliance. In his preface to the White Paper, Balladur reinforced the argument of the 1980s that French defence was at least in part contingent on defence and security in Europe. Furthermore France's

> defence policy must contribute to building, little by little, a common European defence, with the entry into force of the European Union Treaty. The political identity of the European Union must eventually be expressed, and maintained, in the area of defence.[85]

The Defence Minister Léotard was equally forthright about the prospect of French participation in European defence, with all the 'sacrifices' which that entailed.[86] Moreover, cooperation was to be wide-ranging, extending to renewed joint ventures in arms production, to approach standardisation of capabilities between the European partners, as well as the more overtly cooperative military and political measures.[87] At the same time, the *Livre blanc* maintained that 'NATO remain[ed] the principal defence organisation',[88] while recognising the continually changing nature of the American commitment to Europe.

However, while the government's will to pursue European, and Atlantic, defence and security commitments was reaffirmed, the challenges to the notion of a European defence capability were gaining voice outside the immediate political sphere of leadership. This was the case both practically and politically, and encompassed the true depth of commitment to such a course. Much of the adverse commentary was focused on the Eurocorps, and its implications for broader European defence – unsurprising in the event of there being little else of substance to consider.

The French commitment to a European defence, it was argued, was rhetorical, at best, and was highly vulnerable, as was the rest of French defence planning, to domestic political considerations. For example,

> on the subject of defence, the month of May 1992 was marked by a series of measures indicative of the government's manner of dealing with the problem: giving the impression of moving towards a European defence, while reducing the means which [were] allocated to it.[89]

The announcement of the creation of the Franco-German Corps (May 1992) had been preceded by notification of ever more defence cuts in France, which necessarily called into question the depth and capacity of France's commitment. Associated with continued force reorganisations in the conventional sphere, and Mitterrand's amendments to the nuclear forces, the main impression was one of uncertainty.

Neither was the German commitment beyond question. A 'growing scepticism' could be perceived over the strength of Germany's commitment to a deeper European cooperation than that constituted by a free-market area, especially as results, rather than initiatives, had been somewhat lacking in the early 1990s, beyond the conclusion of the Maastricht Treaty.[90] In addition, the German role in the early recognition of Slovenia and Croatia in the former Yugoslavia, together with Germany's lack of support for the French proposal for an international conference to resolve the crisis, further called into question the commitment of Bonn to the sort of Europe envisaged in Paris.[91] As was argued by *Le Monde*, Germany had 'two irons in the fire'[92] in terms of European security; on the one hand, following the preferred French path towards indigenous European capabilities, and on the other, maintaining the Atlantic linkage at all cost, and additionally, cementing the ties between France and NATO. This was inevitably regarded with some concern.

Furthermore, the Eurocorps seemed to have acclimatised public and political opinion to the potential unification of European armies, when in fact 'it [went] without saying that this idea [was] false'.[93] It was false because in a Europe still built, and for the foreseeable future, on respect for national identities – despite the Maastricht Treaty – 'it would be paradoxical, to say the least, to "supranationalise" the armies',[94] for such a force would be militarily paralysed. In view of the difficulties of gaining effective agreement on action, the need for political consensus across the Union, in order that a military course could be adopted, would be almost impossible to achieve in a Europe of states. In spite of the agreements concluded between France and Germany, and the intention for the Eurocorps to advance the cause of European integration, the Corps 'still [did] not master, however, all the problems concerning its command and its missions, over which the shadow of NATO, well-known to [France's] German friends, continu[ed] to fall'.[95] Indeed, for 11 of the 12 EU members, 'European defence [could] be the obedient instrument of Atlantic defence; in no case must it want to be its substitute'.[96] In short, a European army respond[ed] to no clearly definable need. Far from being the shortcut that [was] imagined, it [was] only an illusory detour leading to an impasse. The living proof of this [was] provided by the Eurocorps ... it [was] an end in itself.... It serv[ed] neither the defence of Europe, nor its independence, nor its individual security, nor collective security. It must be concluded that European defence, at least such as it [was] conceived in France, [was] only an empty concept,... a simple illusion.... Rather than to objective arguments, European defence respond[ed] to reckless urges, and more than to a need for security, to a dream of power....[97]

Finally, even the ideal of a European defence was widely argued to be fundamentally unrealistic. Such an argument was advanced to explain the lack of debate around the Maastricht defence provisions in the closely fought French referendum campaign of September 1992: the ends seemed 'too far away and uncertain to mobilise opinion', for states were unlikely, in any calculation, to renounce the sovereignty conveyed by national control of foreign and defence policy.[98] Moreover, the prevalence of a preferred alternative to the European security approach was a constraining factor; 'whoever [said] "European forces" presuppos[ed] a common defence policy and a European executive capable of taking the necessary decisions in a reasonable time.... [However] certain [allies] had subscribed to the North Atlantic Treaty, and therefore to a physical participation in the joint defence, within the framework of NATO, very often because within this Organisation the American presence was predominant.'[99] The dilemma was insurmountable: to improve the European position within NATO,

it would be necessary to proceed to the harmonisation of the Europeans' status within NATO, which [could] only be done by the alignment of the Allies with the French model, or by France's alignment with that of its integrated allies. But, of these two solutions, everyone [knew] that the first would be the most reasonable but that it [was] unrealistic, and that the second would be the simplest but that it [was] absurd. Moreover, the problem [was] so far from being resolved that no one even dar[ed] to pose it, as if it could disappear by dint of being ignored![100]

The position was fundamentally constrained by the impossibility of maintaining real debate over the idea of a European defence. 'Thus

with defence: it [was] enough to call it European to shield it from any
questioning. Possibly you [could] ask yourself "when",... "how",... or
"how much" ... but never "if" and "why". The necessity for a
European defence [did] not need to be demonstrated: it must only be
affirmed.... It [was] no longer the time to quibble over its principle;
the only urgency [was] to pass to its execution.'[101]

Thus, while the development of a European defence capability,
building on the capabilities and reassurance of the commitment of the
Atlantic Alliance to European security, became an increasingly firm
French policy commitment during Mitterrand's second presidential
term, such a position was in fact contested, despite the apparent
French commitment to the cause of European defence since at least
the 1980s. As the Cold War ended, the scale of the challenge to
France's European security interests, the prevarication of the President
and the government in responding to that challenge, and the reac-
tionary position into which the leadership was compelled by the pace
of international change, served to highlight the authorities' inability
to dictate the European course. However, the underlying lack of real
consensus, as was the case in the 1980s, was again highlighted when
the President and government attempted to force through the
European option in the early 1990s: notwithstanding the support of
the powerful, unified German ally, the stakes, it seemed, had changed,
and the political debate to which the government's actions were
subject had moved on.

Indeed, as had become clear from the course of events, the French
inability to influence German actions was ever more apparent, even in
the formerly privileged Franco-German sphere of activity that was
Europe. The best means to preserve France's security interests therefore
remained the Atlantic Alliance. However, in the context of the radically different international security situation of the 1990s, the position
to which France had previously subscribed – that of a protected protagonist, in effect – was no longer viable. A more overt support was
required, in order to maintain the very factors that were essential to
France's long-term security in Europe, and against which she had been
rhetorically fighting since the advent of de Gaulle – the American
political and military commitment to Europe, as manifested by the
presence of American troops.

In the context of the changed international security climate, then,
and as the failings of the European approach to French defence and
security were emphasised, the extent of divergence with the leadership's course – including the governments of the Left and the Right of

Mitterrand's second term in this respect – became more apparent. Not only was the European orientation contested in detail, but even the grand design was under threat, and by more mainstream analysts than the marginalised, and still Moscow-supporting, *Parti Communiste Français*. Such was almost without precedent in Mitterrand's presidential term. A firm direction was needed in security policy, one which Mitterrand had increasingly failed to give over the time of change which dominated his second term.

9
The New French Interventionism

Since the end of the Algerian War, more than thirty years ago, the French army [had] never been so much engaged outside the national borders. One soldier in five – some 47 000 of its men in total – [was] serving outside metropolitan France. That [was] the distinguishing feature of the last five years in military matters. This [was] what the Head of the Armed Forces, M. François Mitterrand, [had] wanted.[1]

Mitterrand's second *septennat* certainly saw a proliferation of the forums in which French armed forces were engaged. The new spirit of interventionism contrasted sharply with the hostility which had characterised the Socialists' perspective on armed involvement outside France's borders prior to Mitterrand's election,[2] and the will with which French forces were committed to national and multilateral initiatives also contrasted with the ambivalence and uncertainty which had surrounded the beginnings of the operations in Lebanon and Chad. Despite its lack of resources, and its difficulty in effecting the transition to the post-Cold War circumstances, the French military establishment was now active in a plethora of overseas missions. By the time of the second *cohabitation* French troops were deployed in Bosnia, Somalia, Cambodia and Iraq, as well as in continuing missions in Europe and Africa.[3] It had indeed become 'an army on which the sun never [set]'.[4]

The reasons for such a change were perhaps more evident in the political, than in the strictly military sphere, and were closely linked to the debate which was emerging in France, and beyond, on the continued justification for France's occupancy of a permanent seat on the United Nations Security Council. However, the reactions to the new interventionism encompassed military as much as political concerns. The debate exacerbated difficulties which had been demonstrated over defence planning and the degree to which French defence could be Europeanised. Militarily, the engagements in the Gulf War, in the former Yugoslavia and in Rwanda in the early 1990s, all highlighted disagreement over France's military capabilities, force structures, and military doctrines – and the perennial problem of finance. Politically, the national authorities were often perceived to be reacting to events, especially in the former Yugoslavia, doing too little too late, and acting as much from concern over domestic political calculations as from concerns to further the rule of international law.

France and the Gulf War

The outbreak of the Gulf crisis in August 1990 found the world's major powers preoccupied with events in a more familiar theatre – Europe – and with the general difficulties of adapting to the post-Cold War environment. Nevertheless, according to the accounts of his closest advisers, Mitterrand quickly established a firm position against the Iraqi aggression. While his firmness largely found favour with the main Opposition parties, both before and after the commitment of French forces, it had less appeal for elements of the Left.

Mitterrand's leading role in delineating French reactions to the Gulf crisis, and the divergences to which this gave rise with his Defence Minister, Chevènement, have been considered above.[5] More broadly, however, the leadership took care to engender national support for France's actions through regular speeches, broadcasts and press conferences by the President, and through consultation with Parliament. Mitterrand's approach was grounded at least in part on the primacy of international law, and condemnation of its 'intolerable violation' by the Iraqi invasion and annexation of Kuwait.[6] His support for an international embargo against Iraq, his commitment of troops to help to police it, and his reinforcement of that troop commitment after the sacking of the French embassy in Kuwait, demonstrated his desire to resolve the crisis by international means – including military means if necessary.

According to H. Védrine, the President's firmness included a conscious effort to prepare French public opinion for possible military action.[7] His concerns were reflected in his overt call for national unity in this matter, as in his message to the Assemblée Nationale of August 1990. He declared himself convinced that beyond the natural differences which justifiably separat[ed the deputies], and which guarante[ed France's] democracy, the Parliament of the Republic [would] be able to mobilise the country around the simple message which guid[ed] France's actions, so well expressed since 1946 by the Preamble of the Constitution: 'the French Republic, faithful to its traditions, conform[ed] to the rules of public international law. It [would] undertake no war with a view to conquest and [would] never use its forces against the liberty of any nation ...'.[8]

The accord sought by the leadership on these points seemed to have been achieved by the time of the parliamentary vote approving France's military commitment to the Gulf War in January 1991. Indeed, of 556 votes cast by the parliamentarians, 523 were in favour.[9] However, this figure in isolation fails to convey the extent of political dissent over the course of action to be taken.[10]

The divergences in parliamentary opinion were apparent between, and even among, the political groupings, bearing on issues relating perhaps more to foreign policy concerns than to strictly military calculations. Four areas prevailed. Firstly, the sacrifice of Paris' interests to those of Washington was a theme of such unlikely allies as the PCF and the *Front National*, but was not their sole preserve. Like the PCF, the *Front National* believed that the Gulf hostilities were concerned solely with the interests of American oil companies, and that Mitterrand's alignment with the United States was destroying all of France's previous policy towards the Arab States.[11] The leadership of the PCF insisted that France had 'nothing to do with this war',[12] and claimed widespread public opposition to French involvement.[13] In short, 'France must refuse to commit herself in a war which [could] not be her own, and must withdraw her troops from the region'.[14]

Secondly there was divergence over the government's consideration of the Gulf crisis as a single issue. Among the Opposition a much wider view of the Middle East conflict was taken, including the continuing hostilities between Israel and the Palestinians, and the situation in Lebanon. Concerns were also voiced about Moscow's repression in its Baltic Republics, particularly Lithuania.[15] While largely prepared to approve the implementation of UN resolutions in the Gulf, partly to ensure a place at any Middle East peace table for France, the parliamentarians nonetheless indicated recognition that their government and others were rather selective in their application of the international law on which their Gulf action was ostensibly based.

Thirdly, Mitterrand's six-point peace plan, proposed before the Security Council in the last hours before the expiry of the UN ultimatum, also engendered discord. While the Socialists and Communists supported the initiative[16] the Right was highly critical. Léotard condemned the President for having broken ranks with the diplomatic solidarity of the UN,[17] while further Right Lellouche derided the 'dubious French peace initiatives',[18] and J.-M. Le Pen insisted that the move had been little more than a gesture to public opinion.[19] The onset of war was not necessarily welcomed; but peace at any price was viewed with no more enthusiasm.

The final major source of divergence concerned the French military capabilities themselves. These had been in question since the beginning of the crisis due to their technical inadequacies, and to the political constraints of autonomy.[20] By January 1991, the difficulties of command and control had been addressed: autonomy was preserved, since the President's authority was that which committed France's forces to action, but the matter of day-to-day operational command could thereafter be left to the Americans. The problems of out-dated, inadequate equipment, lack of sufficient air cover and lack of basic artillery remained, however, causing great anxiety for the UDF and the RPR.[21] Considering the continued limitations of the defence budget, it was recognised that 'France [could] only commit herself, in an affair like that of the Gulf, with difficulty and for a modest result.'[22]

Discord between the parties was reinforced by discord within the parties, on the Right and Left. For the Right, leading figures as Léotard, Pasqua and Séguin all had reservations about the Gulf commitment while the Baltic and Lebanese crises were not addressed.[23] Chirac, and still more so his adviser Lellouche,[24] were much firmer in their advocacy of strong military action. Also, while the Centre Right called for increased solidarity with France's coalition partners, the RPR was divided. As Pompidou's Foreign Minister, M. Jobert argued, 'France [had] nothing to do with this conflict. None of [her] basic interests [was] at stake.'[25] Moreover her influence would have counted for more 'if she had abstained from being present militarily in a coalition led entirely by the Americans for the defence of American interests'.[26] Differences were similarly evident within the ranks of the PS. While party leaders such as Mauroy and Fabius gave full support to the government, nine Socialists actually voted against the government in the parliamentary debate of 16 January, running second only to the PCF in terms of the number of negative votes cast.[27] Furthermore it was alleged that had the ballot been secret, rather fewer Socialist deputies might have voted in line with party requirements.[28]

While it was largely Chevènement's supporters who voted against the government,[29] Socialist opposition was more widespread. In a parliamentary meeting on 15 January 'in their vast majority, the Socialist deputies who spoke did not hide that this war was not really their own'.[30] The majority support for the government, ultimately, was perhaps attributable only to a lack of any alternative to secure Iraqi withdrawal from Kuwait,[31] and to a desire to support the line taken by the President. For one Chevènementiste, who had voted with the government, 'it [was] not a matter of conscience, but of discipline or of tactics'.[32] Similarly R. Léron and M.-J. Sublet, both of whom supported Chevènement, had nevertheless voted with the government solely in order to demonstrate confidence in Mitterrand and to preclude a government crisis.[33] Socialist disunity was seized upon by the members of the Opposition as justification for Chevènement's resignation. Quite simply 'since he [was] speaking through intermediaries, M. Chevènement must resign'.[34] Concern over Chevènement's position was also held in broader circles. As one newspaper commented,

that a fringe of the Socialist Party balk[ed], whatever the circumstances, at voting for a resort to force, so be it. That this fringe should be led and directed by the serving Minister of Defence, at a time when French troops [were] preparing to do battle, that [was] what [was] most difficult to explain....[35]

Consequently, the massive vote in favour of the commitment of French troops to military operations in the Gulf did not convey conviction in the justification for, or appropriateness of, France's actions, even among the majority. Rather, it seemed that in response to public opinion, which polls showed by January 1991 to be mostly favourable to such a course, politicians had avoided questioning seriously the government's plans.[36] Ominously however, as Chirac cautioned, an occasion to air disagreements would return.[37] In the meantime, it was observed that in fact, 'François Mitterrand [found] himself again the principal beneficiary of these divergences, since only a low profile seem[ed] to allow the Opposition to maintain a relative cohesion.'[38] Thus it was argued, not favourably for the President, that 'this desert [would] give M. Mitterrand a platform from which he would try to be equal to the developments'.[39]

Notwithstanding Chirac's apparent restraint, France's actions during the Gulf War did not go entirely unchallenged. Two particular issues occasioned discord. The first concerned the supposed limitation of French military action to Kuwaiti objectives only. In a press conference of 9 January Mitterrand, evidently keen to counter remaining opposition to the prospect of war in the Gulf, had insisted that 'it [was] not a matter of organising some sort of war of destruction against Iraq, it [was] a matter of liberating Kuwait'.[40] Although he qualified his statement immediately, so as not to exclude the possibility of an attack on Iraq, sufficient imprecision remained to add credence to Chevènement's announcement, in the aftermath of the first French air raid of the war, that a 'protocol of agreement'[41] had been reached with the US, to restrict French actions to Kuwait. The issue quickly became 'explosive'[42] as criticisms mounted.

Most vociferous in his denunciation of the decision was Giscard d'Estaing. Questioning the legitimacy of attacking the aggressed, while sparing the aggressor,[43] he demanded to know whether France would have accepted the attack of German targets in occupied France in the Second World War, while Nazi Germany remained secure.[44] For J.-F. Deniau the French risked being seen as 'part-time allies',[45] while for F. Bayrou France was only a 'second rate actor'.[46] More measured in tone, but equally critical, G. Longuet of the *Parti radical* maintained that 'a conditional commitment, limited to Kuwait alone, [was] incomprehensible, ineffective and unacceptable'.[47] In a swift reaction to the criticisms France's position was hardened, as Mitterrand confirmed in a television interview,[48] and the new stance was demonstrated by a French air raid over Iraq.[49]

The second controversy arose over France's response should Iraq use chemical or biological weapons against the UN coalition. Interviewed on television, Mitterrand stated categorically that France would use 'neither chemical weapons, nor biological weapons, nor nuclear weapons'[50] against Iraq. Chirac retorted that Mitterrand's statement was contrary to the 'logic of deterrence';[51] the whole point of which was to leave a potential adversary uncertain as to one's reactions. This position was shared by Giscard d'Estaing.[52] The incident coincided with an increase in Right-wing criticism of Mitterrand, albeit tempered by the President's residually high ratings in opinion polls.[53] Nevertheless, for Chirac, the President was ever compounding the 'diplomatic deficit',[54] if not 'patent failure'[55] of his policies. Simultaneously, Balladur criticised 'a certain number of ambiguities'[56] in Mitterrand's stance, while P. Séguin argued for more flexibility in ending the war, regarding for example the Iranian offer to mediate.[57] The rhetoric of consensus (Giscard: 'My country is at war. I support my country'[58]) may not have been overcome, but it was certainly under sustained attack.

Lessons of the Gulf War

If many of the debates before, and during, the war related to political rather than strictly military considerations, the course of debate in the aftermath of the conflict undoubtedly redressed the balance. Five areas figured prominently: France's continuing difficulties of force projection; the inadequacies of military equipment and planning; the shortcomings of a conscript army; the absolute requirement for a space-based military intelligence capability; and the slim prospects for a European defence identity in the foreseeable future. As one Army colonel lamented, when French forces arrived in Saudi Arabia in August 1990 – and it had taken them some time to arrive – they had 'no real anti-missile protection, it [was] difficult for [them] to see and hear, through a lack of electronic means, and [they] lack[ed] heavy weaponry in the event of an Iraqi attack'.[59] Given such a starting-point, it is perhaps unsurprising that the Gulf War should have highlighted so many shortfalls in France's armoury, which had hitherto remained unproved.[60]

On the plus side for France, the prepositioning of troops in the Indian Ocean meant that a naval presence could be sent to the Gulf relatively quickly in August 1990.[61] Thereafter however, difficulties increased. As a consequence of the shortage, felt since the mid-1980s, of France's declining capabilities for long-range troop transportation, naval vessels and aircraft were, of necessity, commandeered from the civilian sector. This was partly successful: however, it was noted that 'if the requisition of civilian ships succeeded beyond all the hopes of the military, the call to airliners [was] not so simple'.[62] The Army's ageing transport planes (DC-8s, C-130 Hercules, and C-160 Transall) were 'notoriously inadequate'[63] to cope, even with the assistance of the jumbo-jets of Air France.

Moreover, once the equipment was in place, it was argued that the Gulf War underlined all the inadequacies of France's military planning,[64] especially for the Army and Air Force. The matter of tanks (an issue linked with the question of a professional army) was significant. The US wanted use of AMX-30s, of which the Army had 1300, but only two squadrons of the 501 tank regiment comprised professional soldiers. Most of France's career soldiers were trained to use AMX-10s, which were lighter and less heavily armoured, and therefore less well suited to possible ground war against Iraq.[65] The Air Force also experienced difficulties. It was observed that France made only a modest contribution to air strikes, making 1 per cent of sorties in total, and less than that of the high-precision raids;[66] an issue complicated by the French Jaguars' lack of night-sight capabilities and the problem – a consequence of France's prolific arms sales to Iraq since the 1970s – that France's Mirages could be confused with those of the Iraqi air force.[67] Thus, the claim by Mitterrand's military aides that France's Jaguar missions were particularly dangerous because of low-altitude flight[68] cut little ice. Still worse, action was further limited for both the Army and Air Force since they lacked sufficiently accurate weapons systems, and adequate supplies of ammunition, leading Heisbourg to conclude that these were two of the greatest military lessons to be drawn from France's participation in the Gulf War.[69] Neither was the Navy spared criticism. Due to concerns over equipment and conscript manpower, both of France's aircraft carriers, the *Foch* and the *Clemenceau*, had remained in port in Toulon until February. Only from 4 February, after changing crews, did the *Clemenceau* even begin to train off Toulon in order to set sail subsequently for the Gulf.[70] Such were the signals emanating from the crisis that *Le Figaro* condemned the 'formidable gaps in [France's] defence system', and the 'worrying weakness of [France's] means'.[71]

Difficulties were exacerbated by the structure and organisation of France's armed forces. Mitterrand's announcement in a press conference on 9 January that conscripts would not serve in the Gulf increased the constraints on French action. At that time, 140 conscripts were already aboard French ships in the area of the Gulf, and the logistics of re-manning the aircraft carriers, given that approximately 500 of each of their crews of 1800 were conscripts, posed considerable difficulty.[72] The solution was again found through 'voluntary conscripts': those who signed up for military service of either three years, or the duration of the war, enabling them to be sent overseas.[73] Nevertheless, France could still send only 10 000–15 000 troops to the Gulf (depending on whose estimate, and when), while comparisons to the effect that Great Britain had succeeded in dispatching 35 000 soldiers were common.[74] The criticisms were challenged by Védrine, who commented that 'beyond this self-denigration, all of France discovered, and not without surprise, that since she did not want to risk the lives of her conscripts, ... it was difficult for her to send more than 15 000 men 4000km away ...'.[75] Nonetheless, notable military figures such as General Lacaze, Mitterrand's former Chief of Staff of the Armed Forces, lent their voices to those elements of the Right advocating that France 'must move on to a professional army'.[76]

Fourthly, intelligence was a serious concern for France after the Gulf War. Chevènement's replacement, Joxe, was a keen advocate of improved capabilities for France in this area, and used all means at his disposal to counter the difficulties faced by France in the Gulf (such as dependence on the US for all intelligence, and the restrictions on autonomy that this imposed).[77] As he commented in a prominent speech, 'it was the United States that provided [France] with the bulk of the information necessary for conducting the conflict, as and when it wished'.[78] French military intelligence capabilities in the Gulf had not only been underequipped but also undermanned, requiring the secondment of American soldiers to interpret even the most basic data.[79] Thus, the conflict was a timely confirmation to France that the foundations of her military strategy were painfully inadequate in the modern era.[80]

Finally, the question of a European defence identity was also raised. As initiatives by Mitterrand and Kohl had multiplied in recent years, 'something' might have been expected from 'Europe' in relation to the Gulf crisis and conflict, but this was not to be the case. The importance of naval action under the auspices of the WEU, while lauded in some parts in France,[81] was more realistically assessed in others. As Heisbourg argued, 'Europe remain[ed] an idea, and not a reality, in the field of international security.'[82] In addition for the Right, 'Europe was the great absentee in the victory of the coalition.'[83]

'France intends to be present ...'

The uncertainties of the post-Cold War period weighed heavily on French political and military calculations in the early 1990s, as the bases of France's rank and status in world affairs were increasingly challenged. This was most symbolic in respect of France's permanent seat on the United Nations' Security Council, as suggestions that economic giants, such as Japan, now had a greater claim to that position than a medium-sized, albeit nuclear-armed, power like France. The subsequent preference, as expressed by many high-ranking French figures, to strengthen and extend the role of the UN – and France's active military participation therein – can thus be seen as indicative of attempts to preserve the Gaullist axioms of French power in a changing world. This was indeed a consideration for Mitterrand. As he had recognised at the time of Iraq's invasion of Kuwait,

> the changes under way throughout the world foreshadowed more demanding and more difficult times for France, [and he] was not sorry to find an area where [France] could be committed militarily and could reiterate her rank as a permanent member of the Security Council.[84]

The opportunities provided by the UN's increased ambitions after 1990 were seized by France in pursuit of this end.

The optimism with which the United Nations' future was viewed in France had been evident from the beginning of President Mitterrand's second *septennat*, when France supported the UN General Assembly's adoption, in 1988, of a much firmer position on humanitarian issues. Subsequent French diplomacy took such concerns as its spearhead.[85] This was highlighted by the reaction of Prime Minister Bérégovoy to the decision to commit forces to Somalia in December 1992: 'France intend[ed] to be present, always under the auspices of the United Nations, when law [had] to be respected or human lives protected.'[86] Indeed, the difference between early French attitudes to the UN, and those displayed in the 1990s, was considered nothing less than 'spectacular'.[87]

The implications of this development were equally recognised. Primary among them, for Saulnier, was the responsibility of the permanent members of the Security Council to designate intervention forces for the UN.[88] A strong French contribution, through a military-humanitarian doctrine, would justify the maintenance of France's seat, and would provide a guaranteed world military presence, and opportunities for acclimatising troops to combat conditions.[89] However, given that the UN was increasingly burdened with almost insoluble conflicts,[90] the difficulties for states contributing blue berets were manifest. Hence, far from the large French manpower commitment to UN military actions after the Gulf War bringing only benefits, it was also a source of consternation, associated in part with domestic financial considerations. The extra costs of France's involvement in the former Yugoslavia alone in spring 1992, prior to the height of the commitment, were estimated at one million francs per day,[91] and this at a time when the military budget for 1992 had been cut by nearly 3.3 billion francs. Moreover, the costs were political and military, as well as financial. Participation in UN operations meant a dilution of national command and sovereignty, as had been amply demonstrated in the Gulf, and its military implications 'risk[ed] ... accentuating the weakness already revealed by Opération Daguet'.[92] Nevertheless, the new direction in France's strategy of military intervention was likely to be maintained: as was explicitly acknowledged, with the reduced influence of nuclear capabilities in the post-Cold War period, France needed the UN for her own diplomatic ends.[93]

The Yugoslav tragedy[94]

The Gulf War had provided the occasion for at least a semblance of national unity over the course and forms of action to be taken. Such was not to be the case regarding the disintegration of Yugoslavia from 1991. Notwithstanding France's willingness to bring the Yugoslav crisis to international attention, as with its referral to the WEU to consider the despatch of a military force to separate the protagonists,[95] the policies of Mitterrand and his governments gave rise to repeated criticism. The official French reluctance to accept any break-up of the Yugoslav federation, after the Slovenian and Croatian declarations of independence in June 1991, was alleged to have 'illustrated this French incapability of understanding the movement which [had] shaken Europe since the fall of the Berlin Wall'.[96] This was reflected by ill-will to afford full diplomatic recognition to the former Yugoslav republics, even as the European Community decided to take this step, in January 1992.[97] Moreover, the even-handedness which the French leadership attempted to apply to the civil war, apparently avoiding explicit recognition of Serb aggression or atrocities, similarly attracted adverse reaction from across the political spectrum. The government's position proved so contentious that H. Védrine devotes a 90-page chapter of his chronicle of the Mitterrand presidency to justification of France's position during the Yugoslav crisis.[98]

Criticism of France's Balkan policies was heightened in 1992, after the extension of war to Bosnia-Herzegovina, and the siege of Sarajevo, and after knowledge emerged of Serb atrocities, including concentration camps and ethnic cleansing, against other ethnic populations. From this point, criticism of the humanitarian position to which the government had committed itself and its troops was amplified, and calls for direct military action grew. Nevertheless, it is difficult to identify party-political divisions other than the position of the Communists, who were implacably opposed to any 'military adventure'[99] in the Balkans. Opinion across the wider political spectrum was less unified, less constant and less consistent.

Troops were committed to the former Yugoslavia from spring 1992 in a peacekeeping and humanitarian role under UNPROFOR, according to Resolution 743 of the United Nations Security Council. According to Defence Minister Joxe the initial French commitment would number 2062 men, and would include conscripts.[100] The humanitarian aspect of France's stance was emphasised by the despatch of aid convoys to Yugoslavia from Easter; and by the President's lightning visit to Sarajevo in June 1992 to secure the opening of Sarajevo airport to two French aircraft carrying humanitarian supplies. However, by this time the body of cross-party opinion which considered such action to be inadequate was clearly growing.

While the French commitment to UNPROFOR at first attracted little criticism[101] the inadequacy and almost irrelevance of the humanitarian basis for military presence was soon a source of contention. As Millon (UDF) argued, it was 'insufficient',[102] and the former Socialist Prime Minister Fabius agreed that 'humanitarian initiatives [were] essential, but they [were] not enough'.[103] Notwithstanding Mitterrand's assessment that political benefits would accrue from a military-humanitarian presence, stronger action was called for. For Fabius, Serb responsibility must be clearly recognised.[104] Likewise for Chirac, France's, and particularly Mitterrand's, hitherto 'excessive' pro-Serb sympathies must be ended, for they constituted a 'historic mistake'.[105] For the Serbs, humanitarian measures had 'no deterrent effect';[106] much firmer diplomatic and military measures were necessary.

Pressure for graduated action was widespread among the Centre and the Right. Jean Lecanuet (UDC) believed that 'the atrocities committed in the former Yugoslavia demand[ed] a political, and if necessary a military action of greater scale',[107] and Millon also advocated this position.[108] Further Right, a yet stronger position was widely sought. N. Sarkozy (RPR) insisted that 'the international community could not have done what it did for Kuwait, outside Europe, and not act when comparable events [took] place in Europe itself'.[109] Such action, for Chirac, involved three facets; the implementation of a real, respected embargo, coupled with immediate air strikes against Serb artillery, and the extended protection of aid convoys by the use of force.[110] Moreover, for the Centre and Right, France should take a leading role in these actions.[111]

Notably, such views were also expressed on the Left, including prominent Socialists among their proponents. A. Billardon considered that if the existence of Serb concentration camps was proven the UN would have to act, even militarily, and he welcomed the prospect of French participation.[112] Le Gall concurred, asserting that military action was all the more necessary to counter suggestions, like that of Sarkozy, that international law was only applicable in the Gulf.[113] Fabius favoured the aerial bombardment of Serb military targets; and 'France, which [had] been at the forefront of international pressure, [could] and must participate in these initiatives. They [were] in accordance with [her] tradition in favour of human rights and peace.'[114] That Laurent Fabius should have taken this position was indeed significant. Given the strength of his longstanding personal and political ties with Mitterrand, and with Bérégovoy, it was considered that public perception would inevitably expect a firmer government line thereafter.[115]

Despite such pressures, however, Mitterrand excluded this possibility. Working on the principle that France would not compound the conflict situation he rejected international air strikes for political and military reasons. Neither would France act alone:

there [was] no action possible for her but within the framework of the United Nations. There [could] not be a question of an isolated action ... a properly military campaign would constitute a formidable test. France [was] not proposing it.[116]

Only the Communists championed Mitterrand's announcement.[117] On the Right A. Juppé accused the government of 'shady dealing'[118] and Chirac even argued that Mitterrand's preference for non-intervention made him 'a party to the pursuit of a war of territorial conquest, and to the atrocities which [were] committed day after day'.[119] Nevertheless, former president Giscard d'Estaing shared Mitterrand's reluctance for military intervention,[120] and Fillon (RPR) similarly believed that 'no military solution exist[ed]'[121] for the crisis in the former Yugoslavia. However, it was observed that of the political groupings, 'it [was] among the PS that the discomfort and cacophony [were] most evident'.[122] Although Fabius had purported to speak for the Socialist Party, he was openly opposed by such figures as R. Dumas, P. Joxe, B. Kouchner and J. Lang.[123]

Added to political considerations were more military concerns. It was considered that too great a commitment would be required, for too long, incurring too many casualties.[124] For French planners, a military commitment of the nature proposed would be near-impossible for France. General Schmitt alleged that the Serbs had 1800 tanks, 1800 heavy guns and 450 aircraft – figures in excess of French capabilities.[125]

This theme was reiterated by M.-F. Garraud, a former adviser to Pompidou, who argued that after ten years of 'disarmament' under Mitterrand, France no longer possessed the means for such an intervention.[126] Difficulties notwithstanding, however, it seemed that there was a strength of feeling in favour of action at least among those most clearly implicated. According to government figures, four conscripts were volunteering for each conscript post available to serve in the former Yugoslavia.[127]

From the end of 1992 it seemed that a degree of accord was in fact emerging around the prospect of firmer intervention in the Balkans, based on military means – even if the exact form of that intervention remained open to question. As the Sarajevo situation worsened, and the hard-line Milosevic was re-elected to the Serbian presidency, the president of the Assemblée Nationale, H. Emmanuelli, wrote to the Prime Minister to inform him that 'a very broad majority of deputies desir[ed] a firmer French commitment'[128] to the former Yugoslavia; the implication being, in the guise of a military action. It seemed, simultaneously, that the government was also moving towards this position. Following an American attack on an Iraqi plane violating the Middle Eastern no-fly zone, and the declared willingness of the US to impose the UN's resolutions by force if necessary, R. Dumas stressed in a televised interview that 'France [would] take her part in military action when it [was] decided.... It seem[ed] as [had] just happened in Iraq, that examples must be made to have the Security Council's decisions [of 9 October] forbidding the overflight of Bosnia respected.'[129] Even the Communists now moderated their opposition, no longer excluding appropriate pan-European military action under the auspices of the UN.[130]

If the political obstacles to a firmer commitment could thus be overcome, the military difficulties nonetheless remained. As was made clear by soldiers to the *Secrétaire d'Etat à la défense*, J. Mellick, French troops in the former Yugoslavia believed they lacked both a clear mission, and the means to implement it. They were regularly subject to direct or indirect attack, and could do little to respond.[131] Two more French soldiers were killed in September,[132] and a further attack at the beginning of 1993 brought the total to eleven deaths since the previous June.[133] France's Army seemed physically 'at the limit of its capabilities',[134] as troops were committed at the end of 1992 in UN operations in Europe, the Middle East, Africa and East Asia.[135] The subsequent dispersal of its professional soldiers, and residual problems of ageing equipment, meant that the Army was somewhat stretched,

and *matériel* sent to Bosnia in January 1993 to reinforce French positions was considered little more than a gesture.[136] Moreover, the
financial position relative to the armed forces remained poor. The cost
to the Defence Ministry of external operations in 1992 would be 3.5
billion francs which the Finance Ministry refused to reimburse,[137] and
the prospect of payment by the UN was largely hypothetical, given
its own deficit.[138] The result was further reduction in equipment
expenditure.

Consequently, France's military commitment in the former
Yugoslavia was a complex issue by the second *cohabitation*, from
March 1993. Under the Right-wing Balladur government a firmer
stance was adopted towards the Serbs, but as the Prime Minister,
Foreign Minister and Defence Minister seemed to be in competition
for policy control, discord and confusion continued to characterise
France's commitment. The fragility of the consensus was again in
evidence: as the government reversed some of the demands it had
made for military intervention while in Opposition, divisions were
accentuated, and calls from the military establishment itself for a
reassessment of France's role in UN operations were heard.

Despite the Centre-Right's many calls for a firmer military position
against the Serbs, in government its approach was much less belligerent. As Juppé pledged only weeks after acceding to the Foreign
Ministry, France would not increase her troop presence in the area
even in implementation of any peace plan.[139] He was supported by the
Defence Minister Léotard, who acknowledged the government's difficulties in committing to a strong military engagement.[140] However,
more broadly, the relationship between Juppé and Léotard was more
prone to conflict. Their divergence, especially from the end of 1993,
over troop-withdrawal, was difficult to contain. Léotard's preference
for this option, if a political solution to the Yugoslav crisis was not
found by spring 1994,[141] did not concur with that of Juppé. 'Persistent
rumours' suggested that an inner cabinet meeting chaired by
Mitterrand had revealed a 'serious clash' between them.[142] Indeed, the
discord coincided with Juppé's efforts to gain a stronger military reaction from the international community – from NATO and the United
States – to continuing atrocities in Bosnia, as at the NATO summit in
Brussels in January 1994.[143]

As politicians disagreed over the relative merits of remaining in
Bosnia, the military establishment was also making some harsh decisions over the costs and benefits of participation in UN military
missions. As Lanxade had indicated at the end of 1992, the military

hierarchy was not altogether convinced that the latter outweighed the former. Constituting 10 per cent of the total UN forces deployed around the world by mid-1993 (8100 men out of 80 150), the French military sought more precision about 'the location, the length and the conditions' of the commitments.[144] This was all the more relevant as United Nations operations were viewed with little faith, given 'the problem of the debatable military effectiveness of UN structures and procedures ...'.[145] It was considered that 'because she [had] decided to become the primary "contributor" of the United Nations and that she [made] a political argument of it to show that she [was] fulfilling all her responsibilities as a permanent member of the Security Council, [France] must seek to obtain guarantees before launching her army into such actions'.[146] On this point at least, it seemed that the government and the military were in accord. Such was the line that Léotard had taken since March 1993,[147] and he had also acted to regroup France's forces gradually in the former Yugoslavia, in order to ensure they were better protected.[148] Moreover, France had taken ever more determined steps to secure the active participation of American troops on the ground,[149] to relieve some of the burden on France, and to help to effect a workable solution.

Thereafter, it was argued in the media that the approach to the Yugoslav/Bosnian affair was more consensual, particularly after the Serb shelling of the Sarajevo market-place and the instigation of air strikes against the belligerents.[150] However, the consensus was only superficial; only a month after the Parliamentary debate on Yugoslavia Léotard and Juppé again disagreed over the prospect of reducing France's military commitment to the Balkans.[151] What the debate over that commitment had shown since the beginning of the conflict in 1991 was that discord, even in the matter of military intervention, was rarely far from the surface of French politics. Moreover in military terms, where the Gulf War had shown that France's military capabilities in 1991 were ill-adapted to, and inadequate for, demands of that type of coalition intervention, the Yugoslav experience showed that such problems were exacerbated as the number of missions in which French forces participated increased. Transportation might not be the main problem; relief of the contingent vied for this distinction. Given the lessons which could be drawn from these two instances, the Rwandan intervention reflected changes in France's approach to military action abroad.

Opération Turquoise

After military concerns expressed over France's external interventions, the *Livre blanc* of 1994 and the subsequent Rwandan intervention seemed to take account of such questions, showing a tendency to selectivity and conditional action. According to the *Livre blanc*, if military action by France's defence forces was to occur increasingly in a multilateral framework, especially within the United Nations, 'the participation of French forces [would] only be contemplated if the mandate and the operation fulfil[led] certain political and military criteria'.[152] This was proven to be the case for the Rwandan intervention; while France would intervene in the period between the withdrawal of the first UN mission in Rwanda, and its reinforcement after the assassination of the Rwandan Hutu president and the outbreak of genocide which followed it, the operation had to be explicitly sanctioned by the Security Council, it had to be limited in duration, and it had to have a primarily humanitarian goal.[153] UN sanction was obtained on 22 June 1994, the mission was to last for a maximum of two months, and the aim was to establish a humanitarian safe zone to protect civilians.[154]

The likelihood of French intervention in Rwanda was increased by the close ties which had existed since Rwandan and Burundian independence from Belgium in 1959. Mitterrand had taken a close interest in Rwandan affairs since his accession to the presidency, advocating democratic reforms to President Habyarimana, and a peaceful settlement of the country's ethnic tensions, since at least January 1991.[155] French troops had been present in Rwanda from 1990 until December 1993, and France had facilitated the signature of a power-sharing agreement between Hutus and Tutsis in August 1993. There was, therefore, a precedent for French interest in the area at the time of renewed violence in 1994. Nonetheless, the prospect of intervention after Habyarimana's assassination caused divisions within the government, including again Léotard and Juppé.[156] The Defence Minister and his military advisers maintained that such an operation, at a distance of 8000 kilometres from France, in a situation of brutal civil war, was far too dangerous and difficult an option.[157] On the other hand, Juppé believed France had a duty to intervene. While Balladur initially favoured Léotard's position, Mitterrand favoured French action.[158] After consultation with the President, Balladur supported a limited operation,[159] but the restrictions on its duration emanated directly from the Prime Minister's office.

More broadly, however, opinion was not wholly favourable to the French government over Rwanda at this time. Responsibility for arming Rwanda, and maintaining President Habyarimana's monopoly on power from 1975 to the beginning of the 1990s,[160] was laid directly at the French door. Criticisms were accentuated by perceptions that the planned military intervention was ill-conceived and imprecise;[161] and P. Messmer denounced it as 'ill-founded, ineffective and dangerous'.[162] For *L'Humanité*, it would be 'a serious error with incalculable consequences'.[163] Nevertheless, the argument prevailed that if France failed to intervene, no one else would; France was 'the only Western power which [was] still engaged in Africa, she [was] the only one to possess credible military means there'.[164]

Despite uncertainties at the outset of the action, Opération Turquoise was implemented in June–August 1994. Two thousand five hundred troops, all professionals, were deployed from 24 June,[165] a number which was regularly reinforced[166] until the end of July, before being scaled down.[167] In Rwanda, protected areas were established for the safety of refugees, and a humanitarian safe zone was declared.[168] The duration of the mandate was scrupulously respected; France withdrew by 22 August 1994, two days before its expiry,[169] and this despite pleas from the United Nations for its prolongation.[170] Given the limitations within which they worked, Admiral Lanxade, the Chief of Staff of the Armed Forces, considered that the troops had effected a successful operation: it

> could not bring back peace, nor restore normal living conditions to Rwanda, but in the very short time of its mandate it [had] allowed a halt to genocide, avoided a medical catastrophe and contributed if not to moving forward human rights in Africa, at least to having their systematic violation condemned.[171]

More widely, opinion similarly viewed French actions as positive; indeed, 'having become specialists in the matter, the French soldiers exercised their talents as rescuers brilliantly'.[172]

Nevertheless, two related military factors were again underlined by the Rwandan operation – prepositioned forces, and force-projection capabilities. Lanxade cited the prepositioning of troops in the Central African Republic as one of the operation's facilitators, a lesson to consider for the future.[173] Over force projection, such was the requirement for heavy equipment in Rwanda, notwithstanding the use of forces in the CAR, that the Air Force had to commit around 40 aircraft to the transportation effort.[174] However, French capabilities alone were still insufficient for the task, giving rise to the requisitioning of aircraft from other sources. Unlike in the Gulf effort, though, the aircraft of Air France could not be used: the deployment coincided with the holiday season and aircraft were unavailable.[175] Transportation was therefore undertaken with the use of chartered Russian Antonov and Ilyushin cargo planes, highlighting again the discrepancies of France's global ambitions and her military means.

The new French interventionism

Military interventions overseas were a feature of Mitterrand's second term, and served not only the declared aims of furthering international law and human rights, but also the less altruistic, more manipulatively political concern of safeguarding what remained of France's status as a world power. Moreover, this was a conscious choice by the President, and demonstrated again his tendency to use the armed forces, and issues relating to them, for his own political ends.

This extension of missions and responsibilities for the French forces highlighted the deficiencies which affected them. The high technology of the Gulf War, and the opportunity for direct comparison with the United States, proved this beyond doubt. But the shortcomings were not only technological: in terms of manpower, regardless of whether Védrine appreciated comparisons with Britain, the disparity of commitment by similar-sized powers remained. While the Socialist government thereafter attempted to modify certain aspects of France's military position, through increased investment in space-based intelligence capabilities and adjustments to conscription, it was incapable of achieving significant improvement. Indeed, the extra resources committed to intelligence necessarily constrained the resources available for other out-dated areas of the armed forces, like force projection capabilities. There had certainly been no significant increase in the amount of professional manpower available for commitment to Bosnia, as shown by the number of conscript troops employed. The timeliness, in fact the urgency, of the major reforms announced by Chirac in February 1996 was underlined by the interventions of the later Mitterrand years; indeed, as *Le Figaro* noted, in relation to the Gulf in particular, but which could be more widely applied, 'even beyond [France's] problem of mobilisation, [she had] demonstrated the obsolescence of her forces. After ten years of Mitterrandism, it must be fully recognised that [France] alone could hardly face up to the threat of a third world army ...'.[176]

Missions in the Gulf, the former Yugoslavia, and Rwanda also demonstrated the extent to which debate and discord characterised questions of troop deployment in external operations. What was easily apparent was the President's ability to by-pass conflicting government and parliamentary opinion, in order to impose his own preferences on the course of military action. The *domaine réservé* was alive and well, it seemed, in the 1990s. Moreover, it was overtly used to serve Mitterrand's own political ends, as with his troop reinforcements, and firmer tone, in the weeks preceding the legislative elections of 1993. In each case, assertions of consensus were usually only that, lacking in substance and often hiding a myriad of divergences even, and especially, at the highest levels.

Conclusion

When François Mitterrand acceded to the French presidency in 1981 the international security context was one of East–West hostility – détente was over; Europe was no less divided than it had been for the previous 35 years; and the coincidence of Brezhnev, Reagan and Thatcher in power in Moscow, Washington and London would seem to augur ill for a thaw in Cold War tensions. By the end of Mitterrand's presidency, the Cold War had ended; the Soviet Union no longer existed; Communism had lost its grip on Central and Eastern Europe, while integration spread from the West; new regional power centres were emerging; and Mitterrand had outlasted all the major political leaders who had shared his early years in office.

The changes that these developments portended had global repercussions. Their effects were particularly felt in France, where the foundations of the defence and security position of 1981 had been completely undermined by 1995. Nuclear deterrence had been seriously questioned, the role of conventional forces had been reasserted, and the feasibility and function of alliances had been challenged by the demise of the Warsaw Pact and subsequent adaptations within NATO. The Gaullist tenets of national defence – the primacy of the State, the concern for prestige and status, autonomy of decision and action, and the possession of a modern military capability based on an atomic armoury – had been exposed for their inadequacy in the rapidly shifting strategic environment, and the wisdom of their continuity was questionable. Moreover, that element of defence asserted to be so peculiar to France, the alleged defence consensus, was likewise undermined and in itself debatable.

It has been the contention of this book that the defence consensus, in so far as it existed, was neither as convincing, nor as comprehensive, as many in France would like to imply. It has similarly been argued that the defence debate, broadly speaking, had been far more apparent than some were prepared to acknowledge. I have aimed to demonstrate that Mitterrand's role in relation to France's defence planning and execution was not only prominent, but principal, in many instances, despite a public projection which might have indicated otherwise. Finally, it has been suggested that although the external security environment in which France operated presented almost innumerable opportunities for change in the defence position, the Mitterrand presidency failed to take advantage of them, even when change was sorely needed – and that this was often due to the preferences and priorities of the President himself. Moreover, the analysis of debate and consensus has also indicated broader issues arising in consideration of the structures, and means, of France's defence.

What was the consensus?

It can be seen from the evidence that there were perhaps three aspects around which a degree of consensus can be suggested. Firstly, there was some accord that France should possess a nuclear weapons capability. However, consensus in this respect extended across the breadth of the political spectrum for only a very short space of time, from about 1978 until the mid-1980s. Previously, the PCF and the PS had not yet rallied to this point; thereafter, the PCF had moved away from it, at least rhetorically, in favour of a reduced defence effort, a redistribution of resources, and a reduction of the nuclear capability (towards a zero-level by the turn of the century, at one stage). For the more mainstream political positions, the importance of a maintained nuclear capability was more consistently recognised, even if that importance was perhaps more associated with concerns of prestige and status than with military utility. Thus, the Gaullist preoccupation with concerns of rank and status remained a point of accord in French defence under Mitterrand.

Secondly, there was concurrence that, as far as possible, France should retain her autonomy of decision-making and action in defence and military matters. On this point, consensus was perhaps more comprehensive than it was over the issue of nuclear weapons. None of the political parties advocated any real dilution of French independence in matters military. This was true on the Left, where the Communists and others regularly alleged that Mitterrand's governments were sacrificing French independence, to the United States in particular, especially with reference to the commitment of French troops in external operations. It was also true on the Centre-Right, where groupings such as the UDF and the UDC, who called for greater commitment to, and solidarity with, France's allies, nevertheless retained a basic belief in the benefits of autonomy. It was still more true on the Right, where notwithstanding the potentially fundamental shifts in attitude of the 1990s, echoes of de Gaulle's antipathy towards military cooperation or collaboration with the US remained. Indeed, even after France's return to certain of NATO's military structures, such as the Council of Defence Ministers and the Military Committee, under the presidency of Mitterrand's successor Jacques Chirac, the Defence Minister C. Millon suggested that renewed French participation would only occur within 'appropriate NATO military bodies which [did] not encroach on her sovereignty'.[1] In these questions, one of the advantages of the purported consensus was in fact its imprecision. Although it was argued that by the early 1980s 'a consensus [had] finally been achieved in France on independence and nuclear deterrence',[2] and this statement was perhaps true, it only served to highlight the extent to which similar arguments did not apply to the wider aspects of defence.

Thirdly, and on this point there seems to have been little dispute, a consensus surrounded the issue of presidential responsibility for defence concerns. The role and function of the Presidency, as provided for in the Constitution of the Fifth Republic, did not seem to feature in the debates which have been considered. This was perhaps partly because one of the main proponents of serious change in the duties and powers of the office had been François Mitterrand, and many of his arguments dissipated considerably after 1981. Moreover, the big challengers to various developments in the course of defence planning and execution, such as Giscard, Chirac and Balladur, all had presidential aspirations of their own, and therefore had little incentive to challenge the President's Constitutional prerogatives in defence and military concerns. In short, the *domaine réservé*, that peculiar feature which had stemmed from de Gaulle's interpretation and implementation of the French presidential office, thrived under Mitterrand, and demonstrated little prospect of alteration.

Nevertheless, while there was a degree of consensus around these three points, it should be emphasised that the agreement possible on broad outlines was not usually mirrored in the details. Consequently, limitations can be applied even to the matters of the nuclear capability, and national autonomy, named above.

Firstly, although there was a degree of accord around the premise that France should possess a nuclear weapons capability, it can be argued to have been little more than superficial. The reservations of the *Parti Communiste* have already been mentioned. More widely, while the mainstream parties concurred over the possession of a nuclear armoury as the basis of France's defence posture, its size and composition, as well as the strategic justification on which it rested, were areas of divergence. This was apparent during the discussion of the *loi de programmation militaire* for 1987–91, especially considering the debates it portended about the future composition of France's strategic triad. It was also true in relation to the changes imposed by Mitterrand in the 1990s. Hence, while the limitation of the tactical nuclear weapons capability was broadly accepted in the light of post-Cold War events, despite its previous support by much of the political spectrum, measures limiting nuclear testing, and their implications for the credibility of the French nuclear deterrent into the next century, were certainly not widely supported.

Secondly, qualifications must be attached to any assertion of consensus relating to the retention of France's autonomy. While the principle was accepted, the detail was open to question. Therefore, the extent to which France should improve her relations with her European and Alliance partners, and particularly the United States, recurred in discussion of successive governments' decisions and actions. Mitterrand himself had always favoured close relations between France and the United States, and in this respect his views were undoubtedly coloured by the postwar context of the Fourth Republic which had characterised his early political career. Nevertheless, limitations were apparent even in his own position. Although one of his first actions as President had been to despatch his military adviser, General Saulnier, to Washington to discuss rights of access to French ports for American nuclear submarines,[3] agreement on many other issues, such as overflight rights for the bombing of Libya and SDI, was out of the question. Even where agreement was possible support was often nuanced, as over the Gulf War. Indeed, such was the poor state of Franco-American relations as the war approached that the US Secretary of State, James Baker, accused the French of being 'congenitally difficult'.[4] The differences in approach and attitude were amply demonstrated over moves towards Europe and NATO in the early 1990s, and served to indicate that the degree of *rapprochement* envisaged at separate points on the political spectrum could be quite different.

It was suggested by an official of the French Defence Ministry at the beginning of this book that opportunities for parliamentary debate of defence issues were, and remain, limited.[5] To an extent, this work accepts his view. They were especially restricted in consideration of those occasions when debate could lead to substantive change in the preferred policy course of the government of the day. In this respect the legal framework instituted by de Gaulle to maximise the President's control over matters pertaining to defence was, and is, highly effective. Nevertheless, this does not imply that the Parliament was impotent under Mitterrand's presidency in such questions, nor that debate did not exist. The role of the parliamentary Committees, as indicated by the testimonies of their *rapporteurs* in defence debates, certainly seems to have been significant in relation to military planning. In addition, the parliamentary forum was well used for the expression of opposition to governments' proposals, indicated as early as the debate over the defence budget for 1982, and reiterated in consideration of subsequent planning. While the impact of such debate is difficult to quantify, given that parliamentary discussion of a measure is the last stage in its genesis, debate nevertheless existed, and the parliamentary process did not merely constitute a rubber-stamping exercise.

Furthermore, while occasions for formal parliamentary discussion were constrained, the defence debate flourished elsewhere. In this respect, newspapers in particular constituted a ready organ for the expression of criticism, and parliamentarians showed themselves, in general, well-disposed to take advantage of this. Perhaps for obvious reasons, military criticisms were less readily available in this format. Nonetheless observations and analyses were widely found in the professional journals, especially *Défense Nationale*, and despite the semi-official nature of this publication the critiques of policy contained therein were often harsh. Therefore, it would be hard to contest the view of H. Védrine – somewhat atypical of senior figures in the French polity on this matter – that 'it [was] inaccurate, even if it [was] ritual, to speak of a "French consensus" on the problems of defence. This consensus [was] superficial, more verbal than real.'[6]

Mitterrand and continuity

While this has not been a study of defence policy formulation in France during the Mitterrand years, it is nevertheless possible to ascertain from the evidence available that François Mitterrand's role in the definition of France's defence priorities was considerable. He undoubtedly assumed the full mantle of the presidency, as de Gaulle had designed it, and assumed with it the Constitutional responsibilities for defence and national security. Moreover, Mitterrand also took advantage of grey areas, in terms of the division of responsibility between himself and his governments, and particularly his prime ministers – notwithstanding the efforts of certain of the latter to maximise their own position. In this respect, continuity was certainly the order of the day in Mitterrand's interpretation of his own authority and responsibility over French defence, and the search for grandeur and prestige remained.

However, it has been argued that Mitterrand went further in his exploitation of the *domaine réservé* for his own political advantage. This was apparent through his spectacular use of the presidential initiative, as with his trips to Beirut, the South Pacific and Sarajevo, and his manipulation of defence matters for potential political gain. It could be also seen during the presidential election campaign of 1988, with his *Lettre à Tous les Français*, and subsequently, with the reduction in the length of military service, the nuclear testing moratorium, and the despatch of more weighty military means to Bosnia, in 1993. Furthermore, it was evident in Mitterrand's determination to retain full responsibility for the commitment of French troops to external actions, particularly in Africa.

As Mitterrand's interpretation of his presidential role in defence suggested broad continuity with what had gone before, so too did the continued dependence on nuclear deterrence as the cornerstone of France's defence and security. In this respect, Mitterrand allayed fears from the beginning of his term of office, through his advocacy of an expanded nuclear submarine fleet, and the strengthening of the land-based missiles of the Plateau d'Albion from the mid-1980s. Indeed, throughout the 1980s, Mitterrand advanced a self-image as the dogged protector of the French nuclear deterrence capability, in the face of internal challenges to strategy and doctrine during *cohabitation* with the Chirac government, and in the face of external challenges such as SDI and arms control. In addition, there was continuity in that the nuclear force retained the political connotations that it had had from its inception. It remained one of the major justifications, in the French view, for the maintenance of France's international status and standing, and not least of her permanent seat on the United Nations Security Council.

Continuity also prevailed, it seemed, for the conventional forces, especially in relation to manpower. Although successive reorganisations of the armed forces occurred during Mitterrand's presidency, and some significant changes were made, he failed to address the basic problem of France's conscript-based services. Improvements were made to conscripts' living and working conditions, but the fundamental difficulty remained: despite armed forces numbering 225 000 men even after the reductions of the early 1990s, France struggled to commit more than a few thousand men to military action at any given time. The extent of the problem was proven by the Ministry of Defence's continuing need to call upon 'volunteer conscripts' to bolster interventions from Lebanon to Bosnia. In this respect Mitterrand's arbitrary and unexpected reduction of the length of military service, to ten months, caused only confusion, and exacerbated the problems associated with conscript manpower.

Neither was the problem of relative under-emphasis on, and under-investment in, the conventional forces addressed under Mitterrand. These characteristics had been evident under de Gaulle and Pompidou, and despite the attempts of the Giscard presidency to redress the balance little was achieved. By the onset of the 1980s, and the advent of the new Socialist president, the consequences of this situation had become apparent. Nonetheless the changes made by Hernu initially, and his successors in the 1990s, proved sadly lacking in measures capable of improving the situation. Even the creation of the *Force d'Action Rapide* was inadequate, at best, and at worst irrelevant, in addressing the limited capabilities of the French armed forces for external intervention. This was particularly demonstrated with the Gulf War. Although the exploits of the *Division Daguet*, composed in a large part of forces from the FAR, were portrayed as successful, this was more attributable to the fact that 'as with French air forces, French ground forces were assigned only the tasks they were deemed capable of accomplishing'.[7] Neither were problems addressed with the subsequent interventions in Europe and Africa. Furthermore, successive governments did little to combat effectively the perennial problem of limited resources with which the services were faced. Decreased financial resources, and increased responsibilities, became the norm under the Mitterrand presidency.

Where Mitterrand demonstrated a degree of innovation was in the realm of defence within Europe. Indeed the President proved to be a driving force in improving security relations with his German neighbour, and extending the amelioration thus achieved to the rest of Europe, at least in embryo. Although the principle of improved relations with (the then) West Germany had been apparent under de

Gaulle, and in defence terms had been a primary factor in the 1963 Franco-German Elysée Treaty, the practicalities of the measure had eluded the General and had not figured strongly in the presidencies of either Pompidou or Giscard. The years of the Mitterrand presidency, on the other hand, witnessed increasingly formal military commitments by France to (West) Germany, including a degree of nuclear commitment, and more extensive cooperation arrangements in conventional terms, via the Franco-German Brigade, the Franco-German Corps, and later the Eurocorps. In this area at least, it seemed that Mitterrand was following a certain defined path in defence and military matters.

While Mitterrand's modifications to France's defence position in relation to (West) Germany and Europe were in general favourably received, it is important to note that the President did not seem to act through any particular concern to promote or preserve the alleged consensus. Although he did not undertake any radical alterations to the structure of France's defence, neither did he refrain from pursuing courses of action likely to challenge the received wisdoms, and to expose divergences cloaked by assertions of consensus. This was in direct contrast to his careful positioning in the debates of the *Parti socialiste* in the 1970s, where he took pains to minimise the occasions for publication of the party's internal discussions and divisions on defence questions. On the contrary, during his presidency, Mitterrand seemed keen to promote his own preferences on certain matters, as he indicated strongly during the first *cohabitation* over SDI and other nuclear-related questions, and also later over financial provision, and again over nuclear issues, where he enforced his preferences in the matters of nuclear systems and testing, despite the tensions in the consensus to which these decisions gave rise.

Finally, then, it seems that there was continuity in discord. Despite the profusion of commentators within and outside France who applauded the French defence consensus in the Mitterrand presidency, debate and disagreement were as much in evidence as they had been at any other time in the Fifth Republic. In fact, given the conditions pertaining to the defence debate in 1981–95 – the length of Mitterrand's occupancy of the Elysée Palace, the economic conditions prevailing, their effects on defence in particular, and the international upheavals with which they coexisted – debate and discord were perhaps heightened, providing the context necessary for the profound reorganisation undertaken by Mitterrand's successor.

Broader issues arising

Analysis of the defence debate, and of the proffered defence consensus, has raised a number of supplementary questions about the functions and forms of the French defence establishment. The first of these concerns the type of defence ultimately envisaged by France. The years of the Mitterrand presidency exposed the severe, and indeed worsening, weaknesses with which the armed forces had to contend. If the French forces had been overstretched at the time of the overlap in their commitments to Lebanon and Chad, they were sorely tested by the extension of their role and responsibilities in the 1990s, not only in manpower, but also in equipment and operational flexibility.

The military planning undertaken since 1981 had exacerbated, rather than eradicated, the difficulties already apparent under Giscard. The tendency to maintain the majority of military programmes in defence planning laws, while lessening their immediate cost by extending or reducing their ultimate production runs, meant that equipment became significantly out-dated, if not obsolete. Furthermore, the likelihood was that replacement programmes would also be out-dated by the time they entered service, later than originally anticipated, in lesser quantities, and usually considerably over budget. This was even the case with prestige programmes such as the seventh nuclear submarine ordered by Mitterrand within weeks of taking up office, the aircraft carrier proposed in the Socialists' first *loi de programmation militaire*, the Leclerc tank series for the Army, and the Rafale fighter for the Air Force.

The inadequacies of military planning under Mitterrand inevitably detracted from the abilities of France's armed forces to act efficiently and effectively in combat situations. This was particularly identified in the Gulf War with the complete inability of France's aircraft to operate at night. Moreover, the failure to address existing shortcomings meant that problems such as France's inadequate force projection capabilities, condemned at the beginning of the 1980s, remained in the mid-1990s. Such factors did not augur well for France's future capacity to participate in international military actions relying increasingly on airpower, or in distant missions requiring a troop presence on the ground, both of which seemed to be an increasing feature of the post-Cold War order. As indicated above, neither was the FAR a response to the difficulties: deprived of adequate means and *matériel*, it was little able to alleviate the limited capabilities of the French forces beyond their borders.

If equipment was one of the major difficulties faced by the armed forces by the 1990s it was certainly not the only one. Given the apparent inability of the French military hierarchy, up to and including the Head of the Armed Forces, the President, to adapt to the changing security environment with any coherence, questions were raised about the discrepancies of French strategic thought and subsequent military planning, and their relevance to modern times. The *Livre blanc* of 1994 highlighted such concerns. While the government of the day had an ideal opportunity to give France a defence mechanism for the twenty-first century, through the first such document for over 20 years, that opportunity was largely missed. Although it attempted to set priorities for France's future defence missions, it failed to make the decisive choices necessary to implement those missions. The nuclear force retained the same deterrence doctrine it had gained in the 1960s; conscription remained; and the strains on equipment were aggravated by the extension of the armed forces' roles. In such a situation, how could military planning possibly provide effectively for the future? In short it could not. By the end of the Mitterrand presidency, French defence was in a parlous condition.

The difficulties were compounded by the extension of the armed forces' roles implemented by Mitterrand and codified by Balladur's White Paper. Financially, the services had barely enough money to pay for day-to-day operational costs, let alone the resources to fund the political goal of maintaining France's international prestige through military action outside her borders. This was expressed by Joxe with particular clarity when he expressed the costs of the Bosnian operation in the cuts he was compelled to make in equipment expenditure, as a direct result.[8] The dichotomy between France's ambitions, on the one hand, and the means available on the other, was stark. Such was the gravity of the resource dilemma by the 1990s that criticism became a tacitly accepted method of challenging a government's position on defence. It became a means widely used by politicians to express their 'shared concerns' over the defence effort: or rather, to question the bases of a government's defence analysis, and express dissatisfaction and disagreement, without openly undermining the alleged basic consensus.

The broadening of France's defence missions, and the extension of the forums in which her armed forces were engaged in the early 1990s, had political as well as military and financial implications. This, together with the explicit reorientation of France's external military actions towards a cooperative framework, raised questions about the very independence and autonomy to which the political classes professed themselves attached. Mitterrand's imperatives of improving cooperation in the defence and military fields with Germany, and subsequently Europe, through the quest for a Common Foreign and Security Policy, and a European Security and Defence Identity, suggest that the original Gaullist concept of autonomy was perhaps somewhat fluid. Potentially, this was a significant change in the French defence position under Mitterrand. The challenge to independence of decision-making and action was clearly apparent during Operations Desert Shield and Desert Storm, when political contortions were necessary on the part of Paris and Washington to maintain the nuances of French autonomy, and in the context of wider operations, under the auspices of the United Nations, to which France was committed in the 1990s.

It can therefore be seen that despite the apparent simplicity in assertions of consensus and continuity in French defence, these were in fact far more complex issues during the Mitterrand era. Indeed, while there may have been continuity in the broad outlines of French defence, it was often simply a continuity in insufficiency. Moreover, in terms of consensus, the French defence debate was sound, and at times vibrant, most notably during the years of Mitterrand's presidency, providing for no more than the most vague consensus on the basic orientations of the nation's defence. Even this degree of accord on the military undertakings of the leadership was only facilitated by its lack of precision and definition, thus allowing significant discord to be expressed under the umbrella of basic agreement. Nevertheless, the notion of a consensus was promoted, often by those who at times least agreed with the policy directions of the government, demonstrating that the suggestion of agreement had become a rallying cry that approximated on occasion to patriotism: one could not be for France if one was against France's defence. Thus, especially in the parliamentary framework, consensus was a tool of argument, used widely to engender support for measures relating to military planning, even those which patently raised questions about the future of the military forces they were supposed to equip. It was little more than an instrument of political expediency, whose fragility was in fact most often underlined by the actions of the Constitutional guardian of France's military might, the President himself – François Mitterrand.

Notes

Introduction

1. Such works are already available and include, for example, P. H. Gordon, *A Certain Idea of France: French Security Policy and the Gaullist Legacy* (Princeton, NJ; Princeton University Press, 1993), and T. R. Posner, *Current French Security Policy: the Gaullist Legacy* (Westport, CT; Greenwood Press, 1991).
2. 'Toute ma vie, je me suis fait une certaine idée de la France.' C. de Gaulle, *Mémoires de Guerre, tome I: L'appel, 1940–1942* (Paris; Plon, 1955), p. 1.
3. J. Marcus and B. George, MP, 'The Ambiguous Consensus: French Defence Policy under Mitterrand,' *The World Today*, 39, x (1983) 369–77, p. 369.
4. S. F. Wells, Jr, 'The Mitterrand Challenge,' *Foreign Policy*, 4 (Fall 1981) 57–69, p. 59.
5. According to a SOFRES poll published in the journal *L'Expansion*, 6.5.83, which asked if the nuclear deterrent was perceived to be positive or negative for France. Cited in J. Marcus and B. George, MP, 'The Ambiguous Consensus,' p. 369.
6. P. Favier and M. Michel-Roland, *La Décennie Mitterrand vol. 1: Les Ruptures (1981–1984)*, (Paris; Seuil, 1990), p. 266. Favier and Martin-Roland were journalists with Agence France-Presse, who were assigned to the Elysée Palace during the Mitterrand Presidency. Their work is based on knowledge acquired at the time, a substantial number of interviews and consultation of confidential archives.
7. Interview with J. Attali, 23.5.96.
8. Medium-term military planning law.
9. The situation whereby the government is not of the same political leaning as the President, which occurs due to the French electoral system which elects its President for seven-year terms, but its legislature for five-year terms. Consequently, when Mitterrand won the Presidency in 1981 he dissolved Parliament and a Left-wing majority was thereafter elected, but their victory was not repeated in the legislative elections of 1986, thus giving rise to the *cohabitation* of the Socialist President Mitterrand and the Gaullist Prime Minister Jacques Chirac and his Right-wing government. On Mitterrand's re-election in 1988 a Leftist majority was again returned to Parliament, but this was once more overturned at the legislative elections of 1993, thereby creating a second period of *cohabitation*, this time under Prime Minister Edouard Balladur.
10. J.-P. Chevènement, in the *Journal Officiel de la République française, Débats Parlementaires, Assemblée Nationale* (hereafter *J.O., A.N.*), 2nd sitting, 8.4.87, p. 116. Dates given refer to the date of the debate, and not the date of publication of the *Journal Officiel*, which is generally the following day.
11. M. Rocard, *J.O., A.N.*, 1st sitting, 9.4.87, p. 125.
12. P. Pascallon, *J.O., A.N.*, 2nd sitting, 8.4.87, p. 115.

13. L. Bouvard, *J.O., A.N.*, 1st sitting, 9.4.87, p. 140.
14. See Chapters 4 and 7 below.
15. J.-M. Boucheron, *J.O., A.N.*, 1st sitting, 3.10.89, p. 3023.
16. J. Chirac, 'La Politique de Défense de la France: Allocution du Premier Ministre, le 12 septembre 1986, lors de la séance d'ouverture de la 39e session de l'Institut des Hautes Etudes de Défense Nationale,' *Défense Nationale*, 42, 11 (November 1986) 7–17, p. 7.
17. J.-M. Boucheron, *J.O., A.N.*, 1st sitting, 3.10.89, p. 3026.
18. Ibid.
19. J.-P. Chevènement, ibid., p. 3035.
20. Ibid., p. 3036.
21. J. Chirac, 'La Politique de Défense de la France,' p. 7.
22. P. Quilès, *J.O., A.N.*, 2nd sitting, 8.4.87, p. 111. He specified accord in three areas: the necessity of independent decision-making for France, the strategy of deterrence of the strong by the weak (*la dissuasion du faible au fort*), and the importance of solidarity with friends and allies.
23. P. Quilès, ibid., p. 112. The areas of discord were concerned with the extension of a French nuclear guarantee to other countries, the doctrine for the use of tactical nuclear weapons, chemical weapon capabilities, the defence budget, approaches to disarmament and ideas of a European defence.
24. J. Isnard, 'Impossible Consensus,' *Le Monde*, 20.5.83.
25. Interview with a senior official in the French Ministry of Defence, 21.5.96.
26. A notable exception is J. Howorth and P. Chilton (eds), *Defence and Dissent in Contemporary France* (London; Croom Helm, 1984), although as this was published in 1984 an account dealing with the rest of the Mitterrand presidency is quite justifiable.

1 Years of Discord

1. F. Mitterrand, *J.O., A.N.*, 1st sitting, 2.12.64, pp. 5770–1.
2. In the Presidential election of December 1958 de Gaulle received 78.5 per cent of votes cast.
3. The legislative elections of November 1958 constituted a landslide victory for the Right-wing association of Gaullists and conservatives in the Assemblée Nationale. The Gaullist UNR won 196 seats, and the conservatives 132. By contrast the Centre and Left were routed – 23 Radicals, 44 Socialists and only 10 Communists were elected. Among those who lost their seats were P. Mendès-France and E. Faure, former leaders of the Fourth Republic, F. Mitterrand, and the Socialists G. Defferre and J. Moch. See J. Lacouture, *De Gaulle, the Ruler: 1945–1970* (London; Harvill, 1991), p. 221. Translated from the French by A. Sheridan.
4. S. Hoffmann, 'Gaullism by any Other Name,' *Foreign Policy*, 57 (Winter 1984–85) 38–57, p. 38.
5. T.R. Posner, *Current French Security Policy*, and P. H. Gordon, *A Certain Idea of France*, are but two recent examples of this suggestion.
6. C. de Gaulle, *Mémoires de Guerre, tome III: Le Salut, 1944–1946* (Paris; Plon, 1959), p. 1.
7. J. Lacouture, *De Gaulle*, p. 211.
8. De Gaulle had particularly quarrelled with General Eisenhower at the turn

of 1944–45, over the provision of defence for Strasbourg in the face of the German offensive in the Ardennes and Alsace.

9. C. de Gaulle, *Mémoires de Guerre I*, p. 70.
10. C. de Gaulle, *Discours et Messages III: Avec le Renouveau, Mai 1958–Juillet 1962* (Paris; Plon, 1970), p. 126. Speech to the École Militaire, 3.11.59.
11. C. de Gaulle, *The Army of the Future* (London; Hutchinson, 1940), pp. 11–17.
12. De Gaulle was preoccupied with the idea that these three powers might actually conspire together against France, to deny the latter the opportunity to enhance her prestige and military capabilities through the acquisition of an atomic weapons capability. Regarding the three nuclear powers' attempts to secure an end to nuclear weapons testing in the late 1950s, de Gaulle categorically refused French adherence: 'the day approach[ed] when [France], in [her] turn, [would] carry out testing. Perhaps this circumstance [had] counted in the fact that Washington, Moscow and London [had] thought simultaneously that the suspension of testing was suddenly desirable ...'. C. de Gaulle, *Discours et Messages III*, p. 58. Press conference, 23.10.58.
13. C. de Gaulle, ibid., p. 126. Speech to the École Militaire, 3.11.59. Italics added.
14. See O. D. Menard, *The Army and the Fifth Republic* (Lincoln, Nebraska; University of Nebraska Press, 1967), p. viii and pp. 87–101; also E. S. Furniss Jr, *De Gaulle and the French Army: a Crisis in Civil–Military Relations* (New York; Twentieth Century Fund, 1964), pp. 47–9.
15. J. Lacouture, *De Gaulle*, p. 165.
16. A. Clayton, *The Wars of French Decolonization* (London; Longman, 1994), p. 164. The Algerian War, and its resolution by de Gaulle and his governments, will not be treated in detail here as it arguably constituted as much of a domestic political problem as a direct challenge to future defence directions and structures. For further reference to the Algerian conflict, Clayton's study is useful, as is the greatly detailed A. Horne, *A Savage War of Peace: Algeria 1954–1962*, revised edn (London; Papermac, 1996).
17. M. L. Martin, *Warriors to Managers: the French Military Establishment since 1945* (Chapel Hill; University of North Carolina Press, 1981), p. 39.
18. Unsigned, 'Les attributions des chefs d'État-major sont modifiées par décrets,' *Le Monde*, 13–14.7.58.
19. Over 79 per cent of voters in Metropolitan France voted for the Constitution (a figure over 80 per cent in Algeria). J. Lacouture, *De Gaulle*, p. 206.
20. Translation of the French Constitution of 4 October 1958, by W. Pickles. Cited in D. Pickles, *The Fifth French Republic: Institutions and Politics*, 3rd edn (London; Methuen, 1965), pp. 234–55, p. 235.
21. Ibid., p. 238.
22. Ibid.
23. Ibid., p. 239.
24. Unsigned, 'Les textes concernant la défense,' *Le Monde*, 26–27.4.64.
25. Ibid.
26. See *Le Monde*, 13.2.60, pp. 1–5 for a variety of articles covering the explosion; also W. Grainger Blair, 'France explodes her first A-bomb in Sahara test,' *New York Times*, 13.2.60.

27. On the planning law, see D. S. Yost, 'French Defense Budgeting: Executive Dominance and Resource Constraints,' *Orbis*, 23, 3 (Fall 1979) 579–608, in particular p. 581.
28. G. A. Kelly, *Lost Soldiers: the French Army and Empire in Crisis, 1947–1962* (Cambridge, Mass.; MIT Press, 1965), p. 17.
29. M. S. Alexander and P. C. F. Bankwitz, 'From *Politiques en Képi* to Military Technocrats: De Gaulle and the Recovery of the French Army after Indo-China and Algeria,' in G. J. Andreopoulos and H. E. Selesky (eds), *The Aftermath of Defeat: Societies, Armed Forces and the Challenge of Recovery* (New Haven and London; Yale University Press, 1994), pp. 79–102, p. 98.
30. See, for example, C. de Gaulle, *Discours et Messages III*, p. 375. Speech broadcast and televised from the Palais de l'Élysée, 29.12.61.
31. See, for example, ibid., pp. 185–6, Speech delivered at Ottawa, 19.4.60, pp. 189–94; Press conference held at the National Press Club of Washington, DC, 23.4.60, pp. 297–8; press conference held at the Palais de l'Élysée, 11.4.61.
32. Ibid., p. 134. Press conference held at the Palais de l'Élysée, 10.11.59.
33. Ibid.
34. W. Mendl, *Deterrence and Persuasion: French Nuclear Armament in the Context of National Policy, 1945–1969* (London; Faber and Faber, 1970), p. 18.
35. C. de Gaulle, *Discours et Messages III*, p. 93. Press conference held at the Palais de l'Élysée, 25.3.59.
36. Ibid., p. 248. Press conference held at the Palais de l'Élysée, 5.9.60.
37. On these points, see ibid., pp. 92–3, press conference held at the Palais de l'Élysée, 25.3.59, pp. 248–9; press conference held at the Palais de l'Élysée, 5.9.60.
38. For the text of this Memorandum, see J. Lacouture, *De Gaulle*, pp. 216–17.
39. J. Newhouse, *De Gaulle and the Anglo-Saxons* (London; Andre Deutsch, 1970), p. 272.
40. W. L. Kohl, *French Nuclear Diplomacy* (Princeton. NJ; Princeton University Press, 1971), p. 137.
41. Cited in J. Lacouture, *De Gaulle*, p. 376.
42. C. de Gaulle, *Discours et Messages IV: Pour l'effort, Août 1962–Décembre 1965* (Paris; Plon, 1970), pp. 75–6. Press Conference held at the Palais de l'Élysée, 14.1.63.
43. J. Lacouture, *De Gaulle*, p. 213.
44. C. de Gaulle, *Discours et Messages IV*, p. 126. Press conference held at the Palais de l'Élysée, 29.7.63.
45. De Gaulle's Foreign Minister, Maurice Couve de Murville, said of the Test Ban Treaty, 'what [was] at stake [was] not to disarm those who [were] armed, but to prevent those who [were] not armed from arming, and that [was] what [France] … [could] not find satisfactory.' Cited in W. L. Kohl, *French Nuclear Diplomacy*, p. 167.
46. C. de Gaulle, *Discours et Messages IV*, p. 127. Press conference held at the Palais de l'Élysée, 29.7.63.
47. See J. Newhouse, *De Gaulle and the Anglo-Saxons*, p. 245.
48. See W. L. Kohl, *French Nuclear Diplomacy*, pp. 167–8.
49. Rather than risking a critical defeat for the Government's military plans, de Gaulle's Prime Minister M. Debré had required the National Assembly

to engage in three votes of confidence in his government. Under the terms of the 1958 Constitution, the Assembly's failure to overturn Debré's Government on the third attempt was taken as implicit approval of its actions, including the military planning law. See W. Grainger Blair, 'De Gaulle victor on nuclear force,' *New York Times*, 19.10.60; W. Grainger Blair, 'Atom bill beaten in French Senate,' *New York Times*, 10.11.60; W. Grainger Blair, 'Debré again sets atomic bill test,' *New York Times*, 18.11.60; Unsigned, 'Senate again balks French atomic plan,' *New York Times*, 1.12.60; and W. Grainger Blair, 'France enacts bill for nuclear force,' *New York Times*, 7.12.60.

50. R. Schmitt, *J.O., A.N.*, 3rd sitting, 18.10.60, p. 2587.
51. P. Villon, ibid., pp. 2594–5.
52. R. Schmitt, ibid., p. 2587.
53. M. Lauriol, ibid., p. 2593.
54. R. Schmitt, ibid., p. 2587.
55. P. Villon, ibid., p. 2595.
56. P. Ferri, ibid., p. 2575.
57. Unsigned, 'Savants decry A-bomb,' *New York Times*, 12.3.60. This reflected the situation of the 1950s when scientists of the *Commissariat à l'Énergie Atomique* (CEA), who were involved in developing an atomic capability for France, were particularly averse to the prospect of its military use.
58. H. Dorey, *rapporteur spécial de la Commission de l'économie, des finances et du plan*, *J.O., A.N.*, 1st sitting, 18.10.60, p. 2550.
59. P. Villon, *J.O., A.N.*, 3rd sitting, 18.10.60, p. 2594.
60. J. Planchais, 'Le chemin sera long de la première bombe A à la force de frappe nucléaire,' *Le Monde*, 16.2.60.
61. H. Dorey, *J.O., A.N.*, 1st sitting, 18.10.60, pp. 2547–55.
62. J. Le Theule, ibid., pp. 2555–9.
63. R. Schmitt, *J.O., A.N.*, 3rd sitting, 18.10.60, p. 2585. However, according to observers, the situation had improved little even by 1968: the military correspondent of *Le Monde*, J. Isnard, commented that even by 'the most optimistic hypothesis, France [would] have a nuclear capacity of about thirty megatons around 1975. In other words,... what one American bomber carr[ied] in its hold.' J. Isnard, 'La France disposera en 1975 d'une capacité nucléaire égale à celle d'un B-52 américain,' *Le Monde*, 11.7.68.
64. H. Dorey, *J.O., A.N.*, 1st sitting, 18.10.60, p. 2549.
65. P. Villon, *J.O., A.N.*, 3rd sitting, 18.10.60, p. 2594.
66. M.-R. Simonnet, ibid., p. 2583.
67. R. Aron, cited in P. H. Gordon, *A Certain Idea of France*, p. 40.
68. F. Japiot, *J.O., A.N.*, 3rd sitting, 18.10.60, p. 2597.
69. M.-R. Simonnet, ibid., p. 2581.
70. M. Lauriol, ibid., p. 2591.
71. J. Le Theule, *J.O., A.N.*, 1st sitting, 18.10.60, p. 2556.
72. H. Dorey, ibid., p. 2551.
73. D. S. Yost, 'French Defense Budgeting,' p. 581.
74. P. Reynaud, *J.O., A.N.*, 2nd sitting, 18.10.60, p. 2564.
75. M. Schumann, *J.O., A.N.*, 1st sitting, 18.10.60, p. 2559.
76. A. Rossi, *J.O., A.N.*, 2nd sitting, 18.10.60, p. 2569.
77. M. Junot, *J.O., A.N.*, 3rd sitting, 18.10.60, p. 2600.

78. See, for example, C. Nay, *Le Noir et le Rouge* (Paris; Grasset, 1984); F.-O. Giesbert, *François Mitterrand ou la Tentation de l'Histoire* (Paris; Seuil, 1977); W. Northcutt, *François Mitterrand: a Political Biography* (New York; Holmes and Meier, 1992).

79. Long a subject for speculation among both contemporary political associates and subsequent biographers, the emergence of a semi-official commentary on Mitterrand's early life in P. Péan, *Une Jeunesse Française* (Paris; Seuil, 1994) would seem to confirm that Mitterrand worked for the Vichy regime less as a cover for Resistance activities, and more out of personal conviction, than has previously been suggested. See also J. Hellmann, 'Wounding Memories: Mitterrand, Moulin, Touvier, and the Divine Half-lie of Resistance,' *French Historical Studies*, 19, 2 (Fall 1995) 461–86, particularly pp. 461–70; and J.-P. Rioux, 'François Mitterrand: "Speech in Defence of the Indefensible" in the "Year of Farewells",' *Contemporary European History*, 5, 1 (1996) 129–32.

80. A. Cole, *François Mitterrand: a Study in Political Leadership* (London; Routledge, 1994), pp. 3–4.

81. Ibid., p. 5.

82. His hostility was immediately apparent. See F. Mitterrand, *J.O., A.N.*, 1st sitting, 1.6.58, p. 2585.

83. F. Mitterrand, *Ma Part de Vérité: de la Rupture à l'Unité* (Paris; Fayard, 1969), p. 42.

84. A. Ballet, 'Le premier ministre expose devant l'Assemblée sa conception du fonctionnement des institutions,' *Le Monde*, 26–27.4.64.

85. F. Mitterrand, *Ma Part de Vérité*, p. 24.

86. F. Mitterrand, *J.O., A.N.*, 1st sitting, 2.12.64, p. 5774.

87. F. Mitterrand, *Journal Officiel de la République Française, Débats Parlementaires, Sénat*, 12.6.62, p. 475.

88. F. Mitterrand, *J.O., A.N.*, 1st sitting. 2.12.64, p. 5771.

89. F. Mitterrand, *Ma Part de Vérité*, p. 193.

90. H. Kamm, 'Mitterrand outlines policy as candidate in French election,' *New York Times*, 22.9.65.

91. H. Kamm, 'Communists will back Mitterrand in bid for Presidency of France', *New York Times*, 24.9.65.

92. Unsigned, 'De Gaulle to speak to nation Nov. 4,' *New York Times*, 28.10.65.

93. A. Cole, *François Mitterrand*, pp. 24–6.

94. R. Barrillon, 'L'élection présidentielle: la conférence de presse de M. François Mitterrand,' *Le Monde*, 23.9.65.

95. R. Barrillon, 'M. François Mitterrand formule vingt-huit propositions constituant «la ligne de départ» de la Gauche moderne,' *Le Monde*, 19.11.65. Reiteration of R. Barrillon, 'L'élection présidentielle: la conférence de presse de M. François Mitterrand,' *Le Monde*, 23.9.65, and repeated again in *Combat Républicain*, 25.11.65, and *Combat Républicain*, 2.12.65.

96. P. Braestrup, 'Mitterrand bids Paris end A-force,' *New York Times*, 2.12.65.

97. F. Mitterrand, *J.O., A.N.*, 1st sitting, 2.11.67, p. 4326.

98. R. Barrillon, 'M. Mitterrand: la disparité des revenus s'accroît de façon constante,' *Le Monde*, 16.12.65.

99. F. Mitterrand, *J.O., A.N.*, 1st sitting, 17.6.65, p. 2206.

100. R. Barrillon, 'L'élection présidentielle: la conférence de presse de M. François Mitterrand,' *Le Monde*, 23.9.65.
101. P. Braestrup, 'Mitterrand bids Paris end A-force,' *New York Times*, 2.12.65.
102. R. Barrillon, 'M. François Mitterrand: de Gaulle a fait toutes les politiques depuis sept ans,' *Le Monde*, 15.12.65.
103. Combat Républicain, 25.11.65. On the dangers of proliferation, see also F. Mitterrand, *J.O.*, *A.N.*, 1st sitting, 2.12.64, p. 5770.
104. H. Tanner, 'De Gaulle fights for votes on TV', *New York Times*, 12.12.65.
105. P. Viansson-Ponté, 'M. François Mitterrand dénonce le caractère national-iste de la politique du régime et souhaite régler le «contentieux» avec le Parti communiste,' *Le Monde*, 5.11.66.
106. H. Tanner, 'Leftists' leader scores de Gaulle,' *New York Times*, 4.11.66.
107. P. Braestrup, 'Mitterrand bids Paris end A-force,' *New York Times*, 2.12.65.
108. F. Mitterrand, *Ma Part de Vérité*, p. 197.
109. F. Mitterrand, 'Mitterand (sic) says – France is no longer a democracy,' *New York Times*, 29.5.66, Section VI.
110. F. Mitterrand, *J.O.*, *A.N.*, 3rd sitting, 24.1.63, p. 1650.
111. H. Kamm, 'Mitterrand outlines policy as candidate in French election,' *New York Times*, 22.9.65.
112. H. Tanner, 'De Gaulle denies charge he is anti-American,' *New York Times*, 15.12.65.
113. See F. Mitterrand, *J.O.*, *A.N.*, 3rd sitting, 24.1.63, p. 1650.
114. F. Mitterrand, *J.O.*, *A.N.*, 1st sitting, 2.12.64, p. 5771.
115. Unsigned, 'Les déclarations de personnalités politiques françaises,' *Le Monde*, 10.3.66.
116. Unsigned, 'Le discours du président de la Fédération,' *Le Monde*, 14.6.66.
117. Unsigned, 'M. Mitterrand: Nous ne prendrons pas les voix de l'extrême gauche pour aller nous allier ensuite avec d'autres,' *Le Monde*, 19–20.6.66.
118. F. Mitterrand, 'Mitterand (sic) says – France is no longer a democracy,' *New York Times*, 29.5.66, Section VI.
119. Unsigned, 'M. Mitterrand: votre politique est une sorte de poujadisme aux dimensions de l'univers,' *Le Monde*, 16.4.66.
120. Unsigned, 'Paris to stress deadline,' *New York Times*, 15.4.66.
121. H. Tanner, 'De Gaulle wins French runoff with 54.7 per cent vote,' *New York Times*, 20.12.65.
122. P. Viansson-Ponté, 'L'accord entre le PC et la Fédération vise à assurer le succès du «candidat de gauche le mieux placé»,' *Le Monde*, 22.12.66.
123. Unsigned, 'Le texte du communiqué commun,' *Le Monde*, 22.12.66.
124. Unsigned, 'Le texte intégral de la déclaration commune de la Fédération et du Parti communiste,' *Le Monde*, 25–26.2.68.

2   Towards a Defence Consensus?

1. *Section Française de l'Internationale Ouvrière* [French Section of the Workers' International] behind such prominent figures in French postwar politics as G. Mollet and P. Mendès-France.
2 At Epinay the Parti Socialiste issued a 'Call to the French People', recog-nising that 'Capitalism [was] unable to reduce the suffering of men ... [and] it multipli[ed] instead the forms of exploitation and oppression. This

working class [would] liberate itself only by a total rupture with this exploiting system ...'. By contrast, the 1969 'Declaration of Principles' of the SFIO, renamed the *Parti Socialiste*, stressed the more moderate goal of 'Liberat[ing] the human being from all alienations which oppress him ...'. See F. L. Wilson, 'The French Left in the Fifth Republic,' in W. G. Andrews and S. Hoffmann (eds), *The Fifth Republic at Twenty* (Albany; State University of New York Press, 1981), pp. 172–90, p. 181.

3. Ibid., p. 182.
4. Mitterrand received 49.3 per cent of the vote, compared to Giscard d'Estaing's 50.7 per cent. F. Lewis, 'France elects Giscard President for 7 years after a close contest,' *New York Times*, 20.5.74.
5. The Party was successful in seventeen Assemblée Nationale by-elections between 1974 and 1977, in the cantonal elections of 1976 and in the municipal elections of 1977. F. L. Wilson, 'The French Left in the French Republic,' p. 183.
6. Parti Socialiste, *Changer la Vie: Programme de Gouvernement du Parti Communiste* (Paris; Flammarion, 1972).
7 Parti Socialiste, *Programme Commun de Gouvernement du Parti Communiste Français et du Parti Socialiste (27 juin 1972)* (Paris; Editions Sociales, 1972).
8. Parti Socialiste, *Changer la Vie*, p. 204.
9. Parti Socialiste, *Programme Commun de Gouvernement*, p. 171.
10. Ibid.
11. The *110 Propositions for France* are alleged to have been Mitterrand's personal commitment to the French electorate. They are reprinted in D. Macshane, *François Mitterrand: a Political Odyssey* (London; Quartet, 1982), pp. 259–72.
12. Ibid., p. 259.
13. Ibid., p. 272.
14. For a concise description of the relationship between France's nuclear and conventional forces in the postwar period, to the end of the 1970s, and the increased emphasis on the former in proportion to the de-emphasis on the latter, see J. Baylis, 'French Defense Policy', in J. Baylis, K. Booth, J. Garnett and P. Williams, *Contemporary Strategy, Volume II: The Nuclear Powers*, 2nd edn, revised (New York; Holmes and Meier, 1987), pp. 168–96, pp. 178–83.
15. The proportion of the national budget devoted to defence averaged over 22 per cent in the years 1959–72, though decreasing over the same period to a figure of 17 per cent by the latter date. See France, Ministère de la Défense, *Livre Blanc sur la Défense Nationale, Tome 1* (Paris; Ministère de la Défense Nationale, 1972) p. 58. See also P. H. Gordon, *A Certain Idea of France*, pp. 36–7.
16. R. Lagre, 'La coopération gaullo-soviétique prend tournure ...,' *Rivarol*, 15.2.73.
17. J. Le Lagadec, 'Debré et Marette accusent l'opposition de démoraliser l'esprit public,' *L'Humanité*, 1.6.73.
18. F. Cornu, 'Les neuf soldats du 19e régiment d'artillerie sont toujours détenus au camp de Canjuers,' *Le Monde*, 14.9.74, and M. Vivès, 'Le chasseur Jean Fournel a été incarcéré au camp de Carpiagne,' *Le Monde*, 14.9.74.
19. Parti Communiste, *Programme Commun de Gouvernement*, p. 173.

20. J.-P. Mithois, 'Quand les socialistes courent après les militaires,' *Le Figaro*, 9.4.74.
21. Unsigned, '«Le parti socialiste cherche à développer sa capacité d'ouverture dans le milieu militaire» affirme M. François Mitterrand,' *Le Monde*, 11.3.75.
22. Ibid.
23. F. Mitterrand, *J.O., A.N.*, 2nd sitting, 9.6.70, p. 2369.
24. F. Mitterrand, *J.O., A.N.*, 6.4.71, p. 913.
25. Mitterrand and several of his colleagues had proposed a Bill for the reduced length of military service in 1963: J. Chamant, *J.O., A.N.*, 7.6.63, p. 3257. He advocated major reforms during a debate in 1965: F. Mitterrand, *J.O., A.N.*, 2nd sitting, 26.5.65, p. 1564. Further concerns over conscription had featured during the 1965 Presidential election campaign: R. Barrillon, 'M. François Mitterrand: de Gaulle a fait toutes les politiques depuis sept ans,' *Le Monde*, 15.12.65.
26. Unsigned, 'Le parti socialiste propose d'aligner les droits et les devoirs des cadres militaires sur ceux de la fonction publique,' *Le Monde*, 13.7.74.
27. S. O'Dy, 'Armées: création d'une Convention des Appelés Socialistes,' *Le Quotidien de Paris*, 21.7.75.
28. T. P., 'Le parti socialiste propose la mise en place de comités représentatifs élus au scrutin secret par tous les soldats dans chaque unité,' *Le Monde*, 9.12.75.
29. See G. Claisse, 'Le grand dessein des généraux,' *L'Express*, 6.8.73.
30. Ibid.
31. R. Galley, '«Malgré les orages et la houle de la subversion ...», Texte intégral du discours prononcé le 13 mai à Lille, par M. Robert Galley, Ministre des Armées,' *L'Express*, 21.5.73.
32. F. Chatel, 'Dans le collimateur des gens d'armes du pouvoir,' *L'Humanité*, 7.6.73.
33. F. Mitterrand, *La Paille et le Grain: Chronique* (Paris; Editions Livres de Poche, 1996), pp. 189–92. Also in English translation, F. Mitterrand, *The Wheat and the Chaff* (London; Weidenfeld and Nicolson, 1982), pp. 77–81. Translated from the French by R. S. Woodward.
34. N. Copin, 'Au-delà d'un budget,' *La Croix*, 8.11.73.
35. Unsigned, 'Sur l'armement nucléaire, le programme commun s'inspire plus de considérations politiques et morales que de préoccupations militaires,' *Le Monde*, 16.10.73.
36. From a statement by the *Bureau politique* of the French Communist Party, cited in F. Chatel, 'Dans le collimateur des gens d'armes du pouvoir,' *L'Humanité*, 7.6.73.
37. Cited in Unsigned, 'Sur l'armement nucléaire, le programme commun s'inspire plus de considérations politiques et morales que de préoccupations militaires,' *Le Monde*, 16.10.73.
38. Mitterrand was careful to maintain a distance. See F. Mitterrand, *La Paille et le Grain*, pp. 192–5. Also in English translation, F. Mitterrand, *The Wheat and the Chaff*, pp. 79–82.
39. M. Rocard, 'Une armée, mais pour défendre quoi?' *Le Figaro*, 6.11.73.
40. N. Copin, 'Au-delà d'un budget,' *La Croix*, 8.11.73.
41. M. Rocard, 'Une armée, mais pour défendre quoi?' *Le Figaro*, 6.11.73.

42. Ibid.
43. C. Hernu, *Soldat-Citoyen: Essai sur la Défense et la Sécurité de la France* (Paris; Flammarion, 1975), p. 95.
44. J. Isnard, 'M. Sanguinetti, partisan de la stratégie indirecte, réclame un renforcement des moyens classiques,' *Le Monde*, 26.1.72.
45. In June 1974, inflation was running at 16 per cent. Unemployment by the end of that year was approaching one million. See I. Derbyshire, *Politics in France: From Giscard to Mitterrand*, revised edn (London; Chambers, 1990), p. 42. This compared with an unemployment figure of 300 000 in 1973. See R. F. Kuisel, 'French Post-war Economic Growth: a Historical Perspective on the *Trente Glorieuses*,' in G. Ross, S. Hoffmann, and S. Malzacher (eds), *The Mitterrand Experiment: Continuity and Change in Modern France* (Cambridge; Polity Press, 1987), pp. 18–32, p. 28.
46. The almost thirty years of rapid economic growth, low inflation, low unemployment and stable exchange rates in France, that had followed the end of the Second World War.
47. Y. Pitette, 'M. Le Theule: «L'effort a été fait là où il le fallait mais les investissements sont médiocres»,' *La Croix*, 31.10.75.
48. P. Th., 'Giscard au Plateau d'Albion: Pas de Changement dans notre politique de défense,' *Le Figaro*, 31.10.75. The significance of Debré's threat was considerable: in France, financial provisions for individual concerns, such as defence, are made within the wider context of the whole of the national budget. If a single element of that budget was to prove unacceptable to the deputies, and was rejected, the vote could quite easily be overridden according to the Constitution as the government could require a vote on the whole of the national budget instead – if this was accepted, then by implication that part referring to the initial problem area was also agreed. However, if as Debré suggested, the entire budget was rejected, the situation would be much more serious for the government.
49. Unsigned, 'Le Gouvernement pratique une politique de pourrissement pour s'orienter, carrément vers l'armée de métier et la réintégration dans l'OTAN, déclare M. Jean-Pierre Chevènement (PS),' *Le Monde*, 16.12.75.
50. J. D., 'Le projet de programmation militaire, Le Theule: «imprécision et ambiguïté»,' *Le Figaro*, 13.5.76.
51. Ibid.
52. Y. Gayard, 'Défense: critiques tous azimuts,' *Le Quotidien de Paris*, 20.5.76.
53. J. D., 'Le projet de programmation militaire, Le Theule: «imprécision et ambiguïté»,' *Le Figaro*, 13.5.76.
54. Unsigned, 'L'episcopat français aurait jugé inopportune la publication d'une note sur le désarmement,' *Le Monde*, 9.1.73.
55. See Mgr G. Riobé, and Mgr P. Boillon, cited in S. Maffert, 'Orléans, Verdun et la bombe atomique,' *Le Monde*, 29.9.73.
56. J. Isnard, 'Des chefs militaires déçus ou exaspérés,' *Le Monde*, 18.7.73.
57. Unsigned, 'Commentaires et réactions,' *Le Monde*, 18.7.73.
58. J. Isnard, 'Des chefs militaires déçus ou exaspérés,' *Le Monde*, 18.7.73.
59. Construction at Canjuers had begun at the end of 1970. At Larzac 107 agricultural concerns would be negated, and 527 people would have to move from the 16 700 hectares designated for the extension of existing military facilities.

60. Canjuers would cover 35 000 hectares of what was previously countryside, and would constitute an eighth of all the land the Army possessed within France. Moreover, economic benefits which might have been expected to accrue to the region had not materialised, as much of the construction and associated work had been undertaken by firms from outside the area concerned. According to a local economist, any future jobs created would go to career military personnel, and economic activity for local inhabitants would stagnate because tourism would suffer, due to the proximity of such extensive military facilities. P. Coste, 'Le camp de Canjuers: une commune rayée de la carte,' *Combat*, 25.11.72.

61. Unsigned, 'Rassemblement de solidarité à 16 heures à la Bourse du Travail,' *L'Humanité*, 13.1.73.

62. G. Toulet, 'La fête de la moisson au Larzac: un succès grandissant d'année en année … mais une ombre au tableau,' *La Croix*, 20.8.74.

63. Ibid.

64. That these texts were the basis of the Party's stance on defence was confirmed in an interview given by Charles Hernu in 1975. Y. Pitette, 'M. Charles Hernu: le pouvoir responsable de la dislocation de l'esprit de défense,' *La Croix*, 1.2.75.

65. C. Hernu, 'Une question de fond au-delà d'un programme de legislature,' *Le Monde*, 21.7.73.

66. C. Hernu, *Soldat-Citoyen*, p. 91.

67. F. Mitterrand, *Ma Part de Vérité*, p. 193. Mitterrand had written, 'During my presidential campaign of 1965 I said that I would ban the *force de frappe*. I will not be able to say that in future. General de Gaulle's military policy has been approved by the French people, who re-elected him, before electing a successor of his line. In seven years our atomic armament will be an irreversible reality. We cannot drown it like puppies.'

68. J.-P. Mithois, 'Le PS convoque une convention nationale sur la sécurité,' *Le Matin*, 13.5.77.

69. Unsigned, 'M. Hernu: prévenir toute manoeuvre d'intimidation directe,' *Le Monde*, 5.1.72.

70. J. Howorth, 'Defence Policy under François Mitterrand: Atlanticism, Gaullism or 'Nuclear Neutralism?' in P. G. Cerny and M. A. Schain (eds), *Socialism, the State and Public Policy in France* (London; Frances Pinter, 1985), pp. 108–28, pp. 108–9. On the many PS factions more generally, see G. A. Codding, Jr and W. Safran, *Ideology and Politics: the Socialist Party of France* (Boulder; Westview Press, 1979), pp. 217–21.

71. G. A. Codding, Jr and W. Safran, *Ideology and Politics*, p. 219.

72. Unsigned, 'M. Bérégovoy: inefficace sur le plan militaire, illusoire sur le plan diplomatique,' *Le Monde*, 5.1.72.

73. Unsigned, 'Le prochain comité directeur du parti socialiste devrait fixer la date de la convention sur les problèmes militaires,' *Le Monde*, 20.7.77.

74. For example, see Unsigned, 'M. Mitterrand a évoqué les grands thèmes de l'actualité,' *Le Monde*, 13.3.75.

75. D. de Montvallon, 'Le double langage du PS,' *Le Point*, 19.4.76.

76. Unsigned, 'Les dirigeants socialistes ont amorcé une réflexion approfondie sur la défense,' *Le Monde*, 15.6.76.

77. Ibid.

78. Unsigned, 'La gauche au pouvoir devra tenir compte du fait nucléaire, estiment MM. Hernu, Pontillon, Chevènement,' *Le Monde*, 9.11.76.
79. Ibid.
80. E. Bergheaud, 'Mitterrand devra arbitrer entre les pro et les anti-nucléaires,' *Le Figaro*, 6.1.78.
81. Unsigned, '«Il n'y a pas de modifications significatives de nos missions de défense pour le moment» précise M. Jacques Soufflet,' *Le Monde*, 14.10.74.
82. See J. Isnard, 'M. Giscard d'Estaing retouche la politique militaire,' *Le Monde*, 13.11.75; Unsigned, '«Nous rejetons toute idée de plafonnement de la force nucléaire»,' *Le Monde*, 13.11.75; and R. Faure, 'Adaptée à tout péril, annonce Giscard à la télévision,' *L'Aurore*, 13.11.75.
83. J. Goldsborough, 'Army chief writes of shift in French military strategy,' *International Herald Tribune*, 2.6.76.
84. Unsigned, 'L'interview du Chef de l'Etat à TF1,' *Le Monde*, 7.5.76.
85. Général G. Méry, 'Une armée pour quoi faire et comment,' *Défense Nationale*, 32, 6 (June 1976) 11–34.
86. V. Giscard d'Estaing, 'Allocution de M. Valéry Giscard d'Estaing, Président de la République, à l'occasion de sa visite à l'Institut des Hautes Etudes de Défense Nationale, Paris, le 1er juin 1976,' *Défense Nationale*, 32, 7 (July 1976) 5–20.
87. See J. Isnard, 'Le débat sur la programmation militaire n'a pas résolu la question de la conscription,' *Le Monde*, 27.5.76.
88. Unsigned, 'Sanguinetti: non à la programmation,' *Le Quotidien de Paris*, 20.5.76.
89. Unsigned, 'Sanguinetti rompt avec Giscard,' *Le Quotidien de Paris*, 3.6.76.
90. Unsigned, 'Commentaires et Réactions,' *Le Monde*, 4.6.76.
91. Ibid.
92. Y. Gayard, 'Défense: Critiques tous azimuts,' *Le Quotidien de Paris*, 20.5.76.
93. Unsigned, 'Jean Kanapa: une politique de boutefeu,' *L'Humanité*, 3.6.76.
94. Ibid. Bold text in original.
95. Ibid.
96. J.-M. Caradec'h, 'Une section socialiste face à la force de frappe,' *Libération*, 7.6.77.
97. J. Huntzinger, 'Giscard et la doctrine Méry,' *L'Unité*, 21.11.75.
98. C. Hernu, 'Par-dessus la tête de l'Assemblée,' *Le Quotidien de Paris*, 3.6.76.
99. Unsigned, 'Commentaires et Réactions,' *Le Monde*, 4.6.76.
100. Unsigned, 'Les dirigeants socialistes ont amorcé une réflexion approfondie sur la défense,' *Le Monde*, 15.6.76.
101. It has been argued that the Communists' decision was as much attributable to electoral calculations as any strategic doctrinal concerns, designed to redirect the support of disaffected Gaullists from the majority Centre-Right coalition towards the PCF, and to enhance its own position in relation to the growing strength of the PS, in the run-up to the legislative elections of 1978. F. L. Wilson, 'The French CP's Dilemma,' *Problems of Communism*, xxvii, 4 (July/August 1978) 1–14, p. 12.
102. Unsigned, 'M. Mitterrand reste nuancé sur l'armement nucléaire et l'Alliance Atlantique,' *Le Monde*, 10.1.72.
103. See, for example, J. Isnard, 'M. Charles Hernu répond au PCF sur les problèmes militaires,' *Le Monde*, 27.7.73, and J. Isnard, 'Les divergences

s'accusent entre Socialistes et Communistes sur l'armement nucléaire et l'Alliance Atlantique,' *Le Monde*, 18.3.75, p. 13.

104. Unsigned, 'Les dirigeants socialistes favorables à la force de frappe,' *L'Humanité*, 11.3.75.

105. Ibid.

106. J. Isnard, 'Les divergences s'accusent entre Socialistes et Communistes sur l'armement nucléaire et l'Alliance Atlantique,' *Le Monde*, 18.3.75, p. 13.

107. J. M. C.'H., 'Le PS «remué» par l'arme nucléaire,' *Libération*, 28.5.77.

108. The important legislative elections, which considering recent good electoral performances, the Left hoped to win, thus bringing them to the government of France.

109. J. M. C.'H., 'Le PS «remué» par l'arme nucléaire,' *Libération*, 28.5.77.

110. Unsigned, 'Le prochain comité directeur du parti socialiste devrait fixer la date de la convention sur les problèmes militaires,' *Le Monde*, 20.7.77.

111. J.-P. M., 'La gauche et l'arme nucléaire: le dossier du grand débat,' *Le Matin*, 13.6.77.

112. See F. L. Wilson, 'The French CP's Dilemma,' pp. 4–5; and D. S. Bell and B. Criddle, *The French Socialist Party: the Emergence of a Party of Government* (Oxford; Clarendon, 1988), pp. 95–8.

113. J.-P. Mithois, 'Dans une interview au Matin, Mitterrand: le PS et l'arme nucléaire,' *Le Matin*, 8.8.77.

114. Interview with H. Védrine, 12.6.96.

115. J. Isnard, 'Désaccord PS–PC sur la défense,' *Le Monde*, 26.7.77.

116. D. S. Bell and B. Criddle, *The French Socialist Party*, p. 98.

117. J.-P. Mithois, 'Dans une interview au Matin, Mitterrand: le PS et l'arme nucléaire,' *Le Matin*, 8.8.77.

118. E. Bergheaud, 'Mitterrand devra arbitrer entre les pro et les anti-nucléaires,' *Le Figaro*, 6.1.78.

119. K. Evin, 'PS: la poussée des «antinucléaires»,' *Le Nouvel Observateur*, 25.12.77.

120. Unsigned, 'Les principaux compléments apportés par le PS au programme commun,' *Le Monde*, 6.1.78.

121. K. Evin, 'PS: la poussée des «antinucléaires»,' *Le Nouvel Observateur*, 25.12.77.

122. R. Mauthner, 'A man who never quite made it,' *Financial Times*, 12.4.72.

123. Hernu's biographer, J. Guisnel, implies that something of a debt of gratitude on Hernu's part was involved here; Hernu, who had been interested in questions of defence and foreign affairs throughout his career as a journalist, had been maintained in the political fold by M. Mitterrand at the turn of the 1960s and 1970s after a series of personal and political scandals. He was given the defence portfolio because at the time it was considered that he could do no harm there. J. Guisnel, *Charles Hernu ou la République au Coeur* (Paris; Fayard, 1993), Chapter 4.

3   Mitterrand and Defence: an Overview

1. J. Isnard, 'Entretien avec M. Charles Hernu,' *Le Monde*, 11.7.81.

2. G. B., '«Non au comités de soldats, oui au Larzac»,' *Libération*, 4.6.81.

3. Ibid. The neutron bomb was an enhanced radiation warhead, intended for tactical military usage.

4. P. Krop, 'Une nouvelle politique de défense pour la France,' *Le Matin*, 9.6.81.
5. P. Darcourt, 'Charles Hernu précise ses intentions,' *Le Figaro*, 12.6.81.
6. For a concise yet comprehensive summary of the French economic position in the postwar period, see J. Szarka, *Business in France: an Introduction to the Economic and Social Context* (London; Pitman, 1992), Chapter 1.
7. In the context of the previous ten years' economic downturn, of which the past seven could be called serious recession, it was not untoward that the Socialists should intend to focus their efforts on that matter. Mitterrand and his ministers set out to end the recession by stimulating growth and industrial output, reducing unemployment, and curbing inflation. So, between 1981 and 1982, old age pensions were increased by 62 per cent, and family allowances by 50 per cent. At the same time the minimum wage level, the SMIC, went up by 10.6 per cent. Housing allowances were increased twice in 1981 alone. Additional Socialist measures included a fifth week of annual paid leave for workers, reduction of the working week to 39 hours, and reduction of the retirement age to 60. However, the Socialists' measures only exacerbated the existing economic difficulties. See ibid., p. 27.
8. The support of, or at least the lack of firm opposition to, the Socialists' initial moves in defence was demonstrated by the adoption of the Defence Budget for 1982 by the National Assembly. Former President Giscard d'Estaing's UDF party voted with the Socialists, while Chirac's Gaullist RPR abstained. Unsigned, 'Priorité à la force de frappe,' *La Croix*, 17.11.82.
9. Y. Pitette, 'L'austérité pousse à privilégier la seule dissuasion nucléaire,' *La Croix*, 4.11.82.
10. Unsigned, 'Priorité à la force de frappe,' *La Croix*, 17.11.82, and C. Hernu, 'Une défense, des choix, des moyens,' *Le Figaro*, 30–31.1.82.
11. Y. Pitette, 'L'austérité pousse à privilégier la seule dissuasion nucléaire,' *La Croix*, 4.11.82.
12. M.-C. Davet, 'Défense: la fin du consensus,' *Le Nouveau Journal*, 12.11.82.
13. J. Isnard, 'Un ministre au pied du mur,' *Le Monde*, 12.11.82.
14. C. Hernu, 'Une défense, des choix, des moyens,' *Le Figaro*, 30–31.1.82.
15. J. Isnard, 'Un ministre au pied du mur,' *Le Monde*, 12.11.82.
16. Unsigned, 'Un nouveau modèle d'armée de terre,' *Le Monde*, 30.11.82.
17. P. Mauroy, 'Vers un nouveau modèle d'armée: Allocution du Premier Ministre, le 20 septembre 1982, lors de la séance d'ouverture de la 35e session de l'IHEDN,' *Défense Nationale*, 38, 11 (November 1982) 9–28.
18. D. Housego, 'French pledge to strengthen land forces in Europe,' *Financial Times*, 1.12.82.
19. P. Krop, 'Armées: création d'une nouvelle force d'intervention,' *Le Matin*, 21.4.83.
20. Unsigned, '«Le gouvernement organise l'inadaptation de l'appareil militaire aux nécessités vitales de notre défense» estime le RPR et l'UDF dans une déclaration commune,' *Le Monde*, 23.4.83.
21. P. Krop, 'Loi de programmation militaire: des échanges à fleurets mouchetés,' *Le Matin*, 20.5.83.
22. Proposition no. 4 of Mitterrand's *110 Propositions for France* reasserted his intention to reorientate France's formerly overt pro-Arab bias in the

Middle East. D. MacShane, *François Mitterrand*, p. 259.

23. P. Favier and M. Martin-Roland, *La Décennie Mitterrand: I*, p. 371.

24. As the French perceived in the American plans for a simultaneous with-drawal of Israeli and Syrian forces from Beirut, after the installation of a multinational peacekeeping force. The lack of provision for the Palestinians was pointed out to the US Secretary of State, Alexander Haig, by the French Foreign Minister, Claude Cheysson. Ibid., p. 371.

25. Mitterrand's changing attitude was demonstrated in a communiqué issued by the Palais de l'Élysée on 14 June. Ibid.

26. See Chapter 5.

27. P. Favier and M. Martin-Roland, *La Décennie Mitterrand: I*, pp. 369–84, *passim.*

28. Ibid., p. 411.

29. Ibid., p. 416.

30. J. Attali, *Verbatim, tome I: Chronique des Années 1981–1986* (Paris; Fayard, 1993), p. 487. Diary entry for 9 August 1983.

31. By the twin-track decision of December 1979 the NATO members under-took to deploy American Ground-Launched Cruise Missiles and Pershing II missiles, as a response to the perceived aggressive Soviet arms build-up of intermediate-range Backfire bombers and SS-20 missiles, from 1983. The second strand of the decision required attempts to negotiate the removal of the SS-20s with Moscow, thus rendering the potential NATO counter-measures unnecessary.

32. Speech given by President Mitterrand to the West German Bundestag on the occasion of the Twentieth Anniversary of the Franco-German Élysée Treaty of 1963, on 20 January 1983. F. Mitterrand, *Réflexions sur la Politique Extérieure de la France: Introduction à Vingt-Cinq Discours (1981–1985)* (Paris; Fayard, 1986), pp. 183–208, especially pp. 192–5.

33. Speech given by President Mitterrand at the Kremlin, during his first offi-cial visit to the Soviet Union since his election, on 21 June 1984. Ibid., pp. 161–70, especially p. 165.

34. The Americans had successfully intercepted a ballistic missile in 1984, and in 1985 a satellite was destroyed by a missile launched from an F-15 fighter bomber. Moreover additional progress had been made in the use of laser beams to destroy missiles.

35. As expressed, for example, by Hubert Védrine, Mitterrand's Diplomatic Adviser with responsibility for strategic affairs, during a radio interview on 30 January 1985. Unsigned, 'La crédibilité de la dissuasion nucléaire française n'est pas réduite par les armes spatiales à rayons, assure M. Védrine, le conseiller diplomatique de l'Elysée,' *Le Monde*, 1.2.85.

36. I. Legrand-Bodin, 'Hernu: Dissuasion d'abord, guerre des étoiles après,' *Le Matin*, 26–27.1.85.

37. J. George, 'De Bonn à Brest,' *L'Humanité*, 27.5.85.

38. B. Jasani, 'EUREKA – How Much of a European SDI?' in J. Holdren and J. Rotblat (eds), *Strategic Defences and the Future of the Arms Race: a Pugwash Symposium* (London; Macmillan, 1987) pp. 171–8.

39. Unsigned, 'M. Hernu crée un état-major de l'espace,' *Le Monde*, 5.6.85.

40. J. Isnard, 'Défense: l'obsession de l'espace,' *Le Monde*, 23.11.85.

41. Ibid.

42. J. Isnard, 'La défense spatiale ne rend pas caduque l'arme nucléaire,' *Le Monde*, 18.12.85.
43. F. Mitterrand, *Lettre à Tous les Français*, Paris, 8 April 1988.
44. F. Mitterrand, *Réflexions*, p. 19.
45. J. Isnard, 'M. Mitterrand, professeur de stratégie,' *Le Monde*, 11.2.86.
46. J. Attali, *Verbatim, Tome II: Chronique des Années 1986–1988* (Paris; Fayard, 1995), p. 11. Diary entry for 15 March 1986.
47. Before the diplomatic press on 22 May, Chirac had declared that France could not remain outside the 'inevitable, irreversible and justified grand movement' which was SDI. He further approved the US plan on both the military and technical levels. See B. Frederick, 'Orbite américaine,' *L'Humanité*, 23.5.86.
48. F. Muracciole, 'Général Mitterrand,' *Le Matin*, 28.5.86.
49. Ibid.; J. Guisnel, 'Mitterrand/Chirac: ping-pong dans les étoiles,' *Libération*, 28.5.86; and J. Isnard, 'M. Mitterrand réaffirme que la France ne doit pas s'insérer dans un dispositif de défense limitant sa liberté d'action,' *Le Monde*, 29.5.86.
50. J. Isnard, ibid.
51. The exchange was reported in J. Attali, *Verbatim II*, p. 29. Diary entry for 26 March 1986.
52. See J. Isnard, 'Cohabitation stratégique,' *Le Monde*, 11.4.86; and Unsigned, 'La France ne participera décidément pas à l'IDS,' *Tribune de l'Economie*, 4.7.86.
53. Unsigned, ibid.
54. Cited in J. Isnard, 'Cohabitation stratégique,' *Le Monde*, 11.4.86.
55. Ibid.; and I. Legrand-Bodin, 'Les rapports Mitterrand–Chirac à l'épreuve du missile SX,' *Le Matin*, 14.4.86.
56. I. Legrand-Bodin, ibid.
57. Unsigned, 'Défense: Chirac entend «pleinement exercer» son role,' *Le Quotidien de Paris*, 11.7.86.
58. Unsigned, 'M. Chirac se félicite «de l'accord profond qui rassemble les Français sur leur défense»,' *Le Monde*, 13.9.86.
59. J. Isnard, 'M. Mitterrand prend ses distances envers la politique de défense préconisée par MM. Chirac et Giraud,' *Le Monde*, 15.10.86.
60. Ph. M., 'Continuité et rupture,' *Le Quotidien de Paris*, 11.3.87.
61. Interview with J. Attali, 30.5.96.
62. J. Isnard, 'Cohabitation stratégique,' *Le Monde*, 11.4.86.
63. Unsigned, 'M. Chirac se félicite «de l'accord profond qui rassemble les Français sur leur défense»,' *Le Monde*, 13.9.86.
64. C. Page, 'Mitterrand welcomes German plan for joint defence force,' *The Guardian*, 22.6.87.
65. F. Mitterrand, *Lettre à Tous les Français*, pp. 8–10, particularly p. 10.
66. Commented upon in J.-P. Ravery, 'L'avocat du surarmement,' *L'Humanité*, 14.7.88.
67. J. Baumel, 'Ne pas toucher à la défense,' *Le Figaro*, 4.8.88.
68. P.-H. Desaubliaux, 'Défense: des choix s'imposent,' *Le Figaro*, 27.12.88.
69. Ibid.
70. Y. de l'Ecotais, 'Défense,' *L'Express*, 28.4–4.5.89, and J. Guisnel, 'Défense: des pertes sur le champ de bataille,' *Libération*, 18.5.89, being but two examples.

71. J. Guisnel, ibid.
72. Reported in P. Darcourt, 'Une politique de non-choix,' *Le Figaro*, 25.5.89.
73. Ibid. The pressures to which Chevènement had been subjected by these other branches of the government, supported by President Mitterrand, was further commented in J. Bothorel, 'Pacifisme feutré,' *Le Figaro*, 29.5.89.
74. P. Marcovici, 'Ne pas baisser la garde,' *Le Quotidien de Paris*, 19.5.89; P. Darcourt, 'Une politique de non-choix,' *Le Figaro*, 25.5.89; and J. Bothorel, ibid.
75. J.-M. Boucheron, Socialist president and *rapporteur* of the National Defence and Armed Forces Committee in the National Assembly, *J.O., A.N.*, 1st sitting, 3.10.89, p. 3024.
76. J.-P. Chevènement, ibid., pp. 3030–6.
77. See Chapter 7.
78. J. Schmitt, 'Mitterrand: la défense élastique,' *Le Point*, 23.7.90.
79. D. Chivot and A. Fouchet, '«Pas d'économies au détriment de la défense»,' *La Croix*, 1.7.89.
80. Ibid.
81. XXX (an anonymous group of senior officers), 'Avons-nous une politique de défense?' *La Croix*, 2.10.89.
82. S. Rak, 'Alain Lamassoure: «Suspendons ce plan caduc»,' *La Croix*, 3.9.90.
83. I. Legrand-Bodin, 'Vers un nouveau paysage stratégique,' *La Croix*, 11.2.88.
84. F. Mitterrand, 'Allocution de M. François Mitterrand, Président de la République, devant les auditeurs de l'Institut des Hautes Etudes de Défense Nationale, le 11 octobre 1988,' *Défense Nationale*, 44, 11 (November 1988) 13–27. See also J. Guisnel, 'Mitterrand bétonne sa ligne de défense européenne,' *Libération*, 12.10.88; P. Jacobson, 'France rejects dual role,' *The Times*, 12.10.88; and Unsigned, 'M. Mitterrand, chef des armées,' *Le Monde*, 13.10.88.
85. J. Fitchett, 'Mitterrand mutes objections to U.S. proposals on Europe,' *International Herald Tribune*, 19.12.89.
86. F. Mitterrand, cited in J.D., 'Chevènement monte au front,' *L'Express*, 13.7.90.
87. J.D., ibid.
88. J. Attali, *Verbatim, tome III: Chronique des Années 1988–1991* (Paris; Fayard, 1995), p. 558. Diary entry for 9 August 1990.
89. J. Pimlott and S. Badsey (eds), *The Gulf War Assessed* (London; Arms and Armour Press, 1992), p. 275.
90. J. Attali, *Verbatim III*, p. 568. Diary entry for 16 August 1990.
91. Ibid., p. 577. Diary entry for 28 August 1990.
92. Details were published in the satirical investigative weekly *Le Canard Enchaîné*. Reported in ibid., p. 574. Diary entry for 22 August 1990.
93. Statement given to Agence France-Presse on 21 August 1990.
94. Mitterrand's very public role during the crisis was extensively reported in newspaper coverage of his press conferences, speeches and televised pronouncements, many of which were reproduced in F. Mitterrand, *François Mitterrand et la Crise du Golfe (Discours et Messages: 9 août 1990–16 janvier 1991)* (Paris; T. Mage, 1991); and F. Mitterrand, *François Mitterrand et la Guerre du Golfe (Discours et Messages: 20 janvier–3 mars 1991)* (Paris; T. Mage, 1991).

95. J. Phillips, 'Jaguars join in attack on Kuwait,' *The Times*, 18.1.91.
96. J. Pimlott and S. Badsey, *The Gulf War Assessed*, p. 276.
97. C. Marchand, 'Un pas de plus,' *L'Humanité*, 25.1.91.
98. P. Lacoste, 'L'heure des choix,' *Le Figaro*, 23.5.91.
99. Mitterrand had specified when he called for the debate in March that nuclear deterrence would not be called into question, and that, rather, opinions were sought on the equipment and organisation of the conventional forces. P.-H. Desaubliaux, 'Défense: l'année des décisions,' *Le Figaro*, 5.3.91.
100. I. Legrand-Bodin, 'L'Assemblée remet la défense à plat,' *La Croix*, 6.6.91.
101. E. Marcuse, 'Armée: la soustraction des divisions,' *L'Express*, 1.8.91.
102. M. C., 'Une aubaine pour les budgets militaires,' *La Croix*, 23.8.91.
103. Unsigned, 'La défense encaisse mal les dividendes de la paix,' *Le Quotidien de Paris*, 24-25.8.91.
104. See below.
105. A. Chastagnol, '... dans un monde riche de dangers,' *Le Quotidien de Paris*, 15.11.91.
106. Y. Cuau, 'La rigueur et la démagogie,' *L'Express*, 23.4.92.
107. See Chapter 9.
108. A. Chastagnol, 'A la sauvette,' *Le Quotidien de Paris*, 24.7.91.
109. P. Boniface, 'Dissuasion d'abord,' *Libération*, 19.2.92.
110. J.-C. Rufin, 'Nos acquis militaires,' *Le Quotidien de Paris*, 15.2.93, and P.-H. Desaubliaux, 'Défense: la mort lente du consensus,' *Le Figaro*, 2.4.93.
111. See Chapter 7.
112. For the opinions of P. Séguin and E. Balladur, see I. Legrand-Bodin, 'La France s'interroge sur sa défense,' *La Croix*, 6.12.89; for those of F. Fillon see F. Fillon, 'Défense: réduire nos forces conventionnelles', *Le Figaro*, 21.2.90; for those of Balladur again, see E. Balladur, 'Pour une nouvelle politique de défense,' *Le Monde*, 6.3.91; and for those of P. Lellouche, see P. Lellouche, 'Défense française: ce qui doit changer,' *Le Figaro*, 12.4.91.
113. P.-H. Desaubliaux, 'Défense: la mort lente du consensus,' *Le Figaro*, 2.4.93.
114. The decision was to become effective in October 1991.
115. S. Rak, 'Léotard sur le théâtre des restructurations,' *Le Quotidien de Paris*, 28.5.93.
116. J. Nundy, 'Balladur under fire on troop cutbacks,' *The Independent*, 31.5.93.
117. The text of the White Paper can be found in France. Ministère de la Défense, *Livre Blanc sur la Défense, 1994* (Paris; Editions 10/18, 1994).
118. Unsigned, 'Un Livre blanc très cohabitationniste,' *Le Quotidien de Paris*, 24.2.94.
119. D. Buchan, 'France maps out military strategy into next century,' *Financial Times*, 24.2.94.
120. P.-H. Desaubliaux, 'Les grands choix de la défense,' *Le Figaro*, 8.12.93.
121. D. Garraud, 'Défense: un livre blanc sous contrôle de Mitterrand,' *Libération*, 16.2.94.
122. Ibid.
123. See J.-C. Rufin, 'Nos acquis militaires,' *Le Quotidien de Paris*, 15.2.93; P.-H. Desaubliaux, 'La mort lente du consensus,' *Le Figaro*, 2.4.93.
124. P.-H. Desaubliaux, ibid.

125. Unsigned, 'Léotard maintient: il faut reprendre les essais nucléaires,' *Le Quotidien de Paris*, 24.2.94.
126. D. Buchan, 'France maps out military strategy into next century,' *Financial Times*, 24.2.94.
127. F. Léotard, 'Un consensus actif,' *Le Figaro*, 4.3.94.
128. D. Garraud, 'Défense: les députés jugent le livre blanc trop flou,' *Libération*, 4.3.94.
129. P.-H. Desaubliaux, 'Les députés estiment acceptable le livre blanc,' *Le Figaro*, 4.3.94.
130. Ibid.
131. P. Boniface, 'Le rôle de la France dans l'OTAN,' *Vendredi*, 7.5.93.
132. Unsigned, 'La France multiplie les exercices d'état-major avec l'OTAN et l'UEO,' *Le Monde*, 19.11.94.

4   Defence Planning in the First Term

1. P. Mauroy, 'La cohérence d'une politique de défense: allocution du Premier Ministre, le 14 septembre 1981, lors de la séance d'ouverture de la 34e session de l'IHEDN,' *Défense Nationale*, 37, 10 (October 1981) 15–28, pp. 27–8.
2. P. Favier and M. Michel-Roland, *La Décennie Mitterrand: I*, p. 465.
3. J.-Y. Lhomeau, 'M. Mitterrand annonce la mise en chantier d'un septième sous-marin nucléaire,' *Le Monde*, 26.7.81.
4. Unsigned, 'Priorité à la force de frappe,' *La Croix*, 17.11.81; and P. Favier and M. Michel-Roland, *La Décennie Mitterrand: I*, pp. 467–8.
5. J.-Y. Lhomeau, 'M. Mitterrand annonce la mise en chantier d'un septième sous-marin nucléaire,' *Le Monde*, 26.7.81.
6. Televised interview. J.-Y. Lhomeau, 'Un homme aux mains libres,' *Le Monde*, 18.11.83.
7. Speech to the West German Bundestag, 20 January 1983. F. Mitterrand, *Réflexions*, pp. 184–208, p. 195. See also Speech to NATO Foreign Ministers, meeting in Paris for the first time since 1966, 9.6.83. *Réflexions*, pp. 209–15.
8. J. Lacaze, 'Politique de défense et stratégie militaire de la France: Exposé du chef d'état-major des armées devant l'Institut des Hautes Études de Défense Nationale, le 3 mai 1983,' *Défense Nationale*, 39, 6 (June 1983) 11–29, p. 11.
9. P. Mauroy, 'Vers un nouveau modèle d'armée ...,' p. 20.
10. Y. Pitette, 'L'austérité pousse à privilégier la seule dissuasion nucléaire,' *La Croix*, 4.11.82.
11. J.-L. Mathieu, *La Défense Nationale*, Collection Que Sais-Je? no. 2028 (Paris; Presses Universitaires de France, 1996), p. 18.
12. Ibid.
13. Hernu had decided as early as June 1981 to allow an extra year for completion of the previous planning law, for 1976–82, because of the extent of delays and shortcomings which had been accumulated in its execution. P. Krop, 'Une nouvelle politique de défense pour la France,' *Le Matin*, 9.6.81.
14. J.-Y. Le Drian, *rapporteur spécial de la commission des finances, de l'économie générale et du Plan, pour la défense, J.O., A.N.*, 2nd sitting, 13.11.81, p. 3642.

15. C. Hernu, *J.O., A.N.*, 3rd sitting, 13.11.81, p. 3660.
16. See, for example, J.-Y. Le Drian, *J.O., A.N.*, 2nd sitting, 13.11.81, p. 3643; and J. Huyghues des Etages, *rapporteur pour avis de la commission de la défense nationale et des forces armées, pour la politique de défense de la France, J.O., A.N.*, 2nd sitting, 13.11.81, p. 3646.
17. C. Hernu, ibid., p. 3661.
18. J.-Y. Le Drian, ibid., p. 3643.
19. L. Bouvard, *rapporteur pour avis de la commission de la défense nationale et des forces armées, pour la section air*, ibid., p. 3651.
20. P. Dabezies, *rapporteur pour avis de la commission de la défense nationale et des forces armées, pour la section marine*, ibid., p. 3650.
21. J.-Y. Le Drian, ibid., p. 3643.
22. P. Mauger, *rapporteur pour avis de la commission de la défense nationale et des forces armées, pour la section commune et pour le budget annexe des essences*, ibid., p. 3648.
23. R. Aumont, *rapporteur pour avis de la commission de la défense nationale et des forces armées, pour la section Gendarmerie*, ibid., p. 3652.
24. J.-Y. Le Drian, ibid., p. 3643.
25. J.-M. Daillet, *J.O., A.N.*, 3rd sitting, 13.11.81, p. 3672.
26. F. Fillon, 'Pour une session extraordinaire,' *Le Monde*, 17.11.81.
27. Y. Lancien, *J.O.,.A.N.*, 3rd sitting, 13.11.81, p. 3670.
28. R. Galley, *J.O., A.N.*, 1st sitting, 14.11.81.
29. J.-M. Daillet, *J.O., A.N.*, 3rd sitting, 13.11.81, p. 3672.
30. F. Fillon, ibid., p. 3675.
31. The Giscardian *Union pour la Démocratie Française.*
32. M. Bigeard, *J.O., A.N.*, 3rd sitting, 13.11.81, p. 3668.
33. P. Mestre, *J.O., A.N.*, 3rd sitting, 12.11.82, p. 7110. *Autorisations de programme* are the upper limit of expenditure which a Minister is authorised to commit for the implementation of programmes extending over several years. *Crédits de paiement* are the upper limit of expenditure which can be made in the year under consideration.
34. A promise made by Pierre Mauroy, which had been delivered to the Assemblée Nationale, by Charles Hernu, during the debate over the defence budget for 1982. C. Hernu, *J.O., A.N.*, 3rd sitting. 13.11.81, p. 3660.
35. Y. Pitette, 'L'austérité pousse à privilégier la seule dissuasion nucléaire,' *La Croix*, 4.11.82.
36. J.-Y. Le Drian, *J.O., A.N.*, 2nd sitting, 12.11.82, p. 7083.
37. Y. Pitette, 'L'austérité pousse à privilégier la seule dissuasion nucléaire,' *La Croix*, 4.11.82.
38. J. Combasteil, *rapporteur pour avis de la commission de la défense nationale et des forces armées, pour la section forces terrestres, J.O., A.N.*, 2nd sitting, 12.11.82, p. 7089.
39. L. Bouvard, ibid., p. 7092.
40. Ibid.
41. J. Gourmelon, *rapporteur pour avis de la commission de la défense nationale et des forces armées, pour la section marine, J.O., A.N.*, 2nd sitting, 12.11.82, pp. 7090–1.
42. R. Aumont, ibid., p. 7093.

43. J.-Y. Le Drian, ibid., p. 7083.
44. J.-M. Daillet, *J.O., A.N.*, 3rd sitting, 12.11.82, p. 7099.
45. M. Bigeard, ibid., p. 7104.
46. Ibid. The theme of stagnation was also taken up by J.-M. Daillet.
47. C. Hernu, ibid., p. 7114.
48. L. Darinot, *président de la commission de la défense nationale et des forces armées, J.O., A.N.*, 2nd sitting, 12.11.82, p. 7094.
49. J.-M. Daillet, *J.O., A.N.*, 3rd sitting, 12.11.82, p. 7100.
50. P. Mauroy, 'La cohérence d'une politique de défense ...,' p. 16.
51. Y. Lancien for F. Harcourt, *J.O., A.N.*, 1st sitting, 14.11.81, p. 3688.
52. Unsigned, 'Un nouveau modèle d'armée de terre,' *Le Monde*, 30.11.82.
53. F. Fillon, *J.O., A.N.*, 3rd sitting, 12.11.82, p. 7107; and Y. Pitette, 'L'austérité pousse à privilégier la seule dissuasion nucléaire,' *La Croix*, 4.11.82.
54. M. Nilès, *J.O., A.N.*, 3rd sitting, 12.11.82, p. 7101.
55. J.-M. Daillet, ibid., p. 7100.
56. C. Hernu, *J.O., A.N.*, 1st sitting, 19.5.83, p. 1217.
57. Some accounts state a financial provision of 705 billion francs at 1983 levels. The more impressive figure of 830 billion francs took account of calculations of expected inflation.
58. An increase of 11 per cent in real terms over the period, according to I. Davidson, 'France rejoins its allies,' *Financial Times*, 3.5.83.
59. For an English-language summary of the military planning law's provisions, see Lt-Col G. Cox, MBE, 'France's Five Year Plan: the Defence Programme 1984–1988,' *The Army Quarterly and Defence Journal*, 114, 1 (January 1984) 22–31.
60. C. Hernu, *J.O., A.N.*, 1st sitting, 19.5.83, p. 1219.
61. Ibid.
62. Ibid., pp. 1218–20.
63. L. Tinseau, *rapporteur de la commission de la défense nationale et des forces armées*, ibid., p. 1226.
64. J.-Y. Le Drian, *J.O., A.N.*, 1st sitting, 19.5.83, p. 1230.
65. G. Istace, *J.O., A.N.*, 2nd sitting, 19.5.83, p. 1267.
66. A. Bellon, ibid.
67. C. Hernu, *J.O., A.N.*, 1st sitting, 19.5.83, p. 1217.
68. Y. Lancien, ibid., p. 1240.
69. L. Bouvard, *J.O., A.N.*, 2nd sitting, 19.5.83, p. 1269.
70. V. Lecasble, '830 milliards sur cinq ans: la poire coupée en deux,' *Les Echos*, 21.4.83.
71. See, for example, E. Daillet, *J.O., A.N.*, 1st sitting, 19.5.83, p. 1232; and F. Léotard, *J.O., A.N.*, 2nd sitting, 19.5.83, p. 1249.
72. L. Bouvard, *J.O., A.N.*, 2nd sitting, 19.5.83, p. 1268.
73. F. Léotard, ibid., p. 1249.
74. F. Fillon, ibid., p. 1253.
75. F. Léotard, ibid., p. 1249.
76. Y. Lancien, *J.O., A.N.*, 1st sitting, 19.5.83, p. 1241.
77. F. Léotard, *J.O., A.N.*, 2nd sitting, 19.5.83, p. 1248.
78. L. Richard, ibid., p. 1263.
79. F. Léotard, ibid., p. 1249.

80. F. Fillon, ibid., p. 1253.
81. J. Baumel. ibid., p. 1261.
82. F. Fillon, ibid., p. 1254.
83. Unsigned, 'Le message du chef de l'État au Parlement,' *Le Monde*, 10.4.86.
84. Ibid.
85. P. H. Gordon argues that Chirac's conduct in this respect was at least in part attributable to his desire ultimately to occupy the post of President of the Republic, and exercise the full powers which went with that office. Hence he was unwilling to dilute Mitterrand's powers excessively by instigating protracted disagreements and promoting fully the role of the Prime Minister in the delineation of defence. However, while he may well have stopped short of major, fundamental divergences with the President, this did not prevent him from asserting his authority whenever possible and practicable: 'rather than an all-out battle for power, then, *cohabitation* became a sort of nonlethal duel ...'. P. H. Gordon, *A Certain Idea of France*, p. 145.
86. I. Legrand-Bodin, 'Chirac: moi aussi, je suis responsable de la défense,' *Le Matin*, 11.7.86.
87. Unsigned, 'Défense: Chirac entend «pleinement exercer» son rôle,' *Le Quotidien de Paris*, 11.7.86. Italics added.
88. I. Legrand-Bodin, 'Chirac: moi aussi, je suis responsable de la défense,' *Le Matin*, 11.7.86.
89. Unsigned, 'Défense: Chirac entend «pleinement exercer» son rôle,' *Le Quotidien de Paris*, 11.7.86.
90. J. Chirac, 'La politique de défense de la France ...,' pp. 7–17; and Unsigned, 'M. Chirac se félicite de «l'accord profond qui rassemble les Français sur leur défense»,' *Le Monde*, 13.9.86.
91. J. Isnard, 'M. Mitterrand réaffirme que la France ne doit pas s'insérer dans un dispositif de défense limitant sa liberté d'action,' *Le Monde*, 29.5.86.
92. J. Isnard, 'M. Mitterrand prend ses distances envers la politique de défense préconisée par MM. Chirac et Giraud,' *Le Monde*, 15.10.86.
93. J. Alia and G. Buis, 'Défense: la bataille a commencé,' *Le Nouvel Observateur*, 31.10.86.
94. Ibid.
95. F. Puaux, 'Une doctrine contestable,' *Le Figaro*, 6–7.12.86.
96. H. Karleskind, 'Faute de dogme ...,' *Le Quotidien de Paris*, 6.11.86; and D. Gerbaud, 'Défense: Mitterrand dissuade Chirac,' *La Croix*, 7.11.86.
97. P. Favier and M. Martin-Roland, *La Décennie Mitterrand, tome II: Les Epreuves (1984–1988)* (Paris; Seuil, 1991), p. 783.
98. See ibid., pp. 782–9, for a detailed, if largely undocumented, account of the extent of divergence between the President and government during 1986 on precisely this issue.
99. Unsigned, 'Le projet de loi de programmation, 1987–1991,' *Le Monde*, 7.11.86.
100. J. Chirac, *J.O., A.N.*, 1st sitting, 8.4.87, p. 89.
101. F. Fillon, *président et rapporteur de la commission de la défense nationale et des forces armées*, ibid., p. 92.
102. A. Giraud, *J.O., A.N.*, 2nd sitting, 8.4.87, p. 103.
103. Ibid., pp. 103–4.
104. Ibid.

105. A. Billardon, *vice-président de l'Assemblée nationale, J.O., A.N.*, 2nd sitting, 9.4.87, p. 186.
106. F. Fillon, *J.O., A.N.*, 1st sitting, 8.4.87, p. 95.
107. Y. Guéna, *rapporteur pour avis de la commission des finances, de l'économie générale et du Plan*, ibid., p. 98.
108. M. Rocard, *J.O., A.N.*, 1st sitting, 9.4.87, p. 126.
109. M. Peyrat, *J.O., A.N.*, 2nd sitting, 8.4.87, p. 107.
110. Ibid.
111. J. Peyrat, *J.O., A.N.*, 1st sitting, 9.4.87, p. 128.
112. M. Peyrat, *J.O., A.N.*, 2nd sitting, 8.4.87, p. 107.
113. G. Marchais, *J.O., A.N.*, 1st sitting, 9.4.87, p. 131.
114. Ibid., p. 133.
115. E. Avice, *J.O., A.N.*, 1st sitting, 9.4.87, p. 141.
116. J.-M. Boucheron, ibid., p. 137.
117. F. Fillon, *J.O., A.N.*, 1st sitting, 8.4.87, p. 90.
118. P. Quilès, *J.O., A.N.*, 2nd sitting, 8.4.87, p. 112. See also P. H. Gordon, *A Certain Idea of France*, p. 147.
119. P. Favier and M. Michel-Roland, *La Décennie Mitterrand: II*, p. 789.
120. J. Chirac, *J.O., A.N.*, 1st sitting, 8.4.87, p. 88.
121. Ibid.
122. A. Giraud, *J.O., A.N.*, 2nd sitting, 8.4.87, p. 105.
123. L. Bouvard, *J.O., A.N.*, 1st sitting, 9.4.87, p. 140. For the majority, consensus was specifically asserted also by F. Fillon, P. Pascallon, Y. Briant, J. Baumel and M. Bigeard.
124. P. Quilès, *J.O., A.N.*, 2nd sitting, 8.4.87, pp. 110–11.
125. Ibid., pp. 112–13.
126. J.-P. Chevènement, *J.O., A.N.*, 2nd sitting, 8.4.87, p. 116.
127. M. Rocard, *J.O., A.N.*, 1st sitting, 9.4.87, p. 126.
128. G. Marchais, ibid., p. 133.
129. C. Hernu, *J.O., A.N.*, 3rd sitting, 12.11.82, p. 7114.
130. J. Baumel, *J.O., A.N.*, 2nd sitting, 19.5.83, p. 1261.

5 Military Intervention in Lebanon and Chad

1. D. MacShane, *François Mitterrand*, p. 259.
2. Mitterrand served as Minister for Overseas Territories in the Pleven administration from July 1950 to February 1951. See P. M. Williams, *Crisis and Compromise: Politics in the Fourth Republic* (London; Longmans, 1964) Appendix III: The Ministers; and A. Cole, *François Mitterrand*, p. 6. Mitterrand was also very briefly *Ministre d'état* with responsibility for Algeria and North Africa in the E. Faure administration from January to February 1952.
3. Mitterrand had voiced concerns in Parliament regarding the motivation for involvement in Chad as early as April 1970. He reiterated his concerns over African policy in the Assemblée Nationale in May and June 1978, and in October 1979. See F. Mitterrand, *J.O., A.N.*, 24.4.70, p. 1290; F. Mitterrand, *J.O., A.N.*, 1st sitting, 18.5.78, p. 1814; F. Mitterrand, *J.O., A.N.*, 1st sitting, 8.6.78, pp. 2676, 2679; and G. Bèche, *vice-président, J.O., A.N.*, 2nd sitting, 10.10.79, p. 8061.

4. H. Cobban, *The Making of Modern Lebanon* (London; Hutchinson, 1987) pp. 181–2, and W. Haddad, *Lebanon: the Politics of Revolving Doors* (New York; Praeger, 1985), p. 76.

5. H. Cobban, ibid., p. 185.

6. W. Haddad, *Lebanon*, p. 79.

7. H. Cobban, *The Making of Modern Lebanon*, p. 188.

8. The attack on the French barracks occurred simultaneously with a similar bomb attack on the American barracks in Beirut, which killed 242 Marines.

9. Unsigned, 'La détermination de M. Mitterrand,' *Le Monde*, 26.10.83; and J. Attali, *Verbatim I*, pp. 526–9. Diary entries for 23 and 24 October 1983.

10. See J. J. Leblond, 'Liban: raid punitif français,' *Le Figaro*, 18.11.83; R. Fisk, 'French jets hit Shia stronghold,' *The Times*, 18.11.83; and J. Flint and P. Webster, '39 die in French raid on Beka'a extremists,' *The Guardian*, 18.11.83.

11. Unsigned, 'Liban: nos troupes sur le départ,' *Le Figaro*, 24–25.3.84; and Unsigned, 'Le contingent français quittera Beyrouth avant le 31 mars,' *Le Monde*, 25–26.3.84.

12. F. Ch., 'La France décide de retirer ses observateurs à Beyrouth,' *Le Monde*, 2.4.86.

13. F. Mitterrand, *Réflexions*, pp. 110–11.

14. H. Védrine, *Les Mondes de François Mitterrand* (Paris; Fayard, 1996), p. 306.

15. Unsigned, 'M. Mitterrand réaffirme la volonté de la France «d'être présente au Liban»,' *Le Monde*, 27.5.82.

16. J. Attali, *Verbatim I*, p. 263. Diary entry for 25 June 1982.

17. Ibid., p. 275. Diary entry for 8 July 1982.

18. P. Favier and M. Martin-Roland, *La Décennie Mitterrand: I*, p. 375. See also T. Carothers, 'Mitterrand and the Middle East,' *The World Today*, 38, x (1982) 381–6, p. 386.

19. J. Attali, *Verbatim I*, p. 276. Diary entry for 10 July 1982.

20. P. Favier and M. Martin-Roland, *La Décennnie Mitterrand: I*, pp. 379–81.

21. In this sense, there was an element in the Franco-Egyptian Plan of bridge-building between the Lebanese situation and the wider Arab–Israeli conflict. While this had important effects in the emphasis of a Lebanese side to the crisis, in its own right, by France, it had the added benefit of allowing Mitterrand some middle ground in the diplomatic quagmire he was entering with his positions on Israel and the Arab nations, particularly the PLO. On the Franco-Egyptian Plan, see J. Marcus, 'French Policy and the Middle East Conflicts: Change and Continuity,' *The World Today*, 42, ii (1986) 27–30, p. 28.

22. P. Beylau, 'La gêne de Mitterrand,' *Le Quotidien de Paris*, 9.6.82.

23. R. Hanna, 'L'honneur de la France,' *Le Monde*, 22.6.82.

24. P. Beylau, 'Mitterrand s'enlise dans les affaires du Levant,' *Le Quotidien de Paris*, 23.6.82.

25. H. Tincq, 'La France devait-elle partir?' *La Croix*, 23.9.82.

26. 'François Mitterrand on Margaret Thatcher: "I admire her ... or is it envy?"' J. Attali, *Verbatim I*, p. 201. Diary entry for 5 April 1982.

27. R. Fisk, 'French bomb Druze and Syrian artillery positions,' *The Times*, 23.9.83.

28. Ibid.

29. M. Delarue, 'La riposte française au Liban,' *Le Monde*, 24.9.83.
30. F. Delattre, 'Le Général Bigeard au *Quotidien*: «Ce qui m'inquiète, c'est demain»,' *Le Quotidien de Paris*, 24–25.9.83.
31. M. Delarue, 'La riposte française au Liban,' *Le Monde*, 24.9.83.
32. P. Tesson, 'Marchais pilonne Mitterrand,' *Le Quotidien de Paris*, 24–25.9.83.
33. L. Guilbert, 'Troupes françaises hors du Liban,' *Lutte Ouvrière*, 24.9.83. This view was shared by the Revolutionary Communist League (Trotskyist). See M. Delarue, 'La riposte française au Liban,' *Le Monde*, 24.9.83.
34. J. Attali, *Verbatim I*, pp. 526–7. Diary entries for 23 October 1983 and 24 October 1983.
35. D. Geddes, 'French parties close ranks despite doubts,' *The Times*, 25.10.83.
36. Unsigned, 'La détermination de M. Mitterrand,' *Le Monde*, 26.10.83.
37. Unsigned, 'Les réactions en France,' *Le Monde*, 26.10.83.
38. Ibid.
39. Ibid.
40. Ibid.
41. J. Vincour, 'French public swings behind Lebanon policy,' *International Herald Tribune*, 1.11.83.
42. Unsigned, 'La détermination de M. Mitterrand,' *Le Monde*, 26.10.83.
43. Unsigned, 'Dans la presse parisienne: une initiative incontestée,' *Le Monde*, 26.10.83.
44. Favilla, 'Savoir ce que l'on veut,' *Les Echos*, 25.10.83.
45. Unsigned, 'Les Super-Etendards frappent à Baalbek,' *Le Matin*, 18.11.83; and D. Geddes, 'Reprisal in Lebanon delights the French,' *The Times*, 19.11.83.
46. J.-J. Leblond, 'Liban: raid punitif français,' *Le Figaro*, 18.11.83. Statement by the Ministry of Defence.
47. D. Geddes, 'Reprisal in Lebanon delights the French,' *The Times*, 19.11.83.
48. J.-J. Leblond, 'Liban: raid punitif français,' *Le Figaro*, 18.11.83.
49. P. Tesson, 'Baalbek la faute,' *Le Quotidien de Paris*, 19–20.11.83.
50. J.-J. Leblond, 'Liban: critiques autour du raid français,' *Le Figaro*, 19–20.11.83.
51. D. Buffin, 'La gauche dans l'embarras,' *Le Matin*, 19–20.11.83.
52. A. Passeron, 'L'opposition durcit sa condamnation de la politique extérieure de M. Mitterrand,' *Le Monde*, 24.11.83.
53. M. Couve de Murville, 'Quelle idée de la France?' *Le Figaro*, 26–27.11.83.
54. R. Fisk, 'French jets hit Shia stronghold,' *The Times*, 18.11.83; and J. Flint and P. Webster, '39 die in French raid on Beka'a extremists,' *The Guardian*, 18.11.83.
55. R. Fisk, 'French reprisal raid leaves militia targets unscathed,' *The Times*, 21.11.83. See also Unsigned, 'Les Super-Etendards ont été «efficaces»,' *Le Matin*, 19–20.11.83; P.-J. F., 'Bouche cousue et cible fantôme,' *Le Monde*, 20–21.11.83; and Unsigned, 'Le doute subsiste sur le raid de Baalbek,' *Le Figaro*, 21.11.83.
56. P. S., 'Baalbek: questions sur un raid,' *Libération*, 21.11.83.
57. J. Garçon, 'Les paras français à Beyrouth: à petits pas vers le retrait,' *Libération*, 26.12.83; and Unsigned, 'Redéploiement du contingent français,' *L'Humanité*, 26.12.83.
58. P. Marcovici, 'La France doit-elle quitter le Liban?' *Le Quotidien de Paris*, 27.12.83.

59. Unsigned, 'Beyrouth: poursuite du redéploiement français,' *Le Figaro*, 28.12.83; and J. Vincour, 'France to shift some of Beirut force to South,' *International Herald Tribune*, 31.12.83; and H. de Kergolay, 'La France retirera 482 soldats de Beyrouth,' *Le Figaro*, 3.1.84.

60. Unsigned, 'Mitterrand wants French unit replaced,' *International Herald Tribune*, 8.2.84; P. Marcovici, 'Contrairement à ce qu'affirme maintenant le gouvernement, la décision d'en appeler à l'ONU pour relever la force multinationale n'a pas été prise de longue date,' *Le Quotidien de Paris*, 9.2.84; and W. Schwarz, 'French prepare to quit Beirut,' *The Guardian*, 2.3.84.

61. P. Servent, '80 diplomates en casque blanc,' *La Croix*, 21.7.84.

62. D. Lagarde, 'Beyrouth: deux observateurs français tués dans une embuscade,' *Le Quotidien de Paris*, 15.1.85.

63. Eight French citizens had been kidnapped, and were still being held, by the beginning of *cohabitation*. M. Dobbs, 'French military presence in Lebanon is reduced after increase in attacks,' *International Herald Tribune*, 2.4.86.

64. F. Ch., 'La France décide de retirer ses observateurs à Beyrouth,' *Le Monde*, 2.4.86.

65. M. Dobbs, 'French military presence in Lebanon is reduced after increase in attacks,' *International Herald Tribune*, 2.4.86.

66. F. Ch., 'La France décide de retirer ses observateurs à Beyrouth,' *Le Monde*, 2.4.86.

67. On the continued troop commitments in Lebanon and Chad, see France. Ministère de la Défense, *1997–2002: Projet de Loi de Programmation Militaire* (Paris; Ministère de la Défense/Service d'Information et de Relations Publiques des Armées, 1996).

68. For the history of Chadian instability since decolonization (1960), and of French interventions therein, see K. Somerville, *Foreign Military Intervention in Africa*, (London; Pinter, 1990); J. C. Hollick, 'Civil War in Chad: 1978–1982,' *The World Today*, 38, vii–viii (1982) 297–304; and J. Gibour, 'Le Conflit du Tchad,' *Défense Nationale*, 41, 6 (June 1985) 127–38. For an account of French intervention in Africa more widely, see J. Chipman, 'French Military Policy and African Security,' *Adelphi Papers*, 201, Summer 1985 (London; International Institute for Strategic Studies, 1985).

69. F. Mitterrand, *Réflexions*, pp. 121–2.

70. The regard in which François Mitterrand was held was indicated by the fact that the Franco-African summit of 1981, held in Paris, was attended by more heads of government than ever before. The summit for 1982, in Kinshasa, was still better attended. See C. Wauthier, 'France and Africa: Socialists Blaze a New Trail,' in C. Legum (ed.), *Africa Contemporary Record: Annual Survey and Documents, 1981-1982*, Vol. XIV (New York; Africana, 1981) A236–A245, p. A236; and C. Wauthier, 'France's Year in Africa: a Policy of Continuity Rather than of Change,' in C. Legum (ed.), *Africa Contemporary Record: Annual Survey and Documents, 1982–1983*, Vol. XV (New York; Africana, 1984) A104–A112, p. A106.

71. F. Mitterrand, *Réflexions*, p. 119.

72. Ibid., pp. 120–1.

73. Ibid., pp. 122–3.

74. J. C. Hollick, 'Civil War in Chad,' p. 303.

236 *Notes*

75. M.D., 'Le gouvernement fera tout pour que le Tchad puisse se relever et retrouver son unité politique,' *Le Monde*, 17.9.81.
76. Unsigned, 'Une mission de techniciens français à N'Djamena,' *Le Monde*, 6.8.81.
77. R. Backmann, 'Tchad: le plan français,' *Le Nouvel Observateur*, 3.10.81.
78. E. Cody, 'France is reported sending arms to Chad in bid to get Libyans out,' *International Herald Tribune*, 27.10.81.
79. P. Webster and A. Brummer, 'France ready to fly Africans to Chad,' *The Guardian*, 24.10.81.
80. N. Waites, 'France under Mitterrand: External Relations,' *The World Today*, 38, vi (1982) 224–31, p. 231.
81. J. C. Hollick, 'Civil War in Chad,' p. 303.
82. J. Attali, *Verbatim I*, p. 247. Diary entry for 7 June 1982.
83. Unsigned, 'Tchad: que peut la France?' *Le Matin*, 8.6.82.
84. Ibid.
85. J. Attali, *Verbatim I*, p. 473. Diary entry for 24 June 1983.
86. Ibid., p. 473. Diary entry for 28 June 1983.
87. Unsigned, '«La France respectera sans limites ses engagements» déclare M. Mitterrand,' *Le Monde*, 29.6.83.
88. J. Garçon, 'La France livre 200 tonnes d'armes au Tchad,' *Libération*, 30.6.83; and F. Hauter, 'La France s'engage au Tchad,' *Le Figaro*, 1.7.83.
89. Unsigned, '«La France n'a aucune raison d'aller au-delà des accords de coopération de 1976» déclare M. Mitterrand,' *Le Monde*, 16.7.83.
90. Unsigned, 'Hernu bars immediate intervention by French forces in Chad's conflict,' *International Herald Tribune*, 8.8.83.
91. P. Lewis, 'France is reported to send 500-man contingent to Chad,' *International Herald Tribune*, 11.8.83.
92. L. Plommer, 'First French casualty killed by mine explosion in Chad,' *The Times*, 20.8.83.
93. J. Chipman, 'French Military Policy and African Security,' p. 18.
94. Favilla, 'Fidélité,' *Les Echos*, 13.7.83.
95. Unsigned, 'M. Chirac: je m'associe parfaitement à la politique du gouvernement,' *Le Monde*, 12.7.83.
96. J. Ficatier, 'Le silence d'Hernu,' *La Croix*, 16.9.83.
97. J. François-Poncet, 'Quatre Ans de Politique Etrangère Socialiste: le Mirage Evanoui,' *Politique Etrangère*, 50, 2 (Summer 1985) 437–47, p. 442.
98. Elce et Hesse, 'La France et la crise du Tchad d'août 1983: un rendez-vous manquée avec l'Afrique,' *Politique Etrangère*, 50, 2 (Summer 1985) 411–18, p. 414.
99. Interview with Pierre Gallois. J. Ficatier, 'Tchad: une dissuasion manquée,' *La Croix*, 15.9.83.
100. Ibid.
101. P. Beylau, 'Le choix de Mitterrand,' *Le Quotidien de Paris*, 4.7.83.
102. P. Webster, 'Chad policy divides French leaders,' *The Guardian*, 2.7.83.
103. P. Lewis, 'France is reported to send 500-man contingent to Chad,' *International Herald Tribune*, 11.8.83.
104. Unsigned, 'Sur la pointe des pieds,' *La Croix*, 11.8.83.
105. C. Picquet, 'Tchad: l'intervention honteuse de Mitterrand,' *Rouge*, 14.7.83.
106. C. Picquet, 'Rappel immédiat des paras français!' *Rouge*, 26.8.83.

107. See F. Mitterrand, *Réflexions*, pp. 123–4; and H. Védrine, *Les Mondes de François Mitterrand*, p. 345.
108. A. Louyot, 'La France en premier ligne', *Le Point*, 30.1.84.
109. Unsigned, 'French pilot is killed in new Chad fighting,' *International Herald Tribune*, 26.1.84. There was some dispute as to the exact nature of the Jaguar's mission, with air operations staff suggesting that it was carrying out a reprisal attack for the raid on Ziguey. It was further suggested that the government would not acknowledge this mission after the fiasco of Baalbek. See C. d'Epenoux, 'Tchad: le poker de Kadhafi,' *L'Express*, 9.2.84.
110. A. Louyot, 'La France en premier ligne', *Le Point*, 30.1.84.
111. Unsigned, 'Le débat en France. M. Kosciuszko-Morizet (RPR): l'immobilisme n'est pas une politique,' *Le Monde*, 28.1.84.
112. C. d'Epenoux, 'Tchad: le poker de Kadhafi,' *L'Express*, 9.2.84.
113. Unsigned, 'Le ministre de la défense fait état d'un accident lors d'un déminage,' *Le Monde*, 10.4.84.
114. D. Buffin, 'Tchad: le temps travaille pour l'opposition,' *Le Matin*, 12.4.84.
115. A. Griotteray, 'Restons au Tchad, mais sachons pourquoi,' *Figaro Magazine*, 5.5.84.
116. R. Sicile, 'Troupes françaises hors du Tchad,' *Lutte Ouvrière*, 18.8.84.
117. Unsigned, 'M. Lionel Jospin: «un succès marquant de la politique française»,' *Le Monde*, 18.9.84.
118. J.-Y. L., 'De gauche à droite aucune réserve,' *Le Monde*, 19.9.84.
119. Ibid.
120. Unsigned, 'L'épineux retrait du Tchad,' *Le Monde*, 26.9.84.
121. L. Zecchini, 'Les troupes françaises marquent une pause dans leur retrait,' *Le Monde*, 6.10.84.
122. E. Weisenfeld, 'François Mitterrand: l'action extérieure,' *Politique Etrangère*, 51, 1 (Spring 1986) 131–41, p. 139.
123. Elce et Hesse, 'La France et la crise du Tchad ...,' p. 418.
124. M. Dobbs, 'France to step up arms delivery to Chad,' *International Herald Tribune*, 14.2.86.
125. R. Bernstein, 'France puts troops in Central Africa on alert after rebel attacks in Chad,' *International Herald Tribune*, 15.2.86.
126. Unsigned, 'La France renforce son dispositif militaire au Tchad,' *Le Quotidien de Paris*, 17.2.86.
127. Ibid.
128. M. Dobbs, 'French planes bomb Chad airfield built by Libya to support rebels,' *International Herald Tribune*, 17.2.86.
129. P. Favier and M. Martin-Roland, *La Décennie Mitterrand: II*, pp. 603–10.
130. D. Geddes, 'France bombs Libyan base in Chad as US flies in help,' *The Times*, 8.1.87.
131. F. Hauter, 'Paris: plusieurs options pour aider Hissène Habré,' *Le Figaro*, 17.12.86.
132. J. Burnet, 'La France prend ses distances,' *Le Figaro*, 11.8.87.
133. Ibid.
134. J. Isnard, 'La «légion» des appelés volontaires dans deux unités françaises,' *Le Monde*, 22–23.8.82.
135. Ibid.
136. J. Chipman, 'French Military Policy and African Security,' p. 17.

137. G. Vincent, 'Liban et Tchad,' *Défense Nationale*, 39, 11 (November 1983) 165–7, p.165.
138. J. Isnard, 'L'armée française sur deux fronts,' *Le Monde*, 10.9.83.
139. G. Vincent, 'Liban et Tchad,' p. 166.
140. D. Buffin, 'Tchad: le temps travaille pour l'opposition,' *Le Matin*, 12.4.84.
141. Interview with Pierre Gallois. J. Ficatier, 'Tchad. Une dissuasion manquée,' *La Croix*, 15.9.83.
142. F. Delattre, 'Le général Bigeard au *Quotidien*: «ce qui m'inquiète, c'est demain»,' *Le Quotidien de Paris*, 24–25.9.83.

6 The Security Challenge of the 1980s

1. See Chapter 3.
2. The widely used term in France for the intermediate-range nuclear forces of both superpowers (SS-20s, Backfire bombers, Pershing II and Cruise missiles in particular), so-called because of the designated target area.
3. "The Euromissiles Crisis", from D. Moïsi, 'La France et la Crise des Euromissiles,' *Défense Nationale*, 39, 8/9 (August/September 1983) 37–46.
4. François Mitterrand in an interview with M. Tatu of *Le Monde*, published on 31.7.80. Reproduced in F. Mitterrand, *Ici et Maintenant*, pp. 226–38, p. 234.
5. The neutron bomb was an enhanced radiation weapon which was specifically designed to 'produce minimum blast effects and maximum prompt radiation', thus allowing its use in a battlefield context to prevent an enemy advance by killing its personnel, without causing excessive collateral damage, and facilitating the earlier return of defensive forces or populations to the affected area. J. Baylis, K. Booth, J. Garnett and P. Williams, *Contemporary Strategy, vol. I: Theories and Concepts*, 2nd edn (New York, Holmes and Meier, 1987), pp. 93–4.
6. Mitterrand alleged he had held this principle since 1980. See Unsigned, '«Je ne peux pas signer la disparition de la France en dehors de son pré-carré»,' *Le Monde*, 18.11.83.
7. Reiterated in J. Reston, 'How Mitterrand views himself and the world,' *The Times*, 5.6.81.
8. Unsigned, 'L'entretien télévisé du Président de la République,' *Le Monde*, 11.12.81.
9. M. Duverger, 'Le discours de l'Ubersee Club,' *Le Monde*, 18.5.82. See also Unsigned, '«Je ne peux pas signer la disparition de la France en dehors de son pré-carré»,' *Le Monde*, 18.11.83, which cited Mitterrand's appeal to the superpowers: 'Negotiate weapons down to the lowest level possible for your security, but maintain your equilibrium, for if there is no longer a balance between one and the other, then war is at our door.'
10. F. Mitterrand, *Réflexions*, pp. 216–35, pp. 218–19. See also Unsigned, '«Il faut affecter au développement des moyens importants qui seraient dégagés par une réduction progressive mais méthodique des dépenses militaires»', *Le Monde*, 30.9.83.
11. Unsigned, 'M. Mitterrand: «J'attends de tous les Français qu'ils mobilisent leurs facultés d'énergie, d'initiative et d'entreprise»', *Le Monde*, 2.1.82.
12. J. Attali, *Verbatim I*, pp. 384–6. Diary entries for 19 and 20 January 1983;

and H. Védrine, *Les Mondes de François Mitterrand*, p. 235. See also P. Favier and M. Martin-Roland, *La Décennie Mitterrand: I*, pp. 318–19.
13. F. Mitterrand, *Réflexions*, pp. 183–208, p. 193.
14. P. H. Nitze, with A. M. Smith and S. L. Rearden, *From Hiroshima to Glasnost: at the Centre of Decision* (London; Weidenfeld and Nicolson, 1990) p. 376.
15. Unsigned, 'Mitterrand: mes nouveaux objectifs,' *Le Matin*, 10.6.82.
16. A. Roulat, 'Euromissiles: M. Mitterrand réaffirme sa position,' *Le Monde*, 15.7.83.
17. P. Lellouche, 'Moscou: un pavé dans l'Otan,' *Le Point*, 20.12.82. Under Andropov's proposals the USSR would have 450 nuclear warheads targeted at Europe thereafter, as each of the SS-20s could carry three warheads, in addition to another 100 SS-20s stationed in Asia. Given the range and mobility of these missiles, they too would potentially be capable of reaching targets in Europe.
18. Unsigned, 'François Mitterrand: «Redonner de l'oxygène à notre économie»,' *Le Figaro*, 3.1.83.
19. F. Mitterrand, *Réflexions*, pp. 216–35, p. 221.
20. D. David and G.-P. Halleman, 'Les Partis Politiques Français et les Euromissiles,' *Défense Nationale*, 37, 2 (February 1981) 67–84.
21. P. Mauroy, 'La Stratégie de la France: Allocution du Premier Ministre, le 20 septembre 1983, lors de la séance d'ouverture de la 36e session de l'IHEDN,' *Défense Nationale*, 39, 11 (November 1983) 5–22, p. 11. This view was shared outside the political framework; see J. Soppelsa, 'Euromissiles et Surarmement pour une Grande Négotiation,' *Défense Nationale*, 39, 7 (July 1983) 43–54, p. 44.
22. Y. Moreau, 'Le surarmement et la France,' *L'Humanité*, 5.10.83.
23. F. Mitterrand, *Réflexions*, pp. 216 35, p. 221. However, according to *Le Monde*, Mitterrand's figures were questionable: the figure of 98 French warheads was derived from the 18 missiles sited on the Plateau d'Albion, and from the fact that each of France's five nuclear submarines could carry 20 warheads, and assuming that at least one would always be out of service, that meant 80 warheads were potentially available at any one time. Mitterrand's figures did not account for France's airborne nuclear strike force, nor the tactical missile forces. However, *Le Monde* argued, neither had Mitterrand included the superpowers' tallies of air-launched missiles and tactical forces in his figure of 8000 to 9000 warheads in the armouries of Washington and Moscow.
24. J. Soppelsa, 'Euromissiles et Surarmement …,' p. 45.
25. P.-M. de la Gorce, 'L'année des missiles,' *Le Figaro*, 12.1.83.
26. P. Lellouche, 'Moscou: un pavé dans l'Otan,' *Le Point*, 20.12.82.
27. A. Duhamel, 'Le triptyque de François Mitterrand,' *Le Quotidien de Paris*, 28.1.83.
28. P.-M. de la Gorce, 'L'année des missiles,' *Le Figaro*, 12.1.83.
29. Before the opening of the first INF negotiations in November 1983, Reagan had proposed the formula of no deployment of superpower intermediate-range forces in Europe – the zero option. Mitterrand was perplexed that some elements of the press should have made this interpretation, as he had not specifically mentioned the zero option in his speech. See J. Attali, *Verbatim I*, p. 387. Diary entry for 21 January 1983.

30. C. Picquet, 'L'alignement de Mitterrand,' *Rouge*, 10–16.6.83.
31. Excerpts from President Reagan's Speech to the Nation, 23 March 1983, reprinted in *Survival*, xxv, 3 (May/June 1983) 129–30, p. 130.
32. Unsigned, 'M. Mitterrand: le projet Eurêka est en bonne voie,' *Le Monde*, 2–3.6.85.
33. L. Fabius, 'La Politique de Défense: Rassembler et Moderniser. Allocution du Premier Ministre, le 17 septembre 1984, lors de la séance d'ouverture de la 37e session de l'IHEDN,' *Défense Nationale*, 40, 11 (November 1984) 7–17, p. 11.
34. Speech by the Defence Minister Charles Hernu in Munich, 9 February 1985. Cited in J. Vernant, 'Comparaison n'est pas Raison,' *Défense Nationale*, 41, 4 (April 1985) 9–14, p. 13.
35. Ibid., p. 12.
36. G.-E. Touchard, 'Candide et l'Initiative de Défense Stratégique,' *Défense Nationale*, 42, 1 (January 1986) 25–38, p. 33.
37. P. Quilès, 'L'avenir de Notre Concept de Défense face aux Progrès Technologiques: Allocution de Monsieur Paul Quilès, Ministre de la Défense, devant les auditeurs de l'Institut des Hautes Etudes de Défense Nationale, le 12 novembre 1985,' *Défense Nationale*, 42, 1 (January 1986) 11–24, p. 16.
38. L. Fabius, 'La Politique de Défense ...,' p. 11.
39. M. B. Froman, A. L. Gardener, S. R. Mixer and A. Poensgen, 'Strategic Implications of SDI for France and West Germany,' *Journal of the Royal United Services Institute for Defence Studies*, 132, 2 (June 1987) 51–6, p. 52.
40. P. Forget, 'Eléments pour une Analyse Politico-Stratégique de l'IDS,' *Défense Nationale*, 42, 3 (March 1986) 21–34.
41. R. Solé, 'M. Reagan relance les recherches pour une nouvelle défense antimissiles,' *Le Monde*, 25.3.83.
42. G.-E. Touchard, 'Candide et l'Initiative de Défense Stratégique,' p. 26.
43. L. Fabius, 'Patriotisme, Indépendance, Solidarité: Allocution du Premier Ministre, le 13 septembre 1985, lors de la séance d'ouverture de la 38e session de l'IHEDN,' *Défense Nationale*, 41, 11 (November 1985) 9–18, p. 13.
44. C. Hernu, 'Equilibre, Dissuasion, Volonté: la Voie Etroite de la Paix et de la Liberté. Discours de M. Charles Hernu, Ministre de la Défense, devant les auditeurs de la 36e session de l'Institut des Hautes Etudes de Défense Nationale, le 15 novembre 1983,' *Défense Nationale*, 39, 12 (December 1983) 5–20, p. 5.
45. P. Mauroy, 'La Stratégie de la France ...,' p. 20.
46. P. Quilès, 'L'avenir de Notre Concept de Défense ...,' p. 16.
47. P.-I. de Saint-Germain, 'L'Initiative de Défense Stratégique: Quel Défi pour la France?' *Défense Nationale*, 42, 6 (June 1986) 123–30, p. 124.
48. In 1984 a ballistic missile had been intercepted, and in 1985 a satellite was destroyed by a missile launched from an F-15 aircraft. Progress had also been made in the use of laser beams to destroy missiles in flight.
49. J. Isnard, '«La dissuasion nucléaire a encore de longues années devant elle» affirme M. Mitterrand,' *Le Monde*, 28.5.85.
50. Unsigned, 'M. Mitterrand: le projet Eurêka est en bonne voie,' *Le Monde*, 2–3.6.85.

51. While limitations were thus placed on the nature of French association with SDI, and with French firms' participation in research, it was nevertheless undesirable that French industries should be excluded entirely from SDI involvement, and lower-key participation by French research and armaments concerns was permitted.

52. J. Isnard, 'M. Mitterrand entend affirmer les intérêts stratégiques de la France,' *Le Monde*, 12.9.85.

53. B. Pellegrin, 'Le troisième coup de théâtre du chef de l'Etat,' *Le Matin*, 11.9.83.

54. J. Lacaze, 'L'avenir de la Défense Française: Conférence du chef d'Etat-major des Armées à l'Institut des Hautes Etudes de Défense Nationale, le 11 mai 1985,' *Défense Nationale*, 41, 7 (July 1985) 15–33, p. 33.

55. See Chapter 3.

56. L. Fabius, 'La Politique de Défense ...,' p. 9.

57. F. Mitterrand, *Réflexions*, p. 7.

58. See speech to the European Parliament at Strasbourg, 24 May 1984. F. Mitterrand, *Réflexions*, pp. 280–97, p. 281. See also F. Mitterrand, *Ici et Maintenant*, p. 236; and F. Mitterrand, *Réflexions*, pp. 67–8.

59. Mitterrand had been concerned that the European Defence Community would be vulnerable to loss of control by the politicians, and to an associated dependence on control by the military. This was unacceptable; developments during his presidency indicated the extent to which political control over military matters was one of his principles.

60. On these points, see A. Cole, *François Mitterrand*, p. 117.

61. F. Mitterrand, *Réflexions*, p. 101.

62. See, for example, Unsigned, 'M. Léotard se déclare satisfait,' *Le Monde*, 22.1.83; and Unsigned, 'Michel Pinton, secrétaire-général d'UDF,' *Le Monde*, 22.1.83.

63. A. Passeron, 'M. Chirac: le scrutin des 6 et 13 mars doit retenir comme un avertissement solennel au gouvernement,' *Le Monde*, 25.1.83.

64. Unsigned, 'M. Marchais approuve le discours de M. Mitterrand à Bonn,' *Le Monde*, 25.1.83.

65. EUREKA was to have primarily civilian objectives, allowing Western Europe to proceed in high-technology areas, although the French Foreign Minister R. Dumas admitted that it could have 'military implications'. Cited in B. Jasani, 'EUREKA – How Much of a European SDI?' in J. Holdren and J. Rotblat (eds), *Strategic Defences and the Future of the Arms Race: a Pugwash Symposium* (London; Macmillan, 1987), pp. 171–8, p. 171.

66. During a visit to the Centre Européen des Recherches Nucléaires, in Geneva. J.-F. A., 'M. Mitterrand invite l'Europe à ne pas manquer la «troisième révolution industrielle»,' *Le Monde*, 15.9.83.

67. F. Mitterrand, *Réflexions*, pp. 267–79, pp. 274–7. Speech delivered at The Hague, 7 February 1984.

68. UDF, *Redresser la Défense de la France* (Paris; UDF, 1985). Cited in J. Howorth, 'Of Budgets and Strategic Choices: Defence Policy under François Mitterrand,' in G. Ross, S. Hoffmann and S. Malzacher (eds), *The Mitterrand Experiment*, p. 316.

69. RPR, *La Défense de la France: Quatre Ans de Gestion Socialiste. Propositions pour le Renouveau* (Paris; RPR, 1985). Cited in ibid., pp. 315–16.

70. Y. Pitette, 'L'austérité pousse à privilégier la seule dissuasion nucléaire,' *La Croix*, 4.11.82.
71. J. Chirac, 'La Politique de Défense de la France ...,' p. 11.
72. J. Chirac, 'La France et les Enjeux de la Sécurité Européenne: Allocution du Premier Ministre, le 12 décembre 1987, devant les auditeurs de l'Institut des Hautes Etudes de Défense Nationale,' *Défense Nationale*, 44, 2 (February 1988) 9–18, p. 16.
73. Ibid., p. 14.
74. A. Giraud, 'La Défense de la France et la Sécurité Européenne: Discours de Monsieur André Giraud, Ministre de la Défense Français, à Chatham House, le 22 mars 1988,' *Défense Nationale*, 44, 5 (May 1988) 11–19, p. 16.
75. A. Giraud, 'Donner à la France une Défense Forte: Discours de Monsieur André Giraud, Ministre de la Défense, à l'Assemblée Nationale, le 12 novembre 1986, à l'occasion de la présentation du budget de la défense pour 1987,' *Défense Nationale*, 43, 1 (January 1987) 11–25, p. 21.
76. J. Chirac, 'La France et les Enjeux de la Sécurité Européenne ...,' p. 15.
77. C. Lambroschini, 'Gorbatchev dévoile son plan de désarmement,' *Le Figaro*, 4.10.85.
78. J. Attali, *Verbatim I*, pp. 857–63. Diary entries for 2, 3 and 4 October 1985.
79. Unsigned, 'M. Mitterrand accueille avec prudence les propositions de M. Gorbatchev,' *Le Monde*, 5.10.85.
80. C. Bourdet, 'Gorbatchev: le doigt sur la détente,' *Témoignage Chrétien*, 14–20.10.85.
81. N. Darbroz, 'Mitterrand garde l'équilibre,' *La Croix*, 5.10.85.
82. C. Lambroschini, 'Gorbatchev dévoile son plan de désarmement,' *Le Figaro*, 4.10.85
83. N. Darbroz, 'Mitterrand garde l'équilibre,' *La Croix*, 5.10.85.
84. P. H. Nitze, with A. M. Smith and S. L. Rearden, *From Hiroshima to Glasnost*, p. 423.
85. J. Attali, *Verbatim I*, p. 914. Diary entry for 15 January 1986.
86. P. Lellouche, 'Pourquoi Gorbatchev embarrasse Paris,' *Le Point*, 27.1.86.
87. P. Lellouche, 'Missiles: le piège qui menace l'Europe,' *Le Point*, 3.3.86.
88. P. Favier and M. Martin-Roland, *La Décennie Mitterrand: II*, p. 800.
89. Ibid., p. 799.
90. Ibid., p. 800.
91. J. Attali, *Verbatim II*, p. 177. Diary entry for 15 October 1986.
92. P. Favier and M. Martin-Roland, *La Décennie Mitterrand: II*, p. 800.
93. Address by Mr. Chirac, Prime Minister of France, 2 December 1986. Assembly of Western European Union, *Proceedings: Thirty-Second Ordinary Session*, Second Part, December 1986, Section IV: Minutes; Official Reports of Debates, pp. 109–12, p. 110.
94. W. Schütze, 'Documents: Les Prises de Position des Hommes Politiques Français sur les Négociations Relatives à l'Elimination des Armes Nucléaires de Portée Intermédiaire en Europe,' *Politique Etrangère*, 52, 2 (Summer 1987) 461–73, p. 462.
95. J. Attali, *Verbatim II*, p. 270. Diary entry for 4 March 1987. These remarks went officially unconfirmed, but were widely commented upon.
96. P. Favier and M. Martin-Roland, *La Décennie Mitterrand: II*, p. 803.

97. W. Schütze, 'Documents: Les Prises de Position des Hommes Politiques Français …,' p. 465.
98. Before the United Nations' General Assembly, Mitterrand had given these as a significant reduction in superpower arsenals, so that they were comparable with that of France; reductions in conventional and chemical weapons capabilities; and a halt to the development of missile defence systems. However, these proposals were somewhat fluid, and by the time of his address to the *Conseil des ministres* simultaneous disarmament by the superpowers had been added, as had reductions in (unspecified) short-range weapons, and control and verification of arms reductions.
99. J. Attali, *Verbatim II*, p. 271. Diary entry for 4 March 1987.
100. M. Thatcher, *The Downing Street Years*, pp. 471–2.
101. J. Attali, *Verbatim II*, p. 272. Diary entry for 4 March 1987.
102. P. Favier and M. Martin-Roland, *La Décennie Mitterrand: II*, p. 803.
103. Ibid., p. 805.
104. P. Lellouche, 'La France et l'Option Zéro: Réflexions sur la Position Française,' *Politique Etrangère*, 52, 1 (Spring 1987) 161–6, p. 162.
105. Ibid.
106. Unsigned, 'M. Mitterrand justifie les négociations sur les euromissiles et réaffirme que «les armes de la France ne sont pas en cause»,' *Le Monde*, 12.3.87.
107. Televised interview, 19.3.87. W. Schütze, 'Documents: Les Prises de Position des Hommes Politiques Français …,' p. 467.
108. J.-M. Benoist, 'A Quoi Bon cet Accord Reagan-Gorbatchev?' *Défense Nationale*, 43, 12 (December 1987) 51–5, p. 51.
109. Général (CPN) M. Forget, 'L'Europe, le Piège et le Sursaut,' *Défense Nationale*, 43, 6 (June 1987) 32–44, p. 43.
110. B. Guillerez, 'Le Gambit des Euromissiles,' *Défense Nationale*, 44, 2 (February 1988) 155–60, p. 158.
111. J.-M. Benoist, 'A Quoi Bon cet Accord Reagan–Gorbatchev?' p. 53.
112. Ibid.
113. D. Moïsi, 'L'Europe entre les Inconséquences de Reagan et les Sourires de Gorbatchev,' *Défense Nationale*, 43, 5 (May 1987) 7–17, p. 15.
114. Colonel H. Paris, 'La France, Ennemi Principal de l'URSS en Europe?' *Défense Nationale*, 44, 1 (January 1988) 51–64; and P. Boniface, 'Le Traité de Washington: Victoire dans les Faits, Défaite dans les Textes?' *Défense Nationale*, 44, 5 (May 1988) 31–9.
115. D. Colard, 'Les Sommets et le Dialogue Stratégique Soviéto-Américain,' *Défense Nationale*, 43, 5 (May 1987) 53–67, p. 65.
116. Vice-amiral J. Chabaud (CR), 'L'Europe de la Défense est-elle Née à Reykjavik?' *Défense Nationale*, 43, 12 (December 1987) 35–50, p. 50.
117. G. Vincent, 'Faut-il Avoir Peur de la Négociation sur les Euromissiles?' *Défense Nationale*, 43, 5 (May 1987) 180–2, p. 182.
118. Le groupe Renouveau Défense, 'Le Défi du Double Zéro,' *Défense Nationale*, 44, 2 (February 1988) 19–37, p. 26.
119. D. Colard, 'Les Sommets et le Dialogue Stratégique …,' p. 66; Général (CPN) M. Forget, 'L'Europe, le Piège et le Sursaut,' p. 44; and Vice-amiral J. Chabaud (CR), 'L'Europe de la Défense est-elle Née à Reykjavik?' p. 50.

7   The End of the Cold War: a Crisis for French Military Planning?

1. F. Bujon de l'Estang, cited in J. Laughland, *The Death of Politics: France under Mitterrand* (London; Michael Joseph, 1994), p. 229.
2. This was a situation of some longevity. See Unsigned, 'French Socialist rebuked,' *New York Times*, 4.9.72; and H. Smith, 'Moscow rebukes critics in France,' *New York Times*, 24.9.72. For an account of relations between Mitterrand and the Soviet Union immediately prior to, and after, his election to the presidency, see F. Mitterrand, *De l'Allemagne, de la France* (Paris; Editions Odile Jacob, 1996), pp. 163–7.
3. The early divergences between Mitterrand and Moscow centred on the former's criticisms of the latter's interventions in Czechoslovakia in 1968. Subsequently, the Socialist leader's criticisms of the meeting between Giscard d'Estaing and Brezhnev in Warsaw in May 1980, after the Soviet invasion and occupation of Afghanistan, indicated firmness in his stance over the USSR: a firmness which was reiterated in No. 1 of Mitterrand's *110 Propositions for France* in 1981 – 'Demand the withdrawal of Soviet troops from Afghanistan'; MacShane, *François Mitterrand*, p. 259. Further criticisms on Mitterrand's part, in relation to the human rights situation in the USSR, were liberally scattered throughout the 1960s and 1970s.
4. For example, F. Mitterrand, *Un Socialisme du Possible* (Paris; Seuil, 1970) p. 23; F. Mitterrand, *Ici et Maintenant*, p. 241; and F. Mitterrand, *Réflexions*, p. 12.
5. For example, his Presidential election campaign of 1965 (see Chapter 1); F. Mitterrand, *Ma Part de Vérité*, p. 197; and F. Mitterrand, *Ici et Maintenant*, p. 241.
6. F. Mitterrand, *De l'Allemagne, de la France*, p. 13.
7. Mitterrand's view of his discussions with Gorbachev alleged no uncertainty over reunification. See F. Mitterrand, *De l'Allemagne, de la France*, pp. 87–96. For a rather different perspective on Mitterrand's apparently considerable concerns, and the contradictions between their public and private expression, which she regarded as 'a tendency to schizophrenia', see M. Thatcher, *The Downing Street Years*, pp. 796–8, p. 797.
8. D. David, 'The Search for a New Security Strategy in a Shifting International Arena,' in T. Chafer and B. Jenkins (eds), *France: from the Cold War to the New World Order* (London; Macmillan, 1996), pp. 65–75, p. 71. Italics in original.
9. Michel Rocard led the first Socialist government of François Mitterrand's second *septennat*; he was replaced by Edith Cresson in May 1991; she in turn was replaced, in April 1992, by Pierre Bérégovoy.
10. J.-C. Casanova, 'Mitterrand stratège,' *L'Express*, 15.4.88; and P. Krop, 'Défense: ce que veut Mitterrand,' *L'Evénement du Jeudi*, 21.4.88.
11. F. Hollande, *rapporteur spécial de la commission des finances, de l'économie générale et du Plan, pour la défense, J.O., A.N.*, 1st sitting, 2.11.88, p. 1581. For a summary of the budget provisions, see also M. Faivre, 'Le Budget de la Défense pour 1989,' *Défense Nationale*, 45, 1 (January 1990) 168-74.
12. P.-H. Desaubliaux, 'Défense: des choix s'imposent,' *Le Figaro*, 27.12.88.
13. A. Paecht, *J.O., A.N.*, 2nd sitting, 2.11.88, p. 1611.

14. F. B., 'Défense: le ministre repart à l'attaque,' *Le Quotidien de Paris*, 28.4.89.
15. J.-F. Augereau, 'Stratégie, stratégies,' *Le Monde*, 14–15.5.89.
16. J. Guisnel, 'Défense: des pertes sur le champ de bataille,' *Libération*, 18.5.89; and J. Amalric, 'M. Mitterrand souhaite sauvegarder tout le programme de défense,' *Le Monde*, 19.5.89.
17. Air-to-surface medium-range missile.
18. J.-P. Chevènement, *J.O., A.N.*, 1st sitting, 3.10.89, p. 3034; and F. Hollande, *J.O., A.N.*, 1st sitting, 3.10.89, p. 3028. For a summary of the law's main provisions, see M. Faivre, 'La Programmation 1990–1993 des Equipements Militaires,' *Défense Nationale*, 45, 12 (December 1989) 169–73.
19. J.-P. Chevènement, *J.O., A.N.*, 1st sitting, 3.10.89, p. 3032.
20. J.-M. Boucheron, *président et rapporteur de la commission de la défense nationale et des forces armées*, ibid., p. 3024.
21. F. Hollande, ibid., p. 3028.
22. G. Hage, *vice-président de l'Assemblée Nationale*, ibid., p. 3042.
23. J. Lorgeoux, *rapporteur pour avis de la commission des affaires étrangères*, ibid., p. 3030.
24. See Chapter 1.
25. J. Boyon, *J.O., A.N.*, 2nd sitting, 3.10.89, p. 3054.
26. F. Fillon, *J.O., A.N.*, 1st sitting, 3.10.89, p. 3037. According to Fillon, by late 1989 France's economic growth was running at 3.5 per cent instead of the 2.8 per cent anticipated.
27. J. Boyon, *J.O., A.N.*, 2nd sitting, 3.10.89, p. 3056.
28. L. Bouvard, ibid., p. 3058.
29. R. Galley, *J.O., A.N.*, 1st sitting, 9.10.89, p. 3309, in the debate over the vote of no confidence.
30. A. Berthol, *J.O., A.N.*, 2nd sitting, 3.10.89, p. 3062.
31. L. Pierna, ibid., p. 3063.
32. J.-C. Gayssot, ibid., p. 3057.
33. L. Pierna, ibid., p. 3063.
34. J. D., 'Chevènement monte au front,' *L'Express*, 13.7.90.
35. J. Schmitt, 'Mitterrand: la défense élastique,' *Le Point*, 23.7.90.
36. F. Hollande, *J.O., A.N.*, 2nd sitting, 7.11.90, p. 4890. For a summary of the budget provisions, see M. Faivre, 'Le Budget Militaire à l'Assemblée Nationale,' *Défense Nationale*, 47, 1 (January 1991) 171–5.
37. J. Briane, *J.O., A.N.*, 2nd sitting, 7.11.90, p. 4898.
38. J.-M. Boucheron, *J.O., A.N.*, 3rd sitting, 7.11.90, p. 4911.
39. L. Pierna, ibid., p. 4915.
40. M. Faivre, 'Le Budget Militaire à l'Assemblée Nationale,' p. 171.
41. For a summary of budget provisions, see M. Faivre, 'Du Bilan Social au Budget et à la Programmation,' *Défense Nationale*, 48, 1 (January 1992) 170–6.
42. M. Faivre, 'Du Budget de 1993 au «Référentiel» de 1997,' *Défense Nationale*, 49, 1 (January 1993) 166–70, p. 166.
43. For an assessment of the provisions of the planning law for 1992-97 as they were known, see M. Faivre, 'Les Equipements Militaires de 1997,' *Défense Nationale*, 49, 2 (February 1993) 172–8.
44. For a summary of budgetary provision, see M. Faivre, 'Du Budget de 1993 au «Référentiel» de 1997.'

45. J. Hoagland, 'Why France's defense minister still feeds with the lions,' *International Herald Tribune*, 12.7.90.
46. As in Mitterrand's reactions; see above. See also Chevènement's analysis of the international changes in the debate over the *loi de programmation militaire* for 1990–93. J.-P. Chevènement, *J.O., A.N.*, 1st sitting, 3.10.89, pp. 3030–6; and P. Darcourt and F.-O. Giesbert, 'Un entretien avec Jean-Pierre Chevènement: «L'intérêt de la France commande la vigilance»,' *Le Figaro*, 30.5.90.
47. P. Mauroy, December 1989, cited in I. Legrand-Bodin, 'Les crédits militaires en question,' *La Croix*, 23.2.90; L. Fabius, cited in P. Lellouche, 'Défense française: ce qui doit changer,' *Le Figaro*, 12.3.91; and M. Debré, 'Priorité à la défense,' *Le Figaro*, 25.3.91.
48. Unsigned, 'La défense encaisse mal les dividendes de la paix,' *Le Quotidien de Paris*, 24–25.8.91.
49. M. Faivre, 'Le Plan «Armées 2000»,' *Défense Nationale*, 45, 10 (October 1989) 177–9. The plan had previously been leaked to *Le Monde*, however, and its main themes had been known since 21.4.89.
50. Interview with Chevènement about *Armées 2000*. D. Chivot and A. Fouchet, '«Pas d'économies au détriment de la défense»,' *La Croix*, 1.7.89.
51. Ibid. According to Chevènement, there were over 1000 separate units and commands within the Army alone, which he said was 'not rational'. For an account of the almost breathtaking complexity of command and operational relations between units, districts and regions prior to the proposed reforms, see J.-F. Lazerges, 'Armées 2000,' *Défense Nationale*, 47, 5 (May 1991) 25–40.
52. For the Army and Air Force; two for the Navy.
53. For a summary of the plan's principal aims and measures, see M. Faivre, 'Le Plan «Armées 2000»,' pp. 177–9.
54. Although a compromise was reached with the residents of Barcelonnette, Chevènement had insisted in July that the interests of national defence superseded all other concerns. See M. Rocard, 'Les Orientations de la Politique de Défense de la France: Discours de Monsieur Michel Rocard, Premier Ministre, le 7 septembre 1989, devant les auditeurs de l'Institut des Hautes Etudes de Défense Nationale,' *Défense Nationale*, 45, 11 (November 1989) 13–29, p. 26; and D. Chivot and A. Fouchet, '«Pas d'économies au détriment de la défense»,' *La Croix*, 1.7.89.
55. Organisation rationelle d'une infrastucture opérationnelle nouvelle. See F. Fillon, *rapporteur pour avis de la commission de la défense nationale et des forces armées, pour la section des forces terrestres, J.O., A.N.*, 1st sitting, 2.11.88, p. 1587.
56. XXX (anonymous group of senior officers), 'Avons-nous une politique de défense?' *Le Figaro*, 2.10.89.
57. F. Fillon, *J.O., A.N.*, 2nd sitting, 6.11.89, p. 4600.
58. I. L.-B., 'La nouvelle Europe secoue la défense française,' *La Croix*, 13.7.90. On the significance of these points for *Armées 2000*, see S. R., 'Bataille autour d'un plan,' *Le Quotidien de Paris*, 3.9.90.
59. Unsigned, 'France announces cuts in armed forces and scraps missile plan,' *The Times*, 24.7.91.
60. Unsigned, 'M. Joxe annonce une centaine de mesures de dissolution ou de

regroupement d'unités militaires,' *Le Monde*, 17.4.92.

61. C. Makarian, 'La révolution Joxe,' *Le Point*, 13.6.92.
62. P. Joxe, 'Défense et Renseignement: Discours de Monsieur Pierre Joxe, Ministre de la Défense, le 6 mai 1991, devant les auditeurs de l'Institut des Hautes Etudes de Défense Nationale,' *Défense Nationale*, 47, 7 (July 1991) 9–21.
63. C. Makarian, 'La révolution Joxe,' *Le Point*, 13.6.92.
64. See M. Faivre, 'Les Restructurations en 1993,' *Défense Nationale*, 48, 6 (June 1992) 178–80; and A. Lavère, 'La Gestion des Restructurations dans l'Armée de Terre,' *Défense Nationale*, 48, 6 (June 1992) 181–3.
65. J.-P. D., '8,000 militaires de carrière et 4,750 civils sont concernés par les restructurations dans l'armée,' *Le Monde*, 18.4.92.
66. Y. Cuau, 'La rigueur et la démagogie,' *L'Express*, 23.4.92.
67. J.-F. S., 'Adieu l'armée,' *Le Monde*, 19–20.4.92.
68. J.-P. D., '8,000 militaires de carrière et 4,750 civils sont concernés par les restructurations dans l'armée,' *Le Monde*, 18.4.92.
69. Ibid.
70. Unsigned, 'Cherbourg plaide sa cause à Matignon,' *Le Monde*, 27.4.92.
71. J.-P. D., '8,000 militaires de carrière et 4,750 civils sont concernés par les restructurations dans l'armée,' *Le Monde*, 18.4.92; and Unsigned, 'Manifestations contre la restructuration des armées,' *Le Monde*, 25.4.92.
72. Unsigned, 'Le gouvernement ne reviendra pas sur le remodelage de l'armée française,' *Le Monde*, 24.4.92.
73. See J. Rivière, 'Les Restructurations dans l'Armée de Terre en 1994,' *Défense Nationale*, 49, 7 (July 1993) 190–3. See also S. Rak, 'Léotard sur le théâtre de restructurations,' *Le Quotidien de Paris*, 28.5.93.
74. J. I., 'Le RPR critique le plan de restructuration militaire,' *Le Monde*, 30–31.5.93. On the other hand, the Socialist mayor of Laval, A. Pinçon, was delighted by the arrival of an Army communications training facility.
75. J. Nundy, 'Balladur under fire on troop cutbacks,' *The Independent*, 31.5.93; and G. Chatain, 'Les élus du Limousin contre le plan de restructuration militaire,' *Le Monde*, 1.6.93.
76. E. Zemmour, 'Pons réclame l'arbitrage de Matignon,' *Le Quotidien de Paris*, 1.6.93.
77. Unsigned, 'Le PR au secours de M. Léotard,' *Le Monde*, 1.6.93.
78. E. Zemmour, 'Pons réclame l'arbitrage de Matignon,' *Le Quotidien de Paris*, 1.6.93.
79. J. I., 'Le RPR critique le plan de restructuration militaire,' *Le Monde*, 30–31.5.93.
80. D. Bernard, 'Jean-Michel Boucheron: «C'est la réduction des crédits militaires qui est dangereuse»,' *Le Quotidien de Paris*, 28.5.93.
81. J. I., 'Le RPR critique le plan de restructuration militaire,' *Le Monde*, 30–31.5.93.
82. For a regular analysis of the limitations of conscription, see M. Faivre, 'Service Militaire, Effectifs et Programmation,' *Défense Nationale*, 45, 5 (May 1989) 171–4; 'Les Formes Non-Militaires du Service National,' *Défense Nationale*, 45, 6 (June 1989) 182–4; 'Les Formes Non-Militaires du Service National (suite),' *Défense Nationale*, 45, 7 (July 1989) 171–6; 'Diversification et Modernisation du Service National,' *Défense Nationale*, 46, 1

(January 1990) 181–5; 'Les Chiffres Actuels et Futurs du Service National,' *Défense Nationale*, 46, 11 (November 1990) 182–3; 'Les Chiffres du Service National,' *Défense Nationale*, 46, 12 (December 1990) 176–81; 'Le Colloque «Conscription et Armée de Métier»,' *Défense Nationale*, 47, 4 (April 1991) 178–81; 'Diversification du Service et Précisions Statistiques,' *Défense Nationale*, 47, 12 (December 1991) 178–82; and 'Le Service National en Question,' *Défense Nationale*, 49, 6 (June 1993) 172–5.

83. M. Faivre, 'Les Formes Non-Militaires du Service National,' p. 183.
84. M. Faivre, 'Diversification et Modernisation du Service National,' pp. 181–2.
85. Unsigned, 'M. Chevènement: le service militaire doit être modernisé et diversifié,' *Le Monde*, 23.5.89.
86. A report by the Socialist deputy G.-M. Chauveau was commissioned in October 1988, which was presented to the Minister in June 1989, and made public at a press conference of 12 October 1989. Unsigned, 'Un rapport parlementaire dénonce les «planqués» du service national,' *Le Monde*, 13.10.89.
87. M. Faivre, 'Service Militaire, Effectifs et Programmation,' p. 172.
88. Ibid.
89. The substance of Mitterrand's announcement had been contested by Chevènement less than a week earlier. Unsigned, 'M. Chevènement évalue à 35,000 hommes la baisse des effectifs militaires avant 1995,' *Le Monde*, 13.7.90.
90. J. Isnard, 'Dix mois de service en 1992,' *Le Monde*, 17.7.90; and Unsigned, 'M. Mitterrand: «Pour l'instant, le problème posé n'est pas de réduire le budget militaire»,' *Le Monde*, 17.7.90.
91. Unsigned, 'L'ironie des Verts et le scepticisme de M. Chirac,' *Le Monde*, 17.7.90.
92. Ibid.
93. J. Isnard, 'Dix mois de service en 1992,' *Le Monde*, 17.7.90.
94. P. Joxe, *J.O., A.N.*, 1st sitting, 2.10.91, p. 4036.
95. F. Hollande, ibid., p. 4060.
96. D. Colin, ibid., p. 4062.
97. M. Voisin, ibid., p. 4063.
98. Ibid., p. 4064.
99. F. Fillon, *J.O., A.N.*, 1st sitting, 2.10.91, p. 4047.
100. Ibid.
101. J.-L. Saux, 'Le RPR se prononce pour l'abandon de la conscription sans consulter ses partenaires de l'opposition,' *Le Monde*, 4.10.91.
102. Unsigned, 'La professionalisation des armées prendrait au moins cinq ans,' *Le Monde*, 1.3.93.
103. Unsigned, 'M. Jacques Baumel (RPR) contre la professionalisation des armées,' *Le Monde*, 3.3.93.
104. F. Fillon, 'Le domaine partagé de la défense,' *Le Monde*, 5.3.93.
105. J. Boyon, 'Consulter le pays,' *Le Monde*, 26.2.93.
106. M. Schmitt, 'Armée de Métier ou Armée Mixte?' *Défense Nationale*, 49, 4 (April 1993) 9–18; and H. Paris, 'Armée de Métier ou de Conscription?' *Défense Nationale*, 49, 5 (May 1993) 89–96.
107. F. Valentin, 'Armée de Conscription ou Armée Professionnelle?' *Défense Nationale*, 49, 6 (June 1993) 9-15.

108. P. Chicken, 'Conscription Revisited,' in T. Chafer and B. Jenkins (eds), *France: from the Cold War*, pp. 93–103, p. 93.

109. France. Ministère de la Défense, *1997-2002: Projet de Loi de Programmation Militaire* (Paris; Ministère de la Défense/Service d'Information et de Relations Publiques des Armées, 1996). Press dossier.

110. A communiqué had been published by the Elysée on 19 October 1990 indicating Mitterrand's concern over the future of the nuclear capabilities, particularly in view of the impending obsolescence of the Plateau d'Albion missiles. Unsigned, 'M. Mitterrand demande à M.. Chevènement des «propositions précises» sur la modernisation de l'arsenal nucléaire,' *Le Monde*, 22.10.90.

111. Unsigned, 'M. Mitterrand propose une réunion du Conseil de sécurité au niveau des chefs d'Etat et de gouvernement,' *Le Monde*, 5.3.91.

112. E. Cresson, *J.O., A.N.*, 22.5.91, p. 2193; and P. Lacoste, 'L'heure des choix,' *Le Figaro*, 23.5.91.

113. J. Isnard, 'La France renonce à développer son missile nucléaire mobile S45,' *Le Monde*, 21–22.7.91.

114. Although the mobile missile had been conceived in the 1970s, it came to prominence in government considerations during the *cohabitation* of 1986–88. Giraud was its primary advocate, and Chirac also supported it in his speech to the IHEDN of September1986, when he called for 'random deployment of major systems' to reduce their vulnerability. The position was supported by the Parliamentary majority, and significantly by senior military figures, such as General Saulnier, the Chief of Staff of the Armed Forces, and General Forray, Mitterrand's personal military adviser. Nevertheless, the planning law for 1987–91 was much closer to Mitterrand's hostility to the mobile missile plan than to the broader advocacy of it. His opposition was subsequently reiterated in his own speech to the IHEDN (September 1988) and thus continuing studies of a mobile missile, the S45, were known to constitute an area for potential cuts at the beginning of the 1990s. See P. Favier and M. Martin-Roland, *La Décennie Mitterrand: II*, pp. 783-5; J. Chirac, 'La Politique de Défense de la France ...' p. 10; F. Mitterrand, 'Allocution de M. François Mitterrand ...,' pp. 17–18; and J. Isnard, 'M. Mitterrand devait choisir entre un missile mobile et un système d'arme nucléaire adapté à l'avion Rafale,' *Le Monde*, 16.1.91.

115. A Chastagnol, 'A la sauvette,' *Le Quotidien de Paris*, 24.7.91; and Unsigned, 'M. Chirac demande à M. Mitterrand de revenir sur l'abandon du missile S45,' *Le Monde*, 25.7.91.

116. P.-A. Wiltzer (UDF). Unsigned, 'L'abandon du missile S45 provoque des réactions dans les milieux politiques,' *Le Monde*, 23.7.91.

117. Unsigned, 'M. Chirac demande à M. Mitterrand de revenir sur l'abandon du missile S45,' *Le Monde*, 25.7.91.

118. Unsigned, 'M. Fabius s'interroge sur l'intérêt de maintenir le programme Rafale,' *Le Monde*, 26.7.91.

119. Unsigned, 'L'abandon du missile S45 provoque des réactions dans les milieux politiques,' *Le Monde*, 23.7.91; and A Chastagnol, 'A la sauvette,' *Le Quotidien de Paris*, 24.7.91.

120. Unsigned, 'M. Fabius s'interroge sur l'intérêt de maintenir le programme Rafale,' *Le Monde*, 26.7.91.

121. Unsigned, 'M. François Léotard approuve l'abandon du missile S45,' *Le Monde*, 31.7.91.
122. Unsigned, 'M. Fabius s'interroge sur l'intérêt de maintenir le programme Rafale,' *Le Monde*, 26.7.91.
123. Unsigned, 'La France crée sa brigade de missiles nucléaires Hadès,' *Le Monde*, 26.7.91.
124. Unsigned, 'La géopolitique de l'Europe a grand besoin d'une théorie des ensembles,' *Le Monde*, 13.9.91.
125. J. Isnard, 'Une autolimitation des armes préstratégiques françaises,' *Le Monde*, 13.9.91.
126. I. Legrand-Bodin, 'La France s'interroge sur sa défense,' *La Croix*, 6.12.89.
127. I. Legrand-Bodin, 'Les crédits militaires en question,' *La Croix*, 23.2. 90.
128. J. Isnard, 'L'armée de terre française va perdre la moitié de ses missiles nucléaires Pluton,' *Le Monde*, 1.4.92.
129. Unsigned, '«Je chercherai, non par la démagogie mais par l'action, à restaurer la confiance et renouer avec espérance»,' *Le Monde*, 10.4.92.
130. Russia had already declared a finite moratorium, although more because of the loss of test facilities to the Republics after the break-up of the Soviet Union than for any altruistic reasons.
131. B. Barrillot, 'French Finesse Nuclear Future,' *The Bulletin of the Atomic Scientists*, 48, 7 (September 1992) 23–6, p. 24.
132. Unsigned, 'Les déclarations du président de la République,' *Le Monde*, 14.4.92.
133. J. Isnard, 'Moratoire sur les essais nucléaires: la dissuasion n'a plus la même priorité,' *Le Monde*, 10.4.92.
134. Unsigned, 'Les Verts: «Un simple infléchissement»,' *Le Monde*, 10.4.92.
135. S. Lepage, 'Satisfaction dans les pays du Pacifique sud,' *Le Monde*, 10.4.92.
136. B. Barrillot, 'French Finesse Nuclear Future,' p. 25.
137. Unsigned, 'Les Verts: «Un simple infléchissement»,' *Le Monde*, 10.4.92.
138. Ibid.
139. Y. Cuau, 'La rigueur et la démagogie,' *L'Express*, 23.4.92. A subsequent report by the Finance Committee of the Assemblée Nationale concluded that as of late 1993 the moratorium had allowed savings of 322 million francs, and another saving of approximately 200 million francs could be expected if the suspension continued until the end of 1994. However, this had to be offset against the costs (estimated at 2 billion francs) of maintaining the sites in working order, and the unquantified military costs of guarding them. Unsigned, 'Deux milliards de francs pour maintenir en état les sites d'essais nucléaires,' *Le Monde*, 10.11.93.
140. J. Chirac, cited in Unsigned, 'Les Verts: «Un simple infléchissement»,' *Le Monde*, 10.4.92. This point was reiterated by a former adviser to Mitterrand at interview, 10.6.96.
141. J.-C. Rufin, 'Nos acquis militaires,' *Le Quotidien de Paris*, 15.2.93.
142. Unsigned, 'Le Mouvement de la paix appelle à manifester contre la reprise des essais nucléaires,' *Le Monde*, 6.5.93; and Unsigned, 'Manifestation des pacifistes sur le Plateau d'Albion,' *Le Monde*, 11.5.93.
143. P. Rouvillois to the Defence Committee of the Assemblée Nationale. Unsigned, 'Le Commissariat à l'énergie atomique s'est mis en situation de reprendre les essais nucléaires après juillet,' *Le Monde*, 4.5.93.

144. Unsigned, 'Le Commissariat à l'énergie atomique s'est mis en situation de reprendre les essais nucléaires après juillet,' *Le Monde*, 4.5.93. See also J. Bétermier, 'Essais Nucléaires et Dissuasion,' *Défense Nationale*, 49, 2 (February 1993) 29–38, p. 32.
145. Unsigned, 'La France prolonge son moratoire sur les essais nucléaires,' *Le Monde*, 6.7.93.
146. Ibid.
147. Air-Sol Longue Portée – air-to-surface long-range missile.
148. Unsigned, 'Les réactions à la prolongation du moratoire sur les essais nucléaires,' *Le Monde*, 7.7.93.
149. Ibid.
150. Unsigned, 'La France prolonge son moratoire sur les essais nucléaires,' *Le Monde*, 6.7.93.
151. J. Isnard, 'La France maintient son moratoire nucléaire,' *Le Monde*, 8.10.93.
152. Unsigned, '«La France est dans l'obligation de procéder à dix ou vingt tirs» déclare M. Chirac,' *Le Monde*, 9.10.93.
153. Unsigned, 'Jean-Louis Debré (RPR) condamne la non-reprise des essais nucléaires français,' *Le Monde*, 10–11.10.93.
154. Léotard in particular was known to consider a renewal of the test cycle as indispensable at a future date. See Unsigned, 'François Léotard: «Il faudra revenir sur certains choix»,' *Le Monde*, 14.7.93; Unsigned, 'L'Elysée et Matignon ont nommé les sept experts du groupe de travail sur les essais nucléaires,' *Le Monde*, 17.7.93; J. Isnard, 'Essais nucléaires: un moratoire jusqu'en mai 1995,' *Le Monde*, 27.10.93; and Unsigned, 'M. Léotard assure que le gouvernement est opposé à tout changement de doctrine nucléaire,' *Le Monde*, 16.11.93.
155. B. Barrillot, 'French Finesse Nuclear Future,' p. 24.
156. J. I., 'La mémoire courte de M. Chirac,' *Le Monde*, 25.2.94.
157. Ibid.
158. R. Galy-Dejean, 'Le piège de Mitterrand,' *Le Monde*, 18.2.94.
159. Ibid.
160. Unsigned, 'M. Chirac: «Il faut lancer d'urgence le programme M5»,' *Le Monde*, 4.3.95.
161. J. Isnard, 'Le missile de la discorde,' *Le Monde*, 7.3.94.
162. Unsigned, 'M. Léotard critique les suggestions de M. Mitterrand sur le programme de missile nucléaire M5,' *Le Monde*, 5.3.94.
163. Unsigned, 'M. Mitterrand a approuvé le report de la fabrication du nouveau missile nucléaire M5,' *Le Monde*, 22.4.94.
164. See, for example, the debate 'L'avenir de la Dissuasion,' in *Relations Internationales et Stratégiques*, 6 (Summer 1992) 44–135.
165. Preface to the *Livre blanc*, by E. Balladur. France, *Livre Blanc sur la Défense, 1994*, p. 6.
166. Ibid., pp. 109–17.
167. Unsigned, 'Satisfaction prudente dans la majorité et dans l'opposition de gauche,' *Le Monde*, 25.2.94.
168. Ibid.
169. Ibid.
170. D. Garraud, 'Défense: un livre blanc sous contrôle de Mitterrand,' *Libération*, 16.2.94.

171. D. Buchan, 'France maps out military strategy into next century,' *Financial Times*, 24.2.94.
172. Unsigned, 'Un livre blanc très cohabitationniste,' *Le Quotidien de Paris*, 24.2.94.
173. F. Léotard, 'Défense: Un consensus actif,' *Le Figaro*, 4.3.94.
174. Unsigned, 'Le Livre blanc reçoit un accueil mitigé à l'Assemblée Nationale,' *Le Monde*, 5.3.94.
175. P.-H. Desaubliaux, 'Les députés estiment acceptable le Livre blanc,' *Le Figaro*, 4.3.94.
176. J. A. C. Lewis, 'French white paper fails to address short term needs,' *Jane's Defence Weekly*, 21, 10 (12.3.94) p. 15.

8   Towards a European Defence?

1. See Chapter 6.
2. F. Mitterrand, *Lettre à tous les Français*, p. 16.
3. F. Mitterrand, 'Allocution de M. François Mitterrand ...,' p. 25.
4. Ibid., p. 27.
5. J. Morizet, 'Le Problème Allemand vu de France,' *Défense Nationale*, 46, 2 (February 1990) 11–23, p. 12.
6. L. Rosenzweig and C. Tréan, '«Ecoutez bien la réponse du président, elle est très importante»' *Le Monde*, 5–6.11.89.
7. Unsigned, 'Stratégie de la tension,' *L'Humanité*, 23.11.89.
8. F. Mitterrand, *De l'Allemagne, de la France*, pp. 87–96, for Mitterrand's own view of the visit to the USSR; C. Tréan, 'M. François Mitterrand a conquis les étudiants de Leipzig,' *Le Monde*, 23.12.89, and C. Tréan, 'M. Mitterrand a su ménager toutes les sensibilités à propos de l'unité allemande,' *Le Monde*, 24–25.12.89.
9. J. Fitchett, 'Mitterrand mutes objections to US proposals on Europe,' *International Herald Tribune*, 19.12.89. See also J. A. Baker III, with T. M. Defrank, *The Politics of Diplomacy: Revolution, War and Peace 1989–1992* (New York; Putnam's, 1995), p. 176.
10. J. Morizet, 'Le Problème Allemand ...,' p. 22.
11. F. Bozo, 'La France et l'OTAN: vers une Nouvelle Alliance,' *Défense Nationale*, 47, 1 (January 1991) 19–33, p. 24.
12. D. Colard, 'Le Couple Franco-Allemand après l'Unification,' *Défense Nationale*, 50, 6 (June 1994) 101–10, p. 106.
13. F. Mitterrand, *De l'Allemagne, de la France*, passim.
14. R. Dumas, *J.O.*, *A.N.*, 1st sitting, 13.12.90, p. 6813.
15. M. Vauzelle, ibid., p. 6813.
16. B. Bourg-Broc, ibid., p. 6815.
17. J.-M. Caro, ibid., p. 6818.
18. R. Montdargent, ibid., p. 6816.
19. Ibid.
20. M. Faivre, 'Débat sur la Défense à l'Assemblée Nationale,' *Défense Nationale*, 47, 8/9 (August/September 1991) 186–8, p. 187.
21. A. Paecht, *J.O.*, *A.N.*, 2nd sitting, 6.6.91, p. 2867.
22. J. Briane, ibid., pp. 2868–9.
23. F. Fillon, ibid., p. 2870.

24. L. Pierna, *J.O., A.N.*, 1st sitting, 6.6.91, p. 2849.
25. M. Faivre, 'Débat sur la Défense ...,' p. 187.
26. J.-P. Chevènement, 'Les Conditions de la Paix et l'Avenir de l'Alliance Atlantique,' *Politique Internationale*, 43 (Spring 1989) 371–8, p. 371.
27. D. Jeambar and C. Makarian, 'Jean-Pierre Chevènement, ministre de la défense: «Non-accès de l'Allemagne aux armes nucléaires»,' *Le Point*, 8.1.90.
28. J.-P. Chevènement, 'Les Conditions de la Paix ...,' p. 377.
29. B. Brigouleix, 'MM. Mitterrand et Schmidt réclament une plus étroite concertation entre l'Europe et les Etats-Unis,' *Le Monde*, 26.2.82. This built on the close coordination of Franco-West German concerns in all areas which Mitterrand had called for six months earlier. See B. Brigouleix, 'M. Mitterrand et la relance de la CEE,' *Le Monde*, 14.7.81.
30. B. Brigouleix, 'MM. Mitterrand et Kohl annoncent un renforcement des consultations militaires et stratégiques entre les deux pays,' *Le Monde*, 24.10.82.
31. J. Attali, *Verbatim I*, p. 699. Diary entry for 22 September 1984.
32. Cited in J. Howorth, 'Of Budgets and Strategic Choices ...,' p. 315.
33. J. I., '«La France et l'Allemagne fédérale partagent des intérêts de sécurité qui sont communs»,' *Le Monde*, 22.6.85.
34. H. Védrine, *Les Mondes de François Mitterrand*, p. 405.
35. B. Brigouleix, 'Paris et Bonn renforcent leur coopération militaire,' *Le Monde*, 1.3.86; and Unsigned, 'La consultation sur les armes stratégiques,' *Le Monde*, 2–3.3.86.
36. H. Védrine, *Les Mondes de François Mitterrand*, p. 458.
37. Ibid., p. 459. See also A. Menon, A. Forster and W. Wallace, 'A Common European Defence?' *Survival*, 34, 3 (Autumn 1992) 98–118, p. 105.
38. H. Védrine, *Les Mondes de François Mitterrand*, p. 475.
39. The text of the Maastricht Treaty was published in a supplement to *The Sunday Times*, entitled 'Maastricht: the Treaty on European Union,' 11.10.92. For the provisions relating to the Common Foreign and Security Policy, and defence, see 'Title V: Provisions on a Common Foreign and Security Policy,' pp. 16–17.
40. J.-P. Chevènement, 'Evolution du Monde, Rôle et Politique de Défense de la France: Discours de Monsieur Jean-Pierre Chevènement, Ministre de la Défense, le 21 mai 1990, devant les auditeurs de l'Institut des Hautes Etudes de Défense Nationale,' *Défense Nationale*, 46, 7 (July 1990) 9–28, p. 15.
41. M. Rocard, 'La France et l'Ordre International: Discours de Monsieur Michel Rocard, Premier Ministre, le 22 octobre 1990, devant les auditeurs de l'Institut des Hautes Etudes de Défense Nationale,' *Défense Nationale*, 46, 12 (December 1990) 9–21, p. 16.
42. J.-P. Chevènement, 'Evolution du Monde ...,' p. 22.
43. Unsigned, 'M. Mitterrand: «La France participera à toute réflexion pour adapter l'Alliance aux exigences des temps à venir»,' *Le Monde*, 7.7.90.
44. P. Bérégovoy, 'Construction Européenne et Intérêt de la France: Discours de Monsieur Pierre Bérégovoy, Premier Ministre, le 3 septembre 1992, devant les auditeurs de l'Institut des Hautes Etudes de Défense Nationale,' *Défense Nationale*, 48, 11 (November 1992) 11–25, p. 24.

45. P. H. Gordon, *A Certain Idea of France*, p. 167; p. 169; p. 170.
46. I. L.-B., 'La nouvelle Europe secoue la défense française,' *La Croix*, 13.7.90.
47. C. Tréan, 'La France «n'entend pas s'intègre» à la force de réaction rapide de l'OTAN, annonce M. Mitterrand,' *Le Monde*, 31.5.91; and I. Davidson, 'France floats global arms control plan,' *Financial Times*, 31.5.91.
48. F. Heisbourg and P. Lellouche, 'Faut-il Enterrer l'Alliance Atlantique?' *Politique Internationale*, 50 (Winter 1990/91) 163–75, p. 166.
49. Ibid., p. 165.
50. I. Legrand-Bodin, 'La France s'interroge sur sa défense,' *La Croix*, 6.12.89.
51. G. Mesmin, *J.O., A..N.*, 1st sitting, 5.6.91, p. 2776.
52. G. Howe, 'The WEU: the Way Ahead,' *NATO Review*, 37, 3 (June 1989) 13–15, p. 14.
53. Sir M. Alexander, 'European Security and the CSCE,' *NATO Review*, 39, 4 (August 1991) 10–14, p. 14.
54. J. Baumel, 'La France, l'OTAN et l'Europe,' *Défense Nationale*, 51, 3 (March 1995) 85–8, p. 86.
55. Sir M. Alexander, 'European Security ...,' p. 14.
56. W. van Eekelen, 'WEU's post-Maastricht Agenda,' *NATO Review*, 40, 2 (April 1992) 13–17, p. 14.
57. W. Christopher, 'Towards a NATO Summit,' *NATO Review*, 41, 4 (August 1993) 3–6, p. 5.
58. L. Le Hégarat, 'Union Politique et Défense Européenne,' *Défense Nationale*, 49, 8/9 (August/September 1993) 75–85, p. 83.
59. P. Fistié, 'La France, Maastricht, et la Défense Européenne,' *Politique Internationale*, 56 (Summer 1992) 129–40, p. 129.
60. H. de Bresson and C. Tréan, 'Paris et Bonn protestent de leur fidélité à l'OTAN,' *Le Monde*, 22.5.92.
61. Ibid.
62. D. Colard, 'Le Couple Franco-Allemand ...,' p. 106.
63. J. Rivière, 'La Coopération Européenne: un Atout Majeure,' *Défense Nationale*, 48, 11 (November 1992) 196–7, p. 197.
64. I. Mitrofanoff, 'L'Eurocorps: Mode d'Emploi,' *Défense Nationale*, 48, 12 (December 1992) 29–36, p. 29.
65. G. Mesmin, 'Contre la politique de la chaise vide,' *Le Figaro*, 12.11.91.
66. G. Schöllgen, 'Putting Germany's Post-Unification Foreign Policy to the Test,' *NATO Review*, 41, 2 (April 1993) 15–22, p. 20.
67. R. P. Grant, 'France's New Relationship with NATO,' *Survival*, 38, 1 (Spring 1996) 58–80, p. 60.
68. F. Mitterrand, *Onze Discours sur l'Europe*, pp. 95–132, p. 124.
69. D. Colard, 'Le Couple Franco-Allemand ...,' p. 106.
70. I. Mitrofanoff, 'L'Eurocorps ...,' p. 35.
71. E. Foster, 'The Franco-German Corps: a 'Theological' Debate?' *Journal of the RUSI*, 137, 4 (August 1992) 63–7, p. 64.
72. L. Le Hégarat, 'Union Politique et Défense Européenne,' p. 78.
73. F. Maurin, 'Avenir de la Défense Militaire Française,' *Défense Nationale*, 49, 12 (December 1993) 23–33, p. 28.
74. P. Moreau Defarges, 'L'Union Européenne après six mois, ou le Rêve Evanoui,' *Défense Nationale*, 50, 5 (May 1994) 79–88, p. 84.
75. E. Cresson, *J.O., A.N.*, 22.5.91, p. 2193.

76. P. Lacoste, 'L'heure des choix,' *Le Figaro*, 23.5.91.
77. E. Cresson, 'Défense et Avenir de l'Europe: Discours de Madame Edith Cresson, Premier Ministre, le 5 septembre 1991, devant les auditeurs de l'Institut des Hautes Etudes de Défense Nationale,' *Défense Nationale*, 47, 11 (November 1991) 9–19, p. 12. Italics added.
78. M. Evans, 'Outmanoeuvred Mitterrand walks out of NATO meeting in a huff,' *The Times*, 9.11.91.
79. Unsigned, 'M. Mitterrand et le «prêchi-prêcha» de l'OTAN,' *Le Monde*, 10–11.11.91.
80. F. Mitterrand, *Onze Discours sur l'Europe*, pp. 95–132, p. 125.
81. Article 5 relating to the collective defence of the member countries.
82. R. P. Grant, 'France's New Relationship with NATO,' pp. 61–2.
83. Unsigned, 'M. Joxe propose que la France participe plus activement aux structures alliés,' *Le Monde*, 30.9.92.; and J. I., 'M. Joxe souhaite que la France participe à la rénovation de l'Alliance Atlantique,' *Le Monde*, 4.12.92. See P. Boniface, 'Le rôle de la France dans l'OTAN,' *Vendredi*, 7.5.93, on Mitterrand's rejection of Joxe's calls.
84. Jacques Chirac to a reception in honour of Parisian reserve officers, 8 February 1993. Cited in R. P. Grant, 'France's New Relationship with NATO,' p. 63.
85. E. Balladur, Préface, in France, *Livre Blanc sur la Défense, 1994* (Paris; Editions 10/18, 1994), p. 6.
86. F. Léotard, Préface, ibid., p. 10.
87. F. Léotard, 'La Rationalisation de l'Industrie de Défense: Discours de Monsieur François Léotard, Ministre d'Etat, Ministre de la Défense, le 8 septembre 1993, devant les auditeurs du Centre des Hautes Etudes de l'Armement,' *Défense Nationale*, 49, 11 (November 1993) 9–19, pp. 10 13.
88. France, *Livre Blanc sur la Défense, 1994*, p. 58.
89. P. Fistié, 'La France, Maastricht ...,' p. 129.
90. P. Maillard, 'Intérêts et Atouts en Politique Extérieure,' *Défense Nationale*, 49, 3 (March 1993) 37–47, p. 45.
91. J. Morizet, 'Le Traité de l'Elysée Trente Ans Après,' *Défense Nationale*, 50, 2 (February 1994) 7–14, p. 11; p. 14.
92. Unsigned, 'M. Mitterrand et le «prêchi-prêcha» de l'OTAN,' *Le Monde*, 10–11.11.91.
93. L. Le Hégarat, 'Union Politique et Défense Européenne,' p. 82.
94. Ibid.
95. P. Maillard, 'Intérêts et Atouts ...,' p. 46.
96. G. Robin, 'Un Concept en Quête de Substance: la Défense Européenne,' *Défense Nationale*, 51, 3 (March 1995) 89–95, p. 92.
97. Ibid., p. 95.
98. H. Conze, 'La Défense de l'Europe: Pourquoi Attendre?' *Défense Nationale*, 49, 5 (May 1993) 75–87, p. 75.
99. F. Maurin, 'Avenir de la Défense Militaire Française,' pp. 26–7.
100. G. Robin, 'Un Concept en Quête de Substance ...,' p. 92.
101. Ibid., p. 89.

9   The New French Interventionism

1. J. Isnard, '«Une armée sur laquelle le soleil ne se couche jamais»,' *Le Monde*, 19.3.93.
2. J. d'Ormesson, 'La France et son armée,' *Figaro Magazine*, 23.1.93.
3. Ibid.
4. J. Isnard, '«Une armée sur laquelle le soleil ne se couche jamais»,' *Le Monde*, 19.3.93.
5. See Chapter 3.
6. F. Mitterrand, Message to the Assemblée Nationale, *J.O., A.N.*, 27.8.90, p. 3213.
7. H. Védrine, *Les Mondes de François Mitterrand*, p. 526.
8. F. Mitterrand, Message to the Assemblée Nationale, *J.O., A.N.*, 27.8.90, p. 3213.
9. J. Patoz, 'Et les députés votèrent la guerre ...,' *Le Quotidien de Paris*, 17.1.91.
10. In fact, the deputies were being asked only to approve France's commitment to the implementation of the UN resolutions; as the Prime Minister observed, a vote in favour of the government's Gulf policy in this respect no way constituted approval of its action overall. M. Rocard, *J.O., A.N.*, 16.1.91, p. 5.
11. M.-F. Stirbois, *J.O., A.N.*, 16.1.91, p. 15.
12. Unsigned, 'Arrêtez la guerre!' *L'Humanité*, 18.1.91.
13. As shown by a street demonstration in Paris while the deputies debated. M. Blachère and J. Teyssier, 'La parole du peuple,' *L'Humanité*, 17.1.91.
14. A. Lajoinie, *J.O., A.N.*, 16.1.91, p. 9.
15. See B. Stasi (UDC), ibid., pp. 5–6; J.-F. Deniau (UDF), ibid., pp. 10–11; J. Chirac (RPR), ibid., p. 14; A. Lajoinie, ibid., p. 7; and M.-F. Stirbois, ibid., p. 15. While the PCF criticised the prospect of action over Kuwait, when the international community would not act over Israel's continued presence in the Occupied Territories, it was noticeably silent over the question of the Soviet Republics.
16. P. Mauroy, *J.O., A.N.*, 16.1.91, p. 12; and A. Lajoinie, *J.O., A.N.*, 16.1.91, p. 8.
17. Unsigned, 'A l'Elysée, il ne restait plus qu'à croire au miracle,' *Le Monde*, 17.1.91.
18. P. Lellouche, 'Que veulent les pacifistes?' *Le Figaro*, 17.1.91.
19. Unsigned, 'A l'Elysée, il ne restait plus qu'à croire au miracle,' *Le Monde*, 17.1.91.
20. M. Aulagnon, 'La France est-elle encore capable de faire la guerre?' *L'Evénement du Jeudi*, 6.9.90.
21. J.-F. Deniau, *J.O., A.N.*, 16.1.91, p. 11; and J. Chirac *J.O., A.N.*, 16.1.91, p. 15.
22. S. Denis, 'Programme minimum,' *Le Quotidien de Paris*, 17.1.91.
23. J. Waintraub, 'Opposition: à chacun sa nuance,' *Le Quotidien de Paris*, 17.1.91.
24. Ibid.; and P. Lellouche, 'Que veulent les pacifistes?' *Le Figaro*, 17.1.91.
25. M. Feltin, 'Michel Jobert: «La duplicité de la France»,' *La Croix*, 17.1.91.
26. Ibid.
27. J. Patoz, 'Et les députés votèrent la guerre ...,' *Le Quotidien de Paris*, 17.1.91.

28. Ibid. See also J. Fitchett, 'France backs US, some seek distance,' *International Herald Tribune*, 17.1.91, who observed that as conscripts were not to be sent to the Gulf, parliamentary approval had not strictly been required. However, the vote had been a useful opportunity to try to enforce party discipline.
29. F. Gerschel, 'PS: l'affront au chef de l'Etat,' *Le Quotidien de Paris*, 17.1.91.
30. P. Jarreau and P. Robert-Diard, 'Les socialistes approuvent l'engagement français mais s'interrogent sur ses finalités,' *Le Monde*, 17.1.91.
31. Hence, the French peace plan must be viewed at least in part as directed at silencing internal party opposition to the prospect of war. As Mauroy had emphasised in the Assemblée Nationale, 'Everything [had] been tried, but in vain. Baghdad [had] never responded.' P. Mauroy, *J.O., A.N.*, 16.1.91, p. 12.
32. D. Motchane, 'La France otage,' *Le Monde*, 17.1.91.
33. P. Robert-Diard and J.-L. Saux, 'Un vote de conscience,' *Le Monde*, 18.1.91.
34. S. Denis, 'Programme minimum,' *Le Quotidien de Paris*, 17.1.91; and P. Robert-Diard and J.-L. Saux, ibid.
35. F. Gerschel, 'PS: l'affront au chef de l'Etat,' *Le Quotidien de Paris*, 17.1.91.
36. See, for example, P. Habert, ''67 pour cent des Français approuvent l'action militaire contre l'Irak,' *Le Figaro*, 19–20.1.91; C. Rebois, '70 pour cent des Français approuvent la participation de notre pays,' *Le Figaro*, 25.1.91; and S. Denis, 'Programme minimum,' *Le Quotidien de Paris*, 17.1.91.
37. J. Chirac, *J.O., A.N.*, 16.1.91, p. 13.
38. J. Waintraub, 'Opposition: à chacun sa nuance,' *Le Quotidien de Paris*, 17.1.91.
39. S. Denis, 'Programme minimum,' *Le Quotidien de Paris*, 17.1.91.
40. Unsigned, 'M. Mitterrand: «A partir du 15 janvier à minuit, le conflit armé sera légitime»,' *Le Monde*, 11.1.91.
41. Unsigned, 'Douze Jaguar français ont bombardé aux côtés de F-16 américains une base irakienne au Koweït,' *Le Monde*, 18.1.91.
42. P. Haski and C. Fauvet-Mycia, 'L'ambiguïté de la doctrine française passe de moins en moins bien,' *Libération*, 19–20.1.91.
43. P. Webster, 'Giscard says France has no firm policy over military role,' *The Guardian*, 21.1.91.
44. J. Fitchett, 'French force to extend its role beyond Kuwaiti sites,' *International Herald Tribune*, 21.1.91.
45. E. Zemmour, 'France: le week-end des ambiguïtés,' *Le Quotidien de Paris*, 21.1.91.
46. Ibid.
47. Ibid.
48. Unsigned, 'L'entretien télévisé du président de la République: «L'ordre donné aux armées c'est de libérér le Koweït, pas d'attaquer l'Irak»,' *Le Monde*, 26.2.91.
49. C. Marchand, 'Un pas de plus,' *L'Humanité*, 25.1.91.
50. Unsigned, 'L'entretien télévisé du président de la République: «Cette épreuve cruelle de vérité aura lieu. Il faut que les Français y préparent leur esprit»,' *Le Monde*, 9.2.91.
51. Unsigned, 'MM. Chirac et Giscard d'Estaing critiquent le rejet de principe des armes non conventionnelles,' *Le Monde*, 10–11.2.91.

52. Ibid.
53. D. Chivot, 'La position de Mitterrand trouble l'opposition,' *La Croix*, 12.2.91.
54. J. Macé-Scaron, 'Le «consensus» se lézarde,' *Le Figaro*, 7.2.91.
55. D. Chivot, 'La position de Mitterrand trouble l'opposition,' *La Croix*, 12.2.91.
56. Ibid.
57. J. Macé-Scaron, 'Le «consensus» se lézarde,' *Le Figaro*, 7.2.91.
58. Unsigned, 'MM. Chirac et Giscard d'Estaing critiquent le rejet de principe des armes non conventionnelles,' *Le Monde*, 10–11.2.91.
59. J. Jublin, 'Nucléaire, conventionnel, engagés ou appelés, la France devra choisir,' *La Tribune de l'Expansion*, 24.1.91.
60. For a detailed English-language consideration of the lessons for France to draw from the Gulf War, see D. S. Yost, 'France and the Gulf War of 1990–1991: Political-Military Lessons Learned,' *Journal of Strategic Studies*, 16, 3 (September 1993) 339–74.
61. G. Valaison, 'Les Forces Navales dans le Golfe,' *Défense Nationale*, 47, 6 (June 1991) 188–91, p. 188.
62. J. Guisnel, 'Le dispositif français est mal adapté au conflit,' *Libération*, 1.2.91.
63. H. Tricot, 'France: les grands programmes militaires relancés?' *Le Quotidien de Paris*, 31.1.91.
64. E. Faudon (pseudonym), 'La guerre avec l'Irak et la programmation militaire française,' *Libération*, 26.2.91.
65. J. Guisnel, 'Le dispositif français est mal adapté au conflit,' *Libération*, 1.2.91.
66. F. Prater, 'La France et la Crise du Golfe,' *Politique Etrangère*, 56, 2 (Summer 1991) 441–53, p. 449.
67. P. Haski and C. Fauvet-Mycia, 'L'ambiguïté de la doctrine française passe de moins en moins bien,' *Libération*, 19–20.1.91; and P. Webster, 'Giscard says France has no firm policy over military role,' *The Guardian*, 21.1.91.
68. J. Jublin, La France à qui perd gagne,' *La Tribune de l'Expansion*, 21.1.91.
69. F. Heisbourg, 'Quelles Leçons Stratégiques de la Guerre du Golfe?' *Politique Etrangère*, 56, 2 (Summer 1991) 411–22, p. 421.
70. J. Guisnel, 'Le dispositif français est mal adapté au conflit,' *Libération*, 1.2.91.
71. Y. Briant, 'Golfe: lacunes de nos armées,' *Le Figaro*, 14.3.91.
72. J.-P. Ravery, 'Moral à zéro,' *L'Humanité*, 5.2.91; and J. Guisnel, 'Le dispositif français est mal adapté au conflit,' *Libération*, 1.2.91.
73. J.-P. Ravery, ibid.
74. See, for example, J. Guisnel, 'Le dispositif français est mal adapté au conflit,' *Libération*, 1.2.91; and H. Védrine's comments on the regularity of such comparisons, in *Les Mondes de François Mitterrand*, p. 538.
75. H. Védrine, ibid. *Le Figaro* commented that '[France had] not been able to send more than 10,000 soldiers against Iraq, while [she was] capable of sending two hundred thousand men to Indochina and more than four hundred thousand to Algeria. Faced with the five hundred thousand Americans, or the thirty-five thousand British, [France could] only therefore claim a very secondary role in the Gulf victory.' Y. Briant, 'Golfe:

lacunes de nos armées,' *Le Figaro*, 14.3.91.

76. See Chapter 7; and M. Colomès, 'Guerre sous expertise,' *Le Point*, 11–17.3.91.
77. See Chapter 7.
78. P. Joxe, 'Défense et Renseignement ...,' p. 10.
79. D. Porch, *The French Secret Services: from the Dreyfus Affair to the Gulf War* (Oxford; Oxford University Press, 1997), p. 493.
80. See also P. Lellouche, 'Défense française: ce qui doit changer,' *Le Figaro*, 12.3.91.
81. G. Valaison, 'Les Forces Navales dans le Golfe,' pp. 188–9.
82. F. Heisbourg, 'Quelles Leçons Stratégiques ...,' p. 415.
83. Y. Briant, 'Golfe: lacunes de nos armées,' *Le Figaro*, 14.3.91.
84. H. Védrine, *Les Mondes de François Mitterrand*, p. 523.
85. M. Torrelli, 'Les Missions Humanitaires de l'Armée Française,' *Défense Nationale*, 49, 3 (March 1993) 65–78, p. 65.
86. P. Bérégovoy, cited in ibid.
87. M. Saliou, 'La France et l'ONU. Des Ambitions Mondiales,' *Politique Etrangère*, 58, 3 (Autumn 1993) 687–95, p. 687.
88. J. Saulnier, 'Missions et Engagement des Forces Françaises,' *Défense Nationale*, 48, 7 (July 1992) 9–16, p. 10.
89. M. Torrelli, 'Les Missions Humanitaires ...,' p. 72.
90. P. Moreau Defarges, 'Quel est l'Avenir des Interventions Humanitaires?' *Défense Nationale*, 49, 8/9 (August/September 1993) 87–95, p. 93.
91. M. Faivre, 'Les Nouvelles Missions des Armées,' *Défense Nationale*, 48, 5 (May 1992) 180–84, p. 183.
92. M. Torrelli, 'Les Missions Humanitaires ...,' p. 73.
93. M. Saliou, 'La France et l'ONU ...,' pp. 687–8.
94. H. Védrine, *Les Mondes de François Mitterrand*, Title of Chapter XVIII.
95. Unsigned, 'France to ask WEU to weigh sending force to Yugoslavia,' *International Herald Tribune*, 6.8.91.
96. F. d'Alançon, 'Le malaise français,' *La Croix*, 6.7.91.
97. C. T., 'La France reste réservée à l'idée de reconnaître la Croatie,' *Le Monde*, 12–13.1.92; and C. Tréan, 'La France s'apprête à ne reconnaître que la Slovénie,' *Le Monde*, 16.1.92.
98. H. Védrine, *Les Mondes de François Mitterrand*, pp. 591–680. The book contains 21 chapters, spread over 760 pages.
99. F. Wurtz, a Communist representative in the European Parliament. Cited in Unsigned, 'Plusieurs responsables politiques pressent le gouvernement d'agir,' *Le Monde*, 9–10.8.92.
100. M. Faivre, 'Les Missions Nouvelles ...,' pp. 182–3.
101. I. Legrand-Bodin, 'Le choix français pour Sarajevo,' *La Croix*, 4.7.92.
102. Unsigned, 'M. Millon (UDF) juge «insuffisante» la solution proposée,' *Le Monde*, 12.8.92.
103. Unsigned, 'M. Fabius demande que «l'Europe intervienne pour arrêter les massacres»,' *Le Monde*, 13.8.92.
104. Ibid.
105. Unsigned, 'Il faut organiser des «opérations aériennes ponctuelles»,' *Le Monde*, 12.8.92.
106. A. Finkielkraut, 'L'insulte et l'abandon,' *Le Monde*, 9–10.8.92.

107. Unsigned, 'Plusieurs responsables politiques pressent le gouvernement d'agir,' *Le Monde*, 9–10.8.92.
108. Unsigned, 'M. Millon (UDF) juge «insuffisante» la solution proposée,' *Le Monde*, 12.8.92.
109. T. Ferenczi, 'Divergences françaises,' *Le Monde*, 12.8.92.
110. Unsigned, 'Il faut organiser des «opérations aériennes ponctuelles»,' *Le Monde*, 12.8.92.
111. T. Ferenczi, 'Divergences françaises,' *Le Monde*, 12.8.92.
112. Unsigned, 'M. Billardon (PS) n'exclut pas que la France participe à une intervention militaire,' *Le Monde*, 6.8.92.
113. Unsigned, 'Plusieurs responsables politiques pressent le gouvernement d'agir,' *Le Monde*, 9–10.8.92.
114. Unsigned, 'M. Fabius demande que «l'Europe intervienne pour arrêter les massacres»,' *Le Monde*, 13.8.92.
115. T. Ferenczi, 'Partage des tâches,' *Le Monde*, 13.8.92.
116. Unsigned, 'M. Mitterrand assure qu'«une campagne proprement militaire constituerait une épreuve redoutable»,' *Le Monde*, 13.8.92.
117. Unsigned, 'M. Chirac juge M. Mitterrand «objectivement complice» de la poursuite de la guerre,' *Le Monde*, 15.8.92.
118. Ibid.
119. Ibid.
120. B. Jérôme, 'Entre faucons et colombes,' *Le Point*, 22.8.92.
121. Unsigned, 'M. Fillon (RPR) estime qu'«aucune solution militaire n'existe»,' *Le Monde*, 21.8.92.
122. B. Jérôme, 'Entre faucons et colombes,' *Le Point*, 22.8.92.
123. Ibid.; and Unsigned, 'M. Lang en «désaccord» avec M. Fabius sur une intervention militaire,' *Le Monde*, 25.8.92.
124. T. de Montbrial, 'Entre l'immobilisme et l'engrenage,' *Le Figaro*, 17.8.92.
125. Cited in C. Franvier, 'La France déchirée par la Yougoslavie,' *Le Quotidien de Paris*, 20.8.92.
126. Unsigned, 'Mme. Garraud estime que la France «est inapte à affronter les Serbes»,' *Le Monde*, 25.8.92.
127. P. Marx, 'Joxe: «Notre armée est engagée pour au moins un an»,' *La Tribune de l'Expansion*, 21.8.92; and Unsigned, 'La France commencera à relever ses «casques bleus» le 10 septembre,' *Le Monde*, 4.9.92. For an account of a conscript's service in Bosnia, and the reasons for it, as well as the positive light in which many conscripts viewed such service, see T. Goisque, 'Voilà à quoi nous servons, nous casques bleus,' *Figaro Magazine*, 28.4.95, pp. 36–41.
128. Unsigned, 'M. Emmanuelli assure qu'une majorité de députés souhaite «un engagement plus ferme» de la France,' *Le Monde*, 25.12.92.
129. C. Tréan, 'La France «prendra sa part» à une action contre l'aviation serbe en Bosnie,' *Le Monde*, 29.12.92.
130. Unsigned, 'M. Fiterman (PC) n'exclut pas «des formes appropriées» d'intervention militaire,' *Le Monde*, 5.1.93.
131. J. Isnard, 'Le désarroi des «casques bleus» français,' *Le Monde*, 1.12.92.
132. E. C., 'Les Bosniaques en question,' *La Croix*, 11.9.92.
133. J. Isnard, 'La France cherche à mieux protéger ses «casques bleus» dans l'ex Yougoslavie,' *Le Monde*, 27.1.93.

134. J.-L. Dufour, 'Intervenir en Bosnie,' *Le Figaro*, 7.1.93.
135. International Institute for Strategic Studies, *The Military Balance, 1992–1993* (London; Oxford University Press for the IISS, 1992), pp. 247–50; and International Institute for Strategic Studies, *The Military Balance 1993–1994* (London; Oxford University Press for the IISS, 1993), pp. 253–60.
136. P. Marcovici, 'Le «Clemenceau» en campagne,' *Le Quotidien de Paris*, 27.1.93.
137. J.-M. Colombani, 'Nourrir la Somalie, mourir pour la Bosnie,' *Le Monde*, 12.12.92.
138. M. Torrelli, 'Les Missions Humanitaires ...,' p. 77.
139. Unsigned, 'La France n'augmentera pas son contingent dans l'ex Yougoslavie, laisse entendre M. Juppé,' *Le Monde*, 6.5.93.
140. P. Haski, D. Garraud and P. Sabatier, 'Léotard: La France attend les alliés en Bosnie,' *Libération*, 21.5.93.
141. Unsigned, 'M. Léotard envisage l'éventualité d'un retrait des casques bleus au printemps,' *Le Monde*, 21.12.93.
142. H. Paillar, 'Bosnie: les divergences dans la majorité,' *Le Figaro*, 27.1.94.
143. D. Garraud, 'Paris souhaite l'implication de l'Otan en Bosnie,' *Libération*, 6.1.94; A. Riding, 'Bosnia plea: diplomatic victory for Paris,' *International Herald Tribune*, 11.1.94; and C. Lambroschini, 'Léotard: à l'Otan, nous avons été suivis,' *Le Figaro*, 12.1.94.
144. J. Lanxade, cited in J. Isnard, 'Les «casques bleus» français ne veulent plus jouer les supplétifs,' *Le Monde*, 28.7.93.
145. General A. Monchal, Chief of Staff of the Army, cited in ibid.
146. Ibid.
147. Unsigned, 'M. Léotard s'en prend au commandement militaire de l'ONU,' *Le Monde*, 24.4.93.
148. Ibid.; and J. I., 'Le dispositif militaire français devrait subir des retouches,' *Le Monde*, 11.6.93.
149. See, for example, Unsigned, 'Alain Juppé souhaite une présence américaine et russe sur le terrain,' *Le Monde*, 19.5.93; P. Haski, D. Garraud and P. Sabatier, 'Léotard: La France attend les alliés en Bosnie,' *Libération*, 21.5.93; and Unsigned, 'La France a demandé à Washington un appui militaire,' *Le Monde*, 7.1.94.
150. F. B., 'Le consensus a remplacé la polémique sur l'attitude de la France en Bosnie,' *Le Monde*, 13.4.94; and A. Fulda, 'Ex-Yougoslavie: Juppé défend sa politique,' *Le Figaro*, 13.4.94.
151. J. I., 'La France devrait retirer 2,500 «casques bleus» avant la fin de l'année,' *Le Monde*, 18.5.94; and C. Lambroschini, 'Militaires et diplomates,' *Le Figaro*, 18.5.94.
152. France, *Livre blanc sur la Défense, 1994*, p. 75. On the applicability of the Rwandan situation to the missions foreseen by the *Livre blanc*, see J. Isnard, 'Le cinquième scénario,' *Le Monde*, 25.6.94.
153. H. Védrine, *Les Mondes de François Mitterrand*, p. 702. In the face of some parliamentary reticence towards military intervention, Balladur proposed five conditions to the parliamentary RPR to underline his concerns that French troops should be as well protected as possible under the circumstances. See Unsigned, 'Les cinq conditions de Balladur,' *La Croix*, 23.6.94.

154. Ibid.
155. Some accounts in fact took a highly critical view of Mitterrand's 'interests' in Rwanda, attributing responsibility for the political divisions and the subsequent genocide to the President.
156. See E. Zemmour, 'Mitterrand en pointe, Balladur en bémol,' *Le Quotidien de Paris*, 23.6.94; and F. Lewis, 'France dares to face the humanitarian challenge in Rwanda,' *International Herald Tribune*, 30.6.94.
157. Léotard acknowledged his own previous reservations in F. Léotard, 'La France doit garder la tête haute,' *Libération*, 22.6.94.
158. C. Lambroschini, 'Mitterrand–Juppé: les alliés objectifs,' *Le Figaro*, 24.6.94.
159. H. Védrine, *Les Mondes de François Mitterrand*, p. 701.
160. See, for example, F. Smyth, 'French money is behind the overarming of Rwanda,' *International Herald Tribune*, 15.4.94; M. Muller, 'Rwanda: Paris directement impliqué dans la tragédie,' *L'Humanité*, 17.5.94; and R. Girard, 'Rwanda: les faux pas de la France,' *Le Figaro*, 19.5.94.
161. Unsigned, 'L'opération Turquoise laisse des bleus à l'armée,' *Libération*, 2.6.94; and Unsigned, 'A rash French venture in Rwanda,' *The Independent*, 21.6.94.
162. M.-P. Subtil, 'Le projet d'intervention française au Rwanda suscite de plus en plus de critiques,' *Le Monde*, 23.6.94.
163. J. Fort, 'Rwanda: la raison ou l'aventure?' *L'Humanité*, 22.6.94.
164. C. Lambroschini, 'L'exemple français,' *Le Figaro*, 21.6.94.
165. P.-H. D., 'Armée de terre: 2,500 hommes,' *Le Figaro*, 24.6.94.
166. J. C. 'Les Mirage et le ministre Léotard arrivent,' *L'Humanité*, 29.6.94.
167. Unsigned, 'Trois cents soldats français doivent quitter le pays avant la fin du mois de juillet,' *Le Monde*, 14.7.94.
168. International Institute for Strategic Studies, *The Military Balance, 1994–1995* (London; Oxford University Press for the IISS, 1994), p. 272.
169. H. Védrine, *Les Mondes de François Mitterrand*, p. 702.
170. Unsigned, 'Paris exclut la prolongation de l'opération «Turquoise» au-delà du 22 août,' *Le Monde*, 24–5.7.94; and Y. Tessier, 'Paris rejects UN call to keep troops in Rwanda,' *The Independent*, 10.8.94.
171. J. Lanxade, 'L'opération Turquoise,' *Défense Nationale*, 51, 2 (February 1995) 7–15, p. 13.
172. M.-P. Subtil, 'Les critiques contre l'opération «Turquoise» se sont tues,' *Le Monde*, 21–22.8.94.
173. J. Lanxade, 'L'opération Turquoise,' p. 10.
174. P.-H. D., 'Armée de l'air: quarante appareils,' *Le Figaro*, 24.6.94.
175. J. Lanxade, 'L'opération Turquoise,' p. 10.
176. Ibid.

Conclusion

1. C. Millon, 'France and the Renewal of the Atlantic Alliance,' *NATO Review*, 44, 5 (May 1996) 13–16, p. 13.
2. J. Baumel. *J.O., A.N.*, 2nd sitting, 19.5.83, p. 1261.
3. H. Védrine, *Les Mondes de François Mitterrand*, pp. 172–3.
4. J. A. Baker, III, with T. M. Defrank, *The Politics of Diplomacy*, p. 314.
5. See Introduction.

6. H. Védrine, *Les Mondes de François Mitterrand*, p. 713.
7. D. S. Yost, 'France and the Gulf War of 1990–1991 …,' p. 346.
8. J.-M. Colombani, 'Nourrir la Somalie, mourir pour la Bosnie,' *Le Monde*, 12.12.92.

Bibliography

Published primary sources

Documents

France, *Journal Officiel de la République Française: Débats Parlementaires. Assemblée Nationale, 1958–95.* Paris; Imprimerie de l'Assemblée Nationale.

France, *Journal Officiel de la République Française: Débats Parlementaires. Sénat, 1960–62.* Paris; Imprimerie du Sénat.

France, *Livre Blanc sur la Défense, 1994.* Paris; Editions 10/18, 1994.

France, Ministère de la Défense, *Livre Blanc sur la Défense Nationale: Tome I.* Paris; Ministère de la Défense, 1972.

France, Ministère de la Défense, *Livre Blanc sur la Défense Nationale: Tome II.* Paris; Ministère de la Défense, 1973.

Parti Communiste, *Programme Commun de Gouvernement du Parti Communiste Français et du Parti Socialiste (27 juin, 1972).* Paris; Editions Sociales, 1972.

Parti Socialiste, *Changer la Vie: Programme de Gouvernement du Parti Socialiste.* Paris; Flammarion, 1972.

Newspaper sources

Aurore, L'
Combat
Combat Républicain
Croix, La
Echos, Les
Evénement du jeudi, L'
Express, L'
Figaro, Le
Figaro Magazine
Humanité, L'
Libération
Lutte Ouvrière
Matin, Le
Monde, Le
Nouveau Journal, Le
Nouvel Observateur, Le

Point, Le
Quotidien de Paris, Le
Rivarol
Rouge
Témoignage Chrétien
Tribune de l'Economie, La
Tribune de l'Expansion, La
Unité, L'
Vendredi

Financial Times, The
Guardian, The
Independent, The
International Herald Tribune
New York Times, The
Times, The

The following files of press cuttings were consulted at the library of the Institut d'Etudes Politiques, rue St. Guillaume, 75006 Paris.

123	Chef de l'Etat: François Mitterrand.
123 bis	Discours et Déclarations du Président de la République.
141/1	Elections Présidentielles.
141/20	Le Parti Socialiste.
211/A	Relations avec l'OTAN.

211/88   Relations Politiques avec le Yougoslavie, puis les états de l'ex-
           Yougoslavie.
212/1   Relations Politiques avec le Moyen Orient.
212/16   Relations Politiques avec le Liban.
213/236   Relations Politiques avec le Tchad.
213/237   Relations Politiques de la France avec le Rwanda.
9.221/29   Conflit du Golfe Persique.
9.282/11   Armement Atomique – Désarmement.

The following press dossier was consulted:

France, Ministère de la Défense, *1997–2002: Projet de Loi de Programmation Militaire*. Paris; Ministère de la Défense/Service d'Information et de Relations Publiques des Armées, 1996.

Diaries and commentaries

Attali, J., *Verbatim I: Chronique des Années 1981–1986*. Paris; Fayard,1993.
Attali, J., *Verbatim II: Chronique des Années 1986–1988*. Paris; Fayard, 1995.
Attali, J., *Verbatim III: Chronique des Années 1988–1991*. Paris; Fayard, 1995.
de Gaulle, C., *The Army of the Future*. London; Hutchinson, 1940.
de Gaulle, C., *Mémoires de Guerre vol. I: L'appel, 1940–1942*. Paris; Plon, 1955.
de Gaulle, C., *Mémoires de Guerre, vol. III: Le Salut, 1944–1946*. Paris; Plon, 1959.
de Gaulle, C., *Discours et Messages III: Avec le Renouveau, Mai 1958–Juillet 1962*.
    Paris; Plon, 1970.
de Gaulle, C., *Discours et Messages IV: Pour l'effort, Août 1962–Décembre 1965*.
    Paris; Plon, 1970.
Hernu, C., *Soldat-Citoyen: Essai sur la Défense et la Sécurité de la France*. Paris;
    Flammarion, 1975.
Hernu, C., *Chroniques d'Attente: Réflexions pour Gouverner Demain*. Paris; Téma-
    Editions, 1977.
Hernu, C., *Nous ... les Grands*. Lyon; F. G. Pres, 1980.
Hernu, C., *Défendre la Paix*. Paris; Lattès, 1985.
Mitterrand, F., *Ma Part de Vérité: De la Rupture à l'Unité*. Paris; Fayard, 1969.
Mitterrand, F., *Un Socialisme du Possible*. Paris; Seuil, 1970.
Mitterrand, F., *La Rose au Poing: Textes Politiques*. Paris; Flammarion, 1973.
Mitterrand, F., *La Paille et le Grain: Chronique*. Paris; Flammarion, 1975.
Mitterrand, F., *Politique I*. Paris; Fayard, 1977.
Mitterrand, F., *L'Abeille et l'Architecte: Chronique*. Paris; Flammarion, 1978.
Mitterrand, F., *Ici et Maintenant: Conversations avec Guy Claisse*. Paris; Fayard, 1980.
Mitterrand, F., *Politique II*. Paris; Fayard, 1982.
Mitterrand, F., *The Wheat and the Chaff*. London; Weidenfeld and Nicolson,
    1982. Translated from the French by R. S. Woodward.
Mitterrand, F., *Réflexions sur la Politique Extérieure de la France: Introduction à
    Vingt-Cinq Discours (1981–1985)*. Paris; Fayard, 1986.
Mitterrand, F., *Lettre à Tous les Français*. Paris, 8 April 1988.
Mitterrand, F., *François Mitterrand et la Crise du Golfe (Discours et Messages: 9 août
    1990–16 janvier 1991)*. Paris; T. Mage, 1991.
Mitterrand, F., *François Mitterrand et la Guerre du Golfe (Discours et Messages: 20
    janvier-3 mars 1991)*. Paris; T. Mage, 1991.

266   *Bibliography*

Mitterrand, F., *Le Coup d'Etat Permanent*. Paris; Editions 10/18, 1993.
Mitterrand, F., *Discours, 1981–1995*. Paris; Europolis, 1995.
Mitterrand, F., *Onze Discours sur l'Europe (1982–1995)*, Collection Biblioteca Europea, no. 8. Naples; Vivarium, 1996.
Mitterrand, F., *De l'Allemagne, de la France*. Paris; Editions Odile Jacob, 1996.
Mitterrand, F., *Mémoires Interrompus*. Paris; Editions Odile Jacob, 1996.

Speeches reproduced in *Défense Nationale*

Bérégovoy, P., 'Construction Européenne et Intérêt de la France: Discours de Monsieur Pierre Bérégovoy, Premier Ministre, le 3 septembre 1992, devant les auditeurs de l'Institut des Hautes Etudes de Défense Nationale,' *Défense Nationale*, 48, 11 (November 1992) 11–25.
Chevènement, J.-P., 'La Défense de la France, la Sécurité et l'Avenir de l'Europe: Discours de Monsieur Jean-Pierre Chevènement, Ministre de la Défense, devant l'Académie de l'état-major général soviétique, à Moscou, le 5 avril 1989,' *Défense Nationale*, 45, 6 (June 1989) 13–34.
Chevènement, J.-P., 'Evolution du Monde, Rôle et Politique de Défense de la France: Discours de Monsieur Jean-Pierre Chevènement, Ministre de la Défense, le 21 mai 1990, devant les auditeurs de l'Institut des Hautes Etudes de Défense Nationale,' *Défense Nationale*, 46, 7 (July 1990) 9–28.
Chirac, J., 'La Politique de Défense de la France: Allocution du Premier Ministre, le 12 septembre 1986, lors de la séance d'ouverture de la 39e session de l'Institut des Hautes Etudes de Défense Nationale,' *Défense Nationale*, 42, 11 (November 1986) 7–17.
Chirac, J., 'La France et les Enjeux de la Sécurité Européenne: Allocution du Premier Ministre, le 12 décembre 1987, devant les auditeurs de l'Institut des Hautes Etudes de Défense Nationale,' *Défense Nationale*, 44, 2 (February 1988) 9–18.
Cresson, E., 'Défense et Avenir de l'Europe: Discours de Madame Edith Cresson, Premier Ministre, le 5 septembre 1991, devant les auditeurs de l'Institut des Hautes Etudes de Défense Nationale,' *Défense Nationale*, 47, 11 (November 1991) 9–19.
Debré, M., 'Les Principes de Notre Politique de Défense,' *Revue de Défense Nationale*, 26, 8/9 (August/September 1970) 1245–58.
Fabius, L., 'La Politique de Défense: Rassembler et Moderniser. Allocution du Premier Ministre, le 17 septembre 1984, lors de la séance d'ouverture de la 37e session de l'IHEDN,' *Défense Nationale*, 40, 11 (November 1984) 7–17.
Fabius, L., 'Patriotisme, Indépendance, Solidarité. Allocution du Premier Ministre, le 13 septembre 1985, lors de la séance d'ouverture de la 38e session de l'IHEDN,' *Défense Nationale*, 41, 11 (November 1985) 9–18.
Giraud, A., 'Donner à la France une Défense Forte: Discours de Monsieur André Giraud, Ministre de la Défense, à l'Assemblée Nationale, le 12 novembre 1986, à l'occasion de la présentation du budget de la défense pour 1987,' *Défense Nationale*, 43, 1 (January 1987) 11–25.
Giraud, A., 'La Défense de la France et la Sécurité Européenne: Discours de Monsieur André Giraud, Ministre de la Défense Français, à Chatham House, le 22 mars 1988,' *Défense Nationale*, 44, 5 (May 1988) 11–19.
Giscard d'Estaing, V., 'Allocution de M. Valéry Giscard d'Estaing, Président de la République, à l'occasion de sa visite à l'Institut des Hautes Etudes de

Défense Nationale, Paris, le 1er juin 1976,' *Défense Nationale*, 32, 7 (July 1976) 5–20.

Hernu, C., 'Répondre aux Défis d'un Monde Dangereux: Discours prononcé par M. Charles Hernu, Ministre de la Défense, devant les auditeurs de l'Institut des Hautes Etudes de Défense Nationale,' *Défense Nationale*, 37, 12 (December 1981) 5–23.

Hernu, C., 'Face à la Logique des Blocs, une France Indépendante et Solidaire: Discours de M. Charles Hernu, Ministre de la Défense, devant les auditeurs de la 35e session de l'Institut des Hautes Etudes de Défense Nationale, le 16 novembre 1982,' *Défense Nationale*, 38, 12 (December 1982) 7–21.

Hernu, C., 'Equilibre, Dissuasion, Volonté: la Voie Etroite de la Paix et de la Liberté. Discours de M. Charles Hernu, Ministre de la Défense, devant les auditeurs de la 36e session de l'Institut des Hautes Etudes de Défense Nationale, le 15 novembre 1983,' *Défense Nationale*, 39, 12 (December 1983) 5–20.

Hernu, C., 'Politique de Défense: une Prospective. Allocution de Monsieur Charles Hernu, Ministre de la Défense, devant les auditeurs de l'Institut des Hautes Etudes de Défense Nationale, le 21 mai 1985,' *Défense Nationale*, 41, 7 (July 1985) 5–14.

Joxe, P., 'Défense et Renseignement: Discours de Monsieur Pierre Joxe, Ministre de la Défense, le 6 mai 1991, devant les auditeurs de l'Institut des Hautes Etudes de Défense Nationale,' *Défense Nationale*, 47, 7 (July 1991) 9–21.

Juppé, A., 'La France et la Sécurité Européenne: Discours de Monsieur Alain Juppé, Ministre des Affaires Etrangères, devant le Forum de la *Wehrkunde*, à Munich, le 4 février, 1995,' *Défense Nationale*, 51, 4 (April 1995) 5–15.

Lacaze, Gén. J., 'La Politique Militaire: Exposé du Chef d'état-major des armées au Centre des Hautes Etudes de l'Armement, le 29 septembre 1981,' *Défense Nationale*, 37, 11 (November 1981) 7–26.

Lacaze, Gén. J., 'Politique de Défense et Stratégie Militaire de la France: Exposé du Chef d'état-major des armées devant l'Institut des Hautes Etudes de Défense Nationale, le 3 mai 1983,' *Défense Nationale*, 39, 6 (June 1983) 11–29.

Lacaze, Gén. J., 'Concept de Défense et Sécurité en Europe: Exposé du Chef d'état-major des armées à l'Institut des Hautes Etudes de Défense Nationale le 19 mai 1984,' *Défense Nationale*, 40, 7 (July 1984) 11–29.

Lacaze, Gén. J., 'L'Avenir de la Défense Française: Conférence du Chef d'état-major des armées à l'Institut des Hautes Etudes de Défense Nationale, le 11 mai 1985,' *Défense Nationale*, 41, 7 (July 1985) 15–33.

Léotard, F., 'Une Nouvelle Culture de la Défense: Discours de Monsieur François Léotard, Ministre d'Etat, Ministre de la Défense, le 15 mai 1993, devant les auditeurs de l'Institut des Hautes Etudes de Défense Nationale,' *Défense Nationale*, 49, 7 (July 1993) 9–19.

Léotard, F., 'L'Effort de Défense: Une Volonté Politique. Discours de Monsieur François Léotard, Ministre d'Etat, Ministre de la Défense, le 2 septembre 1993, devant les auditeurs de l'Institut des Hautes Etudes de Défense Nationale,' *Défense Nationale*, 49, 10 (October 1993) 9–25.

Léotard, F., 'La Rationalisation de l'Industrie de Défense: Discours de Monsieur François Léotard, Ministre d'Etat, Ministre de la Défense, le 8 septembre 1993, devant les auditeurs du Centre des Hautes Etudes de l'Armement,' *Défense Nationale*, 49, 11 (November 1993) 9–19.

Mauroy, P., 'La Cohérence d'une Politique de Défense: Allocution du Premier Ministre, le 14 septembre 1981, lors de la séance d'ouverture de la 34e session de l'IHEDN,' *Défense Nationale*, 37, 10 (October 1981) 15–28.

Mauroy, P., 'Vers un Nouveau Modèle d'Armée: Allocution du Premier Ministre, le 20 septembre 1982, lors de la séance d'ouverture de la 35e session de l'IHEDN,' *Défense Nationale*, 38, 11 (November 1982) 9–28.

Mauroy, P., 'La Stratégie de la France: Allocution du Premier Ministre, le 20 septembre 1983, lors de la séance d'ouverture de la 36e session de l'IHEDN,' *Défense Nationale*, 39, 11 (November 1983) 5–22.

Méry, Gén. G., 'Réflexions sur le Concept d'Emploi des Forces,' *Défense Nationale*, 31, 11 (November 1975) 15–26.

Méry, Gén. G., 'Une Armée pour Quoi Faire et Comment?' *Défense Nationale*, 32, 6 (June 1976) 11–34.

Mitterrand, F., 'Allocution de M. François Mitterrand, Président de la République, devant les auditeurs de l'Institut des Hautes Etudes de Défense Nationale, le 11 octobre 1988,' *Défense Nationale*, 44, 11 (November 1988) 13–27.

Pasqua, C., 'La Défense Civile: Allocution de Monsieur Charles Pasqua, Ministre de l'Intérieur, devant les auditeurs de l'Institut des Hautes Etudes de Défense Nationale, le 16 novembre 1987,' *Défense Nationale*, 44, 1 (January 1988) 11–31.

Quilès, P., 'L'Avenir de Notre Concept de Défense Face aux Progrès Technologiques: Allocution de Monsieur Paul Quilès, Ministre de la Défense, devant les auditeurs de l'Institut des Hautes Etudes de Défense Nationale, le 12 novembre 1985,' *Défense Nationale*, 42, 1 (January 1986) 11–24.

Rocard, M., 'L'Europe et sa Sécurité: Allocution de M. Michel Rocard, Premier Ministre, à la première session européenne de l'Institut des Hautes Etudes de Défense Nationale, le 15 novembre 1988,' *Défense Nationale*, 45, 1 (January 1989) 13–25.

Rocard, M., 'Les Orientations de la Politique de Défense de la France: Discours de Monsieur Michel Rocard, Premier Ministre, le 7 septembre 1989, devant les auditeurs de l'Institut des Hautes Etudes de Défense Nationale,' *Défense Nationale*, 45, 11 (November 1989) 13–29.

Rocard, M., 'La France et l'Ordre International: Discours de Monsieur Michel Rocard, Premier Ministre, le 22 octobre 1990, devant les auditeurs de l'Institut des Hautes Etudes de Défense Nationale,' *Défense Nationale*, 46, 12 (December 1990) 9–21.

Séguin, P., 'La Défense de la France: Discours de M. Philippe Séguin, Président de l'Assemblée Nationale, devant l'Union des Associations de l'Institut des Hautes Etudes de Défense Nationale, le 20 janvier 1994,' *Défense Nationale*, 50, 4 (April 1994) 7–20.

Interview sources

Interview with Monsieur J. Attali, 23.5.96.
Interview with Monsieur H. Védrine, 12.6.96.
Interview with Monsieur P. Boniface, 13.6.96.
Interview with Professor M. Vaïsse, 14.6.96.
Interview with Monsieur J. Boyon, 19.6.96.

I am particularly grateful to these people, and to others who wished to remain anonymous, for their time, consideration and patience in answering my questions.

Published secondary sources

French-language sources: books

Boniface, P., *L'Armée: Enquête sur 300,000 Soldats Méconnus* (Paris; Edition°1, 1990).

Boniface, P. and Gribinski, J.-F., *Les Ecologistes et la Défense* (Paris; Dunod, 1994).

Bozo, F., *La France et l'OTAN: De la Guerre Froide au Nouvel Ordre Européen. Travaux et Recherches de l'IFRI* (Paris; Masson, 1991).

Boulic, J.-Y., *Le Bonheur, la Vie, la Mort, Dieu ...* (Paris; Editions du Cerf, 1981).

Cotteret, J.-M., Emeri, C., Gerstlé, J. and Moreau, R., *Giscard d'Estaing-Mitterrand: 54,774 Mots pour Convaincre* (Paris; Presses Universitaires de France, 1976).

Favier, P. and Martin-Roland, M., *La Décennie Mitterrand, Tome I: Les Ruptures (1981–1984)* (Paris; Seuil, 1990).

Favier, P. and Martin-Roland, M., *La Décennie Mitterrand, Tome II: Les Epreuves (1984–1988)* (Paris; Seuil, 1991).

Giesbert, F.-O., *François Mitterrand ou la Tentation de l'Histoire* (Paris; Seuil, 1977).

Griotteray, A., *Lettre aux Giscardo-Gaullistes: Sur une Certaine Idée de la France* (Paris; Editions Mangès, 1980).

Guisnel, J., *Charles Hernu ou la République au Cœur* (Paris; Fayard, 1993).

Klein, J., *Maîtrise des Armements et Désarmement: Les Accords Conclus Depuis 1945* (Paris; La Documentation Française, 1991).

Krop, P., *Les Socialistes et l'Armée* (Paris; Presses Universitaires de France, 1983).

Lellouche, P., *Légitime défense: Vers une Europe en Sécurité au XXIème Siècle* (Paris; Editions Patrick Banon, 1996).

Manceron, C. and Pingaud, B. (eds), *François Mitterrand: l'Homme, les Idées, le Programme*. Second edn (Paris; Flammarion, 1981).

Mathieu, J.-L., *La Défense Nationale*, Collection Que Sais-Je? no. 2028 (Paris; Presses Universitaires de France, 1996).

Messmer, P. and Larcan, A., *Les Écrits Militaires de Charles de Gaulle: Essai d'Analyse Thématique* (Paris; Presses Universitaires de France, 1985).

Nay, C., *Le Noir et le Rouge* (Paris; Grasset, 1984).

Nay, C., *Les Sept Mitterrand, ou les Métamorphoses d'un Septennat* (Paris; Grasset, 1988).

Péan, P., *Une Jeunesse Française* (Paris; Seuil, 1994).

Schwartzbrod, A., *Le Président qui n'aimait pas la Guerre: dans les Coulisses du Pouvoir Militaire, 1981–1995* (Paris; Plon, 1995).

Vaïsse, M., Mélandri, P. and Bozo, F. (sous la direction de), *La France et l'OTAN, 1949–1996* (Brussels; Editions Complexe, 1996).

Valentin, F., *Regards sur la Politique de Défense de la France: de 1958 à nos jours* (Paris; Fondation pour les Etudes de Défense, 1995).

Védrine, H., *Les Mondes de François Mitterrand* (Paris; Fayard, 1996).

English-language sources: books

Andreopoulos, G. J. and Selesky, H. E. (eds), *The Aftermath of Defeat: Societies, Armed Forces, and the Challenge of Recovery* (New Haven; Yale University Press, 1994).

Andrews, W. G. and Hoffmann, S., *The Fifth Republic at Twenty* (Albany; State University of New York Press, 1981).

Baker, J. A., III, with Defrank, T. M., *The Politics of Diplomacy: Revolution, War and Peace 1989–1992* (New York; Putnam's, 1995).

Ball, D. and Richelson, J. (eds), *Strategic Nuclear Targeting* (New York; Ithaca, 1986).

Baylis, J., Booth, K., Garnett, J. and Williams, P., *Contemporary Strategy I: Theories and Concepts*. Second edn (New York; Holmes and Meier, 1987).

Baylis, J., Booth, K., Garnett, J. and Williams, P., *Contemporary Strategy II: The Nuclear Powers*. Second edn (New York; Holmes and Meier, 1987).

Beckett, I. F. W. and Pimlott, J., *Armed Forces and Modern Counter-Insurgency* (New York; St. Martin's Press, 1985).

Bell, D. S. and Criddle, B., *The French Socialist Party: the Emergence of a Party of Government*. Second edn (Oxford; Clarendon Press, 1988).

Boyer, Y., Lellouche, P. and Roper, J. (eds), *Franco-British Defence Co-operation: a New Entente Cordiale?* (London; Routledge for the Royal Institute of International Affairs, London, and l'Institut Français des relations Internationales, Paris, 1989).

Burrows, Sir B. and Irwin, C., *The Security of Western Europe: Towards a Common Defence Policy* (London; Charles Knight and Co., 1972).

Capitanchik, D. and Eichenberg, R. C., 'Defence and Public Opinion,' *Chatham House Papers* no. 20 (London; Routledge and Kegan Paul/Royal Institute of International Affairs, 1983).

Cerny, P. G. and Schain, M. A. (eds), *Socialism, the State and Public Policy in France* (London; Frances Pinter, 1985).

Chafer, T. and Jenkins, B. (eds), *France: from the Cold War to the New World Order* (London; Macmillan, 1996).

Chipman, J., 'French Military Policy and African Security,' *Adelphi Papers* No. 201, Summer 1985 (London; International Institute for Strategic Studies [hereafter IISS], 1985).

Clayton, A., *The Wars of French Decolonization* (London; Longman, 1994).

Cobban, H., *The Making of Modern Lebanon* (London; Hutchinson, 1987).

Codding, G. A., Jr. and Safran, W., *Ideology and Politics: the Socialist Party of France* (Boulder, Colorado; Westview Press, 1979).

Cole, A., *François Mitterrand: a Study in Political Leadership* (London; Routledge, 1994).

Daley, A. (ed.), *The Mitterrand Era: Policy Alternatives and Political Mobilisation in France* (London; Macmillan, 1996).

Debouzy, O., *Anglo-French Nuclear Co-operation, Perspectives and Problems* (London; RUSI for Defence Studies, 1991).

Deighton, A. (ed.), *Western European Union, 1954–1997: Defence, Security, Integration* (Oxford; European Interdependence Research Unit, St. Antony's College, 1997).

DePorte, A. W., *Europe between the Superpowers: the Enduring Balance* (New Haven; Yale University Press, 1979).

Derbyshire, I., *Politics in France: from Giscard to Mitterrand* (Edinburgh; Chambers, 1990).

Feld, W. J., *The Foreign Policies of West European Socialist Parties* (New York; Praeger, 1978).

Frears, J. R., *France in the Giscard Presidency* (London; George Allen and Unwin, 1981).

Freedman, L., *The Evolution of Nuclear Strategy*. Second edn (London; Macmillan for the IISS, 1993).

Furniss, E. S., Jr., *De Gaulle and the French Army: a Crisis in Civil–Military Relations* (New York; Twentieth Century Fund, 1964).

Furniss, E. S., Jr, *France, Troubled Ally: De Gaulle's Heritage and Prospects* (Westport; Greenwood Press, 1974).

Gordon, P. H., *A Certain Idea of France: French Security Policy and the Gaullist Legacy* (Princeton, NJ; Princeton University Press, 1993).

Grosser, A., *The Western Alliance: European–American Relations since 1945* (London; Macmillan, 1980). Translated from the French by M. Shaw.

Haddad, W. D., *Lebanon: the Politics of Revolving Doors* (New York; Praeger, 1985).

Hanley, D., *Keeping Left? Ceres and the French Socialist Party: a Contribution to the Study of Fractionalism in Political Parties* (Manchester; Manchester University Press, 1986).

Hanley, D. L., Kerr, A. P. and Waites, N. H., *Contemporary France* (London; Routledge and Kegan Paul, 1984).

Harrison, M. M., *The Reluctant Ally: France and Atlantic Security* (Baltimore; Johns Hopkins University Press, 1981).

Hayward, J. E. S., *Governing France: the One and Indivisible Republic*. Second edn (London; Weidenfeld and Nicolson, 1983).

Holdren, J. and Rotblat, J. (eds), *Strategic Defences and the Future of the Arms Race: a Pugwash Symposium* (London; Macmillan, 1987).

Horne, A., *The French Army and Politics, 1870–1970* (London; Macmillan, 1984).

Horne, A., *A Savage War of Peace: Algeria 1954–1962*. Revised edn. (London; Papermac, 1996).

Howorth, J., *France: the Politics of Peace* (London; END/Merlin Press, 1984).

Howorth, J. and Chilton, P. (eds), *Defence and Dissent in Contemporary France* (London; Croom Helm, 1984).

Hudson, M. C., *The Precarious Republic: Political Modernisation in Lebanon* (Boulder, Co.; Westview, 1985).

International Institute for Strategic Studies, *The Military Balance, 1992–1993* (London; Oxford University Press for the IISS, 1992).

International Institute for Strategic Studies, *The Military Balance 1993–1994* (London; Oxford University Press for the IISS, 1993).

International Institute for Strategic Studies, *The Military Balance, 1994–1995* (London; Oxford University Press for the IISS, 1994).

Johnstone, D., *The Politics of Euromissiles: Europe's Role in America's World* (London; Verso, 1984).

Jordan, R. S. (ed.), *Europe and the Superpowers: Essays on European International Politics* (London; Pinter, 1991).

Keeler, J. T. S. and Schain, M. A. (eds), *Chirac's Challenge: Liberalisation, Europeanization and Malaise in France* (London; Macmillan, 1997).

Kelly, G. A., *Lost Soldiers: the French Army and Empire in Crisis 1947–1962* (Cambridge, Mass.; MIT Press, 1965).

Kissinger, H., *Diplomacy* (New York; Simon and Schuster, 1994).

Kohl, W. L., *French Nuclear Diplomacy* (Princeton, NJ; Princeton University Press, 1971).

Kugler, R. L., *Commitment to Purpose: How Alliance Partnership Won the Cold War* (Santa Monica; RAND Corporation, 1993).

Lacouture, J., *De Gaulle, the Ruler: 1945–1970* (London; Harvill, 1991). Translated from the French by A. Sheridan.

Laughland, J., *The Death of Politics: France under Mitterrand* (London; Michael Joseph, 1994).

MacShane, D., *François Mitterrand: a Political Odyssey* (London; Quartet, 1982).

Martin, M. L., *Warriors to Managers: the French Military Establishment since 1945* (Chapel Hill; University of North Carolina Press, 1981).

McInnes, C. (ed.), *Security and Strategy in the New Europe* (London; Routledge, 1992).

McMillan, J. F., *Twentieth Century France: Politics and Society, 1898–1991* (London; Edward Arnold, 1992).

Menard, O. D., *The Army and the Fifth Republic* (Lincoln, Nebraska; University of Nebraska Press, 1967).

Mendl, W., *Deterrence and Persuasion: French Nuclear Armament in the Context of National Policy, 1945–1969* (London; Faber and Faber, 1970).

Morgan, R. and Bray C., *Partners and Rivals in Western Europe: Britain, France and Germany* (Aldershot; Gower, 1986).

Newhouse, J., *De Gaulle and the Anglo-Saxons* (London; Andre Deutsch, 1970).

Nitze, P. H., with A. M. Smith and S. L. Rearden, *From Hiroshima to Glasnost: at the Centre of Decision. A Memoir* (London; Weidenfeld and Nicolson, 1990).

Northcutt, W., *Mitterrand: a Political Biography* (New York; Holmes and Meier, 1992).

Peleg, I., *Begin's Foreign Policy, 1977–1983: Israel's Move to the Right* (New York; Greenwood Press, 1987).

Pickles, D., *The Fifth French Republic: Institutions and Politics*. Third edn (London; Methuen, 1965).

Pimlott, J. and Badsey, S., *The Gulf War Assessed* (London; Arms and Armour Press, 1992).

Porch, D., *The French Secret Services: from the Dreyfus Affair to the Gulf War* (Oxford; Oxford University Press, 1997).

Posner, T. R., *Current French Security Policy: the Gaullist Legacy* (Westport, CT.; Greenwood Press, 1991).

Raymond, G. (ed.), *France during the Socialist Years* (Aldershot; Dartmouth, 1994).

Ross, G., Hoffmann, S. and Malzacher, S. (eds), *The Mitterrand Experiment: Continuity and Change in Modern France* (Cambridge; Polity Press, 1987).

Salem, E. A., *Violence and Diplomacy in Lebanon: the Troubled Years, 1982–1988* (London; I. B. Tauris, 1995).

Scheinman, L., *Atomic Energy Policy in France under the Fourth Republic* (Princeton, NJ; Princeton University Press, 1965).

Schlör, W. F., 'German Security Policy,' *Adelphi Papers* no. 277, June 1993. (London; Brassey's for the IISS, 1993).

Serre, F. de la, Leruez, J. and Wallace, H. (eds), *French and British Foreign Policies in Transition: the Challenge of Adjustment* (New York; Berg for the Royal Institute of International Affairs, London, and Centre d'Etudes et de Recherches Internationales, Paris, 1990).

Somerville, K., *Foreign Military Intervention in Africa* (London; Pinter, 1990).

Story, J. (ed.), *The New Europe: Politics, Government and Economy since 1945* (Oxford; Blackwell, 1993).

Szarka, J., *Business in France: an Introduction to the Economic and Social Context* (London; Pitman, 1992).

Talbott, S., *Deadly Gambits: the Reagan Administration and the Stalemate in Nuclear Arms Control* (New York; Alfred A. Knopf, 1984).

Taylor, T., 'European Defence Co-operation,' *Chatham House Papers* No. 24 (London; Routledge and Kegan Paul/Royal Institute of International Affairs, 1984).

Taylor, T. (ed.), *Reshaping European Defence* (London; Royal Institute of International Affairs, 1994).

Thatcher, M., *The Downing Street Years* (London; HarperCollins, 1993).

Trumpbour, J. (ed.), *The Dividing Rhine: Politics and Society in Contemporary France and Germany* (Oxford; Berg, 1989).

Tuppen, J., *Chirac's France: Contemporary Issues in French Society* (London; Macmillan, 1991).

Williams, P. M., *Crisis and Compromise: Politics in the Fourth Republic* (London; Longman, 1964).

Wright, V. (ed.), *Conflict and Consensus in France* (London; Frank Cass, 1979).

Wright, V. (ed.), *Continuity and Change in France* (London; George Allen and Unwin, 1984).

Yost, D. S., 'France's Deterrent Posture and Security in Europe Part I: Capabilities and Doctrine,' *Adelphi Papers* No. 194, Winter 1984/85 (London; IISS, 1985).

Yost, D. S., 'France's Deterrent Posture and Security in Europe Part II: Strategic and Arms Control Implications,' *Adelphi Papers* No. 195, Winter 1984/85 (London; IISS, 1985).

Young, J. H., 'The French Strategic Missile Programme,' *Adelphi Papers* No. 38, July 1967 (London; IISS, 1967).

French-language sources: articles

Aben. J. and Maury, J.-P., 'Pour en Finir avec l'Inflation Militaire,' *Défense Nationale*, 43, 8/9 (August/September 1987) 111–24.

Ailleret, Gén., 'Opinion sur la Théorie Stratégique de la «Flexible Response»,' *Revue de Défense Nationale*, 20, 8/9 (August/September 1964) 1323–40.

Ailleret, Gén., 'Evolution Nécessaire de nos Structures Militaires,' *Revue de Défense Nationale*, 21, 6 (June 1965) 947–55.

Ailleret, Gén., 'Défense «Dirigée» ou Défense «Tous Azimuts»,' *Revue de Défense Nationale*, 23, 12 (December 1967) 1923–32.

Aladin, 'Tchad, Début 1987,' *Défense Nationale*, 43, 10 (October 1987) 165–9.

Baer, A., 'Réflexions sur les Nouveaux Concepts d'Alliance,' *Défense Nationale*, 42, 2 (February 1986) 44–57.

Baer, A., 'Quelles Armées dans un Nouvel Ordre International?' *Défense Nationale*, 48, 3 (March 1992) 39–51.

Faivre, M., 'Les Chiffres Actuels et Futurs du Service National,' *Défense Nationale*, 46, 11 (November 1990) 182–3.

Faivre, M., 'Les Chiffres du Service National,' *Défense Nationale*, 46, 12 (December 1990) 176–81.

Faivre, M., 'Le Budget Militaire à l'Assemblée Nationale,' *Défense Nationale*, 47, 1 (January 1991) 171–5.

Faivre, M., 'Le Colloque «Conscription et Armée de Métier»,' *Défense Nationale*, 47, 4 (April 1991) 178–81.

Faivre, M., '«Armées 2000»: Des Principes à la Mise en Oeuvre,' *Défense Nationale*, 47, 5 (May 1991) 179–83.

Faivre, M., 'Débat sur la Défense à l'Assemblée Nationale,' *Défense Nationale*, 47, 8/9 (August/September 1991) 186–8.

Faivre, M., 'Le Plan Armées 2000,' *Défense Nationale*, 47, 11 (November 1991) 171–2.

Faivre, M., 'Diversification du Service et Précisions Statistiques,' *Défense Nationale*, 47, 12 (December 1991) 178–82.

Faivre, M., 'Du Bilan Social au Budget et à la Programmation,' *Défense Nationale*, 48, 1 (January 1992) 170–6.

Faivre, M., 'Les Armements Nouveaux Arrivent,' *Défense Nationale*, 48, 3 (March 1992) 168–71.

Faivre, M., 'Les Nouvelles Missions des Armées,' *Défense Nationale*, 48, 5 (May 1992) 180–4.

Faivre, M., 'Les Restructurations en 1993,' *Défense Nationale*, 48, 6 (June 1992) 178–80.

Faivre, M., 'Réorganisation Ministérielle,' *Défense Nationale*, 48, 8/9 (August/September 1992) 184–5.

Faivre, M., 'Participation Française aux Missions de Paix de l'ONU,' *Défense Nationale*, 48, 11 (November 1992) 189–95.

Faivre, M., 'Du Budget de 1993 au «Référentiel» de 1997,' *Défense Nationale*, 49, 1 (January 1993) 166–70.

Faivre, M., 'Les Equipements Militaires de 1997,' *Défense Nationale*, 49, 2 (February 1993) 172–8.

Faivre, M., 'Le Service National en Question,' *Défense Nationale*, 49, 6 (June 1993) 172–5.

Fistié, P., 'La France, Maastricht et la Défense Européenne,' *Politique Internationale*, 56 (Summer 1992) 129–40.

Fontaine, A., 'Diplomatie Française: Un Modèle Gaullien,' *Politique Internationale*, 52 (Summer 1991) 57–67.

Forget, Gén. M., 'L'Europe, le Piège et le Sursaut,' *Défense Nationale*, 43, 6 (June 1987) 32–44.

Forget, P., 'Eléments pour une Analyse Politico-Stratégique de l'IDS,' *Défense Nationale*, 42, 3 (March 1986) 21–34.

Fourquet, Gén. d'Armée Aérienne M., 'Emploi des Différents Systèmes de Forces dans le Cadre de la Stratégie de Dissuasion,' *Revue de Défense Nationale*, 25, 5 (May 1969) 757–67.

François-Poncet, J., 'Quatre Ans de Politique Etrangère Socialiste. Le Mirage Evanoui,' *Politique Etrangère*, 50, 2 (Summer 1985) 437–47.

Gallois, P.-M., 'La France, les SS.20 et la Sécurité de l'Europe,' *Politique Internationale*, 13 (Autumn 1981) 49–64.

Gallois, P. M., 'Désarmement: un Piège pour l'Occident?' *Politique Internationale*, 43 (Spring 1989) 355–69.

Genty, R., 'IDS: Révolution ou Evolution dans l'Art Militaire?' *Défense Nationale*, 43, 4 (April 1987) 119–31.

Gergorin, J.-L., 'Quelles Nouvelles Menaces, Quelles Ripostes, Quelle Dissuasion?' *Défense Nationale*, 48, 6 (June 1992) 43–9.

Gibour, J., 'Le Conflit du Tchad,' *Défense Nationale*, 41, 6 (June 1985) 127–38.

Girard, C., 'L'Avenir de la Guerre,' *Défense Nationale*, 48, 8/9 (August/September 1992) 47–61.

Gorand, F., 'Les Européens et la Politique Européenne de Défense,' *Politique Etrangère*, 49, 4 (Winter 1984) 943–9.

Guillerez, B., 'Sahara Occidental et Tchad: Deux Succès dans la Guerre du Désert,' *Défense Nationale*, 40, 8/9 (August/September 1984) 178–81.

Guillerez, B., 'Tchad: Fin de l'Opération Manta,' *Défense Nationale*, 40, 11 (November 1984) 181–5.

Guillerez, B., 'Au Tchad: La Guerre des Nerfs,' *Défense Nationale*, 41, 1 (January 1985) 175–8.

Guillerez, B., 'Le Tchad Toujours sous la Menace,' *Défense Nationale*, 42, 4 (April 1986) 181–4.

Guillerez, B., 'Le Conflit du Tchad Tourne au Détriment de la Libye,' *Défense Nationale*, 43, 4 (April 1987) 178–81.

Guillerez, B., 'Le Gambit des Euromissiles,' *Défense Nationale*, 44, 2 (February 1988) 155–60.

Guillerez, B., 'Le Tchad Renoue Avec la Libye, mais le Bras de Fer Continue,' *Défense Nationale*, 45, 1 (January 1989) 190–3.

Guillerez, B., 'Les Difficultés Particulières du Rwanda,' *Défense Nationale*, 46, 6 (June 1990) 195–7.

Guillerez, B., 'L'ONU Face au défi Irakien dans le Golfe,' *Défense Nationale*, 46, 10 (October 1990) 170–1.

Guillerez, B., 'Somalie: Les Déchirements d'un Peuple,' *Défense Nationale*, 47, 3 (March 1991) 176–9.

Hassner, P., 'L'Europe Sans Options?' *Politique Internationale*, 37 (Autumn 1987) 97–110.

Heisbourg, F., 'La France Face aux Nouvelles Données Stratégiques,' *Défense Nationale*, 42, 4 (April 1986) 35–47.

Heisbourg, F., 'Réflexions sur la Politique de Défense de la France,' *Politique Etrangère*, 55, 1 (Spring 1990) 157–69.

Heisbourg, F., 'Quelles Leçons Stratégiques de la Guerre du Golfe?' *Politique Etrangère*, 56, 2 (Summer 1991) 411–22.

Heisbourg, F. and Lellouche, P., 'Faut-il Enterrer l'Alliance Atlantique?' *Politique Internationale*, 50 (Winter 1990/91) 163–75.

Huntzinger, J., 'L'Esprit de Défense en France,' *Défense Nationale*, 38, 12 (December 1982) 37–43.

Jeambrun, G., 'La Politique de Contrôle des Satellites Français (1990–2000),' *Défense Nationale*, 43, 2 (February 1987) 129–39.

Jeanclos, Y. and Manicacci, Gén. R., 'Sécurité de l'Europe et Stratégie Nucléaire Intégrale,' *Défense Nationale*, 45, 4 (April 1989) 23–35.

Jospin, L., 'Ni Alignement, ni Slogans,' *Politique Internationale*, 23 (Spring 1984) 41–5.

Paris, H. and Dagiral, C., 'L'Universalité des Théâtres d'Opérations, une Leçon de la Guerre du Golfe,' *Défense Nationale*, 47, 5 (May 1991) 67–73.

Poirier, L., 'La Greffe,' *Défense Nationale*, 39, 4 (April 1983) 5–32.

Polycarpe, G., 'De la Guerre des Etoiles,' *Défense Nationale*, 42, 12 (December 1986) 43–56.

Prater, F., 'La France et la Crise du Golfe,' *Politique Etrangère*, 56, 2 (Summer 1991) 441–53.

Rénier, X., 'Moineau Hardi–Kecker Spatz, le Plus Grand Exercice Franco-Allemand,' *Défense Nationale*, 43, 12 (December 1987) 176–8.

Le groupe "Renouveau Défense", 'Le Défi du Double Zéro,' *Défense Nationale*, 44, 2 (February 1988) 19–37.

Rivière, J., 'La Coopération Européenne: Un Atout Majeure,' *Défense Nationale*, 48, 11 (November 1992) 196–7.

Rivière, J., 'Les Restructurations dans l'Armée de Terre en 1994,' *Défense Nationale*, 49, 7 (July 1993) 190–3.

Robin, G., 'Un Concept en Quête de Substance: La Défense Européenne,' *Défense Nationale*, 51, 3 (March 1995) 89–95.

Rogalski, M., 'Dépenses Militaires et Dividendes de la Paix,' *Défense Nationale*, 48, 6 (June 1992) 119–32.

Roquejoffre, M., 'La Force d'Action Rapide,' *Défense Nationale*, 50, 1 (January 1994) 11–23.

Rose, F. de, 'La Défense de la France et de l'Europe,' *Défense Nationale*, 38, 12 (December 1982) 71–9.

Rose, F. de, 'Les Dilemmes Logistiques et Nucléaires Tactiques de la France,' *Politique Etrangère*, 49, 3 (Autumn 1984) 665–72.

Rose, F. de, 'Dissuader de la Guerre et Dissuader de la Crise,' *Politique Internationale*, 37 (Autumn 1987) 111–21.

Rose, F. de, 'Grands Problèmes Posés par une Petite Unité,' *Défense Nationale*, 43, 10 (October 1987) 9–12.

Rose, F. de, 'La Crise des Stratégies,' *Défense Nationale*, 46, 5 (May 1990) 61–71.

Saint-Germain, P.-I. de, 'L'Initiative de Défense Stratégique: Quel Défi pour la France?' *Défense Nationale*, 42, 6 (June 1986) 123–30.

Saint-Germain, P.-I. de, 'Les Systèmes d'Armes Actuels et Futurs,' *Défense Nationale*, 46, 10 (October 1990) 45–9.

Saint-Germain, P.-I. de, 'Les Forces Nucléaires dans le Nouveau Contexte Stratégique,' *Défense Nationale*, 48, 7 (July 1992) 17–24.

Saliou, M., 'La France et l'ONU. Des Ambitions Mondiales,' *Politique Etrangère*, 58, 3 (Autumn 1993) 687–95.

Saulnier, Gén. J., 'La Stratégie de Dissuasion Nucléaire Française, son Passé et son Avenir,' *Défense Nationale*, 46, 10 (October 1990) 35–43.

Saulnier, Gén. J., 'La Guerre du Golfe; Cas d'Espèce ou Modèle Reproductible?' *Défense Nationale*, 47, 6 (June 1991) 11–21.

Saulnier, Gén. J., 'Missions et Engagement des Forces Françaises,' *Défense Nationale*, 48, 7 (July 1992) 9–16.

Saulnier, Gén. J., 'Les Options Militaires Essentielles,' *Défense Nationale*, 51, 2 (February 1995) 37–44.

Schmidt, C., 'La Portée Economique des Lois de Programmation Militaire,' *Défense Nationale*, 48, 3 (March 1992) 53–67.

Schmitt, M., 'Armée de Métier ou Armée Mixte?' *Défense Nationale*, 49, 4 (April 1993) 9–18.

Schöllgen, G., 'Putting Germany's Post-Unification Foreign Policy to the Test,' *NATO Review*, 41, 2 (April 1993) 15–22.

Schütze, W. (ed.), 'Documents: Les Prises de Position des Hommes Politiques Français sur les Négociations Relatives à l'Elimination des Armes Nucléaires de Portée Intermédiaire en Europe,' *Politique Etrangère*, 52, 2 (Summer 1987) 461–73.

Schütze, W., 'Vingt-Deux Ans Après: Un Concept Français pour un Règlement Panallemand dans le Cadre Paneuropéen,' *Politique Etrangère*, 54, 3 (Autumn 1989) 453–6.

Schütze, W., 'La Réduction des Forces Conventionnelles en Europe,' *Défense Nationale*, 45, 12 (December 1989) 19–31.

Seitz, K., 'La Coopération Franco-Allemande dans le Domaine de la Politique de Sécurité,' *Politique Etrangère*, 47, 4 (December 1982) 979–87.

Sevaistre, O., 'L'Europe Face à l'Initiative de Défense Stratégique,' *Défense Nationale*, 41, 5 (May 1985) 23–33.

Sillard, Y., 'Vers l'Europe de l'Armement,' *Défense Nationale*, 49, 5 (May 1993) 23–7.

Soppelsa, J., 'Euromissiles et Surarmement pour une Grande Négociation,' *Défense Nationale*, 39, 5 (July 1983) 43–54.

Tiberghien, F., 'L'Effort de Défense Depuis 1981,' *Défense Nationale*, 41, 11 (November 1985) 31–70.

Torrelli, M., 'Les Missions Humanitaires de l'Armée Française,' *Défense Nationale*, 49, 3 (March 1993) 65–78.

Touchard, G.-E., 'Candide et l'Initiative de Défense Stratégique,' *Défense Nationale*, 42, 1 (January 1986) 25–38.

Touchard, G.-E., 'Désinformation et Initiative de Défense Stratégique,' *Défense Nationale*, 43, 5 (May 1987) 27–41.

Touraine, M., 'La France Face aux Armes Antisatellites,' *Défense Nationale*, 43, 3 (March 1987) 61–73.

Touraine, M., 'Le Retrait des FNI Soviétiques: Offensive Diplomatique ou Mutation Stratégique?' *Politique Etrangère*, 52, 3 (Autumn 1987) 699–711.

Vaillant, G., 'Le Nouveau Style de la Défense: Changement dans la Continuité?' *Défense Nationale*, 37, 8/9 (August/September 1981) 154–5.

Vaillant, G., 'Le Nouveau Pouvoir et la Défense: Maintien de la Force Nucléaire à un Seuil de Crédibilité, Rejet du Service à Six Mois, Poursuite des Etudes sur la Bombe à Neutrons,' *Défense Nationale*, 37, 10 (October 1981) 148–51.

Vaillant, G., 'En Relisant Deux Discours Récents sur la Défense,' *Défense Nationale*, 37, 11 (November 1981) 167–71.

Vaillant, G., 'Défense: Un Budget Hybride,' *Défense Nationale*, 37, 12 (December 1981) 154–62.

Valaison, G., 'La Loi de Programmation 1990–1993 et le Budget de la Marine pour 1990,' *Défense Nationale*, 46, 1 (January 1990) 188–93.

Valaison. G., 'Les Forces Navales dans le Golfe,' *Défense Nationale*, 47, 6 (June 1991) 188–91.

Valaison, G., 'L'Exercice «Îles d'Or»' *Défense Nationale*, 48, 1 (January 1992) 180–1.

Valaison, G., 'Au-delà de Notre Participation à la Forpronu,' *Défense Nationale*, 48, 6 (June 1992) 184–6.

Cogné, Lt R. L., 'France's Global Reach,' *Proceedings of the United States Naval Institute* (hereafter *Proceedings of the USNI*), 113/3/1069 (March 1987) 76–82.

Cogné, Lt R. L., 'The French Hunt Mines,' *Proceedings of the USNI*, 114/3/1021 (March 1988) 108–12.

Conze, H., 'France's Defence Procurement: Looking to the Future,' *Journal of the RUSI*, 140, 2 (April 1995) 48–51.

Cox, Lt Col G., 'France's Five Year Plan: the Defence Programme 1984–1988,' *The Army Quarterly and Defence Journal*, 114, 1 (January 1984) 22–31.

Cox, Lt Col G., 'France: The Republic's Ordnance,' *The Army Quarterly and Defence Journal*, 114, 2 (April 1984) 160–7.

Criddle, B., 'The French Socialists,' *West European Politics*, 1, 3 (October 1978) 157–61.

DePorte, A. W., 'France's New Realism,' *Foreign Affairs*, 63, 1 (Fall 1984) 144–65.

Dupas, A., 'Military Space: a View from France,' *RUSI and Brassey's Defence Yearbook 1989* (London; Brassey's, 1989) 255–62.

Evans, Lt Col, 'La Légion Etrangère Française,' *The Army Quarterly and Defence Journal*, 111, 1 (January 1981) 44–54.

Fabius, L., 'Excerpts from Speech by M. Laurent Fabius, Prime Minister of France at the Institute of Higher National Defence Studies, 17 September 1984,' *Survival*, 26, 6 (November/December 1984) 280–2.

Fenske, J., 'France's Uncertain Progress toward European Union,' *Current History*, 90, 559 (November 1991) 358–62.

Foster, E., 'The Franco-German Corps: a "Theological" Debate?' *Journal of the RUSI*, 137, 4 (August 1992) 63–7.

Frank. P., 'Twenty Years' Franco-German Treaty,' *Aussenpolitik*, 34, 1 (1983) 17–29.

French Embassy Press and Information Service, 'France's Defense Policy,' *Military Review*, lvii, 2 (February 1977) 26–36.

Fricaud-Chagnaud, Gén., (Retd), 'France's Defence Policy: the Law on the Long-Range Plan for 1984–1988,' *NATO Review*, 32, 1 (1984) 4–9.

Froman, M. B., Gardener, A. L., Mixer, S. R. and Poensgen, A., 'Strategic Implications of SDI for France and West Germany,' *Journal of the RUSI*, 132, 2 (June 1987) 51–6.

Gallois, P. M., 'The Raison d'Être of French Defence Policy,' *International Affairs*, 39, 4 (October 1963) 497–510.

Gallois, P. M., 'French Military Politics,' *The Bulletin of the Atomic Scientists*, 37, 7 (August/September 1981) 21–5.

George, B., MP, and Marcus, J., 'Change and Continuity in French Defence Policy,' *Journal of the RUSI*, 129, 2 (June 1984) 13–19.

George, B., MP, and Marcus, J., 'French Security Policy,' *The Washington Quarterly*, 7, 4 (Fall 1984) 148–58.

Golan, T., 'A Certain Mystery: How can France do Everything that it does in Africa – and Get Away With It?' *African Affairs*, 80, 318 (January 1981) 3–11.

Goodman, E. R., 'France and Arms for the Atlantic Alliance: the Standardisation–Interoperability Problem,' *Orbis*, 24, 3 (Fall 1980) 541–71.

Grant, R. P., 'France's New Relationship with NATO,' *Survival*, 38, 1 (Spring 1996) 58–80.

Guilhaudis, J.-F., 'France's Strategic Options,' *Arms Control: the Journal of Arms Control and Disarmament*, 5, 2 (September 1984) 162–75.

Hassner, P., 'Eurocommunism and Western Europe,' *NATO Review*, 26, 4 (August 1978) 21–7.

Hassner, P., 'Eurocommunism in the Aftermath of Kabul,' *NATO Review*, 28, 4 (August 1980) 6–13.

Hassner, P., 'France, Deterrence and Europe: Rationalising the Irrational,' *International Defense Review*, 17, 2 (1984) 133–42.

Heisbourg, F., 'The European–US Alliance: Valedictory Reflections on Continental Drift in the Post-Cold War Era,' *International Affairs*, 68, 4 (1992) 665–78.

Hellmann, J., 'Wounding Memories: Mitterrand, Moulin, Touvier, and the Divine Half-lie of Resistance,' *French Historical Studies*, 19, 2 (Fall 1995) 461–86.

Highton, S., 'Franco-American Relations: a Retrospective View,' *Journal of the RUSI*, 127, 1 (March 1982) 28–31.

Hoffmann, S., 'Gaullism by Any Other Name,' *Foreign Policy*, 57 (Winter 1984/85) 38–57.

Hollick, J. C., 'Civil War in Chad, 1978–82,' *The World Today*, 38, vii–viii (1982) 297–304.

Howard, Sir M., 'A European Perspective on the Reagan Years,' *Foreign Affairs*, 66 (1987–88) 478–93.

Howe, G., 'The WEU: the Way Ahead,' *NATO Review*, 37, 3 (June 1989) 13–15.

Howorth, J., 'Consensus of Silence: the French Socialist Party and Defence Policy under François Mitterrand,' *International Affairs*, 60, 4 (Autumn 1984) 579–600.

Howorth, J., 'Resources and Strategic Choices: French Defence Policy at the Crossroads,' *The World Today*, 42, v (1986) 77–80.

Howorth, J., 'French Defence: Disarmament and Deterrence,' *The World Today*, 44, vi (1988) 103–6.

Howorth, J., 'France since the Berlin Wall: Defence and Diplomacy,' *The World Today*, 46, vii (1990) 126–30.

Johnsen, W. T. and Young, T.-D., 'Franco-German Security Accommodation: Agreeing to Disagree,' *Strategic Review*, xxi, 1 (Winter 1993) 7–17.

Kolodziej, E. A., 'France and the Arms Trade,' *International Affairs*, 56, 1 (January 1980) 54–72.

Kramer, S. P., 'France Faces the New Europe,' *Current History*, 89, 550 (November 1990) 365–8, 384–6.

Kreile, M., 'French Security Policy under Mitterrand,' *Aussenpolitik*, 35, 1 (1984) 54–66.

Lacoste, Admiral P., 'Balance and Independence: French Security Policies and Force Structures,' *RUSI and Brassey's Defence Yearbook 1988* (London; Brassey's, 1988) 125–34.

Laird, R. F., 'The French Strategic Dilemma,' *Orbis*, 28, 2 (Summer 1984) 307–28.

Lanxade, Admiral J., 'French Defence Policy after the White Paper,' *Journal of the RUSI*, 139, 2 (April 1994) 17–21.

Lellouche, P., 'France in Search of Security,' *Foreign Affairs*, 72, 2 (Spring 1993) 122–31.

Lewis, J. A. C., 'Key Projects Threatened as France Weighs up Its Options,' *Jane's Defence Weekly*, 20, 4 (24 July 1993) 19.

Wauthier, C., 'France and Africa: an Arena of Left–Right Conflicts,' in Legum, C. and Doro, M. E. (eds), *Africa Contemporary Record: Annual Survey and Documents, 1987–1988*, Vol. XX (New York; Africana, 1989) A62–A70.

Wauthier, C., 'France's Year in Africa: the More Things Change,' in Doro, M. E. (ed.), *Africa Contemporary Record: Annual Survey and Documents, 1988–1989*, Vol. XXI (New York; Africana, 1992) A115–A123.

Wells, S. F., Jr, 'The Mitterrand Challenge,' *Foreign Policy*, 4 (Fall 1981) 57–69.

Wells, S. F., Jr, 'Mitterrand's International Policies,' *The Washington Quarterly*, 11, 3 (Spring 1988) 59–75.

Whiteman, K., 'President Mitterrand and Africa,' *African Affairs*, 82, 328 (July 1983) 329–43.

Wilson, F. L., 'The French CP's Dilemma', *Problems of Communism*, xxvii, 4 (July/August 1978) 1–14.

Wolff Metternich, D. von, 'The Franco-German Brigade: a German Perspective,' *Journal of the RUSI*, 136, 3 (September 1991) 44–8.

Woyke, W., 'Mitterrand – Political Change in France,' *Aussenpolitik*, 32, 4 (1981) 344–57.

Yost, D. S., 'French Defense Budgeting: Executive Dominance and Resource Constraints,' *Orbis*, 23, 3 (Fall 1979) 579–608.

Yost, D. S., 'The French Defence Debate,' *Survival*, 23, 1 (January–February 1981) 19–28.

Yost, D. S., 'French Policy in Chad and the Libyan Challenge,' *Orbis*, 26, 4 (Winter 1983) 965–97.

Yost, D. S., 'Radical Change in French Defence Policy,' *Survival*, 28, 1 (January/February 1986) 53–68.

Yost, D. S., 'Franco-German Defence Co-operation,' *The Washington Quarterly*, 11, 2 (Spring 1988) 173–95.

Yost, D. S., 'France, West Germany and European Security Co-operation,' *International Affairs*, 64, 1 (Winter 1987/88) 97–100.

Yost, D. S., 'France in the New Europe,' *Foreign Affairs*, 69, 2 (1990/91) 107–27.

Yost, D. S., 'France and West German Defence Identity,' *Survival*, 33, 4 (July/August 1991) 327–51.

Yost, D. S., 'France and the Gulf War of 1990–1991: Political-Military Lessons Learned,' *Journal of Strategic Studies*, 16, 3 (September 1993) 339–74.

Yost, D. S., 'Nuclear Debates in France,' *Survival*, 36, 4 (Winter 1994/95) 113–39.

Yost, D. S., 'France's Nuclear Dilemmas,' *Foreign Affairs*, 75, 1 (January/February 1996) 108–18.

Index

The name of François Mitterrand is mentioned at such regular intervals in this book that simple citations are not indexed here. Rather, under Mitterrand, François will be found indexed his stance on particular issues.

France – *continued*
new world role after Cold War, 7
peacetime military integration, 166
qualified return to NATO, 172, 201
refuses overflight rights for US
bombing of Libya, 109, 202
relations with USA, 2, 202
risked loss of status in NATO, 35–6
Socialist government and presidency in, 1
troop commitment in (West)
Germany, 60, 62–3, 144, 166
Franco-German Brigade, 62, 166,
169–70, 206
Franco-German Corps, 166, 175, 206
Franco-German relations, and Hadès,
151
François-Poncet, Jean, 106, 111
Front National, 153, 181
Fuchs, Gérard, 152

Gaddhafi, Colonel, 52, 102, 103, 104,
108
Galley, Robert, 34
Gallois, General, 17, 106
Garraud, Marie-France, 192
Gaulle, Charles de, 1, 2, 3, 7, 11, 12,
13, 14, 15, 16, 17, 18, 19, 20, 21,
22, 23, 25, 26, 27, 28, 29, 41, 48,
50, 51, 69, 133, 177, 203, 205
and Atlantic Alliance, 16
belief in France as major power,
15
doubts over allies' reliability, 12
influence on defence, 12
legislates to reinforce political
control over military, 14
relations with French army, 15
relations with USA, 16
Gaullism in defence, 2–3
colonial wars outdated, 13
consequences of, 158
importance of nuclear capability,
12, 15–16, 79
political functions of defence, 13,
15, 16
linkage of defence and national
independence, 12
and military integration, 16

modernisation of armed forces, 13,
20–1
practicalities of, 13–18
principles of, 12-13
Gaullists, *see Rassemblement pour la
République* (RPR)
Gemayel, Bashir, 94, 96
Gendarmerie, 50, 77, 79, 82, 88, 137
Geneva disarmament talks, 26, 27–8
German reunification, 135, 160, 161,
162, 163
consequences, 160, 162
French reservations towards, 161–2
security conditions for, 161
Germany
commitment to Europe questioned, 175
early recognition of Slovenia and
Croatia, 171, 175
Giraud, André, 56, 128, 129
Giscard d'Estaing, Valéry, 28, 32, 35,
36, 41, 42, 47, 51, 104, 123, 142,
184, 185, 191, 201, 205
Atlanticism of, 40, 41, 43, 96
closer defence relations with
Europe, 41
ends atmospheric nuclear testing,
41
French forces to match *Bundeswehr*,
41
reorientation of defence effort, 42
Godefroy, Jean-Pierre, 145
Gorbachev, Mikhail, 58, 125, 130,
135
arms control proposals, 125–6,
127, 128, 129
visit to France, 125
Great Britain, 13
Groupe Socialiste, 25
Guéna, Yves, 89
Gulf War (1990–91), 63, 162, 180–7,
202
advantages of political divergences
for Mitterrand, 183
and American interests, 181
Chevènement's disagreement with,
60
command and control of French
forces, 182, 209